Rethinking
the New Medievalism

Rethinking
the New Medievalism

Edited by
R. HOWARD BLOCH, ALISON CALHOUN,
JACQUELINE CERQUIGLINI-TOULET,
JOACHIM KÜPPER & JEANETTE PATTERSON

Johns Hopkins University Press
Baltimore

© 2014 Johns Hopkins University Press
All rights reserved. Published 2014
Printed in the United States of America on acid-free paper
2 4 6 8 9 7 5 3 1

Johns Hopkins University Press
2715 North Charles Street
Baltimore, Maryland 21218-4363
www.press.jhu.edu

Library of Congress Cataloging-in-Publication Data

Rethinking the New Medievalism / R. Howard Bloch, Alison Calhoun,
Jacqueline Cerquiglini-Toulet, Joachim Küpper, Jeanette Patterson, eds.
    pages cm
    Includes index.
    ISBN 978-1-4214-1240-5 (hardcover : acid-free paper) — ISBN 978-1-4214-1241-2
(pbk. : acid-free paper) — ISBN 978-1-4214-1242-9 (electronic) —
ISBN 1-4214-1240-3 (hardcover : acid-free paper) — ISBN 1-4214-1241-1
(pbk. : acid-free paper) — ISBN 1-4214-1242-x (electronic) 1. Literature, Medieval—
History and criticism. 2. Civilization, Medieval—Social aspects. 3. Middle
Ages in literature. 4. Criticism, Textual. 5. Medievalism. I. Bloch, R. Howard.
II. Calhoun, Alison, 1979–. III. Cerquiglini-Toulet, Jacqueline. IV. Küpper,
Joachim. V. Patterson, Jeanette.
PN671.R48 2014
809'.02—dc23   2013022697

A catalog record for this book is available from the British Library.

*Special discounts are available for bulk purchases of this book.
For more information, please contact Special Sales at 410-516-6936
or specialsales@press.jhu.edu.*

Johns Hopkins University Press uses environmentally friendly book materials,
including recycled text paper that is composed of at least 30 percent
post-consumer waste, whenever possible.

CONTENTS

Rethinking
the New Medievalism

The New Philology *Comes of Age*

R. HOWARD BLOCH

"In medieval studies, philology is the matrix from which all else springs." With that capacious claim, Stephen Nichols famously introduced a special issue of *Speculum,* entitled *The New Philology* (1990), which provoked fiery polemics while spurring disciplinary innovation.[1] In one form or another, the studies in the present volume attest both to the controversy and to the transformation wrought by this movement.

But, as Nichols also pointed out,

> What is "new" in our enterprise might better be called "renewal," *renovatio* in the twelfth-century sense. On the one hand, it is a desire to return to the medieval origins of philology, to its roots in a manuscript culture . . . On the other hand, a rethinking of philology should seek to minimize the isolation between medieval studies and contemporary cognitive disciplines . . . by reminding us that philology was once among the most theoretically avant-garde disciplines (cf. Vico, Goethe, Dilthey, Croce, Vossler, Auerbach, Spitzer, Starobinski, Derrida and Paul DeMan).[2]

Nichols means that philology, like most arts and letters, is most radical when it confronts tradition through renewal, rather than repeal. He recognizes that the Middle Ages, despite an extraordinary record of innovation, invention, and discovery, was an era that resisted change in and for itself. And yet this same veneration of conservative values underlies a fascinating paradox of medieval culture: its delicate and seemingly contradictory balance between stability on the one hand and its ceaseless testing and transformation of almost every aspect of its world—including beliefs, political and ecclesiastical institutions, religious orthodoxy, language, the arts, and literature—on the other.

If that dynamic describes medieval studies itself, it also characterizes the contributors and their essays in this volume. Coming from Europe and the United States, these scholars studied with philologists trained in a narrower, more positivist philology developed in Germany, France, and, later, the United

States. And yet, while respecting the disciplinary rigor imparted by their *maî-tres*, the contributors have also presided over the transformation of medieval studies, a transformation no less than that of the genetic revolution in biology, beginning in both fields in the 1960s. They have had a determining hand in the shaping of medieval studies, and indeed of literary studies more generally, through a series of forward looking publications that took us from the world of Diez, washed upon the shores of North America by exiles like Auerbach at Yale, Leo Spitzer at Johns Hopkins, Werner Jaeger at Harvard, Friedrich Solmsen at the University of Pennsylvania, and Yakov Malkiel at the University of California, Berkeley, to a world in which the initial meaning of philology, as a love of letters, has been restored.

This is not the place to chronicle that transformation, however, beyond saying that the scholars here represented all played major roles. Suffice it to say that *The New Philology* issue of *Speculum* was a landmark event, setting as it did a virtual new agenda for medieval studies in the United States. The factors leading up to this remarkable series of essays as well as the movement's long-term effects are brilliantly articulated in Gabrielle M. Spiegel's contribution, "Reflections on *The New Philology*." Spiegel demonstrates the extent to which medieval studies had at last caught up with the cultural and intellectual context of literary studies more generally, and, in an assessment of the "social semantics" of a shift from semiotics to semantics, she shows where *The New Philology* has led in the years since 1990.

Stephen G. Nichols's own contribution to *The New Philology* issue of *Speculum* on the material conditions of what he called the medieval "manuscript matrix" sowed the seeds of his latest intervention in the field as captured in his contribution to this volume, "New Challenges for the New Medievalism." Here Nichols not only posits the "return to manuscripts as the primary focus of the conceptual study of medieval literature" but also explores the relationship between medieval studies and the new technologies in the transition currently underway "from analogue to digital scholarship."

In his ambitious *Digital Library of Medieval Manuscripts*—undertaken over the last decade or so in partnership with the Bibliothèque Nationale de France and the Sheridan Libraries at Johns Hopkins University—Nichols spearheads the bringing online of some 160 of the 250 manuscripts of the *Roman de la Rose*. It is a project radical in its international scope, uniting as it does specialists from the Bibliothèque Nationale de France as well as from universities in ten countries. But it also pushes to a logical extreme Nichols's 1990 warning that medieval manuscript culture "did not simply live with diversity, but cultivated it." Bernard Cerquiglini's bugaboo of *la variance* and Paul Zumthor's joyous wallowing in the "mobility of the text" seem like weak broth compared to the mass of data to be assimilated in this extreme return to medieval sources.

Nichols recognizes that he has crossed a "line from traditional humanities scholarship based on qualitative analysis of discrete amounts of information to quantitative research based on large data sets necessitating collaborative research teams of the kind that has come to be the norm in the natural and biological sciences. It did not take long for us to realize that this transition entailed a radically different cognitive and even theoretical mode: for we had moved from the world of print-based *philology*, to the infinitely more expansive world of digital *technology*." And yet the questions he seeks to answer, the pressures he exerts on the medieval work, are those that have dogged him throughout a multivalent career and are the very ones that dominate this volume—issues having to do with production and the material conditions of medieval literature; patronage, authorship, and voice; reception of literary language, literary public, and what today is called "intellectual property"; meaning, the world of assumptions, and "cultural preconceptions" surrounding any given work or series of works; and, finally, in an enduring interest going back to his *Romanesque Signs* (1984), the symbolic value of the book and the relationship of literature with the languages of theology and philosophy as well as the other arts, including painting and music.

Turning to the other chapters in the volume, one sees both their adherence to core principles of *The New Philology* and the passion for innovative approaches and topics that it encourages. Daniel Heller-Roazen's essay, "Dialectic of the Medieval Course," is a superb demonstration of the conjunction of the Old Philology and the New. In a close examination of the history of the words used for maritime raiders from Ancient Greece to the present—"pirate," "bandit," "plunderer," "warrior," "pillagers of the sea," "roving sailors," "privateers," "corsair," "free booter," "buccaneer," "sea rover"—Heller-Roazen demonstrates how fine is the line between lawlessness and lawfulness, judicial action and war, private war and public policy. In the history of words, in other words, one finds not only history, *tout court*, but also trenchant fundamental understandings of the nature of the law, the relationship of law to sovereign power, and the distinction between private and public space.

The High Middle Ages represent a particularly interesting period, for it was then that governments first authorized the use of privateers under conditions of war. "Formal legitimacy" was conferred on banditry at sea, license to plunder via letters "patent" or "marques" and rights of reprisal. The medieval condition of banditry did not disappear until the rise of nations in the nineteenth century and the state's "monopoly of the legitimate use of physical force" (Max Weber). Interestingly, the United States was the great holdout as nonsignatory to the Treaty of Paris (1856) abolishing "privateering," thus maintaining the prerogative to hire pirates, as guaranteed by article 1, section 8 of the Constitution, which granted Congress power "to declare war, grant letters of marque and reprisal and make rules concerning capture on land and water." This situation ended only with the Spanish-American War of 1898, a Caribbean war which put an end to the somewhat, sometimes, ambivalent legitimacy of the pirates of the Caribbean, as well as all other pirates, whose space in the late twentieth and early twenty-first century is occupied by the figure of the terrorist, in a strikingly medieval paradigm of sovereign states without means versus those with means but lacking sovereignty.

The questions of conquest, sovereignty, ideology, and law inform Marina Brownlee's "The Possibility of Historical Time in the *Crónica Sarracina*," a carefully crafted account of the confrontation between Christianity and Islam that lasted nearly eight hundred years, "constituting Spain's unique foundational subject matter—on par with the legends of Troy or King Arthur." For Marina Brownlee, the retelling of 711 is about the construction of historical time, the forging of mythic connections in order to legitimize empire in a temporally remote time frame. Written in the early 1430s, Pedro del Corral's monumental *La crónica del rey don Rodrigo con la destrucción de España* (The Chronicle of King Rodrigo with the Destruction of Spain) exploits the *calendric, genealogical,* and *archival* mechanisms of time (Paul Ricoeur) to extraordinary advantage.

She concludes that "the *Crónica* is invested in dramatizing human complexity not only in historical time as Ricoeur conceives it—through the calendar, genealogy, and archive—but Corral also thereby casts doubt on the viability of generic categories, which tend to oversimplify the representation of history and the implementation of ideology." The result is a demythologizing or destabilizing of epic certainties and of romance values, as well. "In the last analysis, we see from Corral's skeptical enterprise that romance proves to be an essential ideological tool that powerfully elucidates the contingencies of history and historical time."

Andrew James Johnston's essay "Ekphrasis in the *Knight's Tale*" explores the ways in which Chaucer makes use of ekphrasis in the service of a specific narrative politics of representation, a politics in which the visual and the verbal on the one hand and the classical and the medieval on the other seem to be locked in ineluctable conflict. Yet, as Johnston shows, the visual and the verbal are always already implicated in each other, and Chaucer uses his awareness of their closeness to test the boundaries of chivalry's ideological claim "to be capable of making use of violence and yet keeping it under control." There are many resonances here, not only with Nichols's 1992 article "Ekphrasis, Iconoclasm, and Desire," but also with his discussion of the relation of photography to reality with reference to Girart Acarie's painting, an illustration of the presentation of a book to François 1er (*Roman de la Rose*, MS Morgan 948) in the current volume.

My own contribution, "From Romanesque Architecture to Romance," picks up on Nichols's writings on Johannes Scotus Eriugena, the reception of the *Pseudo-Dionysius* at Saint-Denis, the question of light and visuality in the making of the first Gothic cathedral, and the relationship of the optical experience of the new architecture to the perceptual modes of what is arguably the first Old French romance—the *Roman d'Eneas*.

Many of the essays that follow deal in one way or another with the question of authorship, a particularly vexed concept under the conditions of the new or material philology. Jan-Dirk Müller's "The Identity of a Text" tests the stability of comparing a stanza of one of Walther von de Vogelweide's love songs and the semantic stability of the words *wîp* (woman) and *frouwe* (lady) against Walther's other writings and against the Minnesänger corpus as a whole. Müller interrogates the importance of the manuscript and the scribal tradition, the imposition of a name to the manuscript, to the text, to the work, to a poetic persona. He poses the basic question of authorship in relation to a medieval work as well as to an individual poet like Walther. Can we identify a unified speaker? A recipient? Are variants in the manuscript variants of an original text? Are the meanings of words the same from one text to another? What is the relation of orality to literacy? Of a work like that of Walther to court culture? Is the integrity of a text a key to its meaning?

In "The *Pèlerinage* Corpus in the European Middle Ages: Processes of Retextualization Reflected in the Prologues," Ursula Peters raises many of the same issues in relation to the process of textual rewriting, another area of concern to New Philology.[3] Rather than focusing upon a single stanza or line, Peters follows the pan-European textual rewritings—in Latin, English, German, Dutch, Spanish, and French—of Guillaume de Deguileville's *Pèlerinage de la vie humaine*, from around 1330. Noting the absence of an Italian version, perhaps due to "overwhelming presence of Dante's *poema sacro Divine Comedy*," Peters underscores the difference between our understanding on a thematic and ideological level of the allegorical journey according to the variables of poetry versus prose, the author's intent as visible in the various prologues and the question of editions, the variable of manuscript versus print, and even different levels of illustration according to manuscript.

Jacqueline Cerquiglini-Toulet's contribution, "Conceiving the Text in the Middle Ages," picks up many of the issues raised by Müller and Peters and places them in the general context of medieval textuality. In the face of multiple manuscript copies of a literary text, Cerquiglini-Toulet poses such questions as: How do we recognize a text? When and how does it end? What's the place of the text in a manuscript? Does it possess a process of individuation? And if so, how can we recognize it? How does it achieve literary identity?

Her ingenious answer to the first question—that a text is writing susceptible to glossing—is followed by a discussion of the *Roman de la Rose* as exemplary of a process of what she terms, resuscitating the thought of Paul Zumthor in his 1963 *Langue et techniques poétiques a l'époque romane*, "monumentalization." A literary text is one that has been monumentalized, and this difference also marks that between past and current medieval studies. Old and New Philology: their difference resides in the way the text is conceived. Is it a document? Or monument?

Jack Abecassis's essay, "Montaigne's Medieval Nominalism and Meschonnic's Ethics of the Subject," is a marvelous exploration of the relationship between language theory and being in the world. He shows how easily and necessarily one moves from a theory of signs and of the name to a practice of writing, and from writing, to ethics and politics. Using the example of Montaigne's reprise of the medieval question of realism versus nominalism, put to new purpose in the service of moral philosophy as opposed to theology, Abecassis demonstrates how, according to Montaigne, a radical nominalism seems logically to deny the possibility of community on one hand, and how a radical realism seems to deny the integrity of the individual on the other. He concludes via a sleight of hand (that is Montaigne's more than his own) that the author of the *Essais* opts for a moderate nominalism, allowing "for Montaigne's skeptical yet active and constructive engagement with political realities, even those of cruel religious civil wars."

A number of the essays in the present volume take up theological questions, or introduce theology to other areas of literary. Andreas Kablitz's "Good Friday Magic: Petrarch's *Canzoniere* and the Transformation of Medieval Vernacular Poetry" poses the question of Petrarch's place in the birth of modern subjectivity versus his status as a Renaissance writer known for his return to antiquity. In the line of Müller and Peters, Kablitz teases out the various meanings of the first word of the *Canzoniere*—*Voi*—in terms of the syntax of the phrase "Voi ch'ascoltate in rime sparse il suono" and in terms of the subject position it implies, as well as its referent and intended recipient. Kablitz concludes that this first phrase puts forth a permanent delay of the identification of the referent of *il suono.* "The first stanza of Petrarch's first sonnet not only poses the syntactic problem of its relation to the continuation of the sentence it opens, it is also characterized by an irritating semantic structure, by a continuous *différance* of meaning."

For Kablitz, such a deferral of meaning points in the direction of a thematics of date, falling in love on Good Friday, along with a deeper theological truth connected to the process of *innamoramento.* In a daring leap of logic and of faith, Kablitz posits a connection between the words used in Saint John's Gospel to describe the capture of Christ—"comprehenderunt Jesum, et ligaverunt eum"—and the terms used by Petrarch to describe his falling in love: "e non me ne guardai ché i be' vostr'occhi, Donna, mi legaro." Petrarch thus becomes a *figura Christi*, the unlimited pains caused by his love to Laura, an imitation of Christ's Passion. In a recognition of the theological underpinnings of impossible love that is at once medieval and modern, the truth of earthly longing is, finally, a condition of being in the flesh, of being in the world, of a waiting to be redeemed, enacted by the deferral of meaning in our understanding of such richly crafted poetry.

The sonnets of the *Canzoniere* are "characterized by a permanent deception of assumptions the text itself produces. The semantic structure of Petrarch's poems becomes itself a mirror of the enigmatic nature of this world. Unlike the *Commedia*, in the *Canzoniere* poetry is no longer a revelation of transcendent truth, but by its permanent variations of the very same subject it offers continuously new insights into the substantially paradoxical character of the perhaps redeemed but, precisely because of this hope, deeply unfathomable world."

Joachim Küpper's "Religious Horizon and Epic Effect: Considerations on the *Iliad*, the *Chanson de Roland*, and the *Nibelungenlied*" draws an important contrast between pagan epics that humanize the gods and Christian epics that divinize the heroes that are the instruments of divine providence. In Homer we encounter a world of gods that mirrors the human world, and the presence of "morality" in the absence of "meaning": "The *Iliad* is the perhaps most impressive literary document of the patriarchal age. The text propagates the basic laws of its historical period, lessons mainly directed to male recipients: never to take serious action on women's advice, never to appropriate other men's sexual property, never to leave one's own sexual property without surveillance."

The *Chanson de Roland*, conversely, is full of transcendental meaning. "The thought of a divinity that asserts itself in the historical process is the necessary complement of monotheism." Both *Roland* and *Le Cid* present a "structure of events perfectly compatible with the optimistic gesture that founds the Christian history of salvation." The *Nibelungenlied*, somewhat of an outlier and third term, provides consciousness of honor, irrational affect, material greed, and shady intrigue, with no transcendental meaning. It is a single enigma, with contingent circumstances, unfolding in narrative.

> What we are presented with here is thus neither the thoroughly human world of the ancient epic, reducible to a play of honor, nor the Christian world of the other great medieval epics with their overarching ceiling of transcendental meaning. The world of the *Nibelungenlied* has—perhaps—a logic and a meaning. But it is one that is unarticulated. It is, in its withdrawal, deeply disturbing. Its power to disturb is increased by the fact that no promise stands at the end of this world, but rather a catastrophe without prospect of compensation in this world or the next.

Küpper explains such difference in the epic as a function of audience, and he sees finally in the *Nibelungenlied* a sign of modernity, of "fascination without reassurance."

"Narrative Frames of Augustinian Thought in the Renaissance: The Case of Rabelais" by Deborah N. Losse works against our received ideas of the Renaissance through her exploration of the extent to which the early Church fathers shaped late medieval and early humanist thinking, particularly the work of François Rabelais, and this despite Rabelais's apparent scorn for medieval scholastic method and theology. Referencing studies of medieval marriage, Losse interrogates Panurge's search in *Le Tiers Livre* for an answer to the question of whether he should marry as an example of the centrality of self-knowledge leading back to Augustine.[4]

The notion of turning inward along with a privileging of free will derives, Losse maintains, from the *Confessions*: "In setting the marriage question within its anthropological context, Rabelais has left us a key to understanding the importance of the Church fathers in his work. Marriage is no longer a disembodied religious ideal examined within a narrow intellectual history, but a social institution that functions within the context of a vibrant and changing Christian community."

Gerhard Regn, in "Virgil's 'Perhaps': Mythopoiesis and Cosmogony in Dante's *Commedia* (Remarks on *Inf.* 34, 106–26)" draws the question of authorship within the "domain of theological authoritative discourse" such that the

Commedia in its totality, though not in particular points, "establishes a suggestive analogy with Holy Scripture." Regn underscores the importance of vision within the *Commedia*, the association with St. Paul's vision, the *topoi* of the numerous medieval accounts and visions of the other world, and the visionary theme in the *proemium* of the *Paradiso*, where the figure of the poet asserts his recent presence in the empyrean by recurring to the visionary mode (*vidi*); all of which establish the conditions for a revelation of hidden truth for the world.

Regn also insists upon an anthropology of space in the *Commedia*, Virgil's location of Jerusalem in relation to Purgatory, at opposite poles of the world, both as part of a divine cosmogony in which Virgil is a forerunner, a "figure of promise whose fulfillment is the poet of the visionary *poema sacro*." Finally, in such an economy of salvation, Dante receives divine grace from the start, the grace that allows him to read the Bible in the "right" way, a way in which "inspired reading and visionary truth appear to converge."

Kevin Brownlee's "Dante's Transfigured Ovidian Models: Icarus and Daedalus in the *Commedia*" picks up Regn's question of models and models of authority within the context of Dante's Christian correction of Ovid's Daedalus and Icarus story. "Dante the protagonist, riding on Geryon's back, is presented as a corrected Icarus figure; and Virgil, as a corrected Daedalus figure (as artist, as father, as guide)." Brownlee pays acute attention to the semantic value of the words *spennare* (*hapax*, or unfeathering), *penne*, the feather motif and its near synonym *ali*, wings; the guide motif; and the human artifice motif—all keys to Dante's reception and rewriting of *Metamorphoses* in a figural articulation of Christian truth "most elaborately demonstrated in the *Paradiso*."

There could be no more fitting nor significant tribute to the lessons of the master than to see the ways in which his lifelong concerns have permeated the thinking and procedures of the work gathered in the present volume. Are these essays the fruits of the new or material philology? The answer to this question is resolutely affirmative. Yet, as Gabrielle Spiegel points out, "Were *The New Philology* to be published today . . . it would look somewhat quaint and even out of date, at least to the extent that there seems to be a growing sense that what was variously called 'the linguistic turn,' 'postmodernism,' or 'poststructuralism' has run its course, wrought whatever changes our disciplines are likely to absorb—while rejecting a significant number of others—and is effectively over." In a reminder of Georges Dumézil's dictum "aujourd'hui j'ai raison, mais demain j'aurai tort" (today I'm right, but tomorrow, I could be wrong), Spiegel identifies this "linguistic turn" with a displacement of semiotics and structural, formal, relational, and its dreary sidekick, relativist, thinking by semantics, and by a move "from culture as discourse to culture as practice and performance," along with a recuperation of history and historical actors as rational subjects, intentional agents.

The essays that follow contain many elements belonging to the New Philology—an attention to the material conditions of the medieval work, especially to the givens of manuscripts and manuscript culture, a questioning of authorship and of authority, an interrogation of the integrity of medieval texts, recognition of the relation between the verbal and the visual.

Many of the defining issues and methods below also belong to what the New Philology took to be the Old Philology—a keen attention to the history of individual words, to influence in the process of writing and rewriting, to the presence of classical models in the literature of the High Middle Ages. And yet there are deeply inscribed concerns that belong neither to the old nor to the New Philology and that are the signs of just how meaningfully assimilated the new and the old really are—a recognition of the importance of the relationship between literature and theology, which has never been a part of official medieval studies, except perhaps in certain corners like Dante studies or the Robertsonians of Princeton; a link between language theory and the lived world of moral philosophy, ethics, and politics; acknowledgment of the importance of the semantic valence of words in the formation of such seemingly transparent notions as sovereignty and law.

The merging of the Old Philology with the new to produce something both older and newer still is proof that communism may be dead, but the dialectic still functions. And it is in the space between the end of the Cold War and the present that the New Philology became old, and then new again.

As long as the superpowers were on the brink of nuclear disaster, the dominant "social semantics" (Spiegel) carried a certain hermeneutic urgency, a thinking of the future in utopic, allegorical terms, which were nowhere more fully articulated than in the French world systems of the late 1960s through the 1980s. With the fall of the iron curtain, right around the time of the *Speculum* volume devoted to the New Philology, history as we knew it collapsed along with the Eastern Bloc, leaving, in the place of the arms race to feed capital, a retrofitting of the military synonymous with the Internet, globalization, and the spectacular disappearance of theory in favor of a return to the past—history, the referent, memory, the body, biography and autobiography, narrative, the archive—a wallowing in ethics and the disappearance of universal theoretical man. These essays represent a synthesis of the theoretical and the universal with the particular and the pointed in what amounts to neither a new old philology nor an old new philology, but a teasing of wide meanings from letters in the original spirit of philology as a love of words.

NOTES

1. Stephen G. Nichols, "Introduction: Philology in a Manuscript Culture," in "The New Philology," ed. Stephen G. Nichols, special issue, *Speculum* 65, no. 1 (1990): 1.

2. Ibid., 1.

3. Stephen G. Nichols, "Why Material Philology? Some Thoughts," in "Philologie als Textwissenschaft: Alte und neue Horizonte," ed. Helmut Tervooren and Horst Wenzel, special issue, *Zeitschrift für deutsche Philologie* 116 (1997): 1–21.

4. Losse's point of departure is Nichols's "An Intellectual Anthropology of Marriage in the Middle Ages," in *The New Medievalism*, ed. by Marina S. Brownlee, Kevin Brownlee, and Stephen G. Nichols (Baltimore: Johns Hopkins University Press, 1991), 70–95.

CHAPTER ONE

New Challenges for the New Medievalism

STEPHEN G. NICHOLS

Scholarship is driven by technology far more often than we may care to admit. And technology is more diverse in its manifestations than one imagines, even difficult to recognize as such, on occasion. At least that seems to be the case for medieval culture, which was a particularly intense period for technological innovation. It should come as no surprise, then, to find that medieval studies adopts technological advance as readily as the period it studies. In the case of New Medievalism, the willingness to explore the frontiers of digital research has come to define its activities by way of a logical extension of its call for a return to manuscripts as the primary focus of the conceptual study of medieval literature.

This is due in no small measure to projects devoted to digitizing medieval manuscripts. The most ambitious of these, and the one with the most extensive corpus of manuscripts of a single work, is the Digital Library of Medieval Manuscripts at Johns Hopkins University (www.romandelarose.org; fig. 1). With some 160 manuscripts of the *Rose* online, including all known codices in France, three private manuscripts not previously available to students, and a growing number of incunabula and early printed editions, this digital repository allows free access to the most popular vernacular work of the Middle Ages at any hour of the day or night from anywhere in the world.

Such projects are a logical outcome of the propositions articulated by the *New Philology* issue of *Speculum* in 1990. In urging readers to accept the fact that the manuscript culture of the Middle Ages "did not simply live with diversity, but cultivated it,"[1] and that in consequence "the manuscript matrix is a place of radical contingencies," we recognized that medieval vernacular literature was not isomorphic, let alone univocal. This observation in turn presupposed a radically new way of looking at the multiple manuscript versions of a given work.

Since *Rose* manuscripts were produced in a variety of centers from the late twelfth century to the early sixteenth century, they offer historical records of the

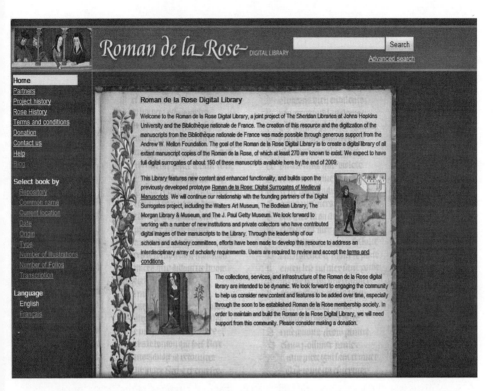

Figure 1. Homepage of the Johns Hopkins Digital Library of Medieval Manuscripts.

work's reception and its geographical itinerary, and provide scholars with significant information about language variation, manuscript design and layout, even changes in artistic style in the case of illuminated manuscripts. In short, by treating the different versions of a work as records of its medieval mode of existence, "new medievalists" take their cue from the God of Love in the *Roman de la Rose* who says that he will equip Jean de Meun "with his own wings and sing him such tunes that once he will have matured and absorbed the doctrine of love, Jean will make our words resound throughout the realm in cross-roads and schools in the language of France."[2] But, to return to my opening assertion that technology drives scholarship, this statement may seem surprising, even misplaced, since it is generally "philology" that one associates with advances in our discipline. That was, after all, how I introduced the *New Philology* special issue of *Speculum* in 1990: "In medieval studies, philology is the matrix out of which all else springs."[3]

While true enough, the statement was polemical. It was intended to remind readers that philology's authority derived above all from its status as an early modern or even nineteenth-century invention aimed at establishing reliable versions of medieval texts through the use of modern scientific methods. My colleagues and I felt that, however laudable its goals, philology so conceived ran the risk of effacing the historical context—what Gabrielle Spiegel called "the social logic"—it ostensibly sought to explain.

Our fears were not exaggerated. Erich Auerbach defined philology as "the need to go back to the sources," a need that took the form of humanists collecting and editing manuscripts, writing "works on the grammar and style of Latin and of their own mother tongues, on lexicography, and on archaeology." The humanists, Auerbach avers, "accomplished an important task of popularization: they were translators of the great works of antiquity."[4] Auerbach saw the printing press—and the culture of the fixed text that it made possible—as a major contributor to philology. For most scholars, however, the origin of philology lies in the nineteenth century, and more particularly in Germany, as Seth Lerer recently observed:

> "Philology" connotes the study of historical linguistics as it developed in the nineteenth century and came to be associated, especially in German universities, with the practices of lexicography, textual criticism, and literary-aesthetic evaluation. This practice centered on two mutually related inquiries: the establishment of historical phonology and the codification of sound changes as the "laws" of diachronic linguistics; and the excavation of the etymologies of individual words, often in the process leading to the recovery of defining social or cultural norms.[5]

Given such entrenched perceptions, our efforts to propose an anthropological philology with its roots squarely in medieval manuscript culture had little chance of overturning received opinion. In retrospect, we should have seen that to propose a philology that would not only return to its sources but also argue that its artifacts should be studied for their own sake and in the context in which they occurred was too radical. It meant spurning established definitions—and practices—of philologists. More importantly, it obscured what we were really trying to do, which, it turned out, was to make the transition from analogue to digital scholarship.

We had no quarrel with philology per se. On the contrary, at the time we simply thought that a perceived split in medieval studies between traditional philology and new theoretical approaches to the field had erected artificial barriers between the study of manuscripts and methods that could shed rather different light—a more historical perspective, in fact—on literary works. We felt, quite rightly as it turned out, that there was no intrinsic opposition between traditional philology and our goals because they entailed different modes with different rationales.[6]

Text editors, for example, using modern methods, sought to reconstruct an ideal conception of a literary work in the form envisaged by its author, or as close to that state as contemporary editorial science could envisage. Our point was simply that the modern critical edition, however erudite and however useful, could not be a faithful representation of an original but was instead a modern reconstruction of an ideal that, from our perspective, never existed. It might evoke the historical moment, but was in no sense *of* it.

That is not how we saw the historical situation. Rather than an individual collaboration between author and publisher, we interpreted the production of multiple versions of a work over time to mean that technologies of manuscript reproduction had a dynamic impact in shaping the nature of the work. Rather than seeing scribal literary transmission over time as adulterating the works they addressed, we perceived the existence of multiple versions as betokening an active milieu of reproduction that could only be called interventionist. It's not that we did not understand that an author might wish to control the "integrity" of his creation. But how would that have been possible in a pre-print culture? For even if writers sought to "protect" their works from change—as some like Dante and Petrarch tried to do—they lacked effective means to do so.

This is not surprising for, after all, manuscripts *were* complex objects produced by artisans skilled in different specialties such as calligraphy, painting, and design, each working within a carefully delimited space on a piece of parchment. In consequence, publication was a collaborative process that produced copies on demand, one at a time, and in many different locales. In the case of popular works like the *Roman de la Rose*, manuscripts continued to be designed long after the writer's death.

Consider figure 2, which shows the incipit folio for a *Rose* manuscript produced in 1520, some 240 years after Jean de Meun completed the poem. On the top half of the folio, we see a writer engaged in composing the work, whose opening lines occupy the bottom half of the page. Iconographic details assure us that it is indeed *this* work and no other that the writer is shown composing or copying. These details include: (1) the bed in which the poet dreams of the events recounted by the poem; (2) the mirror evoking one of the titles of the poem (*le miroër aus amoreus*); (3) the books lying on the shelf above the writer, reminding us of the frequent allusions to classical and other works in the poem; and (4) the idyllic natural landscape through the window where the lover dreams he enters the garden containing the allegorical rose. All that is clear; less evident, however,

Figure 2. Roman de la Rose, MS Morgan 948 (Paris, ca. 1520–25), fol. 5r: Scribe/author writing/copying the poem. The Pierpont Morgan Library, New York. By permission.

is the identity of the writer portrayed. Is it meant to be Guillaume de Lorris, the first author? Jean de Meun, the second? A scribe? Or simply a generic poet?

From the standpoint of this manuscript, which was produced for François 1er, the identity of the original poet is less important than the authority of the renowned work itself. And precisely because this sumptuous version has been rendered "fit for a king," it is the poet/painter responsible, Girard Acarie, who really counts. We don't need to infer this fact. Even before the beginning of the poem, Girard did not hesitate to create a magnificent presentation portrait showing himself on bended knee proffering his work to King Francis (fig. 3).[7]

Figure 3. Roman de la Rose, MS Morgan 948 (Paris, ca. 1520–25), fol. 4r: The poet/painter Girart Acarie presents "his" work to King François 1er. The Pierpont Morgan Library, New York. By permission.

First, the full-page presentation of the scene easily eclipses the half-page author portrait on the following folio, and does so on two counts. First, by its evocation of historical context: the style, décor, and costumes all bespeak the court of François 1er in the early sixteenth century. Lest anyone mistake the sovereign's identity, however, Girard inscribes the king's arms on the facing page of the bifolio, and then makes a full page dedication (fig. 4) to the king on the verso of the presentation portrait that begins: "Tres hault, tres puissant et tres

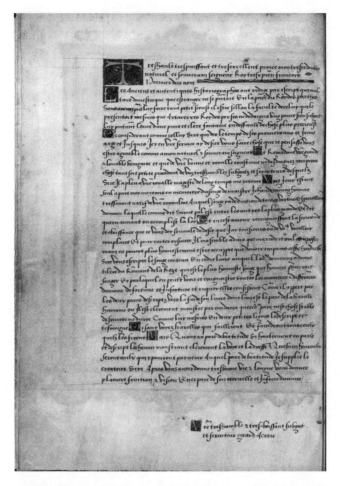

Figure 4. Roman de la Rose, MS Morgan 948 (Paris, ca. 1520–25), fol. 4v: Dedication of the codex by Girard Acarie to King François 1er. The Pierpont Morgan Library, New York. By permission.

excellent prince, mon tres redouté, naturel et souverain seigneur, Roy tres chrestien Françoys, le premier de ce nom" (Most high, all-powerful and most excellent prince, my most redoubtable, rightful and sovereign Lord, Most Christian King François, the first of this name).[8]

Second, even a cursory comparison of the presentation scene with the "author" portrait on folio 5r shows its matter to be drawn entirely from the poem itself. The figure portrayed writing is, like the other figures painted later on in the work, fictional: the poet-lover who figures as protagonist. Girart Acarie and

François 1er, however, like Morgan 948 itself, are real historical figures or artifacts. We'll return to this point later.

Another historical contingency palliated the importance of the author: the nature of the codex itself. Since the manuscript was a complex technology produced by skilled teams working in close coordination, there had to be a single vision, a plan for the whole. The person who guided the process and coordinated the different artisans was called the master scribe. He took responsibility for designing the codex, planning the page layout, determining the number and placement of illuminations and rubrics, and finally for coordinating and supervising the team who executed his plan.

In essence, the master scribe determined how readers would interact with the manuscript as they read or leafed through it. All the components of the individual folio or page had a role to play in guiding the reader. We should not think of illuminations, rubrics, historiated or decorated initials, even bas-de-page images purely in esthetic terms. In the case of the *Rose*, at least, they played a key role in allowing readers to follow a sinuous narrative through its complex excurses, as well as in guiding them back to passages to which the poet subsequently refers. Jean de Meun, in particular, frequently references earlier scenes or passages of the poem as a means of contrasting his vision with that of his predecessor Guillaume de Lorris.

From a critical standpoint, the layout, paintings, rubrics, textual emendations— in short, all the supplements introduced by the master scribe and his team— transformed the codex into an agent of interpretation. In consequence, since no two manuscripts were identical, each has a story to tell about the work it represents: the story of its reception and interpretation by those who produced it.

For us, this way of looking at manuscripts opened dynamic aspects of transmission offering key insights into the sociology of medieval literature. We found it fascinating to witness a literary process where authorship, intellectual property rights, even the concept of "an original work," were all but nonexistent. And while it was exciting to place intellectual value on the study of multiple manuscript versions of a work, it proved much more difficult to put that theory into practice.

The reason was simple: if every version of a work has a potential story to tell about its production and reception, one needs to have access to as many of the manuscripts as possible to be able to determine what that story is, and ultimately to tell it. But given their dispersion in repositories around the world, access was a fairly considerable obstacle. And even if one found a way of surmounting that hurdle, another potentially even greater one loomed: that of data mass. Since there are some 250 extant manuscripts of the *Rose*, produced as we saw over a period of roughly the same number of years, how was one to tabulate all the potential information each manuscript could offer—linguistic, historical, textual, art historical, philosophical, and so on?

Unwittingly, we had crossed a line from traditional humanities scholarship based on qualitative analysis of discrete amounts of information to quantitative research based on large data sets necessitating collaborative research teams of the kind that has come to be the norm in the natural and biological sciences. It did not take long for us to realize that this transition entailed a radically different cognitive and even theoretical mode: for we had moved from the world of print-based *philology*, to the infinitely more expansive world of digital *technology*. The difference is not trivial.

In the former, scholarship, conceptualization, and representation of the object of study are determined by the limitations of the print medium—which is in turn driven by economic and technological constraints. In print, what one can represent of a medieval work—short of simply publishing a facsimile (which is only a static image)—is a rendering of the text transposed from its actual state.

Rather than presenting us with an image of the artifact itself, such transposed representations are the result of structured imagining on the part of scholars whose vision encourages us to see the work in a certain way. That is only natural, since we have traditionally recognized the true work of scholarship as consisting of perceptions arising from arduous research. As long as the critical edition was the only regular access we had to historical works, there was no problem. Now that we have ready access to digital images of the works, however, we must recalibrate the balance between the critical edition and the manuscripts on which it is based. Scholars have long preferred critical texts to manuscripts for at least three excellent reasons: accessibility, "accuracy," and intelligibility.

But things have changed dramatically. It is not simply that we now possess reliable access to manuscripts on a scale never before possible . . . or even conceivable. We can also actually "see" them on our own computer screen, where we have a variety of tools to enhance our reading of difficult or doubtful passages. We can, for example, compare the same scenes in a number of different manuscripts to study differences in vocabulary, wording, illustration, and the like. Furthermore, we can do all this at the same time that others may be consulting those same manuscripts. But it is not just ease of access that has shifted the balance between edition and manuscript. Many of us no longer subscribe to the need for a "master text"—that is to say, a text considered definitive and consequently authoritative. But then New Medievalism never did believe that a "definitive text" was a norm, or even a priority in the Middle Ages, at least for vernacular works.[9] Given these changes in the scholarly landscape, then, it makes sense to take stock of the subtle prejudices undermining the status of manuscripts as reliable textual witnesses.

To take an elementary example, the critical edition inspires confidence by conforming to scholarly norms recognized as "scientific." It has an introduction, tables of various sorts, and a list of manuscripts, and above all it delivers a transcribed and printed text of the work to the reader. These are all good things and we are the richer for them. But let us be clear about what that transcribed and printed text implicitly says about the originals.

As the name implies, manuscripts were copied by hand. But for more than five hundred years, printing has been the recognized medium for public and commercial written documents. This trend has accelerated markedly over the last century with the invention and proliferation of mechanical and now digital writing instruments for personal and business correspondence, reports, medical records, creative and nonfiction writing—in short all forms of written communication. Inevitably, these technological advances have radically transformed the cultural status of handwriting. In education, commerce, law, government, and other activities of daily life, script is discouraged for all but either the most informal uses, or for conventional genres like thank-you notes or letters of condolence. It would be unthinkable today for a job seeker to send a handwritten letter of application, for example. Why? Because of a general consensus that handwritten documents just don't have the same gravitas as print.

In the case of medieval manuscripts, handwriting conveyed yet another stigma: that of the individual scribe, whose hand graphically imposed its presence between the original author and the reader. How could one be certain that the mind and imagination that controlled the scribal hand had not exceeded the strictly mechanical task of copying the author's text? The answer of course was that there was no way that scribe and artist *could* avoid leaving their mark upon the work. It was precisely to correct such interventions that the critical edition adopted a resolutely textual approach, eschewing illuminations and utilizing multiple manuscripts to produce a *printed* critical text reflective of the author's persona, rather than that of the scribe.

Lest anyone doubt that critical editions reinforce cultural prejudices against handwritten copies, they have only to compare the language of the edition to that of the manuscript. The former, having been transcribed, emended, and corrected, assumes a particular status, not simply as Middle French or Middle High German, say, but as a model of the literary language of its time *tout court*.

It may even, by implication, suggest something of the poet's own style, at least as conceived by the editor. In these and other ways, the edition encourages us to read and imagine the work as restored by the textual scholar to represent a best-case scenario of the poet's creation. This "master version" implicitly alters the balance between edition and manuscripts so that the latter fade into the background to play a secondary role as "raw material."

Abetting this nuance are the prejudices that mechanical writing aids have progressively leveled against handwriting: informality, sloppiness, and, above all, inaccuracy. For all these reasons, an editor bases the edition on "scientific" principles that are themselves informed by cultural preconceptions. The critical edition represents structured imagining as to how the work and its language would have been conceived by the original author. The format of the edition seeks to persuade the reader of the accuracy of this informed scenario.[10]

If the edition allows us to experience the medieval literary work as purportedly conceived by its author, the digital library gives us not one, but multiple pictures of how the work looks today and would have appeared to readers of the period when reading the physical object. That means, of course, that medieval readers would experience the work in different manuscript versions, each similar to the others but not identical. Let's take a moment to parse the implications of this fact and the opportunities digital imaging of multiple manuscripts affords us for studying this literature in new ways.

To state the obvious by way of being absolutely clear, photographic images of manuscripts place us in an entirely different relationship with the work in question. It is not the case that photographs of the manuscripts are in any way the same thing as holding the manuscripts themselves in our hands. That point, frequently reiterated, is indisputable. But it is also irrelevant to some extent, because we aren't discussing the merits of the original vis-à-vis digital images of it. The question is rather to distinguish two very different, but necessary, kinds of representation of the medieval work: on the one hand, a critical edition that offers a best-case scenario of the text alone, and, on the other, direct representation of the manuscripts by means of digital images. This boils down to a simple question. What does each do that the other doesn't? We've seen the answer in the case of the edition. Now what about digital photographs?

That question depends on how we construe the relation of the photograph to the object depicted. This is particularly important in ascertaining the utility for scholarship of digital photographs for the study of manuscripts. Initially, some scholars had reservations about the technology, fearing that digital images might deprive the artifact of its materiality, a source of valuable information. Were we advancing digital images as a substitute for all phases of manuscript study, the objection would have merit. But that is emphatically not the case, nor does digitization give rise to apprehension as it did only a few years ago. On the contrary, it is rapidly becoming the most common mode of access to manuscripts, a move enthusiastically endorsed by curators and museums alike as a dynamic merging of those seemingly irreconcilable goals: access and preservation. All too frequently, however, issues of digitization focus primarily on complex technical questions—of which there are many. One tends to take the referential relation between digital image and manuscript as a given. But recent work in aesthetics concerning the relation of seeing and reality suggests that the issue may not be as straightforward as it appears. Indeed, it turns out to open up new avenues of reflection.

Philosopher Kendall Walton offers a bold formula for construing the relation of the photograph to reality. He argues that, unlike other forms of representation, "a *photograph* is always a photograph of something that *actually exists*. Photographs of Abraham Lincoln," he says, "are in some fundamental manner more realistic than painted portraits of him . . . [because] there is a fundamental difference between photographs and painted portraits."[11] He goes on to say that "photography is special and deserves to be called a supremely realistic medium." This is not to say that it is realistic in the sense "of the post-Renaissance quest for realism in painting, or with standard theoretical accounts of realism."[12] The kind of realism Walton has in mind that imbues photography with "a special nature" derives directly from "its contribution to the enterprise of seeing" (85).

He means seeing quite literally, but not in ways we usually think. What Walton has in mind is photography's ability to help us to see what we cannot immediately experience for ourselves and yet is (or was) real nonetheless. Photography can help us to see history "with the assistance of the camera, we can not only see around corners and what is distant or small; *we can also see into the past*. We see long-deceased ancestors when we look at dusty snapshots of them . . . Photographs are *transparent*, we see the world *through* them" (86).

The claim here is not that photography "supplements vision," or that photographs are "duplicates or doubles or reproductions of objects, or substitutes or surrogates for them," but that it makes us really see something that is absent.[13] To underline his point, Walton subordinates the mode of representation to the nature of the represented object. It is the status of the photographed scene that concerns him. This is what he means by saying "photography deserves to be called a supremely realistic medium," whose "special nature" lies in its "contribution to the enterprise of *seeing*." Precisely how the "enterprise of seeing" activates photography's capacity for realism depends upon the link between "the act of seeing" and "what is seen," which he elaborates by asking, "What do we mean by seeing?"

> Our theory needs a term which applies both to my "seeing" my great-grandfather when I look at his snapshot and to my seeing my father when he is in front of me. What's important is that we recognize the fundamental commonality between the two cases, a single natural kind to which both belong. We could say that I *perceive* my great-grandfather but do not *see* him, recognizing a mode of perception ("seeing-through-photographs") distinct from vision . . . [But] I prefer the bold formulation: the viewer of the photograph sees literally the scene that was photographed. (86)

For my purposes, it is the "fundamental commonality" between seeing the snapshot of the deceased great-grandfather and seeing the father in person that can help us to understand how digital photographs can contribute to the "enterprise of seeing" medieval manuscripts. A moment's reflection tells us that, with respect to Walton's example, the medieval codex has a double status: it represents both the snapshot of the great-grandfather and the father standing before the viewer.

We know that if we go to a repository like the Walters Art Museum, the Morgan Library, or the Bibliothèque Nationale, we will be able to see and handle a particular manuscript. Similarly, when we see a digital photograph of that manuscript, we know that we are literally seeing that manuscript and no other. We can be certain that the digital photograph of a specific folio of a given manuscript will correspond exactly to the same page of the physical manuscript. At the same time, we also know whether we have the material object before us or are looking at a digital photograph of it, that what we are seeing is a real medieval artifact, a product of a specific historical context. The parchment was prepared, the text copied, the rubrics inserted, the illuminations painted all at a given moment and at a particular location—say, the Latin Quarter of Paris in the fourteenth, fifteenth, or sixteenth century.

It is in this sense that I would claim that the codex offers the equivalent of a snapshot of all the processes involved in its conception and production. As with any image, it is up to the viewer to decipher the information. But, as I'll suggest in a moment, the aggregation of manuscripts made possible by digital repositories means that, for the first time, we have at our disposal the ability to study and closely compare many versions of a work. We will also be able to pay careful attention to the diachronic evolution of these versions by following the ever-widening temporal gap between the original composition of the work and the production of its many manuscript representations.

Sometimes, and more often than one might think, manuscripts even advertise the primacy of scribe over author. We saw that to be the case with the presentation manuscript of the *Rose* prepared by Girart Acarie that we considered briefly above. Returning once more to this painting (fig. 3), we note that the digital photograph of the folio represents a *mise en abyme* of an actual historical moment—or rather of two historical events, the one real and the other figurative. The photo shows the presentation painting, a real object executed by Girart Acarie sometime between 1520 and 1525.

Because the painting figures as part of a trifolio dedication of the work to François 1er, its full effect could only have been obtained by preparing it *before* the actual event. After all, the painting explains the king's relation to the proffered objet in a positive light that would instantly convey political reasons for accepting it. We must imagine the painting as both pragmatic and idealistic: it not only reveals strong arguments for the king's role as patron, but suggests reasons why patronage of such an historic and culturally significant work would complement and perhaps even enhance François's royal status.

A moment's reflection suffices to confirm the probability of this sequence. To begin, consider the obvious theatricality of the painting; it aims not for historical verisimilitude but dramatic effect. Acarie carefully stages the king at the exact center of the scene. Seven courtiers flank him in receding positions so as to form a V-shaped wedge that thrusts François forward toward the viewer. Behind him, beginning at the top of his head, the arches of an arcade draw the eye out to a landscape showing an estuary with ships, mountains, castles, far-off cities, plains, and forests—in short a symbolic representation of the king's far-flung dominions, the source of his temporal power.

The foreground stages a different kind of authority. It shows the king as a munificent patron of the arts, and more specifically of painting and poetry. The dramatic event commemorated by the foreground of the painting—the kneeling artist-scribe elevating his book as he offers it to the king who grasps it from the top—intersects with the middle ground and background by a different geometric plane. Instead of the V-formation of the main group, the foreground distributes along a diagonal line running from lower left up to the "panache" (or plume) on François's hat and out to a hill receding in the distance. The king and the book occupy the center both vertically and horizontally.

Finally, an ornate frame proclaims the picture's conventional, commemorative status. But just what does it celebrate? Certainly not an event as it actually happened. François certainly must have received the book at some point, and perhaps he even took it from Girard's hands as seen in the painting. But we aren't naïve enough to see the painting as exactly depicting that event. What it does show is the symbolic value of the book as a luxury item in the French court. It also portrays realistically the ideal of the Renaissance king for whom art is as much a part of his persona as statecraft, or rather for whom patronage of the arts *is* a form of statecraft.

Paradoxically, the fact that this event did not happen in the manner portrayed enhances, rather than decreases, the historical information we can draw from it. The painting is part of a bifolio (fig. 5) whose opening shows François's bookplate on the left facing the presentation scene on the right. On the verso of the presentation scene, as already mentioned, Girard places a prose dedication that explains for the edification of the king the significance of the work offered to him (fig. 4). Between the bookplate with the king's arms (folio 3v), the presentation scene (folio 4r), and the prose dedication (folio 4v), there can be no question that this book was executed for François 1er, and, in fact, it did belong to him. Leaving aside what these three folios convey about royal self-presentation, let me simply point to several lines of inquiry they raise about the history of the book on the one hand and, on the other, what they convey about authorship in a culture where intellectual property has yet to be established.

First, the presentation painting evokes the relationship between patron and "author" in a conventional manner that goes back to the twelfth century for vernacular literature. Marie de France and Chrétien de Troyes, writing in the 1160s and 1170s, were among the first to use prologues to link poet and patron as collaborators in producing a work. What is noteworthy in this case—and speaks volumes for the concept of authorship—is that, unlike Marie or Chrétien, who address their patrons directly, this scene claims responsibility for the work by an artist who presents himself as author to his patron, François 1er, some two and a half centuries *after* the date of its original composition. The very boldness of the claim reveals how unexceptional—indeed how normal—it was. This should hardly surprise us, for Girard certainly is responsible, *stricto sensu*, for the book he presents to François.

Moreover, in making a *Rose* according to his own design and illuminations, Girard Acarie joins a long line of writers who "collaborate" with the original poets.

Figure 5. Roman de la Rose, MS Morgan 948 (Paris, ca. 1520–25), fol. 3v–4r: Bifolio showing arms of King François 1ᵉʳ (3v) and Girard Acarie proffering the codex to the king. The Pierpont Morgan Library, New York. By permission.

That in almost all cases these collaborators are anonymous attests to the fact that they are not seeking to eclipse the original poets Guillaume de Lorris and Jean de Meun. On the contrary, given the number of unfinished vernacular literary works in the Middle Ages, creative collaboration was responsible for completing not a few of them, including the *Rose* itself. Few if any of these, however, experienced so aggressive an appropriation and reshaping with eighteen thousand verses added to the relatively modest four thousand lines of Guillaume's original. Jean was not unconscious of this irony, which may be seen from the tongue-in-cheek speech he assigns to the God of Love through whom he identifies himself as author and renames the work:[14]

> Pour ce qu'il est tant mes amys,
> Je l'afluberé de mes esles
> Et luy chanteray nottes telles

Que puis qu'il sera hors d'enfance,

Endoctriné de ma science,

Si flaiollera[15] noz parolles

Par carrefours et par escolles,

Selon le langaige de France,

Par tout le regne en audience,

Que iamais ceulx qui les orront

Des doulx maulx d'aymer mourront

Pour qui le croyent seurement;

Car tant en lira proprement

Que trestous ceulx qui ont a vivre

Debvroyent appeller ce livre

Le Miroër aux Amoureulx,

Tant y verront de bien pour eulx, [fol. 105v a]

Mais que Raison n'y soit pas creüe

La chetive la malostrüe.[16]

Because he'll be so devoted, I'll give him my wings and sing him such airs that once he's grown and learned in my science, Jean will make our words resound throughout the realm in cross-roads and schools in the language of France, so that those who hear him will never die from love's sweet torments provided they believe him surely. For all those to come who read it correctly must call this book *The Mirror of Lovers*, so much will they find rewarding in it, provided they do not pay heed to Reason, the good-for-nothing, worthless baggage.

This passage is part of a much longer speech (over 110 lines in most manuscripts) that Jean ascribes to Amor, the God of Love. Its ostensible purpose is to introduce (and name for the first time) the two poets, Guillaume and Jean. But Jean invests Amor's discourse with much greater scope. He transforms the moment of authorial identification into a poetics of love poetry—a *miroër* or *speculum* in the thirteenth-century sense of a treatise, with the complementary connotation of revealing insights about the nature of life.[17] Besides learning Amor's complex doctrines, poets must embody his principles in order to give them lyric voice.

In enumerating the long line of poets who have served him, Amor cites such classical greats as Catullus and Ovid continuing on down to Guillaume de Lorris. The list effectively establishes a hierarchy of love poets into whose company Jean will be born, with Amor presiding over his birth, nursing, and education.[18] Although often seen—not incorrectly—as self-promoting, the passage offers a more nuanced interpretation whose key lies in the musical terminology Amor introduces: "Et luy chanteray nottes telles. Si flaiollera noz paroles."

The thirteenth century was a highpoint of musical innovation for the Middle Ages, and Paris was its epicenter. At the heart of this musical ferment lay polyphony, called by some the most significant innovation in the history of music. Discovered in the ninth century, polyphony allowed the simultaneous performance by two, three, four, or more voices of different melodies that harmonized while remaining distinct. As Margo Schulter notes, polyphonic intervals "range along a subtle scale of tension from the most purely blending to the most strongly discordant. While such distinctions are often relative, the absolute distinction between stable and unstable intervals is vital."[19] "The music of the 13th century," she remarks, "boldly exploits the entire spectrum of intervals from the most blending to the most aggressively discordant." Key to the effect of polyphony is "the tension created among the unstable intervals," "flexibility and bold contrast," and "an amazing variety and richness of multi-voice combinations and cadences."[20] In other words, polyphony involves multiple voices singing both with and "against" one another to create a whole in which harmony and discord, assertion and contradiction, orthodoxy and heterodoxy, tradition and innovation fuse to take musical performance to new heights. This achievement could not happen without the collaboration of composers and singers— many of them anonymous—each dedicated to common principles and themes evolving over decades and centuries.

Beyond the creation of individual works, new music participated in a much broader cultural evolution that fostered multivoiced dialectic and manuscript production. Given the complexity of polyphony, parts needed to be written and recorded in manuscripts.[21] The latter offered ocular evidence of concurrent vocal parts in musical "dialogue" that had so captivated their hearers. They also showed how these compositions could achieve such a high degree of theatricality by consciously pitting different voices against one another.

They were far from an idiosyncratic cultural development in thirteenth-century Paris, however. One has only to look to one of its principal "industries" of the period, the training of clerks at the university or of lawyers in the Basoche—as the Parisian law courts were known—to find a parallel example. In both the university and the Basoche, quodlibetal *disputationes* (questions, answers, and arguments) played a key role. Thanks to the conscious cultivation of the rhetorical principle of *actio* or delivery, disputation evolved into something akin to theatrical performance replete with spectators. It was Jody Enders's

brilliant insight over twenty years ago that showed how secular training in quodlibetal debate—by definition a multivoiced activity—gave rise to vernacular medieval drama.[22]

In the same vein, we should not overlook another impressive thirteenth-
century innovation: the *chansonniers*, or manuscript collections of lyric poetry.
Rather than presenting the work of individual troubadours or *trouvères*, they
aggregate a certain number of poets and their songs in a single manuscript. By
bringing lyrics originally composed at different times and places into the same
space, *chansonniers* demonstrate the culture of imitation and contrafaction present in troubadour and *trouvère* lyric from the beginning. In effect, songbooks re-
cast the cult of the individual singer into a spectacle of creative competition in
which poets in a *chansonnier* may be perceived in "dialogue" with one another as
they imitate, parody, revise, remake, and critique songs of their precursors or contemporaries. For it is the particular "magic" of the songbook to allow poets who in
life were widely separated chronologically to engage one another within the same
space.[23]

Viewed from the perspective of thirteenth-century culture, the lyric doctrine that Amor adumbrates in the passage quoted above also involves a multi-
tude of singers separated by space and time: Tibullus, Catullus, Ovid, the troubadours, Guillaume, Jean, and so on. They constitute the voices—sometimes
harmonic, sometimes discordant—in the "flexible and boldly contrasting cadences" of medieval love poetry. In Jean de Meun's account, it is Amor who
confers the lyric soul or psyche on the poet, thereby intimately binding poet
and muse.

Others before Jean have made this claim. What is different about his treatment is the dramatic emphasis he places on the role of death and continuity—
the death of love poets and the continuity of love poetry—as a performative
phenomenon. It is as though the poetic psyche migrates from a dead poet to his
successor: "le poète est mort, vive le poète." Jean's theme is the collectivity of
poets—like a chorus constantly depleted and renewed—innovating and renew-
ing love's themes for over a thousand years.

In the spirit of the new music of his age, Jean stresses the multivoiced combinations, cadences, and tensions between the ever-evolving shapes and sounds
of love poetry. Tibullus's love poems and elegies written in the first century BCE
would have sounded quite different to Jean than, say, a poem by the twelfth-
century troubadour Bernart de Ventadorn, even allowing for the difference in
language. Yet for Jean, each serves Amor in celebrating, as does Catullus or

Guillaume de Lorris, their desire for and attachment to a woman whose true name they conceal but whose being they transpose into their verse—indeed whose being *becomes* their song.

Jean dramatizes the intimate bond between poet and Amor via the latter's lament as he recalls the death of Tibullus, by way of illustrating his theme of death and continuity:[24]

> Puis que Tibullus m'est faillis,
> Qui cognoissoit si bien mes teches, [fol. 74v b]
> Pour quel mort je brisay mes fleches,
> Cassay mes arcs et mes cuirees,
> Laissay trestoutes dessirees
> Dont je euz d'angoisses telles,
> Qu'a son tombel mes lassés elles
> Traynay toutes desrompues
> Tant les eu de deul debatues . . .
> En noz plors n'ot ne frains ne brides.
> Gallus Catillus et Ovides,
> Qui bien sorent d'amours trectier,
> Nous feïssent ores bon mestier;
> Mais chascun d'eulx gist mort porris
> Vezcy Guillaume de Lorris:
> Cui Jalousie sa contraire
> Fait tant d'angoisse et de deul traïre,
> Qu'il est en peril de mourir,
> Se je ne pens du secourir . . .
> Si seroit ce molt grant dommages,
> Se si loyal sergent perdoye,
> Com secorre luy puisse et doye
> Qui m'a si loyalment servi;
> Qu'il a bien vers moy desservi
> Que j'assaille et que je m'atour
> Pour rompre les murs de la tor . . .
> Et plus encor me doit servir, [fol. 75r a]
> Car pour ma grace acquerir
> Doit il commencer le rommant
> Ou sont mys tuit my command.[25]

When Tibullus died, he who did my work so well, I broke my arrows, shattered my bow and armor, renounced desire, and felt such anguish that I let my fractured and bedraggled wings—hard beaten in my grief—drag in the dust before his tomb . . . nothing can moderate our tears for him. [Then] Gallus, Catullus, and Ovid, all masters in the art of love, came along to serve me well. But each of them now lies dead and rotted; but here comes Guillaume de Lorris, whom Jalousie— his very antithesis—torments terribly and makes him grieve so much that he's in danger of dying, if I don't find a means of succoring him . . . It would be a great shame were I to lose such a loyal disciple, who has served me so faithfully, and whom I should and must succor; he richly deserves that I surround the tower [where he's imprisoned] and breach its walls . . . For he will yet do me great service when, to win my favor, he will begin the book containing all my laws.

While Amor paints a dramatic picture of Guillaume's plight, the reason for his concern appears at the end of the quotation: he has not yet begun "the book containing all my laws." Guillaume will begin it; Jean will finish it. But by Amor's own logic of death and continuity, this cannot be the end of the story. Amor speaks of the performance of the work as ongoing, a matter for the future tense, for audiences as yet unborn. He has repeatedly stressed the mutability of poets, and Guillaume himself will soon depart this earth, we're told. In this context one begins to understand why Amor, rather than Jean himself, articulates the tension between the contingency of creation and performative or creative continuity. Amor—as god and muse—enjoys transhistorical status. Like the work he inspires and whose performative potential he symbolizes, Amor stands for creative continuity.

Creative continuity is a performative principle that assures transmission of a work by participation of a new "voice" responsible for the version being passed down. For the *Rose,* and for the Middle Ages generally, agents of transmission— the performers of the work—were the scribes and artists who produced the manuscripts. So we might think of scribes as having a status akin to singers' understudies, who assume their roles when the stars cannot perform. While scribes and artists do not often achieve the status of principals, like Jean de Meun as he "sings Amor's words on crossroads and in schools," they do assure the transmission of the work as a living tradition. Amor himself casts such creative continuity as performance when he laments the death of one poet, only to celebrate immediately the performance of his successor. For Amor, as Jean dramatizes him, the *Miroër aux Amoureulx* is a live performance with "his" poet—be it Guillaume, Jean or another continually "flaiollant noz paroles / Par carrefours et par escolles, / Selon le langaige de France, / Par tout le regne en audience."

Obviously, each scribe and artist will determine the nature of their participation in accord with their individual sense of the *Rose*. We can only ascertain that by studying each manuscript version. We can say, however, that each scribe and artist embeds historical "snapshots," photographs in Kendall Walton's sense, of the cultural context of their performance. We might think of this as something akin to the watermark that conveys information about the place, date, and manufacture of paper.

As we have already seen, Girard Acarie presents a striking example of Amor's twin principles of contingent creativity and performative continuity. He is not reticent about joining his voice to those of Guillaume and Jean. He does so with striking subtlety in a painting (fig. 6) on folio 44r of Morgan 948 that is both a proleptic gloss on Amor's lament for Tibullus (the concept of death and continuity) and a critical insight on continuation itself. The image shows the dead figure of Amor's protégé, Guillaume de Lorris, laid out on a table awaiting burial. Shelves of books on the walls, and an alcove showing the bed and writing desk that appear on the incipit folio (folio 5r) of this manuscript (fig. 2) identify the corpse as a writer. Contrasted with the recumbent Guillaume, an elegant figure in a red robe—the same color as worn by the poet in figure 2—stands just outside the door to the house. Behind him stretches the countryside with a winding road symbolizing the distance the Lover still must travel to complete his quest. By his youth and posture, we take this figure to represent the Lover, mourning his dead guide. Two facts about this painting suggest that this figure also evokes Jean de Meun's primal creative act in assuming Guillaume's role in leading the Lover to the end foretold by Amor.[26]

That this painting addresses the joining of these different works—more illustrative of tension and bold contrast than blending—may be seen from its location in the manuscript as well as from the identity of the figure framed by the door. The painting on folio 44r occupies the right-hand page of the bifolio where Guillaume's poem ends and Jean's begins (folio 43v). The painting thus poses an aporia: if Guillaume is dead, how can the Lover, who represents his younger self, survive? One of the first things we learn in the poem, after all, is that it's the story of a dream that befell the poet five years earlier, when he was twenty.

By stressing the forty years that elapsed between Guillaume's death and Jean's continuation, Amor reminds us that, if one construes the Lover as an extension

Figure 6. Roman de la Rose, MS Morgan 948 (Paris, ca. 1520–25), fol. 44r: Guillaume de Lorris lies dead, and ready for burial, while the Lover stands outside the room mourning, but prepared to continue his quest. The Pierpont Morgan Library, New York. By permission.

of Guillaume's being, he *has* been dead, or at least living in suspended animation for all that time.[27] On this view, Girard's painting casts Jean's advent as something of a miraculous event. When the painter juxtaposes the spritely figure of the Lover against the realistic corpse of Guillaume in the foreground, he depicts nothing short of a resurrection—not of the dead poet, but of the work itself. Poets may die, but the work goes on so long as creative agents choose to perform it.

But just as the resuscitated work is no longer exclusively Guillaume's, so the Lover is no longer the protagonist of his own, personal *Bildungsleben*. Jean has freed him from Guillaume's *roman* to play a role in a much more ambitious and ambiguous drama in which lovers learn not about *fin'amors* in Guillaume's narrow sense, but about love as a much broader philosophical proposition. In this broader intellectual context, love morphs into a *speculum* or mirror of life itself, just as Amor predicts. It is this transition to love as knowledge—encyclopedic knowledge—that the resurrected Lover cannot assimilate. If Jean manages to give new dimensions to the laws of Love, their expansive range passes over the Lover's head.

Fully cognizant of Jean's epistemological turn, Girard does not portray the road the Lover must henceforth follow as leading to a *hortus conclusus*—the enclosed garden of Guillaume de Lorris's master reveler, Déduit. Instead, his path leads into a larger world, where the Lover, deprived of Guillaume's comforting certitudes, becomes a figure of farce or parody.

Like the precursors he is channeling in this imaginative presentation, Girard Acarie shows that performance can adapt to historical context, to an ever-changing public and to new modes of artistic representation. Yet as original as Girard's portrayal of this scene may be, as much as he deepens our recognition of its discordant notes, he also leads us to recognize Jean de Meun's wisdom in not seeking to resolve its aporia.

NOTES

I would like to express my gratitude to my Hopkins colleagues Michel Jeanneret and Jacques Neefs, who conceived the idea for the colloquium that gave rise to the present volume, and to my German colleagues Andreas Kablitz and Joachim Küpper, who joined with Michel and Jacques to make it possible. Howard Bloch, my close *compagnon de route* for many years, proved his friendship yet again in editing this volume. Alison Calhoun provided invaluable executive assistance coordinating the many complex components of the event. Jeanette Patterson stepped in at a crucial moment to complete the task of bringing the volume to publication. The former executive administrator of German and Romance Languages, Rebecca Swisdak, patiently devoted her superb organizational talent to logistics, expenses, commissary, troubleshooting, and much more besides. For their work and friendship, I am honored and very grateful.

1. Stephen G. Nichols, "Introduction: Philology in a Manuscript Culture," in "The New Philology," ed. Stephen G. Nichols, special issue, *Speculum* 65, no. 1 (1990): 8, 9.

2. "Pour ce qu'il [Jean] iert tant mes amis, / Je l'afublerai de mes eles / Et li chanterai notes teles / Que puis qu'il sera hors d'enfance, / Endoctrinez de ma science, / Si fleüstera noz paroles / Par carrefors o par escoles / Selonc le langage de france." See Guillaume de Lorris and Jean de Meun, *Le Roman de la Rose*, ed. Armand Strubel, vol. 4533, *Lettres gothiques* (Paris: Librairie générale française, 1992), 10,640–47.

3. Nichols, "Philology in a Manuscript Culture," 1.

4. Erich Auerbach, *Introduction to Romance Languages and Literatures* (New York: Meridian, 1961), 147.

5. Seth Lerer, "Philology and Criticism at Yale," *Journal of Aesthetic Education* 36, no. 3 (Autumn 2002): 16.

6. In "Philology and Criticism at Yale" (quoted above), Seth Lerer argues that philology and theory were intertwined at Yale thanks to the pioneering work of William Dwight Whitney (1827–94), professor of comparative philology and Sanskrit beginning in 1853. In the late 1950s and early '60s, the influence of New Criticism, with its emphasis on close reading, and René Wellek's training in the Prague linguistic circle in the early 1930s were very much in evidence to those of us who were graduate students at that time. On Lerer's account, the thread that ran from Whitney to Auerbach, to Cleanth Brooks, to Wellek as well as other eminent Yale faculty at midcentury may be seen in subsequent theoretical movements by Yale-trained critics. He is thinking of such figures as Thomas Greene, Geoffrey Hartman, Fred Jameson, J. Hillis Miller, Paul De Man, Catherine Gallagher, Steven Greenblatt, and the Yale school of deconstruction. Without endorsing such sweeping claims for the hegemony of New Haven on philology and theory in the United States, one can at least cite Lerer's 2002 article as vindication of our efforts in 1990 to bridge the gap between philology and theory.

7. The book was copied circa 1520–25 by Girard Acarie for presentation to King Francis I of France; Acarie copied the text from a 1519 edition printed in Paris by Michel le Noir. Francis is depicted receiving the book on folio 4r, and his coat of arms appears opposite this on folio 3v. The following provenance is from the *Seventeenth Report to the Fellows of the Pierpont Morgan Library, 1972–1974*:

> Provenance: Francis I, king of France, for whom the manuscript was made; John Louis Goldsmid; his sale, London, Evans, 11 December 1815, lot 729; to John North of East Acton, Middlesex; his sale, London, Evans, 25 May 1819, III, lot 806; to William Esdaile; his sale, London, Christie's, 15 March 1838, lot 357; to Henry Bohn, London bookdealer; William Knight; his sale, London, Sotheby's, 2 August 1847, lot 1074; to William Pickering, London bookdealer; Lord Vernon (Sudbury Hall Library, Derbyshire), with bookplate; his sale, London, Sotheby's, 10 June 1918, lot 327; to B.F. Stevens; Cortlandt Field Bishop, with bookplate; his sale, New York, American Art Association–Anderson Galleries, 26 April 1931, lot 1365; to Beatrice Bishop Berle.

The following bookplates are present: The Pierpont Morgan Library; Lord Vernon's bookplate; Cortlandt Field Bishops' bookplate; label "THE GIFT OF Beatrice Bishop Berle in memory of her father Cortlandt Field Bishop 1972." Written in pencil inside front cover: "Cabinet I.a. 1777 in Catalogue [?struck through]." Description prepared by Professor Timothy Stinson and taken from the *Rose* website: http://romandelarose.org/#book;Morgan948.

8. MS Morgan 948, fol. 4v, J. Pierpont Morgan Library, New York. Girard signs the dedication as follows: "Vostre tres humble Et tres obeissant subyect et serviteur Girard Acarie."

9. This is not to say that poets like Dante, Petrarch, and many others did not wish to control the texts of their works. Especially from the fourteenth century onward, we know

this to have become an issue. But they had neither the technology nor the cultural acceptance of what we have come to call "intellectual property" to realize that desire.

10. For the distinction between depiction as a product of structured imagining and the photograph as transparent and belief independent, see Kendall L. Walton, *Marvelous Images: On Values and the Arts* (Oxford: Oxford University Press, 2008): chaps. 5–6, 63–108.

11. Walton, *Marvelous Images*, 84–85.

12. Ibid., 85.

13. Ibid., 86: "I am not saying that photography supplements vision by helping us to discover things we can't discover by seeing. Painted portraits and linguistic reports also supplement vision in this way. Nor is it my point that what we see—photographs—are *duplicates* or *doubles* or *reproductions* of objects, or *substitutes* or *surrogates* for them. My claim is that we *see*, quite literally, our dead relatives themselves when we look at photographs of them."

14. MS Morgan 948, fol. 105r b.

15. *Flaiol(l)er* is the musical sound produced by the *flaiol*, a *flute-à-bec* or recorder, often played in conjunction with a *taborel* (diminutive of *tabour*), a small, shallow drum played with the hands. In his *Dit dou Lion*, Guillaume de Machaut pairs the two instruments: "Et faisoit une reverdie, / Devant toute la compaingnie, / Au flaiol et au taburel, / A tout son sercost de burel." Guillaume de Machaut, *Le Dit dou Lion*, ed. E. Hoepffner, vol. II (Paris: Librairie Firmin Didot, 1911), 1551–54.

16. MS Morgan 948, fol. 105rb–105va; corresponds to Dominique-Martin Méon and Daniel Poirion, *Le Roman de la Rose* (Paris: Hatier, 1973), ll. 10,636–54; and Félix Lecoy, *Le Roman de la* Rose, vol. II (Paris: Champion, 1966), ll. 10,606–24.

17. "MIROIR, s.m. [Compl.] verre poli et étamé, ou métal poli, où l'on peut voir son image réfléchie.—Fig., ce qui donne l'image de qqchose: *Ceste estoire est mireors de vie.* (Chron. de S.-Den., ms. Ste-Gen., f° 1b. *Le vray miroer de la beauté humaine.* (EUST. DESCH., V, 165.) *C'est le mirouer qui esclaire Voz cueurs.* (MARG. DE NAV., Dern. poés., p. 93, Comédie jouée au Mont-de-Marsan, Ab. Lefranc.)—Au moyen âge, titre de recueils contenant des préceptes de morale, de jurisprudence, des récits, etc.: *Le mireour du monde.* (LAURENT, Chavannes, 1854.) *Le miroir de l'ame.* (LAURENT, ms. Maz. 870, f° 192.)" Frédéric Godefroy, *Dictionnaire de l'ancienne langue française et de tous ses dialectes du 9e au 15e siècle* (Paris: Classiques Garnier numérique, 2004).

18. "Puis viendra Jehan Choppinel / Au cuer joly au corps ysnel, / Qui naistra sur Loyre a Meun, / Qui tout a saoul et a jeun / Me servira toute la vie / Sans avarice et sans envie . . . Le cuer vers moy tant aura fin / Que tousiors au moins en la fin / . . . Cil aura le rommant si chier, / Qu'il le vouldra tout parfinir, / Se temps et lieu luy peult venir. / Car quant Guillaume cessera, / Lors Jehan si le commencera, / Apres sa mort que je ne mente / Ans trespassez plus de quarente. / . . . Mais par cestuy ne peult ores ester, / Ne par celluy qui est a naistre. / . . . Car il n'est mye cy presens / Si rest la chose si pesans, / Que certes quant il sera nez, / Se je ne vien tous empenez / Pour luy lire nostre sentence, / Si tost qu'il ystra de s'enfance, / Si vous oz jurer et plevir, / Il n'en pourroit jamais chevir." Bodleian Library, MS Douce 195, fol. 75ra, 75rb.

19. Margo Schulter, "Thirteenth-Century Polyphony," http://www.medieval.org/emfaq/harmony/2voice.html. For those not conversant in music theory, an interval is

the distance between two notes. One ascertains that distance by counting the lines and spaces on the staff. The interval from C to G is a fifth, because five notes are involved: C, D, E, F, G.

20. Ibid.: "The music of the 13th century boldly exploits the entire spectrum of intervals from the most blending to the most aggressively discordant. While the distinction between stable and unstable intervals is absolute, there are various degrees of tension among the unstable intervals . . . Given this approach of flexibility and bold contrast, we should not be surprised to find an amazing variety and richness of multi-voice combinations and cadences."

21. See, for example, Carl Parrish, "Early Polyphonic Notation," in *The Notation of Medieval Music* (New York: W. W. Norton, 1957), chap. 3.

22. Jody Enders, *Rhetoric and the Origins of Medieval Drama* (Ithaca, NY: Cornell University Press, 1992).

23. On the theatricality of the *chansonnier,* see my article: " 'Art' and 'Nature:' Looking for (Medieval) Principles of Order in *Chansonnier N* (Morgan 819)," in *The Whole Book: Cultural Perspectives on the Medieval Miscellany* (Ann Arbor: University of Michigan Press, 1996), 83–121.

24. MS Douce 195, fol. 74v a.

25. Bodleian Library, MS Douce 195, fol. 74v a–74v b, 74v b–75r a.

26. "Jusqu'a tant qu'il aura cueillie, / Sur la branche vert et fueillie, / La tresbelles rose vermeille / Et qu'il soit ior et qu'il s'esveille . . ." Bodleian Library, MS Douce 195, fol. 75r b.

27. Ibid., fol. 74v b: "Car quant Guillaume cessera, / Lors Jehan si le commencera, / Apres sa mort que je ne mente / Ans trespassez plus de quarente."

CHAPTER TWO

Reflections on The New Philology

GABRIELLE M. SPIEGEL

Before reflecting on the goals, nature, and achievements of Stephen Nichols's edited 1990 volume for *Speculum* on *The New Philology*, it might prove helpful to provide some background about how the volume came to be and the furor that it caused in the profession after its publication.

The publication of *The New Philology* as a special issue of *Speculum* represented an unprecedented foray into special issues on the part of the journal. The decision to invite a guest editor occurred after several years of discussion on the part of the executive committee of the Medieval Academy concerning the state of *Speculum*, its apparent inhospitality to new directions in the field, the unconscionable length of time between submission and publication (sometimes amounting to three years or more), and a host of other problems then besetting the journal. In particular, due to the intellectually conservative bent of the editorial board, throughout the late seventies and eighties almost all new work in the fields covered under the general rubric of medieval studies— especially anything that incorporated the rising tide of poststructuralist literary criticism, questions of gender, or linguistic turn historiography—tended to be turned away. To the executive committee's credit, they found this situation unacceptable and after considerable debate determined to create a series of guest-edited issues offering fresh perspectives in the field by publishing representative samples of innovative work dedicated to special themes selected by the guest editors.

How Stephen Nichols came to be chosen to edit the volume I do not know. *The New Medievalism* was to appear only in the following year (1991), but Steve was certainly well known for his writings and collaborative work with other medievalists and sat on myriad editorial boards at the time, so was a logical and intelligent choice. Nor am aware of why he choose the topic of the New Philology or, more mysterious still, how he came to select the five contributors to write on this topic. Indeed, most of us were fairly perplexed about the topic and its substantive focus. Howard Bloch went so far as to note in his article that:

> I do not consider myself a "New Philologist" or a "new" anything, except perhaps a new man; and since part of being a new man implies a certain obligatory return of the subject—a phrase indicating his acquaintance with poststructuralist concepts of the decentered subject—and since the phrase "New Philology" bothers me, I therefore place it in quotation marks. I use the term "New Philology" to refer not to the Italian "nuova filologia," but to a certain unsettling rethinking of medieval literature, especially old French literature.

Why I was asked to participate in the volume is equally perplexing. At the time, I was an associate professor at the University of Maryland, had published a rather traditional survey of the textual and manuscript history of *The Chronicle Tradition of Saint-Denis*, and had for some time been embarked on a study of the rise of vernacular prose historiography in thirteenth-century France. Along the way I was publishing articles, some of which (on the topic of medieval genealogy for example) were akin to work that Howard Bloch was publishing, and I was, like Howard, definitely moving toward work that sought to rethink the medieval enterprise of writing history, both in Latin and Old French, on the basis of my reading of literary theory, and poststructuralism in particular. Whatever the cause, sometime in the fall or spring of 1988, Steve called me up and said, "I am editing a special volume of *Speculum* on current issues in literary studies and I need a historian."

As those who are acquainted with him will readily understand, it is difficult to refuse Steve on such matters, so I agreed, although I had no idea what he meant by "the New Philology." I did try to discover what it might entail by calling up Lee Patterson, whom I knew had also been invited to contribute. "Lee," I asked, "what's the New Philology?" "Damned if I know," he said, "write what you want." I had already told Steve that there was a problem I had been thinking about for a long time, which I conceived in terms of the social logic of the text, so I suggested that I would write on that topic. "I don't know what you mean by that," he said, "but do what you want." And so I came to write my contribution on the social logic of the text, a problem whose relationship to the topic of the New Philology was not, at the time, exactly clear to anyone involved. Lee Patterson similarly decided to write about his own preoccupations, which in his case concerned what he perceived to be the fatal marginalization of medieval studies, and hence medievalists, within the wider professional circles to which they belonged, whether literary or historical. Among the contributions, only the article by Sigfried Wenzel, "Reflections on (New) Philology," mounted a defense of the Old Philology, appropriately updated by noting practices and methods developed since the field's professional founding in the late nineteenth century.

And yet, looking back almost twenty years later, there appears to be an unanticipated degree of coherence to the contributions, at least insofar as all the articles in varying ways sought to move medieval literary study, including the study of medieval historical texts as literary, textual artifacts, beyond the confines of traditional approaches and, as Howard Bloch remarked, to do so in a manner that would unsettle traditional assumptions and approaches. And unsettle them they certainly did. On reflection, it is a minor miracle that *Speculum*, until that time renowned for its intellectual conservatism and *wissenschaftliche* orientation, agreed to publish the volume at all.

No one at the time of its publication, not even the reluctant editorial board, could have envisaged the storm, the *scandal* in fact, that its appearance produced. Steve was denounced by scholars for destroying the field of French medieval literature; conferences attacking the issue in general and Steve in particular were organized; and the looming decline of French medieval studies was loudly trumpeted everywhere. *Speculum* only once again published a guest-edited issue, that time on questions of women's history and gender edited by Nancy Partner ("No Sex, No Gender," *Speculum* 68, 1993), but that issue, too, was considered so scandalous, occasioned so many conferences attacking it, and generated so much controversy that the journal hastily reverted to its normal practices of publishing only submitted and vetted articles.

So what was the scandal about? After all, a series of articles on a topic like philology, old or new, scarcely seemed likely to generate the level of animosity and downright fear for the future of medieval studies created by this slim volume of rather differently oriented pieces on a handful of more or less unrelated topics. Leaving to one side Wenzel's contribution—rather different in character than the others—what underlying thematics were there to the volume as a whole that occasioned such a storm of protest, and yet palpably resonated with a significant segment of the profession who were in sympathy with its goals and approaches, even if they could not all be subsumed, exactly, under the rubric of the New Philology?

Part of the answer, I think, lies in the way the issue was framed by Stephen Nichols's "Introduction: Philology in a Manuscript Culture" and Lee Patterson's conclusion entitled "On the Margin: Postmodernism, Ironic History, and Medieval Studies." Both, in quite different ways and with distinct foci and intentions,

clearly noted the growing irrelevance of traditional approaches to medieval literary studies and called for wholesale revisions to our understanding of medieval
literary culture. Of the two, Nichols's was by far the more respectful of the past
achievements of medieval literary scholars like Spitzer, Curtius, and Auerbach,
and less directly insistent than Patterson on recentering medieval studies
within a postmodern framework. But his desire to ground literary scholarship
in a study of the material manuscript, and hence on the interminable and un-
controllable *variance* that it embodied, called into question once and for all the
philologist's traditional reliance on a hierarchical, printed (and hence stabilized)
version of the text, which reached back to a notional *ur*-text. In brief, as Nichols
described it, the New Philology would develop in opposition to a version of philology that sought to produce "a fixed text, as transparent as possible, one that
would provide the vehicle for scholarly endeavor but, once the work of editing
accomplished, not the focus of inquiry" (3). Such a view of the medieval text, he
noted, was based on an understanding of medieval poetry—or literature more
generally—as "mimesis, rather than semiosis, on direct, rather than mediated,
imitation" (5).

In turning to the material specificity of medieval texts, or what he calls "the
manuscript matrix," Nichols committed himself to exploring the manuscript
culture of the Middle Ages "in a postmodern return to the origins of medieval
studies"; that is, to restoring to philological investigation the "important supplements that were part and parcel of medieval textual production: visual images
and annotations of various forms (rubrics, captions, glosses, and interpolations)"
(7). Moreover, he asserted, when we remember that all manuscripts postdate the
life of the author by decades and even centuries, we recognize "the medieval
matrix as a place of radical contingencies: of chronology, of anachronism, of conflicting subjects, of representation" (8). He then proceeded to argue:

> The multiple forms of representation on the manuscript page often provoke rup-
> ture between perception and consciousness, so that what we actually perceive may
> differ markedly from what poet, artist, or artisan intended to express or from what
> the medieval audience expected to find. In other words, the manuscript space
> contains gaps through which the unconscious may be glimpsed . . . What I am
> suggesting is simply that the manuscript matrix consists of gaps or interstices, in
> the form of interventions in the text made up of interpolations of visual and verbal
> insertions which may be conceived, in Jacques Lacan's terms, as "pulsations of the
> unconscious" by which the subject reveals and conceals itself. (8)

To adopt such a posture toward the interpretation of medieval literary artifacts was to go beyond its textuality as traditionally construed and fatally to destabilize the very textuality that the Old Philology had sought so strenuously to fix in an invariant, printed form. Small wonder that scholars faithful to the traditional notion of philological investigation felt threatened by this new formulation of its aims and character.

Lee Patterson, on the other hand, closed the volume by considering the nature and standing of medieval studies generally, which he claimed were deemed by most of the academic world to be "a site of pedantry and antiquarianism, a place to escape from the demands of modern intellectual life" (87). Denigrated by other branches of academia and willfully self-marginalized, medievalists sought their professional legitimation in the technical difficulties of their work: the lack of instant intelligibility characteristic of medieval texts and the requirement, therefore, for all those learned skills that made the old philologist a heroic figure, since the very strangeness and "difference" signified by the medieval past suggested a special virtue required for its study. "Medievalists," Patterson complained, are wont to wrap their professional identity in an armature of scholarly techniques and competencies, including not just languages, "but paleography, philology, codicology, diplomatics, and a wide range of research techniques, thought to be the essential possessions of the aspiring medievalist" (102). Moreover, in taking refuge in technical virtuosity, medievalists reenacted the grand master narrative of Western civilization according to which modernity was conceived as beginning with the Renaissance, relegating the Middle Ages to an abjected, premodern "other."

Nor did Patterson endear himself or the volume to members of the Medieval Academy when he forthrightly laid part of the blame for the regressive nature of the field on the workings of the Medieval Academy itself, with its hierarchical nature, closely held scholarly authority and control—at the time, the Academy was primarily run by Harvard faculty in Cambridge, where the editorial offices of *Speculum* resided—and lack of openness to discussion, all of which, he asserted, were "inimical to the cooperative spirit to which the Academy is dedicated." And these harmful attitudes, he added, "were fostered by the very structure of the Academy, with its self-perpetuating Fellowships [i.e., the body of fellows, restricted in number to one hundred at any given moment] and its reliance on a nominating committee to produce normally unopposed candidates for the senior offices" (103).

Notwithstanding these inherited difficulties, Patterson held out hope that postmodernism could offer a means to redeem medievalists, because in the "postmodern condition," he quoted Terry Eagleton, "what was previously displaced to the margins returns to haunt the very center." Moreover, by dismantling the West's master narratives, à la Lyotard, postmodernism reconfigured the central place and significance of modernity within it and thus possessed the potential for disclosing the intrinsic compatibility of the pre- and postmodern, in which modernity itself becomes problematic. The bulk of Patterson's article went on to illustrate some of these intrinsic similarities and to see in them the professional occasion for the rehabilitation of medieval studies along new, postmodern lines.

It is not difficult to see why the framing of *The New Philology* by these two programmatic pieces would have caused such a furor within the profession at the time, but in many ways, the more modest demonstrations of the workings of a postmodern/poststructuralist approach to medieval texts and discourses in specific contexts in the intervening articles did as much to demonstrate the obsolescence of traditional philological practices and the need for new approaches to medieval textuality. Although somewhat overlooked at the time the volume came out, Suzanne Fleischman's article on "Philology, Linguistics, and the Discourse of the Medieval Text" was a groundbreaking examination of the nature of Old French as a spoken language imperfectly grammaticalized in written form, our only point of access to it. Bringing to bear contemporary linguistics on traditional philological problems, Fleischman did not hesitate to name the coming "crisis of philology" in the face of the challenges posed by postmodernism and to call upon medieval literary scholars "to reexamine the premises and presuppositions of our traditional methodologies and disciplinary practices and to renovate or replace them if need be with alternatives which can make the old texts speak to us in ways more consonant with our modern, now postmodern, episteme" (19).

Like Nichols, Fleischman sought to suggest directions for revitalizing philology by beginning with a recognition of the inherent instability, the endless *variance*, of medieval texts, a recognition achieved by noting the grammatical and verbal incoherencies contained in Old French as it has come down to us in manuscript form. In her case, the gaps and anomalies were less a function of the manuscript matrix as such, but reflected instead the fact that "the language of Old French texts" was "not yet a codified, written idiom." "From the standpoint of grammar and discourse structure," she asserted, "Old French is very much a spoken language, the communicative instrument of a fundamentally oral culture" (21) even though it comes down to us exclusively as a "text language" (24). As anyone who has ever worked with Old French manuscripts knows, medieval vernacular documents are full of grammatical "errors" (or anomalies, as she prefers to call them), at times rendering the text almost incomprehensible. Fleischman noted, for example, the inconsistencies of orthography (with even proper names spelled variously at any given moment), the lack of word boundaries, the dysfunctionality of case markings, tense usages that "seem to defy grammatical logic," not to mention that absence of connective tissue between clauses, inconsistent narrative chronologies and the like (21), all of which make transcribing, not to mention understanding, an Old French manuscript a time-consuming and arduous endeavor.

Fleischman persuasively demonstrated the utility of contemporary linguistics for understanding the modalities of romance orality and textuality and the specific ways in which they violate the linguistic norms stipulated by traditional philological scholarship, which, rather than seeing them as reflective of the pragmatics of a language in the process of transforming itself from a predominantly spoken one to written form, sought to "emend" them to suit later views of linguistic propriety and grammatical correctness. As she asserted:

> As a linguistically oriented philologist, I am convinced that many of the disconcerting properties of medieval vernacular texts—their extraordinary parataxis, mystery particles, conspicuous anaphora and repetitions, "proleptic" topicalizations, and jarring alternations of tenses, to cite but a few—can find more satisfying explanations if we first acknowledge the extent to which our texts structure information the way a spoken language does, and then proceed to the linguistic literature that explores the pragmatic underpinnings of parallel phenomena in naturally occurring discourse. (23)

Fleischman then proceeded to demonstrate, through a minute examination of the "mystery particle *si*," (30) the ways in which a postmodern view of grammar as "emergent," as a set of linguistic transactions continually being negotiated in unstable ways within the context of individual communication (i.e., from the point of view of pragmatics), modifies and enriches our understanding of language "as a code for communication," thereby displacing the traditional philological focus on structure (or *langue*) to one concerned with actual discourse (or *parole*; 31). The result of these investigations conducted along the principles of a discourse-based linguistics, she suggested, poses "a challenge to philologists who bring linguistic expertise to the study of medieval texts, a challenge to rethink certain of the received ideas about early vernacular grammar, to rewrite the grammars in light of important insights afforded by a pragmatically based text linguistics" (34). Only by accepting such challenges, Fleischman affirmed, will philology be able to rise above the crisis of irrelevancy that it faced and to survive by moving in new directions. Although framed quite differently than Nichols's concern with the variance at the core of medieval *written* language within the "manuscript matrix," Fleischman's article complemented his by offering both a telling critique of the Old Philology and an illuminating illustration of the contours that a "new philology"—one informed by the employment of contemporary linguistics—might take. Although it was not subject to the same level of criticism as the other articles in *The New Philology*, in many ways its challenges to traditional philological practices were as profound and compelling as the more theoretical discussions of the other pieces.

"New Philology and Old French" were similarly the concern of Howard Bloch's article. He began by noting that the New Philology shared with the Old Philology certain fundamental presuppositions: "1) the privileging of language over its referent in the production of meaning . . . ; 2) the contextualizing of literature with respect to historical process and with respect to other discourses of man such as philosophy, anthropology and the social sciences; 3) the irreductibility of the letter within the process of literary understanding, or the resistance of poetry to anything like a univocal meaning and of literary studies to the exactitude of a physical science; and 4) . . . given the impossibility of ever exhausting the semantic richness of even the most finite element of medieval poetics, a corollary of the 'New Philology' was the reinscription of something like the *mysterium* of poetry, its realignment . . . with the domain of ontological thinking and yes, even with a certain occulted theological underpinning" (39).

Bloch then traced the rise of philology as a discipline with claims to the stature of an exact science modeled on the natural sciences and its reduction, beginning in Germany in the 1860s, to a method for the establishment, dating, identification, and localization of texts. It was, of course, against this essentially German model of philology, adopted in France after the Franco-Prussian War, that the New Philology defined itself and, in doing so, against the positivism and literary naturalism that constituted its methodological and philosophical basis. I will not rehearse here Bloch's careful recounting of the rise of French philology in the nineteenth century through the labors of scholars like Gaston Paris and Joseph Bédier, for it is surely well known to most scholars of medieval France, except to note that his focus throughout was on the ways in which philology served as a vehicle of literary realism, intrinsic to which was a notion of "the immediate accessibility of the text, which is imagined to be as lucid and direct as the world it depicts." This version of philology developed in France as "the expression of a nationalist desire on the part of the

French for a scientific—that is hard—methodology that might measure up to German philological science" (46).

In sharp contrast to the aspirations of the Old Philology for textual exactitude, transparency, immediacy, and naturalism, the New Philology, Bloch averred, if it had come to mean anything in the decades between World War II and the present, viewed the Old French text as richly complex, as contrived and perverse, as self-contradictory and problematic, as deceptive and falsely seductive, as opaque, and thus as needy of interpretation as any literary work of any age (46).

Nor, he argued, are these characteristics due merely to the "technical problems deriving from the ways in which an essentially oral language might have been graphically transcribed or with the ways in which manuscripts were copied and preserved," on which Nichols and Fleischman had commented. Rather, they were intrinsic to the nature of Old French textuality, which resisted any attempt to reduce its pregnant plays of the letter to univocal meaning and thus made impossible any effort to exhaust the semantic resonances of certain key syllables and words. Although Bloch does not say so explicitly, this characterization of the language of Old French literature placed it squarely within a post-structuralist, Derridean, understanding of the basic instability of signs and the inherent supplementarity of textual production.

To illustrate the operation of these modalities in Old French literature, Bloch proceeded to investigate the *Lais* of Marie de France and to link the notion of *lai* as written residue "to the written law and, finally, to show the extent to which the poetess [i.e., Marie de France] and a certain medieval (and also peculiarly modern) notion of poetry are implicated in what seems in the *Lais* to be an obsession with linguistic transgression" (48). Moreover, he maintained, medieval poetic theory, as exemplified in the case of Marie de France, was thoroughly integrated with poetic praxis and disclosed, in its very linguistic nature, a consciousness on the part of the poet of "the meta-theoretical nature of medieval poetic practice" (47). Evidence of this theoretical awareness can be seen in Marie's general "Prologue" to *Guigemar*, presenting an "*ars poétique*, which prescribes the making of texts as a series of rewritings, which, no matter how perfect, always leave a 'surplus of meaning'" (54). Clearly, at this point, any philological approach to medieval textuality that strove to be consonant with the nature of such texts and the text's own theoretical entailments placed *The New Philology* well within the precincts of postmodernist understandings of language and literature. My own article on the "social logic of the text" seconded this basic position, although it was, for obvious reasons, more concerned with the contextual determinants of the historiographical texts on which I was working at the time, and hence with the theoretical means of articulating the relationship between text and context in light of the challenge posed by semiotics to older models of historiography.

Reflecting back on *The New Philology* from the vantage point of almost twenty years, it seems clear that in their different ways the articles gathered together under this title essentially enacted, to greater and lesser degrees, a moment of literary history associated with the expansion of semiotics and poststructuralism among literary and historical scholars and did so in ways that today seem wholly benign, so accustomed have we become to the basic postulates of poststructuralism and so thoroughly did it penetrate literary and historical criticism around this time. Were *The New Philology* to be published today, I venture to say that it would look somewhat quaint and even out of date, at least to the extent that there seems to be a growing sense that what was variously called "the linguistic turn," "postmodernism," or "poststructuralism" has run its course, wrought whatever changes our disciplines are likely to absorb—while rejecting a significant number of others—and is effectively over. As Michael Roth recently noted, "for the last decade or so, recognition has been spreading that the linguistic turn that had motivated much advanced work in the humanities is over. The massive tide of language that connected analytic philosophy with pragmatism, anthropology with social history, philosophy of science with deconstruction, has receded; we are now able to look across the sand to see what might be worth salvaging before the next waves of theory and research begin to pound the shore."[1] More pointedly still, Nancy Partner has taken to speaking of the "post-postmodern"[2] in literary and historical scholarship.

At issue is a growing sense of dissatisfaction with poststructuralism's overly systematic account of the operation of language in the domain of human endeavors of all kinds. Among historians who have engaged in these debates, one response to the success of the semiotic/linguistic view of culture and society has taken place via a refocusing on the categories of causality, change, human agency and subjectivity, and experience (all placed under erasure by poststructuralism), accompanied by a revised understanding of the master category of discourse that stresses less the structural aspects of its linguistic constructs than the pragmatics of their use. Thus practice and meaning have been at least partially uncoupled from the impersonal workings of discursive regimes and rejoined to the active intentions of human agents embedded in social worlds. Rather than being governed by impersonal semiotic codes, historical actors are now seen as engaged in inflecting the semiotic constituents (signs) that shape their understanding of reality so as to craft an experience of that world in terms of a situational sociology of meaning, or what might be called a social semantics.[3] This shift in focus from semiotics to semantics, from given semiotic structures to the individual and social construal of signs—in short, from culture as discourse to culture as practice and performance—entails a recuperation of the historical actor as a rational and intentional agent, as Amanda Anderson has passionately and cogently argued in her recent book *The Way We Argue Now.*[4]

Interestingly, this position is remarkably similar to that staked out by most of the contributors to *The New Philology*, all of whom insisted on the presence and workings of the poet's, the language user's, and the historiographer's consciousness and intentions in the making of the literary texts under consideration. In that sense, *The New Philology* not only gave expression to a high tide of theoretical speculation among medievalists, but also already pointed to possible avenues of revision to its theoretical presuppositions. As almost all the contributors noted, the fundamental affinity between medieval and postmodern conceptions of language, literature, and history made the turn to theory, whether in the form of the New Philology or otherwise, a more or less natural tendency. At the same time, what Lee Patterson described as the stubborn allegiance of medievalists to a notion of the alterity of the past and "respect for historical particularity" could, he believed, "challenge the universalist claims of contemporary theory and instruct postmodernist criticism in the historical complexity and concreteness of cultural forms" (106). In that sense, he argued, medieval studies is ideally placed to exploit the other, authentically historicist strain of postmodern thinking, and surely this is what has been occurring over the last decade or so.

What is less clear, at least to me, is the place that medieval studies will occupy in the increasingly globalized world that is currently in the making, one that doubtless will generate new intellectual agendas and create new objects of investigation. This is already apparent in the growing concern with questions of diaspora, migration, immigration, and the rapidly developing field of transnationalism, with its focus on what the French literary scholar Françoise Lionnet has termed "minority cultures," which deploys a global perspective that emphasizes the basic hybridity of global cultures in the postcolonial and postmodern world. Where the Middle Ages will fit in these developments and how we will negotiate the inevitable tensions that such a shift almost certainly will produce between those committed to exploring the implications of present developments and those committed to the fundamentally historical and historicist orientations that have for so long guided medieval scholarship remains to be seen. The answers to such questions doubtless will come with time, but it is important, I believe, that as medievalists we not allow ourselves to retreat to that comfortable marginality against which Lee Patterson railed and which medieval studies so often courts as the basis of its legitimacy.

NOTES

1. Michael Roth, "Ebb Tide," *History and Theory* 46 (2007): 66.

2. Nancy Partner, "Narrative Persistence: The Post-postmodern Life of Narrative Theory," in *Re-Figuring Hayden White*, ed. Frank Ankersmit, Ewa Domanska, and Hans Kellner (Stanford, CA: Stanford University Press, 2009), 2. I would like to thank Professor Partner for sharing this chapter with me before its publication.

3. "Semantics" here would pertain not only to "meaning" or "signification" as such, but would include the relationship of propositions to reality.

4. Amanda Anderson, *The Way We Argue Now: A Study in the Cultures of Theory* (Princeton, NJ: Princeton University Press, 2006).

CHAPTER THREE

Virgil's "Perhaps"

Mythopoiesis and Cosmogony
in Dante's *Commedia* (Remarks on *Inf.* 34, 106–26)

GERHARD REGN

One of the undeniable contributions of New Medievalism is its revitalization of the debate concerning medieval authorship—a debate in which fundamental questions about the otherness of medieval auctorial authorities have been reconsidered, while at the same time the unreflective projection of modern conceptions onto a distant past could be more effectively avoided than was previously possible.[1] How productive the authorship discussion initiated by New Medievalism has been and continues to be is especially noticeable in areas that might not have seemed promising at first glance. This is true particularly for those cases in which, already in the context of the Middle Ages, authorship appears to be linked with auctorial individuality. I refer to those cases where a seemingly "strong" author claims personal responsibility for his work and aims decidedly at establishing a permanent form for his text in order to protect it as much as possible against the genuinely medieval practices of "variance."[2] Probably the most prominent representative of this kind of authorship is the Dante of the *Commedia*. On the basis of the previously mentioned criteria, Dante has usually been considered tacitly and self-evidently as a writer who could be understood by applying the concept of authorship that became common currency since the early modern era. The Dante of the *Commedia* thus became the kind of poetic figure, who, although he could tell of a far-off time and impart a medieval knowledge no longer common, nevertheless, in his role as a narrator, seemed to belong to a familiar mental world. Seen from the point of view of the new medievalist debate on authorship, however, a different picture begins to emerge. From this perspective, the strongly individualized authorship, which aims at textual stability, is seen as an expression of a transpersonal authorization based on the universe of medieval discourse in which religion, theology, and philosophy are closely interlinked.[3] The *Commedia* is a text that asserts truth and whose design places it in an analogy to the highest of all authorities: the Bible. Yet Dante's intention is not to follow the manner of numerous biblical epics that recount occurrences in Holy Scripture, but to create instead a text of revelation that stands in a complementary relationship to the Scriptures.[4] With its plot reenacting the redemption, the *Commedia* resembles a "Third Testament" which, considering the still-unrealized *parousia* (the Second Coming) and the still-unbroken power of evil in a world under the influence of the original sin, is intended to provide the work of salvation with new meaning, and thus render it newly fruitful for a humanity fallen into disorder.[5] A significant piece of evidence for the historical validity of this perspective—despite the controversial authorship question—is Dante's letter, contemporary with the *Commedia*, to Cangrande della Scala, in which the methods of biblical exegesis are applied to Dante's poem.[6] This again shifts the *Commedia* into the domain of theological authoritative discourse,[7] and in such a way that in its totality (not only at certain points) it establishes a suggestive analogy with Holy Scripture. The tendency to interpret the *Commedia* according to the pattern of biblical allegoresis has (*inter alia*) a fundamentally important consequence: it foregrounds the literal sense of the *Commedia* as a variation of the *sensus historicus* and thereby invests the narrated story of the journey to the afterworld not only with connotations of symbolic truth but also with those of reality; for in the perspective of biblical exegesis, the *litterae* of the narrative signify *facta*; that is, facts. The journey to the afterworld is therefore meant to be something other than a completely freely invented *favola*.[8]

Admittedly, Dante's claim to reality appears credible primarily by recurring to the discursive mode of the vision widely accessible at the time. In other words, the pretended reality is first of all that of a visionary experience.[9] From the beginning, the question of the factuality of what is reported is thus suggestively and effectively shifted to the manner in which it is transmitted. The factuality of the vision becomes the indispensable guarantee for the truth and reality of what is seen within the vision. For this reason, Dante's epic strives to affirm the factuality of the vision as emphatically as possible. This occurs in various ways. First, the demonstrative association with St. Paul's vision in the second letter to the Corinthians[10] embeds the *Commedia* in a visionary discourse whose authoritative veracity is incontestable;[11] second, the *topoi* of the numerous medieval accounts and visions of the other world are extensively referred to;[12] and, finally, the visionary situation as such is made a central theme, for example, in the prominent *proemium* of the *Paradiso*, where the figure of the poet asserts his recent presence in the Empyrean by recurring to the visionary mode (*vidi*): "Nel ciel che più de la sua luce prende / fu' io, e vidi cose."[13] The visionary experience is the condition for a revelation of hidden truth for the world. While seeing in the earthly paradise the allegorically charged image of the Church as a chariot, which discloses the complete history of salvation, Beatrice gives the wanderer Dante his commission to proclaim the divine truth, which will be realized in the *Commedia*: "in pro del mondo che mal vive, / al carro tieni or li occhi, e quel che vedi, / ritornato di là, fa che tu scrive."[14] The visionary mode requires a homodiegetic narrative,[15] and thus also the central position of the personality of the poet, who is not only mentioned by his real name, Dante,[16] but becomes present in the work with his whole family history and thereby as a historical individual.[17] In other words, the purely structural presence of the narrator in the text is (as it were) absorbed into the figure of the historically attested poet. All in all, we can see that what appears at a superficial glance to correspond with modern conceptions of the poet proves to be a characteristic variant of medieval authorship on closer inspection: in Dante's *Commedia* the author is fashioned as a prophetic *scriba Dei*; his message, however, presupposes an actual visionary experience that can only be granted an individual elected by divine grace. It is precisely this situation that the *Commedia* establishes at its very beginning: through the mercy of the Virgin Mary[18] the wanderer Dante is granted, in the middle of his life— "[n]el mezzo del cammin di nostra vita"[19]—the gift of grace, a view of the world beyond, about which Dante the poet will then report in the reflective mode.

Nevertheless, the *Commedia* is not merely presented as a simple record of a divinely inspired visionary experience; it is also a work of art that makes use of the available resources of worldly poetics. Accordingly, a personally fashioned authorship consists for Dante of two distinct, superimposed authorities. It is this dual presence of spiritual and secular diction that Dante indicates concisely when, at the beginning of Canto 25 of the *Paradiso*, he describes his work as a *poema sacro*: "al quale ha posto mano e cielo e terra."[20]

The relevance of a genuinely secular poetics is so clearly obvious throughout the *Commedia* that a few references to some of the most striking manifestations should suffice at this point:[21] Dante distinctly endeavors, for instance, to carefully avoid the hieronymic *sancta simplicitas* of traditional visionary literature;[22] he has his poet self-confidently claim the Apollonian laurels for what he has done, which introduces the worldly aspiration for fame at a point where it should be completely inappropriate;[23] and he even makes use of the idea of the author's power to dispose over his narrative, and in such a way that the originally claimed status of the divinely established visionary experience of revelation threatens to become precarious. The clearest hint in this direction is given in the address to the reader in *Paradiso* 5.109–11, where the poet says: "Pensa, lettor, se quel che qui s'inizia / non procedesse, come tu avresti / di più savere angosciosa carizia."[24] But this temptation to fashion the narrator as the sovereign power in his history is only the intensification of an inevitable tendency in the *Commedia*; namely, to effectively present the author as a poet, in the original sense of the word: as the maker[25] of the narrated history.

When Dante establishes the concept of a double authorship for his *poema sacro*, the distinct (and clearly hierarchicalized) authorities of the earthly poet and the divinely inspired scribe are so closely interlinked that the definite boundaries that exist between them become unavoidably blurred. Earthly poets are primarily producers of fictions: "poesi[s] . . . est . . . fictio"; this is the definition of poetry Dante gives in *De vulgari eloquentia* (2.4.2). The *Convivio* then specifies this elastic and broadly interpreted definition taken from the discussion about the vernacular (in which mainly the figurative character of rhetorical diction is meant), to the effect that poetic fictions as such tend to verge on the untrue: they take the form of beautiful lies (*bella menzogna*; *Convivio* 2.1.3) within the literal sense of narrative, which then secondarily, by means of poetic allegory, become signs of hidden truth.[26] A conflict with the author as *scriba Dei* is thus predetermined. For, by establishing an analogy between the *Commedia* and the Bible, Dante, from the very beginning, presents his history of the afterworld vision as nonfictive and places it in opposition to the freely invented *favole* referred to in the *Convivio* (2.1.3). When an afterworld view characterized in this way impinges, as a text, on the sphere of secular poetics, it risks being deprived of its essential element: it is in danger of being "infected" with the "virus" of fictitiousness. In order not to endanger his plan, and in order to endow the work of Christian salvation with a new effectiveness by means of a narrative of revelation that is complementary to the Bible, Dante must, during the course of the unfolding narrative of his *poema sacro*, time after time redefine the relationship between the poet and the scriptor, fiction and truth, the literal and the figural. He does this in an effort to master the unavoidable ambivalences so they can even become arguments that do not weaken the truth of the recounted vision of the afterworld but, on the contrary, attest to it. A prominent example of this, much discussed in Dante studies,[27] can be found at the distinctive end of the *Inferno*, where, in a confluent interplay between the earthly poet and the scriptor of God, the brief narrative of the origin of the world becomes, as it refers to the history of salvation, an explanation of the divine purpose of the world.

When the wanderers through the afterworld have arrived at the midpoint of the earth and the descent from the northern hemisphere down into the jaws of hell is, after arduously overcoming gravity, reversed in the ascent to the southern hemisphere, Virgil explains to his inquiring companion what has happened: at the farthest point away from God in the cosmos he informs him about the salvational significance of the construction of the world. His description of the details fulfills an elementary narratological function: it serves to introduce the place that will be the setting of the second *cantica*.

> Ed elli a me: "Tu imagini ancora
> d'esser di là dal centro, ov' io mi presi
> al pel del vermo reo che 'l mondo fóra.
> Di là fosti cotanto quant' io scesi;
> quand' io mi volsi, tu passasti 'l punto
> al qual si traggon d'ogne parte i pesi.
> E se' or sotto l'emisperio giunto
> ch'è contraposto a quel che la gran secca
> coverchia, e sotto 'l cui colmo consunto
> fu l'uom che nacque e visse sanza pecca;
> tu haï i piedi in su picciola spera
> che l'altra faccia fa de la Giudecca.
> Qui è da man, quando di là è sera;
> e questi, che ne fé scala col pelo,
> fitto è ancora sì come prim' era.
> Da questa parte cadde giù dal cielo;
> e la terra, che pria di qua si sporse,
> per paura di lui fé del mar velo,
> e venne a l'emisperio nostro; e forse
> per fuggir lui lasciò qui loco vòto
> quella ch'appar di qua, e sù ricorse."[28]

Virgil concisely sets forth the elements that constitute the cosmos, which underlies the otherworldly journey. In accordance with Aristotelian-Ptolemaic cosmography, he mentions the spherical shape of the universe, with its northern and southern halves.[29] The landmass inhabited by human beings lies, exactly as medieval geography assumed, in the northern hemisphere: Dante speaks, following the formulation in Genesis 1:9 (*arida*), of *la gran secca* (*Inf.* 34:113). Its highest point—*'l cui colmo* (*Inf.* 34:114)—is Jerusalem, which is described metonymically as the site where Christ's act of redemption took place, and which, both in the Bible and by the Fathers of the Church, is considered to be the center of the world.[30] On the other hemisphere, otherwise completely covered with water, rises the mountain of Purgatory, whose massive size we already know about from the Odysseus canto and on whose summit, we learn in the course of the second canticle, the earthly paradise is situated.[31] In the *Purgatorio* this site will then be (so to speak) rationally measured in accordance with contemporary categories of scientific cosmography. For the mountain of Purgatory, as Virgil explains a few cantos later, lies on the opposite side of the earth, antipodal to Jerusalem:

> imagina Sïòn
> con questo monte in su la terra stare,
> sì, ch'amendue hanno un solo orizzòn
> e diversi emisperi.[32]

In constituting the cosmology that he sketches at the conclusion of the *Inferno* and then completes in the course of the *Commedia*, Dante relies at first on authorized knowledge; within this context it is principally the rationality of medieval *scientia* that is brought to bear. He obviously does this, however, above all in order to render a concept believable that did not have a sufficiently concrete form in the cultural knowledge of the time: the concept of Purgatory.[33] The idea of Purgatory had only become an official tenet of Church doctrine shortly before the appearance of Dante's work, namely in 1274.[34] In spite of the relevance Purgatory possesses for the history of mentalities,[35] it was rather weakly determined conceptually (particularly concerning its relation to the earthly paradise). Most importantly, however, Purgatory usually had no precise geographic location.[36] Dante's procedure makes the floating island of the mountain of Purgatory a fixed constructive feature in a cosmos whose form is supposed to appear plausible, even from a scientific perspective. The elaborated astronomic references that are so important for construing the site of Purgatory are an unequivocal indication of this intention.[37]

It is hardly surprising that Dante does not allow an authorization in which the rationality of medieval science plays the central role to suffice. Instead, presenting the meaning of cosmos as a constitutive part of the history of salvation necessarily requires a recursion to explanatory patterns that are appropriate within the context of a genuinely theological discourse. In other words, the cosmology of the *poema sacro* necessarily exceeds the scientifically focused description of the world of the *Questio de aqua et terra*, most probably written by Dante, which did not include the mountain of Purgatory.[38] In the *poema sacro* the mountain of Purgatory and Jerusalem are conceived as antipodes, since a cosmos so structured can make the principal features of the history of salvation topographically meaningful. For, with the earthly paradise on its summit, the mountain of Purgatory is at the same time the site of the fall of man, and this makes it a mirror image of Mount Zion, the site of the act of redemption. The relationship of the two places is a typological one, as Old Adam, who was driven from paradise, is nothing other than a prefiguration of Christ, whose passion enabled the existence and deliverance of the "new" man.

In order to be able to relate the structure of the world to the constitutive dimension of the history of salvation required for the *Commedia*, Dante supplements the cosmology with a cosmogony that draws on the development of a central motif in biblical mythology. The subject in question is the fall of Lucifer, conceived as God's punishment for the original sin of *superbia*. The relevant Bible passages—especially Luke 10:18, Isaiah 14:12, and Revelation 12:9—briefly mention the fall: "How you are fallen from heaven, / O Day Star, son of Dawn! / How you are cut down to the ground, / you who laid the nations low!" (Isaiah 14:12–16). Dante then expands the biblical motif, making it the cause for the origin of the structure of the cosmos: for fear of Satan, who plunged down into the southern hemisphere, the landmasses that had originally spread out there, covered themselves with water, and fled to the north, where they are to have given the *gran secca* its current form. Simultaneously, at the center of the globe where Satan was supposed to be frozen solid in eternal ice at the point farthest from God, the landmass also attempted to avoid contact with him and formed an empty space—the *natural burella*—by pushing from the inside out and piling itself up into the towering mountain of Purgatory.[39]

Dante recounts—conveyed through Virgil, the secondary narrator—the story of the origin of the world. He does so by continuing a central theological motif, the fall of Lucifer, beyond the Bible text, while nevertheless retaining its discursive mode: a briefly suggested mythical motif from the Bible, which as such possesses the value of truth, is spun out into a "full" mythic narrative. One of the essential stylistic devices is the personification of the landmasses, which become anthropomorphized agents of a story. They experience fear, they cover themselves with a veil like someone wanting to hide, they flee in various directions. This is obviously a technique of rhetorical writing and thus constitutes what Dante emphasized in *De vulgari eloquentia* as the defining characteristic of poetry: a metrically composed "fictio rethorica . . . poita."[40] For, in the context of the tract on the vernacular, *fingere* means first of all (in addition to everything else it may mean) the composition of a text, while recurring to the figures of rhetoric. It is important to consider this because the "fictiveness" of the story Virgil tells about the origin of the world does not necessarily refer to what, in the multilayered medieval reflections on allegory, is occasionally called the *sententia litteralis* of the narrated story.[41] For this is supposed to be, according to the inherent poetics of the *poema sacro*, an analogue of the biblical myth; in this function it is true, substantial, and real. In other words, Virgil's story is not merely a *favola* or *bella menzogna*, as are, according to the *Convivio*, the freely invented narratives of worldly poets.[42] What is fictitious, in the first place, are only the words in which the narratives are clothed linguistically; it is the *parole fittizie* that the *Convivio* speaks of in this context.[43] Thus the prevailing tendency in Dante criticism up to now, which views the story of the origin of the world as no more than poetic fiction, does justice neither to the complexity of Dante's procedure nor to the many dimensions of his cosmogony—a tendency (by the way) that was already apparent in Dante's son Pietro, who also made use of the fiction argument, especially in relation to the cosmogony problem,[44] in order to defend his father's *magnum opus* against the increasingly intensive attacks of contemporaries.

Dante's cosmogony does not conform to the wording of the creation story in Genesis. But this does not inevitably restrict its ability to represent truth. On the contrary: Dante's myth of the origin of the world is meant to be understood instead as a narrative biblical commentary that considers the story of creation with regard to its ramifications in the Scriptures as a whole. As might be expected, in this context it also takes part in the extensive theological discussion of Lucifer's fall,[45] and this accords with Dante's basic pursuit in his *Commedia*: to make the work of salvation newly meaningful for his own time. An initial hint in this direction is given in Canto 29 of the *Paradiso*, where the theme of Lucifer is taken up again and associated with the cosmogony question. This is done differently than in the *Inferno*, however, by reducing the narrative style to an intentionally theoretical one through referring to biblical exegesis. In dissociation with Thomas Aquinas and in agreement with Bonaventura[46]—as we know, both doctors of the Church have a chance to speak extensively in Cantos 11 and 12 of the third canticle—the *Paradiso* passage integrates Lucifer's fall into time, and thus invests the creation of the earth with a sense of process that differs from the time frame of the creation story as reported in Genesis. Of the angels' fall and its consequences for the assumedly preexisting world we are told concerning *terra*, the earth, as the heaviest, and thus lowest, of the elements:

Né giugneriesi, numerando, al venti
sì tosto, come de li angeli parte
turbò il suggetto d'i vostri alimenti.[47]

The fall of Lucifer, to which the words of Isaiah 14:16—*qui conturbavit terram* "who made the earth tremble"—may be considered to allude, as it brings about the displacement of landmasses, is an important topic in creation theology. Although there are many conflicting views among the various authorities involved, this does not alter the principal claim to validity of the position to which Dante subscribes: theological controversies about the true meaning of revealed truth are, of course, not the exception, but the rule in the scholarly culture of Dante's time. The doctrinal explanations Dante presents in the *Paradiso* about the connection between the cosmogony and Lucifer's fall intentionally retain a more general theological-philosophical terminology, whereas the speech about the origin of the earth in the *Inferno* is deliberately composed in a concrete narrative style. In the *Paradiso* Dante thus transforms the myth of the *Inferno* into theory. In doing so, he provides an inherent doctrinal horizon—even though it is only a generic one—for a narrative whose entire composition and especially its most important part, the geographically situated mountain of Purgatory, are not in accord with theological authorities. But that is not the whole of it. Dante attempts to stabilize the precarious status of his cosmogony in yet another way, particularly by indicating that many of its constitutive elements—the nexus of Lucifer's fall and the origin of the ice, Satan's abyssal position, the transformation of water into land, the concealment motif—are sanctioned by biblical exegesis. As Zygmunt G. Barański has shown, Dante particularly conflates Gregory the Great's *Job* commentary, which links the creation to Satan's fall and the *Job* exegesis of Aquinas,[48] which examines the origin of the world scientifically, *per scientiam*, on the literal sense level while excluding the Lucifer motif. Dante synthesizes the two authorities by turning Gregory's moral-allegorical commentary into a literal one, while retaining, unlike Thomas, the motif of Satan's fall. The myth is thus rendered literal again and assumes the position held by scientific argument in Thomas's commentary. This is in fact the central aspect, to which Barański incidentally paid little attention. Dante's subtle manner of dealing with the theological authorities he refers to confirms that he did not want the cosmogony of the final *Inferno* canto to be considered merely from the perspective of a poetic allegoresis. If that were the case, then the truth of the myth would be nothing other than a poetically constructed *fictio poetica*, which would point to a hidden truth, in the manner of conventional rhetorical allegory. But it is exactly this that would contravene the fundamental concern of the *Commedia*. As we have seen, in its innermost core the *Commedia* makes the claim of being a truthful revelation experienced as a vision, a revelation that is suggestively placed in an analogical relationship to the Bible. This inevitably entails a reversion to biblical narrative patterns, among which it is mainly the myths of Holy Scripture that are important. When, however, in the course of their narrative elaboration the biblical myths begin to slip into an area that is not confirmed theologically, or not sufficiently so, as occurs in the retelling of Lucifer's fall (despite the many caveats), there is danger of a fundamental shift: the story that, in its function as a *sacra historia*,[49] is meant to be and must be considered truth with a visionary foundation threatens to be drawn into the vortex of mere fictitiousness. At the end of the *Inferno* Dante's representation of the origin of the world thus involves him in a narrative dilemma. This dilemma concentrates as in a burning glass the entire problematic nature of his epic project, in which the relationship between the worldly poet and the scriptor of God is continually being redefined. But, just as in other places in the *Commedia*, Dante also knows here how to overcome the difficulty with a virtuoso interplay of oppositional authorities, thus making the "mythopoiesis" of his *poema sacro* the instrument of a narrative in which the truth and reality of the narrated story converge.

The story of how the world acquired its salvational structure with the antipodes of Jerusalem and the mountain of Purgatory is not reported by the primary narrator; that is, not by the poet Dante but by Virgil. As the wanderer's guide, Virgil is a privileged authority on knowledge. He is foremost among the poets of the past and at the same time the highest representative of earthly reason.[50] It is this "rational" poet-figure who presents the theologically insufficiently corroborated cosmogony, which Dante nevertheless needs for his design of a meaningful world in his history of salvation. Virgil therefore gives an account of the biblically referenced cosmogony as it must appear from the perspective of earthly reason: not as revealed truth but as mere hypothesis, as conjecture.[51] Exactly at this point where the speech comes to the origin of the "unvalidated" mountain of Purgatory, Virgil modulates his narrative with an adverb that expresses doubt. And Dante, the poet, makes use of this little word to create the greatest possible effect. Not only does he place the *forse* in verse 124 in the prominent rhyme position, he isolates it and also gives it the maximal accentuation with a strongly marked *rejet*. Dante focuses perception on the *forse* with such emphasis that Virgil's entire cosmogony is then biased by the reservation expressed in that "perhaps."

As already mentioned, such a cosmogony, marked by the uncertainty of this "perhaps," would not be adequately understood if it were only seen as a plain analogue of a poetic fiction freely invented for allegorical purposes.[52] Instead, the text makes it unequivocally and emphatically clear that it is a supposition, which could be true, but whose truth a narrator limited by reason cannot confirm. For the reader of the *poema sacro* this truth potential is already underlined, as the cosmogony is produced through the narrative unfolding of a revelationary core explicated by biblical exegesis—that of Lucifer's fall, with its wide diversity of theological interpretations. And it is reinforced as well by the product of the cosmogonic event itself; for in the very next canto, the mountain of Purgatory that appears in the two wanderers' astronomically measured field of perception, is taken for granted as a fact in the logic of the vision, notwithstanding all the additional symbolism it conveys. What can be no more than mere conjecture, from the viewpoint of limited human reason, is meant, in the perspective of Dante's vision, to attain the quality of a revelation that renders the work of salvation fruitful once again. This presupposes (not least) the association of theology with the narrative unfolding of a Christian mythopoiesis, whose constitutive components include the salvational cosmogony. In this context of modeling the history of salvation, Virgil's "perhaps" at last acquires a typological significance. Virgil, who, within the limitations of reason, speaks of truth merely as conjecture, is distinguished as a forerunner, as a figure of promise whose fulfillment is the poet of the visionary *poema sacro*. The poet's divine inspiration is most apparent, however, in the gift of grace that enabled him to read the Bible and its commentaries in the "right" way: in which his inspired reading and visionary truth appear to converge.

NOTES

1. See the important collection of essays of Andersen et al. (1998); Brownlee and Stephens (1989); Brownlee, Brownlee, and Nichols (1991); and Schlesier and Trinca (2008).

2. On the constitutive importance of "variance" for the text culture of the Middle Ages, see Cerquiglini (1989).

3. On the dialectic of personal identity and role constructs in the development of a new concept of authorial identity in the twelfth century, see the seminal study by Meier (2004). In placing the relationship between the personalization of authorship and the claim of representing a transpersonal truth at the center of her discussion, Meier points out how much this manner of writing constitutes a preliminary step to Dante's project.

It is therefore only logical that she begins her commentary on the twelfth century with a reference to Dante.

4. A decisive prerequisite for this is the establishment of the idea that the divine revelation was basically incomplete, a notion developed in connection with the adaptation of the pseudo-Dionysian teaching about the visionary theologian. See Meier (2004, 209n3). On Dante's understanding of the biblical background, see Hawkins (1993).

5. See Andreas Kablitz's work on the *Commedia*, especially Kablitz (1999).

6. *Ep.* 13.20–22. On the controversial authorship question, see Hollander (1994) and—as concise as it is well balanced—Lieberknecht (1999), 4–5. Regardless of how the authorship question is answered in detail, as a document belonging to the immediate context of the work, the Cangrande letter nevertheless provides a historically possible interpretational horizon, whose at least partial relevance for the understanding of the work can be confirmed by a structural analysis of the *Commedia*.

7. See Hollander (1980, 39–89).

8. On the relationship of *historia*, *historia sacra*, and *allegoria in factis*, see also Barański (2000, 111–26), with a critical view of the still-widespread thesis in Dante criticism of the plot of the *Commedia* as a *favola* or *fictio rhetorica*.

9. Dante employs a flexible concept of vision and systematically uses the possibilities of alternating between visions, in a limited sense, and vision-related genres, like prophetic speech. On the range of visionary literature, see Frenschowski and Mette (2003). On the structural importance of the vision for the *Commedia*, see Mercuri (1991); Segre (1990, 25–48); Barolini (2005); Regn (2007).

10. *Inf.* 2.27–30. The *Commedia* quotations are taken from Chiavacci Leonardi (1991–97), which is largely based on Petrocchi's text; the English translation is taken from the edition by Hollander and Hollander (2000, 2004, 2007).

11. As a result of its incontestable veracity, the Pauline vision taken from 2 Cor. 12:1–4 that is initially evoked in *Inf.* 2.27–32 functions as the point of integration for all further references to the visionary mode in the *Commedia*. It also presents especially the Virgilian *katabasis* of Book 6 of the *Aeneid* as a true occurrence in a typological sense: "Io non Enëa, io non Paulo sono" (I am not Aeneas, nor am I Paul; *Inf.* 2.32). It is on the Pauline letter as well that the interaction, or tension between the physical and mental vision, is based, with Dante, in view of the theological conception of hell and purgatory, emphasizing for this part of his journey, what Augustine, following Paul, called the *visio corporalis* (of Aeneas's descent to the underworld, it says in *Inf.* 2.13–15: "Tu dici che di Silvïo il parente, / corruttibile ancora, ad immortale / secolo andò, e fu sensibilmente" (You tell of the father of Sylvius / that he, still subject to corruption, went / to the eternal world while in the flesh); whereas for paradise, he refers explicitly to the Pauline ambivalence of the "sive in corpore, sive extra corpus, nescio, Deus scit" (2 Cor. 12:3).

12. See Morgan (1990).

13. *Par.* 2.4–6: "I was in that heaven which receives / more of His light. He who comes down from there / can neither know nor tell what he has seen."

14. *Purg.* 32.103–5: "to serve the world that lives so ill, / keep your eyes upon the chariot and write down / what now you see here once you have gone back."

15. It is not unusual for visions to be conveyed in the form of an attested report by a third party; this is, however, only a secondary representational procedure. As the logically primary point of reference, we always have to posit a first-person narrator.

16. In *Purg.* 30.55, Beatrice addresses the wanderer by name.

17. This occurs impressively, particularly in the Cacciaguida cantos in the middle of the *Paradiso* (15–17).

18. A basic indicator that Dante's vision is a gift of mercy is the symbolic relationship to the Trinity. Mary acts within a Trinitarian constellation: she has mercy on Dante, ensnared in his sinful state, and sends St. Lucia, as a figure of Dante's future enlightenment, to his minne-lady Beatrice, who then initiates the journey to the afterworld. The wanderer's guides also constitute a Trinitarian constellation—Virgil, Beatrice, and St. Bernard. Parodies of the Trinity are the *tre fiere* and the three-headed Satan.

19. *Inf.* 1.1.

20. *Par.* 25.1–2: "this sacred poem, / to which both Heaven and earth have set their hand."

21. On this aspect, see particulars in Regn (2007).

22. This applies especially to visions of the afterworld. For broad areas of mystical visionary literature, the situation is different.

23. Dante's quest for fame cannot be conceptionally compared with that of the "spiriti attivi per desiderio di gloria" in the heaven of Mercury: in contrast to them, Dante's quest for fame is posterior to his experience of the afterworld; it expresses itself against better (postmortal) judgment and in opposition to the *sancta humilitas* that should be brought about by the "reenactment" of the Act of Redemption; that is, the journey to the afterworld. The apollonian aspiration for fame is an indicator of worldy attachment and is not free of the temptation of *superbia*.

24. *Par.* 5.109–11: "Merely consider, reader, if what I here begin / went on no farther, how keen would be / your anguished craving to know more."

25. "Maker" does not mean the same thing as "inventor"; the term "maker" points to the poet as the supreme authority in conveying an occurrence of which he is not (or not necessarily) the author.

26. On the term "fiction" in Dante, see Paparelli (1960).

27. A list of the most important research positions on the end of the last canto of the *Inferno* appears in Mele (2003).

28. *Inf.* 34.106–26: "And he to me: 'You imagine you are still / beyond the center, where I grasped the hair / of the guilty worm by whom the world is pierced. / So you were, as long as I descended, / but, when I turned around, you passed the point / to which all weights are drawn from every side. / You are now beneath the hemisphere / opposite the one that canopies the landmass– / and underneath its zenith that Man was slain / who without sin was born and sinless lived. / You have your feet upon a little sphere / that forms Judecca's other face. / Here it is morning when it is evening there, / and the one whose hair provided us a ladder / is fixed exactly as he was before. / It was on this side that he fell from Heaven. / And the dry land that used to stand, above, / in fear of him immersed itself in water / and fled into our hemisphere. And perhaps / to escape from him the land we'll find above / created this lacuna when it rushed back up.'"

29. Despite the biblical view of the earth as a disc, in learned circles during the Middle Ages (and not only in the late Middle Ages) it was a commonly held opinion that the earth had a spherical shape. See Tattersall (1981) and Woodward (1985). On Dante's cosmography, see Hausmann (1988, 12), who however assumes that the advocates of the spherical form tended to be outsiders.

30. See Hausmann (1988).

31. *Inf.* 26. On the topography of the earthly paradise before Dante and on Dante's geographical association of the earthly paradise and purgatory, see Morgan (1990, 160): "But there is considerable evidence to suggest that, rather than placing the Earthly Paradise on the summit of the mountain of Purgatory, Dante placed Purgatory on the slopes of the mountain of the Earthly Paradise—that is, that his mountain has its origin not in any traditional iconography for Purgatory, for there was none, but in the learned traditions of Eden and of Jerusalem. These traditions are also reflected in the popular representations of Paradise as manifested in the vision literature."

32. *Purg.* 4.68–71: "picture Zion / and this mountain positioned so on earth / they share the same horizon / but are in different hemispheres."

33. Dante's cosmology in the *Commedia* aims at combining (not at contrasting) the biblically sanctioned knowledge of revelation and *scientia*. See Nardi (1959).

34. On the history of the doctrine of purgatory, see Michel (1936) and Ombres (1978, 1981).

35. See LeGoff (1981).

36. In the *Tractatus de Purgatorio Sancti Patricii*, a suggestive geographical localization of the otherworld is realized by describing its entrance, which is located on an island in a lake in northwestern Ireland. The Purgatory there is admittedly more of an entrance to the otherworld than to one of the afterworld realms; see Pontfarcy (1995). But in the *Vita Sancti Patricii* by Jocelin of Furness (ca. 1185), St. Patrick's Purgatory is shifted to a mountain, the Croagh Patrick, which is conceived of here also as a legendary innerworldly place of St. Patrick's purification and not as an afterworld realm.

37. The *Purgatorio* begins with the typical genre invocation to the muse Calliope, followed immediately by an extensive astronomic periphrase, which serves as a "mapping" of the mountain of Purgatory and is intended to render it credible as a place in the world (and in time). See *Purg.* 1.19–30. See also the detailed commentary by Chiavacci Leonardi (1991–97, 13–16, 36–37).

38. On the still not definitely decided question of the authorship of the *Quaestio*, see Manlio Pastore Stocchi, "De quaestio de aqua et terra," in *Enciclopedia Dantesca*, edited by Umberto Bosco (Rome: Istituto della Enciclopedia Italiana, 1984), 4:761–65. While Nardi (1959, 66) considers the tract a fake—"una falsificazione bella e buona"—Mazzoni (1966) is the most avid defender of the opinion widely advocated today in support of Dante's authorship. More serious than the dispute about the question of authorship are the differing views concerning the interpretation of the tract and its relationship to the *Commedia*. The scope extends from a reading as scholarly innovative (Mazzoni 1966), through an interpretation of the tract as normal medieval scholarship (Padoan 1966), as academically rather retrograde (Nardi 1959) to a critique of medieval science based on biblical hermeneutics (Barański 2000, 199–219). A historically appropriate understanding presumably

lies somewhere between the extreme positions outlined here; the *Questio de aqua et terra* is thus to be evaluated rather as an inconspicuous example of medieval cosmology; see also Ley (1983). Regarding the relationship to the *Commedia*, this would mean that the *poema sacro*, as a work with a revelationary claim, surpasses in its significance the cosmological tract, whose function would then require a more precise classification (perhaps as a tactical *retractatio* or as a document concerning the concept of the Two Truths).

39. The cosmogonic dimension that is developed in *Inf.* 34.121–26 concerns the origin of Purgatory, which—other than is often assumed in Dante criticism—is not connected with the genesis of the *Inferno*: the inner-earthly landmasses, which avoid contact with Satan, simply form a *loco voto* (*Inf.* 34.125, "this lacuna"; *Inf.* 34.126), the *natural burella* (*Inf.* 34.98, "a natural dungeon") at the midpoint of the earth, and not the pit of hell as a whole. On the basis of the structural consistency of the work (see the details on the origin of the *Inferno* in *Inf.* 3.5–8), where the *vox Dei* declares: "Dinanzi a me non fuor cose create / se non etterne" [Before me nothing was but things eternal]), as well as on the basis of the theological assumptions, nothing other than this would have been expected: according to Holy Scripture, the origin of hell, unlike the fall of Lucifer, coincides with the beginning of time. As can be seen, in designing his cosmogony, Dante makes an effort to avoid theologically precarious contradictions of the wording of the Bible. For a corresponding interpretation of Lucifer's fall and the *loco voto* in *Inf.* 34.125, see also Forti (1986).

40. *De vulgari eloquentia* 2.4.2.

41. The "fictiveness" simply refers to the rhetoric of the *voces* and is described as *sensus litteralis primarius*, while the *sententia litteralis* constitutes their fundamental meaning; see Meier (1976).

42. *Con.* 2.1.2–3.

43. *Con.* 2.1.3.

44. In the third version of his commentary, Pietro Alighieri opposes the "fictiveness" of the journey to the afterworld and its cosmogony to the "non ficte et transumptive loquendo" of the *Questio de aqua et terra*; see (with the citation of the appropriate section), section of the Pietro commentary, Mazzoni (1966). On the fiction argument being Pietro's defensive strategy when he was accused of failing to comply with theological orthodoxy, see Barański (2000, 202).

45. A useful presentation of the theological question is provided by Nardi (1959, 15–28).

46. See the commentary on Canto 29 by Chiavacci Leonardi (1991–97, 804n62), with further references on the theological question.

47. *Par.* 29.49–51: "Then, sooner than one might count to twenty, / one band of angels had disturbed / the lowest of your elements."

48. Barański (2000, 213–19).

49. Ibid., 118–21.

50. On Virgil as the guide to "felicità terrena che si raggiunge *per philosophica documenta*," see Mercuri (1991, 228–31). This allegorical interpretation of Virgil has existed since the beginning of Dante-exegesis. See, for instance, the commentary by Dante's son Pietro, who, as might be expected, also stresses the fictive aspect: "Ideo fingit se ita

ruendo Virgilium invenisse, in cuius persona amodo consideranda est dicta rationalis philosophia esse figurate" (Della Vedova and Silviotti 1978, 42). In addition to the allegorical interpretation of the Virgil figure, there is of course also a typological one (Virgil seen as the conveyor of a knowledge of revelation to which he himself had no rational access); the allegorical and typological interpretations do not represent a contradiction: rather, they are complementary.

51. The fact that the Virgil of the *Commedia* is actually allowed to formulate such a hypothesis is, however, due entirely to the typological dimension of his interpretation.

52. Virgil's *forse* is hardly acknowledged in Dante criticism. Where it actually is, it is read—in contrast to here—as an indicator of fictiveness. This is the case, for example, with Chiavacci Leonardi (1991–97, 1:1027), who speaks in her commentary of the *bellissimo forse*: "[che] rivela l'invenzione dell'ardita fantasia che non vuol dare per scientificamente certo ciò che ha immaginato" (Chiavacci Leonardi of course also attempts to disconnect what Dante freely imagined from the medieval concept of a poetics of *integumentum*). Barański (2000, 218n37), too, discusses the *forse* but understands it as a kind of *retractatio* (*sembra quasi un ripensamento*) intended to aim at obscuring the conflict with Holy Scripture, or at least taking the sting out of it and simultaneously making it harmonize with the *Questio*. Barański's interpretation suffers primarily from his reading of the cosmogony formulated by Virgil as a statement about the origin of hell—"la sua ipotesi riguardo la nascita dell'Inferno"—which it is not: it is "only" an assumption about the also geographically located birth of the Purgatorium, about which the Bible is silent. Dante does nothing more than attempt to develop out of this silence a language accompanied by biblical exegesis for his message about salvation.

BIBLIOGRAPHY

Andersen, Elizabeth, Jens Haustein, Anne Simon, and Peter Strohschneider, eds. *Autor und Autorschaft im Mittelalter*. Tübingen: Niemeyer, 1998.

Barański, Zygmunt G. *I segni di Dante: Saggi per una storia intellettuale di Dante Alighieri*. Naples, Italy: Liguori, 2000.

Barolini, Teodolinda. "Why Did Dante Write the *Commedia?* Dante and the Visionary Tradition." *Dante: Rivista internazionale di studi su Dante Alighieri* 2 (2005): 11–32.

Brownlee, Kevin, Marina S. Brownlee, and Stephen G. Nichols, eds. *The New Medievalism*. Baltimore: Johns Hopkins University Press, 1991.

Brownlee, Kevin, and Walter Stephens, eds. *Discourses of Authority in Medieval and Renaissance Literature*. Hanover, NH: University Press of New England, 1989.

Cerquiglini, Bernard. *Éloge de la variante: Histoire critique de la philologie*. Paris: Edition du Seuil, 1989.

Chiavacci Leonardi, Anna Maria, ed. *Commedia*. By Dante Alighieri. 3 vols. Milan: Mondadori, 1991–97.

Della Vedova, Roberto, and Maria Teresa Silviotti. *Il Commentarium di Pietro Alighieri nelle redazioni ashburniana e ottoboniana*. Florence: Olschki, 1978.

Forti, Carla. "Nascita dell'Inferno o nascita del Purgatorio: Note sulla caduta del Lucifero dantesco." *Rivista di letteratura italiana* 4, no. 2 (1986): 241–60.

Frenschowski, Marco, and Norbert Mette. "Vision." In *Theologische Realenzyklopädie*, edited by Gerhard Müller, 35:117–50. Berlin: de Gruyter, 2003.

Hausmann, Frank-Rutger. "Dantes Kosmographie—Jerusalem als Nabel der Welt." *Deutsches Dante-Jahrbuch* 63 (1988): 33–54.

Hawkins, Peter S. "Dante and the Bible." In *The Cambridge Companion to Dante*, edited by Rachel Jacoff, 120–35. Cambridge: Cambridge University Press, 1993.

Hollander, Robert. *Studies in Dante*. Ravenna: Longo, 1980.

———. *Dante's Epistle to Cangrande*. Ann Arbor: University of Michigan Press, 1994.

Hollander, Robert, and Jean Hollander, trans. *The Inferno of Dante*. New York: Anchor, 2000.

———. *Purgatorio of Dante*. New York: Anchor, 2004.

———. *Paradiso of Dante*. New York: Doubleday, 2007.

Kablitz, Andreas. "Poetik der Erlösung: Dantes *Commedia* als Verwandlung und Neubegründung mittelalterlicher Allegorese." In *Commentaries–Kommentare*, edited by Glenn Most, 353–79. Göttingen: Vandenhoeck and Ruprecht, 1999.

LeGoff, Jacques. *La Naissance du Purgatoire*. Paris: Gallimard, 1981.

Ley, Karl. "Dante als Wissenschaftler: Die *Quaestio de aqua et terra.*" *Deutsches Dante-Jahrbuch* 58 (1983): 41–71.

Lieberknecht, Otfried. *Allegorese und Philologie: Überlegungen zum Problem des mehrfachen Schriftsinns in Dante's* Commedia. Stuttgart: Steiner, 1999.

Mazzoni, Francesco. "La Questio de aqua et terra." In *Contributi di Filologia dantesca*, 38–79. Florence: Sansoni, 1966. First published in *Studi danteschi* 34 (1957): 163–204.

———. "Il punto sulla *Questio de aqua et terra.*" In *Contributi di Filologia dantesca*, 80–125. Florence: Sansoni, 1966. First published in *Studi danteschi* 39 (1962): 39–84.

Meier, Christel. "Überlegungen zum gegenwärtigen Stand der Allegorie-Forschung: Mit besonderer Berücksichtigung der Mischformen." *Frühmittelalterliche Studien* 10 (1976): 1–68.

———. "Autorschaft im 12. Jahrhundert: Persönliche Identität und Rollenkonstrukt." In *Unverwechselbarkeit: Persönliche Identität und Identifikation in der vormodernen Gesellschaft*, edited by Peter von Moos, 207–66. Cologne: Böhlau, 2004.

Mele, Veronica. "La reazione della terra alla caduta di Lucifero (*Inf.* 34.121–126): Qualche appunto linguistico." In *Leggere Dante*, edited by Lucia Battaglia Ricci, 345–63. Ravenna: Longo, 2003.

Mercuri, Roberto. "Commedia." In *Letteratura italiana: Le opere*, vol. 1, *Dalle origini al cinquecento*, edited by Alberto Asor Rosa, 211–329. Torino: Einaudi, 1991.

Michel, A. "Purgatoire." In *Dictionnaire de la théologie catholique*, edited by Alfred Vacant, Eugène Mangenot, and Émile Amann, 13:1163–326. Paris: Letouzey et Ané, 1936.

Morgan, Alison. *Dante and the Medieval Other World*. Cambridge: Cambridge University Press, 1990.

Nardi, Bruno. *La caduta di Lucifero e l'autenticità della "Quaestio de aqua et terra."* Torino: Società Editrice Internazionale, 1959.

Ombres, Robert. *The Theology of Purgatory*. Butler, WI: Clergy Book Service, 1978.

————. "The Doctrine of Purgatory According to St Thomas Aquinas." *Downside Review* 99 (1981): 279–87.

Padoan, Giorgio. "Cause, struttura e significato del *De situ et figura aque et terre.*" In *Dante e la cultura veneta*, edited by Vittore Branca and Giorgio Padoan, 347–66. Florence: Olschki, 1966.

Paparelli, Gioacchino. "Fictio: La definizione dantesca della poesia." *Filologia romanza* 7 (1960): 1–83.

Pastore Stocchi, Manlio. "De quaestio de aqua et terra." In *Enciclopedia Dantesca*, edited by Umberto Bosco, 4:761–65. Rome: Istituto della Enciclopedia Italiana, 1984.

Pontfarcy, Yolande de. "The Topography of the Other World and the Influence of Twelfth Century Irish Visions on Dante." In *Dante and the Middle-Ages*, edited by John C. Barnes and Cormac O'Cuilleanain, 93–115. Dublin: Irish Academic Press, 1995.

Regn, Gerhard. "Double Authorship: Prophetic and Poetic Inspiration in Dante's Paradise." *MLN* 122, no. 1 (2007): 167–85.

Schlesier, Renate, and Beatrice Trinca. *Inspiration und Adaptation: Tarnkappen mittelalterlicher Autorschaft.* Hildesheim: Weidmannsche Buchhandlung, 2008.

Segre, Cesare. *Fuori del mondo: I modelli nella follia e nelle immagini dell'aldilà.* Torino: Einaudi, 1990.

Tattersall, Jill. "Sphere or Disc? Allusions to the Shape of Earth in Some Twelfth Century and Thirteenth Century Vernacular French Works." *Modern Language Review* 76 (1981): 31–46.

Woodward, David. "Reality, Symbolism, Time and Space in Medieval World Maps." *Annals of the Association of American Geographers* 75 (1985): 510–21.

CHAPTER FOUR

Dialectic of the Medieval Course

DANIEL HELLER-ROAZEN

Whether ancient, medieval, or modern, seafarers share one common trait: despite the havoc they may wreak, they cannot all be considered equally illegitimate. Many sources indicate, admittedly, that maritime explorers are generally to be feared; but it is significant that, no matter the force they may exert, sailors rarely claim the title of bandit for themselves. Both times Odysseus and his companions are asked whether they are not "pirates [ληϊστῆρες] who roam the seas, risking their lives and bringing harm to others," the Homeric hero declines to answer in the affirmative.[1] There can be no doubt that the question put to him was comprehensible. The actions of the great Achaeans during war bore more than a passing resemblance to those of robbers, and in the Homeric world it was no easy thing to distinguish between the varieties of armed men traveling by ship. Once at least, Odysseus joyfully recalled how he forsook the land for the sea: "I reveled in long ships with oars; I loved polished lances, arrows in the skirmish, the shapes of doom that others shake to see. Carnage suited me; heaven put those things somehow in me. Each to his own pleasure!"[2]

Then, admittedly, the crafty Ithacan was in disguise, claiming, as he did more than once, that he was a Cretan.[3] That mask fit the Homeric hero almost too well. Odysseus competed with the other Greeks for a fame that would depend, at least in part, on the booty to be seized from the sacked city of Troy, and his distinction in battle was to be measured by the magnitude of that which he would take back with him from his raids. As a scholar has recently remarked, "it would seem, therefore, difficult for the modern student of Homeric society to determine exactly, or even approximately, where any boundaries between warfare and piracy might be drawn."[4] This much seems to have changed little in later antiquity. It appears that the people of the classical antiquity, like Goethe's Mephistopheles, held "war, commerce and piracy" (*Krieg, Handel und Piraterie*) to be essentially "three in one" (*dreieinig*), "not to be disjoined" (*nicht zu trennen*).[5] From the archaic age of Greece through to the end of the Roman period, the promise of plunder remained, as Servius observed, the most common reason why anyone—citizen or criminal—would set sail.[6] The ancient lexicon of seafaring is to this degree significant. In Greek as in Latin, a reference to "pirate ships" (ληστρικὰ πλοῖα, *piratica navigia*) remains resolutely ambiguous. It may point to vessels of two very different sorts: those belonging to bandits, and so, too, to those belong to the appointed representatives of a lawful state.[7]

The ancient authors show every sign of having been well aware of the formal difference that may separate the two varieties of violent seafarers. Numerous sources indicate that the writers of the classical age could distinguish, when necessary, between the roving standard-bearers of cities who sacked and pillaged their enemies, on the one hand, and on the other, the raiders who preyed on the sedentary inhabitants of the Mediterranean without claiming any rights. Some scholars have argued that the awareness of this distinction is as old the records of Greek culture and that already in the Homeric world, the warrior and the bandit were not considered to be of the same kind. It suffices, some have argued, to recall the relatively marginal place of the term "pirate" (or "plunderer," ληστής) in the epic vocabulary. In the *Odyssey* and the *Iliad*, this expression refers exclusively to characters of minor status and negligible dramatic importance, and although many of the major Achaean and Trojan figures commit rapacious acts at sea in search of booty, not one suffers the dishonor of finding himself designated by the iniquitous epithet. The philological evidence suggests a conclusion, therefore, that cannot but perplex: although perfectly aware of the distinction between the legitimate and the illegitimate pillagers of the sea, the ancients did not assign to it any single name. The classical authors disposed of no term, be it Latin or Greek, by which they might divide among the wide expanse of roving sailors, separating in a single gesture the lawful maritime raiders from the lawless.

That was to be an achievement—for better or for worse—of modernity. But the sources of the postclassical innovation lay, as so often, in the long interval that followed the end of antiquity. The Middle Ages witnessed the emergence of a term unknown to the ancients, which, once coined, would accompany that old noun, "pirate" (*pirata*), in Latin, Greek, and all the emerging vernaculars of modern Europe. The novel medieval expression was *cursarius*, "corsair." This Latin noun derived from verbal expressions indicating the maritime "course" (*cursum*) run by ships as they raided goods along the coast of the Mediterranean (*cursum facere, ire ad cursum,* and simply *currere*). Numerous medieval administrative and legal documents refer to such "corsairs" and their "course," employing a variety of related forms in Latin and Greek (*cusarii, cursales, corsalia,* κυρσάριοι).[8]

By the last centuries of the Middle Ages, if not sooner, the usage could also be found in literary works. Thus the pirate Paganino,[9] introduced in the *Decameron* as "a very famous corsair" (*molto famoso corsale*), and that other rover of the second day of Boccaccio's tales, Landolfo Ruffolo. The medieval author describes this seaman's exploits in some detail, relating that after he lost his boat at sea, Landolfo "bought a light wooden ship to run the course [*da corseggiare*], arming and decorating it with every thing suited to that purpose," such that "within a year, he had stolen and taken so many ships from the Turks that he had not only regained the goods he had lost but had more than doubled them."[10] Similar expressions for the "course" soon acquired common currency in the other Romance languages. Such terms lasted well into the modern period, furnishing works of literature of the seventeenth, eighteenth, and nineteenth centuries with many of their most memorable figures: of countless cases, one might recall, as a single example, the infamous *corsaire de Salé* who boards and raids the ship of a hapless Candide in Voltaire's exemplary tale.

By the early twentieth century, the medieval distinction had long become a staple element in the technical vocabulary of European international law. In jurisprudential terms, the term "corsair" was not to be confused with that older word, "pirate," though, if one believes the specialists, many of the age continued to do precisely that. "Every day, in common speech," Henri Brongniart deplored in a monograph published in 1904, *Corsairs and Maritime War*, "we see the most enlightened people indifferently using the words *corsair* and *pirate*. This," he continued, not without some severity, "is to confuse the voluntary soldier with the thief, the hero with the bandit. The *course* is one means among others to wage maritime war. Its legitimacy in natural right, at least, may not be contested. Piracy—all authors agree on this point—is a crime against the right of nations. The pirate can be captured by any warship and even, under certain conditions, by merchant ships."[11] In such a sense, the "corsairs" of the Romance jurists corresponded with precision to the legal and political figure the Anglo-Saxon legal authorities regularly termed "privateers." These, as one could read in the W. E. Hall's 1924 *Treatise on International Law*, are "vessels belonging to private owners, and sailing under a commission of war empowering the person to whom it is granted to carry on all forms of hostility which are permissible at sea by the usages of war."[12] As such, they could be clearly contrasted with pirate ships, whose aggressive actions bear no such legitimacy, being "done under conditions which render it impossible or unfair to hold any state responsible for their commission."[13]

One might well wonder when the pirate and the privateer, the common sea thief and the legal rover, definitively parted ways. Historians and lexicographers provide no single answer to the question. Discussing the development of the English terminology of sea plunder, J. G. Lydon has noted that "before 1700, in referring to vessels, the terms *freebooter, buccaneer, sea rover,* and *privateer* were used almost synonymously with the word *pirate.* With the passage of time, the name *privateer* lost its stigma of illegality."[14] In the opening pages of *Elizabethan Privateering,* K. R. Andrews similarly cautioned, despite his title, that the term *privateering* "did not come into use until the seventeenth century and was therefore unknown to the Elizabethans."[15] It is certain, in any case, that when the term "corsair" first appeared in the Middle Ages, its signification could not be clearly opposed to that of "pirate." Numerous medieval documents refer to measures taken "against corsairs and pirates" (*contra cursales atque pirates*), treating under a single rubric activity deemed to be "corsair-like or piratical" (*corsaria ouero piratica*).[16] In his pioneering edition of the maritime code of Rhodes, Ashburner long ago commented on this fact:

> the indiscriminate use of the two words points to a close similarity in the characteristics of the two classes . . . When the Pisans in A.D. 1165 asked Trepedicinus, a distinguished Genoese corsair, where he was going, "I am going," was the answer, "to capture you and your goods and persons and to cut off your noses." It must have been at least as difficult for Pisa or Genoa to keep their corsairs within the bounds of legality as it was for the British Government in the eighteenth century to keep their privateers within the terms of the strict instructions which were given them when war broke out.[17]

Nevertheless, it seems that toward the end of the medieval period, a decisive criterion emerged, which would henceforth allow for the rigorous separation of institutions, if not of terms. "By the late thirteenth century," Frederic L. Cheyette has argued, "lawyers, ambassadors, and scholarly theorists had made the required distinction."[18] To the question of the point at which illegitimate plundering at sea could be told apart from legitimate depredation—that of "the line," in other words, "where wrong became right"—these various authorities furnished a single answer: "it is not the act that renders itself legitimate, nor the actor, but the authorization."[19]

In time, the consequences of this simple principle proved to be immense, for it allowed the medieval and modern authorities to confer formal legitimacy on banditry at sea, producing a legal thing unknown to the ancient world: a veritable license to plunder. Classical Greek and Roman law, to be sure, were familiar with rights that could permit one party forcibly to seize, in peace and in war, things belonging to another. As evidence, it suffices to recall the practices of reprisals illustrated by the law of "capture" (συλᾶν) and its suspension in sites declared places of "asylum." Such institutions had hardly vanished in the Middle Ages; with the development of trade between the Christian and the Muslim coasts of the Mediterranean, rights of reprisal had become, if anything, more various and more effective. But once it could be argued that a violent action at sea could be considered licit or illicit according to no rule other than that of its sanction by a sovereign power, the law of maritime raiding acquired a distinct and recognizable new form. It did so in the later medieval period, through the institution of a branch of jurisprudence that was to play a decisive role in the history of the Europe: that field, namely, involving what the jurists of the epoch termed the "letter," "patent," or "license of marking" (*licentia marcandi*).

Records of this convention in France can be found as early as the first decade of the thirteenth century. By the fourteenth, they abound throughout the European continent.[20] The first document of such "patents" in the administrative history of England dates from 1295, the year Edward I officially allowed and even commanded a captain in his service to plunder from the Portuguese as much as had been already spoiled by "the men and subjects of the realm of Portugal."[21] In times of peace, the English sovereign thus granted the lawful seafarer a "letter," which would enable him to transgress the borders that separated one state from another, passing beyond the limit—the "mark," from the Old High German *marcha*—that restricted the field in which he could otherwise act with legitimacy.[22] An early type of "passport" to the sea, as Merrien has suggested,[23] the license thereby allowed the rover to board vessels belonging to the sailors of another state, for a single purpose: to carry out an act of licit raiding, to whose institution the jurists of medieval Europe, developing the vocabulary of their art, soon gave a host of Latin names (*marca, pigoratio, represaliae, pignorationes, pignora, clarigatio, queminae, cambium, laus,* and *laudes represaliarum*).[24]

Such "letters" were declared in times of peace. Licenses of a similar nature could be issued during war. In an epoch in which state navies, in any modern sense, did not exist, this much was, to a certain degree, inevitable: private vessels manned by seafarers who worked for gain were the classic instruments of war at sea, and no sovereign power could forgo them. Hired seamen had naturally been common in maritime warfare for some time. G. T. Griffith has noted that already in the Hellenistic period, "pirates could be, and were, used as mercenaries through the connivance of their leaders."[25] With time, the force of that convention had not waned. Examples in the field of maritime and political history are hardly lacking, but medieval literature also contains its records.

One might recall, as a single example, how in the *Saga of the Faroese* King Olaf employs Karl, the Mœre-man, who "hinn verið víkingur og hinn mesti ráns-maður" (had been a great Viking and the worst of robbers), to set sail to subjugate the unruly inhabitants of the Faroese archipelago to the Norwegian crown.[26] By the end of the Middle Ages, however, the juridical condition of the hired sea bandit underwent a decisive change. Pirates who acted in the name and interests of the state now acquired, for the first time, an accepted place in the field of public law, even if it was not to be formulated, in its specificity, for some time still. One must await the eighteenth century for the most precise, if subtle, definition of these lawful raiders. Then jurists such as Christian Wolf knew to name that which most properly characterized the lawfully hired pillagers: namely, the fact of "non privatum sed publicum privatim bellum gerunt" (waging, by private means, not a private but a public war).[27]

One of the earliest and most striking records of the altered legal status of the sea bandit can be found in an Old French romance of the thirteenth century, *Eustace the Monk* (Wistasse le Moine).[28] Thought to have been composed sometime between 1223 and 1284, this anonymous work recounts the life and deeds of a churchman of unusual distinction.[29] A French nobleman by birth, Eustace, the romance relates, travels in his youth as far as Toledo. There he studies necromancy and, once a master in its arts, spends a winter and a summer "sous terre en I. abisme" (under ground, in a pit), in constant communication with no less an authority in the field than "the Devil, himself, who taught him the tricks and the ruses [*l'enghien et l'art*] that deceive everyone."[30] Returning to northern France, Eustace resolves to cultivate a different social circle: he enters a Benedictine monastery, which, however, he must soon forsake to avenge the unexpected murder of his father. That obligation exemplarily discharged, Eustace devotes the remaining years of his life to a career as soldier-seafarer in the service of French and English monarchs. This is the period on which the medieval romance focuses with the greatest attention. In the central portions of the work, Eustace finds himself commissioned by King John of England, Philip Augustus, and, still later, Prince Louis of France. The seaman battles and plunders in the Channel for both states, in often-startling alternation, yet always on the official command of at least one sovereign legal authority. The romance closes with the decease of its eponymous protagonist, put to death on his own ship. The Devil, we learn, had long before prophesied that event, announcing from his Spanish crypt that Eustace would be "en la mer occis seroit" (killed at sea) having "rois et contes guerriëroit" (waged war against kings and counts).[31] But the most notable fact in the narrative went unmentioned by the evil one, despite his foresight. It seems the thirteenth-century Devil was still bound, in his imaginings, to rules of combat soon to be outdated. The truth is that erstwhile monk waged war not only "against kings and counts"; with far greater novelty, he did so lawfully, and on their command. Eustace was to be, for this reason, not only pirate but also privateer, the first seafarer in French letters to plunder and to pillage by the right of kings.

Historians have observed that the rights to plunder granted seafarers in the Middle Ages were not all of a single kind. Two varieties of letters, in particular, may be distinguished. Some "marques" were issued to individual merchants, enabling them to secure transactions that could not otherwise be guaranteed. Once licensed to pillage for the sake of commerce, seamen, for example, could lawfully exact reparations for economic wrongs that they had suffered or that, alternately, that they might still suffer; one such instance was the right termed *pignoratio*, "the taking of security by an injured party to guarantee payment of damages."[32] A second type of patent, by contrast, was explicitly political. Licenses to commit *depredationes, rapinae, extorsiones,* and *represalia* were of this order. These were all weapons of war, which permitted the pillaging of enemy ships during times of battle; after the end of hostilities and the reconfiguration of alliances, the "problems" they raised had, therefore, immediately to be "settled."[33] To the modern eye, the distinction between such rights to pillage seems in principle quite clear. One belonged to times of peace, the other pertained to warfare; one facilitated transactions in the private sphere, the other involved the actions of the public domain; one implied, in all rigor, no more than a reprisal; the other, by contrast, authorized privateers.

Yet there are several reasons to doubt that the medieval licenses could so neatly be opposed. In his valuable study of the legal institutions of depredation in the fourteenth century, Frederic L. Cheyette has argued that, in truth, in the Middle Ages "the right of reprisal or marque existed in a no man's land between judicial action and war."[34] One could point to numerous such cases drawn from the maritime histories of England and France in particular.[35] But it is perhaps more important to recall several fundamental facts, which in the Middle Ages rendered any rigorous distinction between the two types of authorized pillagers at sea difficult, if not impossible, to achieve. It is worth noting that those who held a letter of reprisal for commercial reasons and those who, by contrast, were formally hired for battle were, in any case, drawn from a single class of rovers, which included pirates. Among such seamen, a variety of legal offices could easily be exchanged. Moreover, the deeds committed by sailors with private patents and by sailors with public licenses were, as a rule, of one nature.

Despite their juridical variety, these seafarers—again, in this, much like their lawless counterparts—were all specialists in violent depredation.

But there is more. Even when carried out by seafarers who could be distinguished among themselves in form, the two varieties of legal plundering, private and public, could also fade into each other. That which began as a punctual "reprisal," delimited by private law, could slide into public conflict, rendering the legally armed trader, de facto if not de jure, a privateer. Such developments long outlasted the Middle Ages; they remained commonplace in the early modern period. Historians of the fifteenth, sixteenth, and seventeenth centuries have devoted considerable scholarly attention to the "indiscriminate" legal use—or abuse—of licenses to plunder at sea in this age.[36] It is certain that the people of the early modern period held few illusions about the delicacy of the distinctions between legal pillagers. For evidence, it suffices to look to the books of the founding figures of modern international law, which distinguish the rights of private and public plunderers while simultaneously pointing to the multiple possibilities of their confusion. In his *Law of War* of 1539, Vitoria thus alluded, albeit discretely, to the fact that belligerent privateers could be employed to carry out private reprisals. Any prince who orders a war "for his own profit," "appropriating public revenues for his own aggrandizement," he wrote, deserves to be denounced as not a legitimate king but a "tyrant."[37] The inverse, too, could all too easily come to pass; a martial operation authorized by a sovereign, in other words, could acquire the unmistakable characteristics of a common reprisal. Grotius recalled this possibility in his *Law of War and Peace* of 1625. "It sometimes happens," he observed, "that on the occasion of a public war, a private war is born; for example, when someone, confronted by his enemies, runs the risk of losing his life and possessions."[38] Between the two classes of legal plunderers—those private individuals commissioned for the public good, and those, by contrast, publicly licensed to redress a private wrong—the lines of demarcation, for various reasons, could be difficult to draw.

One major phenomenon of the early modern age testifies, perhaps more vividly than any other, to the intractability of all distinctions between types of lawful pillagers at sea. It is the long and complex span of skirmishes between the sailors of Europe and North Africa traditionally designated as the "Barbary wars."[39] Chroniclers have often described these maritime battles as the instances of a single conflict, which divided the two shores of the Mediterranean for centuries. Christian and Muslim corsairs, it has been said, confronted each other from the end of the Middle Ages through to the eighteenth century to wage a war at sea, if, indeed, it was not a series of successive wars. From an historical as well as a legal perspective, however, references to belligerent activity in any accepted sense run the risk of propagating some confusion in this setting. For the conflict of the Mediterranean corsairs, while open, was quite dissimilar to any other. "Unlike normal wars," Peter Earle has written, "the war of the corsairs had neither beginning nor end. It was an *eternal war*."[40] "The maritime prolongation of the holy war between the Cross and the Crescent," this long series of encounters at sea "displayed two features that brought it very close to piracy," as Fontenay and Treneti have argued. "Perpetual and permanent, it did not admit of any truce; total and universal, it could hardly bear the notion of neutrality. Yet the people of the time were formal and generally refused to employ the word 'pirate' to designate its protagonists."[41]

For centuries, Christian and Muslim seamen plundered freely in the Mediterranean, capturing goods as well as persons according to juridical principles that, while widely accepted to be valid, could not easily be defined. The historical and ideological complexities of this "course" were multiple, as numerous historians have shown. First there was the question of the dubious identities of the seafarers themselves. P. Earle has commented that the Christians, while licensed by public authorities, were "often little more than pirates who sought their fortunes under the star-spangled green banner of Algiers rather than the Jolly Roger."[42] The "war" in which they fought, moreover, could hardly be defined in the terms of any established and respected *ius belli*, for while the conflict was stable, the "enemies" whom the Christians were to fight consistently eluded any precise determination. "Even after specific treaties had been signed in the 1620s," for instance, "the question of whether Turkish and Algerine should be treated as pirates or public ships of a sovereign power was still undecided."[43] Finally, the theological dimension of the holy battle, though in principle apparent, assumed historical forms far more obscure than often recalled. The activity of the Maltese, the greatest of the Christian corsairs, is especially telling in this regard. The appointed defenders of the Cross at sea, the Christian islanders dutifully pillaged whatever Muslim ships they could. But the pious corsairs did not limit their efforts there, for the Maltese of the sixteenth and seventeenth centuries, much to the consternation of the eastern coreligionists, also raided the vessels of whatever Greek merchants they could intercept at sea.[44]

The Mediterranean corsairs may present the most searing example of pillagers whose legality, while in some sense established, could not be defined with any satisfactory legal exactitude. They were far from being the only such authorized depredators of the modern age. In the conflicts between England and Spain, the

British "sea dogs," for instance, played a somewhat similar role to the Christians corsairs; licensed by the English crown, these Elizabethan seafarers famously wreaked havoc on the Dutch, the Spanish, and the Portuguese.[45] "Privateers" to the English, they were naturally no more than "pirates" to their victims. After them came many waves of violent sailors in the Atlantic and the Indian Oceans, from the Jacobean pillagers to the Buccaneers, the Madagascar seafarers, the "corsairs of the French Republic," and beyond, each of which once detained rights of some kind to plunder at sea in the service of one European sovereign state.[46] That the savage seamen could turn against the interests of the power that had sponsored them was a fact demonstrated more than once. One might recall, as an example, the fate of Captain Kidd, once "privateer," then "pirate," finally judged for his exploits at sea and hanged in 1701.[47] There was a logic to these early modern phenomena, which Janice Thomson has defined, in its basic pattern, with admirable lucidity: "The state would authorize privateering, which was legalized piracy, during wartime. When the war concluded, thousands of seamen were left with no more appealing alternative than piracy. The state would make desultory efforts to suppress the pirates, who would simply move somewhere else. With the outbreak of the next war, the state would offer blanket pardons to pirates who would agree to serve as privateers, and the process would start all over again."[48]

In the Middle Ages and the early modern period, this movement seemed inevitable. But the situation was soon to change. Privateers would not last forever. The states of modern Europe were soon to consolidate the "monopoly on the legitimate use of physical violence" that Max Weber would one day grant them as their defining trait.[49] By the end of the eighteenth century, not one but several European sovereign powers could conclude that licensed plunderers caused a host of ills that far outweighed any benefits they could provide. It is worth recalling how, in the later eighteenth century, the formidable British insurance companies formally protested to their government the losses they suffered on account of raiding privateers.[50] Their complaints were taken seriously. For reasons of their own, the Russians, to be followed by various other nations, subsequently issued declarations against the practice of allowing their ships conveying goods to be boarded by foreign privateers.[51] The first great blow to the old institution of licensing sea raiders came in 1856, when the representatives of the governments of Britain, France, Prussia, Russia, Austria, Sardinia, and Turkey all signed the Treaty of Paris, whose aim was "to establish a uniform doctrine" on the divisive question of "Maritime Law in times of War." The first statement of the treaty sounded the decisive judgment. "Privateering," it read, "is, and remains, abolished."[52]

That bold assertion did not pass unchallenged. The United States, notably, objected immediately to the terms and intent of the Paris Declaration, replying formally that "the right to resort to privateers is as clear as the right to use public armed ships, and as uncontestable as any other right appertaining to belligerents."[53] That claim was not surprising, for long before, the legal charter of the American nation had established its prerogative to hire pirates in no uncertain terms. Article 1, section 8 of the U.S. Constitution granted Congress the power "to declare war, grant letters of marque and reprisal and make rules concerning capture on land and water."[54] The Americans were not alone in clinging to the medieval institution. In France, too, dissenting voices could be heard. As late as 1904, H. Brogniart insisted "not only on the legitimacy, the necessity and the possibility, but also the *fatality* of employing corsairs at the present hour."[55] The legal scholar argued:

> Wrongly viewed as an inheritance of barbaric times, the privateer, nonetheless so fitting to the modern democratic idea of the armed nation, is essentially suited to humanizing maritime war. While a battleship can be sunk in an instant, pierced by an invisible submarine, the privateer is only after merchandise. He has no need for bloodshed . . . To develop the "course," to make it into the principal basis of maritime war—could one not find there a solution to the problem of imagining maritime war without the sacrifice of human life?[56]

That striking question had been formulated vivaciously and with real enthusiasm. But by 1904, any call to defend the privateer must already have sounded somewhat quaint. Only a few years after objecting to the judgment of the Declaration of Paris, the United States, plunged into civil war, retreated before its initial stance; invoking the decision to which it had once taken issue, the American government called on Britain and France to treat the Confederate privateers as no more than pirates, outlawed by the law of nations.[57] The seizing of goods at sea by private vessels employed by states was fast becoming a practice no modern power would officially condone. In 1897, an American jurist writing on the history of the right to privateers, Francis R. Stark, could comment, without any trace of hesitation: "The right of capture of private property on the high seas in time of war was once universally recognized. At some time in the future, it will not be recognized at all."[58] One year later, in 1898, at the time of its war with Spain, the United States formally issued a presidential proclamation indicating that it would henceforth abide by all the stipulations of the declaration of 1856, including the outlawing of privateers.[59] By the end of the nineteenth century, the situation therefore appeared to many, if not all, indubitable: centuries after being named, identified, diversified, and variously contested, the legal pillager had run his course. The dialectic of sea dogs was at an end.

The fact may once have seemed remarkable, but in retrospect it is not astonishing. With sufficient time and effort, it is possible, after all, successfully to remove from the books of jurisprudence a positive right, especially one instituted, as one was privateer's, at a date in relatively recent memory. The same can hardly be said of the ambiguous person of the law who so long predated the licensed plunderer in the law of nations. Since the Middle Ages, that immemorial pillager— the privateer's old double—had hardly vanished. For several centuries, the unlicensed rover had, perhaps, receded from clear view, concealed behind the more modern seaman and his sovereign letter. But he and his exceptional criminality had nonetheless persisted, both in the open seas, where illegitimate depredations did not disappear, and in the law of nations, which never ceased to reserve a special place in its titles for the outlawed raider of exceptional illegality, who in ancient times had been declared "the common enemy of all" (*communis hostis omnium*) and who was now more often dubbed, in the increasingly precise terms of modern international law, "the enemy of the human kind" (*hostis generis humani*). The inverted image of the licensed plunderer, the pirate remained in the law at least as long as the official privateer. Indeed, the shadow—if it ever was one—lasted longer.

NOTES

For Steve Nichols, who shows his students how to find their course in the uncharted Middle Ages.

1. See Homer, *Od.* 3.71–74; 9.252–55.

2. Homer, *Od.* 14.222–34.

3. Cf. Homer, *Od.* 17.424–33.

4. Philip de Souza, *Piracy in the Graeco-Roman World* (Cambridge: Cambridge University Press, 1999), 21. On piracy in Homer, see Benedetto Bravo, "Sulân: Représailles et justice privée contres les étrangers dans les cités grecques (étude du vocabulaire et des institutions)," *Annali della scuola normale superiore di Pisa* 10, no. 3 (1980): 975–77; Werner Nowag, *Raub und Beute in der archaischen Zeit der Griechen* (Frankfurt: Haag/Herchen, 1983), chap. 2 and 3; Alastar H. Jackson, "War and Raids for Booty in the World of Odysseus," in *War and Society in the Greek World*, ed. John Rich and Graham Shipley (London: Routledge, 1993), 64–76; and Alastar H. Jackson, "Privateers in the Ancient Greek World," in *War and Society: Historical Studies in Honour and Memory of J. R. Western, 1928–1971*, ed. M. R. D. Foot (London: Paul Elek, 1973), 214–53.

5. Goethe, *Faust* II, act 5. On the relations between trade and piracy in the Hellenistic world, see Vincent Gabrielson, "Economic Activity, Maritime Trade and Piracy in the Hellenistic Aegean," *Revue des études anciennes* 103, nos. 1–2 (2001): 219–40.

6. "Haec apud veteres maxima erat navigandi causa ut popularentur terras": cited by Johannes Scheffer, "*De militiâ navali veterum*," in *Le droit maritime international considéré dans ses origines*, ed. Eugène Cauchy (Paris: Guillaumin et Compagnie, 1862), 8, 1:343

7. See Cauchy, *Le Droit maritime international*, 1:344.

8. On the history of the corsair lexicon, see Charles du Fresne Du Cange, "*Glossarium ad Scriptores mediae et infimae Graecitatis*," in *The Rhodian Sea-Law*, ed. Walter Ashburner (Oxford: Oxford University Press, 1909), cxliv–cxlv.

9. Giovanni Boccaccio, *Il Decamerone*, ed. Vittore Branca (Turin: Einaudi, 1980), 1:306.

10. Ibid., 1:168.

11. Henri Brogniart, *Les corsaires et la guerre maritime* (Paris: Augustin Challamel, 1904), 5. Italics mine.

12. William Edward Hall, *A Treatise on International Law*, 8th ed. (Oxford: Clarendon Press, 1924), 620–21.

13. Ibid., 310.

14. James G. Lydon, *Pirates, Privateers, and Profits* (Upper Saddle River, NJ: Gregg Press, 1970), 25.

15. Kenneth R. Andrews, *Elizabethan Privateering: English Privateering during the Spanish War, 1585–1603* (Cambridge: Cambridge University Press, 1966), 5.

16. See Ashburner, *Rhodian Sea-Law*, cxliv–cxlv.

17. Ibid., cxlv.

18. Frederic L. Cheyette, "The Sovereign and the Pirates, 1332," *Speculum* 45, no. 1 (1970): 45–68, esp. 48.

19. Ibid.

20. On the development of the *lettre de marque*, see René de Mas Latrie, *Du Droit de marque, ou droit de représailles au Moyen-Âge* (Paris: A. Franck, 1883); Pierre-Clément Timbal, "Les Lettres de marque dans la France médiévale," *Recueils de la société Jean Bodin* 10, no. 2 (1958): 109–38; Francis Raymond Stark, *The Abolition of Privateering and the Declaration of Paris* (New York: Columbia University, 1897), esp. 49–60.

21. See Alfred P. Rubin, *The Law of Piracy*, 2nd ed. (Irvington-on-Hudson, NY: Transnational Publishers, 1998), 31n102.

22. On the etymology of the term "marque," see Stark, *The Abolition of Privateering and the Declaration of Paris*, 52–53.Cf. Rubin, *Law of Piracy*, 31–32n103, who refers to the Indo-European root *merg- (basing himself on *The American Heritage Dictionary*, 1st ed., s.v. "boundary, border").

23. See Jean Merrien, *Histoire des corsaires* (Saint-Malo, France: L'Ancre de Marine, 1992), 30.

24. See René de Mas Latrie, *Du Droit de marque*, 11. Cf. Timbal, "Les Lettres de marque dans le droit de la France Médiévale."

25. Guy Thomson Griffith, *The Mercenaries of the Hellenistic World*, 2nd ed. (Cambridge: Cambridge University Press, 1968), 262.

26. See Ólafur Halldórsson, ed., *Færeyinga saga* (Reykjavík: Stofnun Árna Magnús-sonar á Íslandi, 1987), chap. 48; and Frederick York Powell, trans., *The Tale of Thrond of Gate: Commonly called Foereyinga* (London: D. Nutt, 1896), chap. 45.

27. Cauchy, *Le Droit maritime international*, 1:64.

28. There have been two editions of the Old French text: Wendelin Foerster and Johann Trost, eds., *Wistasse Le Moine: Altfranzösischer Abenteuerroman des XIII. Jahrhunderts nach der einzigen Pariser Handschrift* (Halle: Niemeyer, 1891), and more recently Dennis Joseph Conlon, ed., *Li Romans de Witasse le moine, Roman du treizième siècle, édité d'après le manuscrit, fonds français 1553, de la Bibliothèque Nationale, Paris* (Chapel Hill: University of North Carolina Press, 1972). An English translation can be found in Glyn S. Burgess, *Two Medieval Outlaws: Eustace the Monk and Fouke Fitz Waryn* (Cambridge: D. S. Brewer, 1997), 51–78.

29. On the dating of the romance, see Burgess, *Two Medieval Outlaws*, 4. Burgess notes that various archival sources, such as patents and charters, mention Eustace, albeit "tersely"; fourteenth- and fifteenth-century chroniclers, such as Roger of Wendover and Matthew of Paris, discuss him at greater length.

30. Conlon, *Li Romans de Witasse le Moine*, vol. 1–16; Burgess, *Two Medieval Outlaws*, 50.

31. Conlon, *Li Romans de Witasse le Moine*, vol. 37–38; Burgess, *Two Medieval Outlaws*, 50.

32. Cheyette, "The Sovereign and the Pirate," 56.

33. Ibid.

34. Ibid., 65.

35. Ibid., 56.

36. There is a vast scholarly literature on privateers from the end of the Middle Ages through the eighteenth century. Among many others, see Kenneth R. Andrews, "Sir Robert Cecil and Mediterranean Plunder," *English Historical Review* 87, no. 344 (1972): 513–32; Andrews, *Elizabethan Privateering*; Lydon, *Pirates, Privateers, and Profits*; Michel Mollat, "De la piraterie sauvage à la course réglementée (XIVe–XVe siècle)," *Mélanges de l'École française de Rome* 87 (1975): 7–25; Michel Mollat, "Essai d'orientation pour l'étude de la guerre de la course et la piraterie (XIIIe–XVe siècles)," *Annuario de estudios medievales* 10 (1980): 743–49; Hugh F. Rankin, *The Golden Age of Piracy* (Williamsburg, VA: Colonial Williamsburg, 1969); Marcus Rediker, *Between the Devil and the Deep Blue Sea: Merchant Seamen, Pirates and the Anglo-American Maritime World 1700–1750* (Cambridge: Cambridge University Press, 1987); Hugh F. Rankin, *Villains of All Nations: Atlantic Pirates in the Golden Age* (Boston: Beacon Press, 2004); Violet Barbour, "Privateers and Pirates of the West Indies," *American Historical Review* 16, no. 3 (1911): 529–66; Jacqueline Guiral-Hadziiosif, "Course et piraterie à Valence de 1410 à 1430," *Anuario de estudios medieavles* 10 (1980): 759–65; Jacqueline Guiral-Hadziiosif, *Valence, port méditerranéen au XVe Siècle* (Paris: Publications de la Sorbonne, 1986); Evandro Puzulu, "Pirati e corsari nei mari della Sardegna durante la prima metà del secolo XV," in *IV Congreso de historia de la corona d'Aragón: Actas Y Communicaciones* (Palma de Mallorca, 1959), 1:155–79; Irene B. Katele, "Piracy and the Venetian State: The Dilemma of Maritime Defense in the Fourteenth Century," *Speculum* 63, no. 4 (1988): 865–89; Anna Unali, *Mariners,*

Pirates i corsaris catalans a l'època medieval, trans. María Teresa Ferrer i Mallol and Maria Antònia Oliver (Barcelona: Edicions de la Magrana, 1986); María Teresa Ferrer i Mallol, "Productes de commerç catalano-portuguès segons una reclamació per pirateria," *Miscellània de Textos Medievals* 6 (1992): 137–63; María Teresa Ferrer i Mallol, *Corsarios castellanos y vascos en el mediterráneo medieval* (Barcelona: Consejo Superior de Investigaciones Científicas, Institución Milá y Fontanals, Departamento de Estudios Medievales, 2000); Anne Merlin-Chazelas, "Ordonnance inédite de François Ier pour la répression de la piraterie," *Bulletin philologique et historique (jusqu'à 1610) du comité des travaux historiques et scientifiques* 1 (1966): 87–93; Philippe Rigaud, ed., *Pirates et corsaires dans les mers de la Provence, XVe–XVIe siècles: Letras de la costiera* (Paris: Éditions de la CTHS, 2006); Philippe Rigaud, "Pirates et corsaires sur le bas-Rhône: IVXe–XVe siècles," in *Guerre et commerce en Méd.térranée IXe–XVIe siècles*, ed. Michel Vergé-Franceschi (Paris: Éditions Veyrier, 1991), 37–57; Alberto Tenenti, "I corsari in mediterraneo all'inizio del cinquecento," *Rivista Storica Italiana* 72 (1960): 234–87; Alberto Tenenti, "Venezia e la pirateria nel levante: 1300 c.–1460 c.," in *Venezia e il Levante fino al secolo XV*, ed. Agostino Pertusi (Florence: Olschki, 1973), 705–71; Alberto Tenenti, *Venezia e i corsari, 1680–1615* (Bari: Laterza, 1961); Michel Fontenay and Alberto Tenenti, "Course et piraterie méditerranéennes de la fin du Moyen Âge au début du XIXe siècle," *Revue d'histoire maritime* 6 (2006): 173–228; Anne Pérotin-Dumon, "The Pirate and the Emperor: Power and the Law of the Sea, 1450–1850," in *The Political Economy of Merchant Empires*, ed. James Tracy (Cambridge: Cambridge University Press, 1991), 196–227; the articles collected in Michel Mollat, ed., *Course et piraterie: Études présentées à la commission internationale d'histoire maritime à l'occasion de son XVe colloque internationale pendant le XIVe congrès international des sciences historiques*, 3 vols. (San Francisco: Institut de Recherche et d'Histoire des Textes, Centre National de Recherche Scientifique, 1975).

37. Francisco de Vitoria, "On the Law of War, §12," in *Political Writings*, ed. Anthony Pagden and Jeremy Lawrence (Cambridge: Cambridge University Press, 1991), 303.

38. "Evenit autem interdum, ut occasione belli publici nascatur bellum privatum, puta si quis in hostes inciderit, et vitae aut rerum adeat periculum." Hugo Grotius, *De Jure Belli Ac Pacis Libri Tres, in Quibus Jus Naturae & Gentium, Item Juris Publici Praecipua Explicantur*, 3.18 (Washington, DC: Carnegie Endowment for International Peace, 1946), 565.

39. On the Barbary "wars," see, among many others, Peter Earle, *Corsairs of Malta and Barbary* (London: Sidgwick and Jackson, 1970); Godfrey Fisher, *Barbary Legend: War, Trade and Piracy in North Africa, 1415–1830* (Oxford: Clarendon Press, 1957); Jacques Heers, *Les barbaresques: La course et la guerre en Méditerranée, XIVe–XVIe siècle* (Paris: Perrin, 2001); Salvatore Bono, *Les corsaires en Méditerranée*, trans. Ahmed Somaï (Paris: Paris, 1998); John B. Wolf, *The Barbary Coast: Algiers under the Turks* (New York: Norton, 1979); Luca Lo Basso, *In traccia de' legni nemici: Corsari europei nel mediterraneo del settecento* (Ventimiglia: Philobiblon, 2002); Fernand Braudel, *La Méditerranée et le monde méditerranéen à l'époque de Philippe II* (Paris: A. Colin, 1966), 2:190–212.

40. Earle, *Corsairs of Malta and Barbary*, 3.

41. Fontenay and Tenenti, "Course et piraterie méditerranéennes de la fin du Moyen-Âge au début du XIXe siècle," 79.

42. Earle, *Corsairs of Malta and Barbary*, 30–31

43. Ibid., 34.

44. Ibid., 115–20.

45. On the English privateers and "sea dogs," see, among others, Andrews, *Elizabethan Privateering*; Harry Kelsey, *Sir Francis Drake: The Queen's Pirate* (New Haven, CT: Yale University Press, 2000), and the works mentioned in note 35 above.

46. See Peter Earle, *The Pirate Wars* (London: Methuen, 2003).

47. See Robert C. Ritchie, *Captain Kidd and the War against the Pirates* (Cambridge, MA: Harvard University Press, 1986).

48. Janice E. Thomson, *Mercenaries, Pirates, and Sovereigns: Extraterritorial Violence in Early Modern Europe* (Princeton, NJ: Princeton University Press, 1994), 54.

49. See the famous terms of *Politik als Beruf*, in *Gesammelte politische Schriften*, ed. Max Weber (Tübingen: Mohr, 1988), 5:505–60, 5:506.

50. Thomson, *Mercenaries, Pirates and Sovereigns*, 70.

51. Ibid.

52. Reprinted in Edward Hertslet, *The Map of Europe by Treaty* (London: Butterworths, 1875), 2:1282–83. On the Declaration of Paris more generally, see Francis Piggott, *The Declaration of Paris, 1856: A Study* (London: University of London, 1919).

53. "Second Marcy Note (Mr Marcy to Count Sartiges, July 28, 1856)," in Piggott, *Declaration of Paris*, 395.

54. Cited in Thomson, *Mercenaries, Pirates and Sovereigns*, 177n16.

55. Brogniart, *Les corsaires et la guerre maritime*, 187.

56. Ibid., 190.

57. The effort failed. See Thomson, *Mercenaries, Pirates and Sovereigns*, 76.

58. Stark, *The Abolition of Privateering and the Declaration of Paris*, 12.

59. Piggott, *Declaration of Paris*, 438, quoted in Thomson, *Mercenaries, Pirates and Sovereigns*, 178n36.

CHAPTER FIVE

Religious Horizon and Epic Effect

Considerations on the *Iliad*, the *Chanson
de Roland*, and the *Nibelungenlied*

JOACHIM KÜPPER

In the *Iliad*, the human and divine worlds are intimately connected, as already
established by their genealogy. The gods fight on the side of men, using natural
and supernatural means, and their interventions decide the course of war. Yet
even this moment of interaction is not the decisive aspect for epic effect; it is the
form of polytheistic divinity itself. The divine world of the Homeric epics is a
mirror of the human world.[1]

The prehistory of the Trojan conflict begins with a battle for supremacy
among women. Three goddesses—Hera, Athena, and Aphrodite—quarrel over
who is first (a constellation repeated on the human level in the dispute between
Agamemnon and Achilles over the right to possess Briseis), and the three of
them seem extraordinarily anthropomorphic, not only in the cause of their dispute but also in the way they stumble upon a solution: blinded by mutual jealousy, they leave the decision to Paris, a man, a mere mortal. They could hardly
have acted more foolishly. From then on, Hera and Athena, whom Paris has
debased, will be the most resolute enemies of Priam's city, and will not rest until Troy lies in ashes. The opening constellation is paradigmatic for the entire
epic. The actions of the gods follow no other logic than that of the warring parties on earth. Their affects—physical desire, envy, jealousy, pride, and offen-
siveness on the one hand, and friendship (for the most part unsteady), love, and
a (largely unstable) loyalty to alliances on the other—are the causes of the action
that unfolds. There is nothing sublime here, nothing mysterious. This heavenly
world is one that corresponds entirely to the measure of the earthly one.

But what are the consequences of such a model of the transcendental world?
Constructing the divine world as a mirror of the human world makes war and
all other actions appear as an endless chain of events that refer only to themselves

and their own motives. If meaning always presupposes an act of translation,[2] the *Iliad* presents a world without higher meaning. The only transcending element remaining here is the fact of separation between gods and men, or in other words, the fact of mortality. If one keeps in mind that the present gods are not the first, but became what they are through a kind of patricide, and that something similar to what befell Chronos could, in principle, threaten them, then even this last remainder of the supernatural seems to dissipate.

What is it, then, that draws the heroes of this meaningless world into battle and, with open eyes, leads them to put their own lives at stake? They do it for themselves. The motive is called "honor" (τιμή). It means the reputation of each individual in the eyes of his equals, and is so central because there would be no stability whatsoever in a warrior society without such imaginary categories of value. Otherwise everyone would have to claim his place in the hierarchy of power by battling others on a daily basis. But because honor is only a symbolic stabilizer of physical power, it is lost as soon as one fails to assert his physical supremacy when it is demanded of him by another. However, the heroism thus founded is unstable on account of just such a foundation. It is, in the end, an (unconsciously) calculating heroism. For, if honor has the function of freeing one from the daily burden of self-assertion, it becomes, for its part, a relative value. It must be weighed against that which it is charged to defend: one's own life. The excess of dead, who give evidence that battling over honor is a precarious business, triggers battle fatigue.[3]

The fundamental structure of the action that develops on the basis of this axiology is the projection of an elemental morality. The losing party, thereafter abandoned to annihilation, is one that has violated the patriarchal law, the respect of other men's sexual property. This violation is also registered as such by the Trojans. But in Priam's city, one opts ultimately for the older law of unconditional loyalty to the (blood) clan, which demands the defense of even those members who have offended the vital interests of a third party. Troy pays for this resistance to the law of a new era with its destruction.

The presence of "morality," the absence of "meaning"; these formulas could perhaps characterize Homer's epic on the destruction of Troy. As grandiose as the text may be rhetorically and in the arrangement of its *histoire*, the construction as a whole is internally fragile. There seems to be no justification for *this* morality to prevail, instead of the alternative one. The implementation of the patriarchal law is characterized neither as preordained by the gods nor as the fulfillment of an immanent logic;[4] it is presented rather as a bare fact, as an irreducible reality without a motivating horizon.

With the *Chanson de Roland* there is a change in the heavens that arch above heroic action. Monotheism has made its way into the epic world. But the medieval text is in no way some form of "religious" epic—on the contrary, the action's logic is first of all that of this world, as it is known from the *Iliad*.

Similarly, in the *Chanson de Roland*, the baser motives of envy and jealousy form the point of departure. Ganelon hates Roland as his stepson and as the most loved and favored of the emperor's knights, both by Charles himself and the other peers. Roland in turn gives cause to Ganelon's treacherous plans by placing his stepfather in a life-threatening situation. When the heroic battle does finally take place, in the certainty that it cannot be won but that one's own life must be sacrificed in the attempt, it is no different here than in the *Iliad*: honor is what motivates the combatants.

At the same time, the *Chanson de Roland*, unlike the *Iliad*, presents a world full of meaning. The heroes' action, driven by an almost-idolatrous valorization of honor, has a "higher" meaning, if one that is only partly conscious and accessible to them. The defeat and total annihilation of the rear guard arouses a desire for revenge—once again a very "earthly" motive—so great in Emperor Charles that he does what he had not done previously; namely, annihilate the unbelievers and lead the survivors before the alternatives of an enforced baptism or summary execution.

The continuation of the story that begins here is not explicitly formulated in the *Chanson de Roland*. But it is stated *that* it continues, and what is said of the subsequent events is sufficiently universal that it can be conceived as one that will repeat itself to the end of days: the "emperor" is exhorted by a messenger of God not to rest, but rather to arm himself for new and greater battles against the unbelievers.[5] The next to play the role of the one charged by God in this story will be Rodrigo Díaz de Vivar, called *El Cid*, whose successors will carry the names Ferdinand and Isabel. They, in turn, are followed by that Charles who will be the fifth German emperor and the first Spanish king of this name, and in the centuries that follow, up to the present, we will periodically find "Caesars" who take upon themselves a mission that converts aggression and a lust for power into a higher, or rather the highest, meaning.

This elevation is made possible by the basic features of the new religion. It would be inconceivable for a God who is the only God, and thus omnipotent, to lower himself to the level of human motives, to "envy" mortals, to be enraged by them, to wish to conquer them, and so on. Since the one God lacks a counterpart of "equal birth" who could allow for anthropomorphic action, his behavior must necessarily be thought of as arcane or as motivated by another, higher logic than human behavior. That other logic is, for its part, constructed out of the essence of this God: that he is the only God. As such, it is given to him that all men pray to him and only to him. Because he transcends every human measure, it is "better" for humans not to resist the cult of this God. As the God whose act of creation founded the principle of taking interest in the material-temporal world, it falls to him to take care that *all* men actually do that which avails them and that to which he alone is entitled: to pray to him.[6] The thought of a divinity that asserts itself in the historical process is the necessary complement of monotheism.

Accordingly, from its very beginning, the conflict in the *Chanson de Roland* is decided in advance. The logic is not of the content; it is instrumental. The accent on morality in the ancient epic has disappeared. Here there is no morality, only transcendental meaning. This likely comprises the immense attraction of the texts under consideration, as well as their modern, secularized, and banal remakes. The world of medieval epic texts like the *Chanson de Roland* or the *Cantar de mío Cid* is not only transparent ex post like that of the ancient epic. Everything in this monotheistic world is also prospectively certain and reliable. The "all-encompassing" world as presented by the texts' narrators sublates chaos, as the fundamental principle of the earthly world, into the cosmos of the one and only God.

The *Nibelungenlied* shares a wide range of characteristics with the epics already discussed; in the first place, genre-constitutive moments: the basic motive of battle, including the unmoved representation of the worst cruelties, and the ideal of heroic honor. Furthermore, there also appears to be an allegorical-moralizing level here, as is almost always the case in premodern literature.[7]

The second important moment of continuity concerns the motivation central to all narrative texts. In long stretches the events of the epic world take place in those lower regions that we know from other epics: Sivrit cannot resist showing his wife the tokens of his manly successes. As in the *Iliad*, a quarrel breaks out between women. Kriemhild allows herself to be carried away to the point of making public Sivrit's boasts. In the thoughtlessness that arises from having been offended, she goes so far as to present the tokens—Prünhild's ring and girdle—and thus thwarts Sivrit's attempt to repair the harm with an oath. The catastrophe takes its course. In the *Nibelungenlied*, too, rationality seems powerless against affect. And no less than in the other epics, here a too-heavily laden plane of material greed interferes with what looks at first sight like a relatively idealistic heroism to modern eyes. It is not the death of Sivrit, but rather the dispute over ownership of the treasure that stands at the beginning of Kriemhild's decision to end the period of passive mourning, to remarry, and to use her new position for revenge.

This broad fund of commonalities, located above all in the syndrome that is composed of a consciousness of honor, irrational affect, material greed, and shady intrigue, should not be allowed to hide the underlying fact that this text, as compared to the others, takes up a singular position. In the first place, the *Nibelungenlied* does not present a play of courage and honor, it stages no world of higher meaning; it is a single enigma unfolding in narrative.

Structurally, the enigma is concentrated in the third adventure, but from there it courses through the text. In this chapter it is first reported that Sivrit, after being dubbed a knight, takes up the service of ladies. Thereupon arrive reports of a beautiful damsel, who is the daughter of the king of Burgundy. Sivrit burns with love and determines to ride out to Worms in order to woo Kriemhild. Up to this point the adventure corresponds to a courtly subschema (*amor de lonh*).

Immediately afterward, the mythical substratum from which the action of the *Nibelungenlied* protrudes is introduced fragmentarily into the adventure's narrative flow. Sivrit rides to Worms with a small entourage. Hagen, the most experienced member of the court at Worms, speculates that the unknown man could only be Sivrit. Then he reports what he knows of the knight (of whose chivalric life to now it has only been heard that he quite recently had been dubbed a knight): that Sivrit had once conquered the Nibelungen. He stumbled upon them as he rode out one day without accompaniment. The Nibelungen were gathered around a "treasure" in order to divide it. Scílbunc and Níbelunc, the sons of the king, were said to have received Sivrit in knightly fashion. By their common counsel they asked Sivrit to attend to the division of the treasure. He initially declined, but then accepted to do what was asked of him. What exactly is meant by "er'n kundez niht verenden,"[8] (he was not able to do it, to completely carry it out) remains unclear. In any case, Sivrit aroused the wrath of the Nibelungen and battled them. Sivrit defeated twelve giants, slew another seven hundred more, and finally killed Scílbunc and Níbelunc, as well. The rest of the Nibelungen submitted to him. But the dwarf Alberich wanted to avenge the death of the two "kings." Sivrit, however, overpowered him, took the cloak of invisibility, and was since then *des hordes herre*,[9] the owner of the treasure. Without situating it temporally or causally in relation to what has been reported until now, Hagen then tells another tale from Sivrit's past that appears even more fantastic in the context of the current world of the court: the slaying of a dragon, bathing in its blood, and the invulnerability that results from it.

On the surface, the entire subsequent course of the action moves according to those wholly transparent causal patterns sketched above in detail that are also constitutive in the other epics. In the end it presents a narrative of the primacy of the affects and its disastrous consequences, shocking in its details, but easily explicable from a Platonic, Stoic, Christian point of view. Twice, however, the mythical substratum breaks through massively once again. The first time even involves an essential element of the action: Prünhild's mythical character alone makes necessary and possible the special courtship and wedding that is itself grounded in the use of mythical-magical objects. The second time the mythical substratum breaks through the plane of the present is immediately prior to the final catastrophe. On the journey, Hagen encounters strange beings, the *wisiu wip* or *merewip*[10] (mermaids), on the banks of the Danube. They prophesy the downfall of the Burgundians, with the exception of the royal chaplain. Hagen throws the clergyman into the water, who survives despite being unable to swim. Afterward, Hagen holds no further doubt as to the foundation of the dire prophecy. He smashes the boat in which the Burgundians crossed the Danube to pieces; there will be no return. As a visionary element, this second mythical incident confronts the listener-reader with the question of what relevance the anthropomorphic, affective motivation has for the action in general.

The narrator himself refers to the things laid in the mouth of Hagen in the middle of the third adventure as *wunder sagen* and *vil séltsaeniu maere*[11] or "marvelous tales" and "tales full of marvel." Thus the break with semantic coherence, as well as the enigmatic, if not paralogical, stamp of the interfering substratum is thematized. But it seems that its exposure has a concealing intention. The narrator, in alluding to the peculiarity of what was narrated, rhetorically withdraws himself from the necessity to which he should actually respond: to supply the information that would establish the coherence not given here.

Why, though, does the narrator report these things at all? Why does he not restrict himself to the "functions" (in the sense of Vladimir Propp) of the standard pattern of epics and courtly novels? He cannot do without them, if he does not want to write an entirely different story than the one that he has decided to write down. In order to construct the plot, he "needs" Prünhild's profile as a mysterious intermediate being—next to the episode of the *merewip* this is the only mythical element that appears on the plane of the narrated story. He needs the cloak of invisibility, not only to lead Gunther's courtship of Prünhild to success, but also above all in order to be able to shape it in such a way that the resulting quarrel between the queens can arise. He needs the mythical duplicity of Sivrit's invulnerability and vulnerability in order to entangle Kriemhild in a complex way in her husband's assassination. And, finally, he needs the story of the treasure in order to lend the deadly enmity between Kriemhild and Hagen such an aggressive virulence that even decades after its inception can lead both parties to their mutual destruction.

But what is puzzling in the world of the *Nibelungenlied* first appears in earnest where the enigma buried in mythical darkness penetrates the text's concrete, "historical" world of action, and the entire narrative flow is allowed to pass over into the exposition of a chain of riddles. Why does the young widow not console herself after an appropriate period of mourning? If she is already incapable of finding consolation, why then does she not direct her aggression against herself as one who shares the guilt, if she does not indeed bear it primarily? Where does the pitiless rigor come from with which she dedicates the rest of her life to revenge against her relatives, both the guilty and the innocent? The will to reappropriate the treasure seems an all too rational motive to explain Kriemhild's unbridled cruelty. What can the figure of Kriemhild "mean," introduced in the text as *ein vil édel magedin*, as *minnecliche(n) meide*[12] or "a most noble and lovely damsel"? Kriemhild, a quasi-tragic figure in the first part insofar as she is punished too severely for the youthful naiveté of her pride and garrulousness, becomes more and more a dehumanized demon,[13] a figure from another world, and it is not made clear why she undergoes this radical transformation.

What is striking in this constellation is that the enigmatic as the most salient feature of the *Nibelungenlied* may have its origin in contingent circumstances. As in the case of the other epics mentioned here, we do not have access to direct documentation of the preliminary stages, which all of the texts certainly had. That said, with the songs of the *Edda* we do have a transcription, slightly later in time than the text of the *Nibelungenlied* known today, of the tradition that precedes the version of the *Nibelungenlied* that has reached us.

One finds in those texts solutions—known in principle from the Mediterranean epics—to all the puzzles that lend the *Nibelungenlied* its abysmal uncanniness. There stands at the point of departure a murder perpetrated by gods against other supernatural, mythical, or even godlike beings.[14] The trouble to come is unknown in the moment of the act. The gods are initially unaware that they have killed an intermediate being and not just an animal. In order to acquire the material compensation demanded by the family of the victim, they commit a second reprehensible act, though aware now of what they are doing. They rob another intermediate being, a dwarf, of his treasure. The dwarf, who cannot prevent the theft, curses the plunder: whoever comes into contact with the gold hoard will perish, though he will first gain supernatural power. And so it comes to pass that the surviving brothers of the victim slay their father in order to come into possession of the hoard. One brother then denies the other his share, in turn provoking Sigurd, the mightiest of all knights, to take the treasure for himself from the greedy brother, who since had been metamorphosed into a dragon. After Sigurd has done so, he then slays the plotter, having heard that he planned on killing him, and becomes the hoard's owner, of whose curse he knows nothing.

But why does the *Nibelungenlied* that has come down to us break the narrative transparence of events by not mentioning the curse? Why is the prehistory of the entire fateful course of events held in silence? Why are those elements crucial to the story of Kriemhild, her brothers, and Sivrit only taken up in fragments?

The version of the *Nibelungenlied* passed down in writing can be placed in the same general time period in which the known versions of the *Chanson de Roland* and the other great Romance epic, the *Cid*, were written down. In the end, the impetus of all three poet-scribes is the same, and is the same that every author still follows today: one writes texts for a public, meaning one composes them in a way in which one expects to speak to the prospective recipients, or at least appear acceptable to them. There was in this period a whole series of points to keep in mind, of which one in particular matters in this context: in a text of the twelfth century about what was one's "own" and not what was "foreign," it was almost impossible to present this world other than how it was taken for granted to be: a Christian world. This was also true for the past phases of one's own world. A consciousness of historicity in the sense of an interest in the past as the opposite of the present did not (yet) exist.

In this regard, the author-scribes of the *Chanson de Roland* and the *Cid* had an easy task. The subject matter in each case presents a story with a happy end, despite the losses along the way. The structure of events is perfectly compatible with the optimistic gesture that founds the Christian history of salvation.[15] One can add to this the opportune circumstance found in both cases: the truly unchristian, bloodthirsty battles, driven to excess and motivated by crass material greed, had in fact taken place in conflict with opponents who were either of a different faith, or who one could stylize without difficulty ex post as being of a different faith.[16]

The *Nibelungenlied* stands out distinctly from these cases. There is no way to give this story of all-consuming destruction a positive turn.[17] A "Christianization" like we find in the *Chanson de Roland* and in the *Cid* would only have been possible at the cost of completely changing the fundamental narrative structure of the story. Ultimately, this would have amounted to taking up the fund of tradition as an inventory of elements to be synthesized in an entirely new way, a way that would have radically distorted that very tradition. Based on the features of the plot, the *Nibelungenlied* itself did not offer those possibilities of a gradual, "Christian" transformation that existed and were put to use in the case of the Arthurian epics, which are, in many regards, parallel. For such a bold engagement with an autochthonous, still-living tradition, as would have been requisite here, even a powerful master of language like the writer-scribe of the *Nibelungenlied* may not have found the necessary understanding in the age before the breakthrough of the poetic concept of Petrarch and Petrarchism.

Thus the narrator leaves it at a few superficial accents: the quarrel between the queens takes place on the steps of the cathedral (and not, as in the saga tradition, while bathing in a stream or in front of a knightly assembly). But neither priest nor bishop shows up to remind the disputants of the vanity of their pretensions and the inappropriateness of their quarrel on the way to worship. Kriemhild has more than a hundred Masses read in three days following Sivrit's death and afterward attends religious services daily for years. But she finds no consolation in a belief in the afterlife. She finds no insight into the guilt she unintentionally shares. Above all, she does not find her way to any form of forgiveness. While it is true that the marriage of the "Christian" woman to the "heathen" Etzel is articulated as a problem, nothing comes of this religious difference: Kriemhild becomes Etzel's wife. On the way to the foreign land the Nibelungen encounter a brother of Ute, Pilgrim, the bishop of Passau. But the encounter with the church dignitary remains a loose end in the narrative structure. It produces nothing and is good for nothing, neither in the positive nor the negative sense.

The biggest problem that faced the writer-scribe of the Nibelungen material in transcribing it during a Christian age, though, was this: what does one make of the beginning of the story, with the greed-caused murder amongst gods and half-gods, with the curse on the hoard? He solves the problem by erasing the prehistory and holding onto only a few fragments that are indispensable for the narrative unfolding of the story to come. The logic he follows can perhaps be most easily measured by the highly conspicuous dissociation between the appropriation of the treasure on the one hand and the granting of (a near-complete) invulnerability on the other. The treasure is divested of all mythical-magical contextualization. Its acquisition follows those patterns shaped in the age of early feudalism, patterns that are familiar, for example, from the *Cid*, as well: as soon as an opportunity presents itself to appropriate the possessions of a third party by means of physical force, it is taken. The mythical element preserved in the *Nibelungenlied* version: the slaying of the dragon, which grounds Sigurd's/Sivrit's supernatural qualities, his invulnerability—his status as a demigod—comes off here as if it were reduced to a few verses with a certain embarrassment, and the author-scribe does not entirely dare to lend the subnarrative the prominence it deserves. But he needs it nonetheless in order to stir up the intrigue of the story he is retelling.[18] The dissociation of the gain of the treasure and the slaying of the dragon permits the precarious moment of the curse[19] to fall into syncope. The author-writer of the *Nibelungenlied* appears to consistently follow the instruction to take up only those pieces of the mythical material that are indispensable for the future course of the action, without being overly concerned about the narrative coherence of the text as a whole. The rest is swept away.

With that, he radically freed himself from the ballast of the polytheistic past. But at the same time he "invented" something that he himself probably did not even realize: the structure of a fatal *causa* without one in whom the cause originates, of a curse without one who curses, of a fate that is not transparent, or even partially transparent, to the ones who fall victim to it. The elements of the sagas would still have been present for his contemporary recipients as distant memories, and for modernity, too, this horizon has come to exist again since romanticism, mediated through the tireless work of reconstruction. But decisive here is that this knowledge of the *causa* of the story told in the *Nibelungenlied* itself is and remains external to it. One would almost like to say that this constellation heightens the uncanny effect: everything that befalls the characters of the Nibelungen world does so for a reason. But they themselves do not have the faintest clue what it is that draws them inescapably to their doom. Granted, at a certain point they know with certainty, or some of them know, that they are doomed. The "why," however, remains, for them, a mystery.

What we are presented with here is thus neither the thoroughly human world of the ancient epic, reducible to a play of honor, nor the Christian world of the other great medieval epics with their overarching ceiling of transcendental meaning. The world of the *Nibelungenlied* has—perhaps—a logic and a meaning. But it is one that is not articulated. It is, in its withdrawal, deeply disturbing. Its power to disturb is increased by the fact that no promise stands at the end of this world, but rather a catastrophe without prospect of compensation in this world or the next.

The way of the world—from a human point of view—is an ineluctable and incomprehensible doom. But the power of this pre- and perhaps also post-Christian myth is not a revealed one, it is not one that is seen, and not even one that is invented. It is one created in absolute contingence. With a view to its human creator, it is probably little more than a solution reached out of embarrassment or even clumsiness. It is this aspect that represents perhaps the most "uncanny" facet of the entire constellation.

What may have attracted (and may still attract) modern readers to take notice of the texts discussed? In terms of aesthetic quality they are outstanding indeed, but it would be difficult to hold that they would dramatically exceed in this respect other prominent texts from our long-lasting Western tradition. Nevertheless, their prestige seems to be unique. As for all texts that narrate a story, the question of their canonical status can hardly be discussed without taking into account the message they convey.

The *Iliad* is the perhaps most impressive literary document of the patriarchal age. The text propagates the basic laws of its historical period, lessons mainly directed to male recipients: never to take serious action on women's advice, never to appropriate other men's sexual property, never to leave one's own sexual property without surveillance.[20] In present times it may be inappropriate to recall that the patriarchal system is the prerequisite of progress. It his highly probable that there was once a matriarchal order, but it seems rather unsurprising that we have practically no material remnants left from that age. The readiness to accumulate wealth that exceeds our personal needs is based on an instinct we share with animals—the instinct to care for our offspring. Civilization, however, is bound to the exclusively human ability of conceptualizing a time that exceeds one's own life span. The patriarchal system has its rationality not primarily in a will to dominance inscribed in males' genetic code, but in the attempt to culturally guarantee what was, until recently, biologically uncertain: the legitimacy of offspring. Only under such conditions are males ready to provide for more than what they need for themselves, only under such conditions may there be established what we call civilization, which is nothing other than an ongoing process of superaccumulation in which each generation builds on the foundation left by the generation before.[21] By staging the transgression of the patriarchal law and by presenting the transgression in a most fascinating way, the *Iliad* evades the banality of a didactic text.

The *Chanson de Roland*'s Christian "fundamentalism" seems to be likewise outdated in modern times, but here, too, a closer look may reveal the reasons for the epic's ongoing resonance. In the end, the text sets the frame for the West's political agenda to today. The "values" for which the modern Occident is ready to fight may seem merely secular, and indeed they are. But their roots are inevitably bound to those religious convictions for which Charlemagne and Roland fight. There are no "human rights" in Aristotle, for instance. From the Stagirite's viewpoint, the "barbaroi"—a term under which he subsumes any humans who are not of Greek culture—cannot pretend to have a status higher than animals.[22] And this holds true with regard to other philosophies and religions, as well. Phenomenally, corporeally, materially, humans considered as individuals are basically unequal. Human rights as a universal principle, however, presuppose that there is something that all humans share, regardless of their apparent differences. But what might that be? Certainly not the genome, which seems to be as individualized as our bodies are. The Judeo-Christian concept of a divinely created soul whose likeness to God accords dignity in itself and equal dignity to every other soul is the highly mythical and at the same time highly useful foundation for all our political action, even today. But it is difficult to posit equality in substance and to tolerate difference as something merely accidental. To put it in abstract terms, it is difficult to differentiate *substantia* and *accidentia*. Monotheism is a great equalizer insofar as it posits the substantial equality of every human being. But it is difficult to limit its equalizing impact to this abstract postulate. Finally, this postulate results in a total leveling of all cultural difference. Texts like the *Chanson de Roland* remind us of the religious or mythical basis of cultural edifices like "democracy" and "globalization" and of the somewhat precarious consequences this descent may have.

The *Nibelungenlied*'s fascination is based, as I tried to show, on its uncanniness, and I meant that in the classical Freudian sense. In Freud, the uncanny is the emotion provoked by our sudden encounter with persons, realities, or structures whom or which we know to exist, but whose existence—or, rather, our consciousness of their existence—we need to repress in order to be able to live.[23] In the case of the *Nibelungenlied*, this knowledge is evidently the knowledge of our mortality, of the world's mortality so to speak, and that of the whole cosmos. If we did not constantly repress this knowledge by creating religions, or by inventing concepts we call progress (or, today, sustainability), we would not be able to live. We would fall prey to resignation or even to despair. We have to repress the knowledge that we as individuals and the world as a whole are doomed without appeal. Conversely, we are, as Freud argued, attracted by phenomena that remind us of this knowledge. The attraction is strong in terms of impetus, but highly ambiguous in terms of emotion. Having read the *Iliad* and *Odyssey* or the *Chanson de Roland* to their end, we may feel comfortable regardless of all the (imaginary) bloodshed we have gone through. In the case of the *Nibelungenlied*, things are different. There is fascination without reassurance. In this sense, it might be that only modernity is able to fully receive this "aborted" version of a text going back to archaic times.[24]

NOTES

1. My argument in this chapter is indebted to Erich Auerbach's famous contrasting of the "classical" and the "Christian" mode of representation. My focus, though, is not primarily on style but on the connection between various religions and the specific narrative structures and features they enable.In addition, I will try to introduce a much sharper distinction between the medieval and the modern variants of "Christian" literature than is suggested by Auerbach's—in many respects extremely useful—thesis of continuity. Erich Auerbach, "Odysseus' Scar," in *Mimesis: The Representation of Reality in Western Literature*, trans. Willard Trask (Princeton, NJ: Princeton University Press, 2003).

2. In the sense that a phenomenon *x* is interpreted as meaning/signifying *y*.

3. See, for example, Homer, *Il.* 2, 3, and 14.

4. This could have been done, for example, by referring to a concept of progress. Patriarchal societies are more effective than matriarchal ones. But at least as it is presented in the *Iliad*, the victory of the "Greeks" seems not to be based on their higher effectiveness as warriors. It is a result of the outcome of several duel combats and the psychological effects the respective defeats and victories generate.

5. *Chanson de Roland* 3993–98.

6. My formulations imply that I consider the first monotheism in history, Judaism, as a monotheism in the state of emergence. Yahweh is the God of the people of Israel, and he is the only God to whom they shall pray, lest they be punished. For the other people or tribes in the region, however, there are other gods, and the text of the Hebrew Bible does not pronounce an unambiguous judgment as to whether these deities are ("real") gods of lesser power than Yahweh or whether they are mere "idols," fabrications by humans without any "objective" status (as the fully developed monotheisms of Christianity and Islam would then have it).

7. The behavior that the text seems to incriminate could perhaps best be labeled garrulousness and pride in terms of traditional moral philosophy.

8. Karl Bartsch and Helmut de Boor, eds., *Das Nibelungenlied*, version B, 18th ed. (Wiesbaden: Brockhaus, 1965), 93:4.

9. Ibid., 97:4.

10. Ibid., 1533:3, 1535:1.

11. Ibid., 89:2, 90:4.

12. Ibid., 2:1, 3:1.

13. Ibid., 1748:4, *válandinne* or "female devil."

14. See Arnulf Krause, ed. and trans., *Die Edda des Snorri Sturluson* (Stuttgart: Reclam 1997), esp. 145–53.

15. This should go uncontested with regard to the *Cid*. As for the *Chanson de Roland*, modern historiography tends to view Charlemagne's (authentic) expedition to Spain as resulting in a catastrophic defeat. The simple fact that Charlemagne went back to France after the "victory" without establishing his rule in northern Spain seems to authenticate this view. The "authentic" events that are at the basis of all premodern epic narratives are, however, not the decisive point. It is rather the story's potential to be reworked by minor changes into a narrative with a "good" outcome that decides its acceptability in

Christian times. With regard to Charlemagne's Spanish campaign (as was the case with Arthurian epic), this could be done simply by substituting the authentic or original ending by a new, optimistic ending. Or, to put it another way, it could be done without rearranging the deep structure of the whole plot.

16. This latter case may apply for the *Chanson de Roland*. It is a widespread, if not generally accepted, view among modern historians that the "Saracens" who inflict a crushing defeat on the rear guard of Charlemagne's army were Christianized tribes living in the valleys of the Pyrenees trying to take booty.

17. The *Nibelungenlied* could have avoided making Kriemhild the pitiless annihilator of her own people, and thus a Christian woman becoming the annihilator of Christians. The price, though, would have been another massive insertion of mythical elements from the tradition of the sagas into the action of the present, namely, the drink of forgetting. When this is given to Gudrun in the saga tradition, it has the effect of discharging the pertinent figure's aggression (bestial here as well as there) not against the brothers, but against the second husband. In the one case as well as the other, however, it is about nothing other than stylizing her into a devil figure, which raises the question of how it can be that this demon triumphs, though at the cost of her own life, above all without opening the bright perspective of a restitution of the "right" power relations between good and evil.

18. The episode in which another mythical object is acquired, the cloak of invisibility, will also come to appear inevitable in light of the following action, and particularly necessary for the courtship of Prünhild. But the introduction of the object is limited to its indispensability for the logic of the action; here as there one reads nothing of a curse that the plundered dwarf might have uttered.

19. Within a Christian context, it pertains to the Almighty alone to curse (and to revoke a curse, if he so wishes). The widespread mythical pattern of fateful curse would contravene the assumption of divine omnipotence. Before the Enlightenment, it was confined to the domain of popular oral literature.

20. As does Agamemnon, who then must pay the price for his lack of circumspection. Ulysses emerges as a contrastive figure to Agamemnon not only because Penelope is, thus contrasting Clytemnestra, the exemplary wife, but even more because he guarantees himself against any danger that might have developed during his absence by carefully investigating the site before he reveals his identity.

21. As we can see in our postpatriarchal times, this basic impetus is still virulent. After a short period in Western history, during which males seemed to have abandoned all questions concerning the legitimacy of "their" children, a science-based substitute for the obsolete patriarchal system of strict surveillance has in the last several years established itself, an instrument compatible with a certain (sexual) freedom of women.

22. Arist., *Pol.* 1252b.5–9, 1254a–56a.

23. Sigmund Freud, "Das Unheimliche," in *Gesammelte Werke*, ed. Anna Freud et al. (London: Imago 1940–52), 12:229–68. Translated by James Strachey et al. as "The Uncanny," in *The Standard Edition of the Complete Psychological Works of Sigmund Freud* (London: W. W. Norton, 1955), 17:218–52.

24. Daniel Heller-Roazen drew my attention to the fact that there are similarities between the *Nibelungenlied* as presented in my reading and a text like Franz Kafka's

Trial, which is not without reason considered to be one of the basic texts of our age. I should perhaps mention that in the entire medieval manuscript tradition, the text of the *Nibelungenlied* was always accompanied by another text, the so-called *Klage*. This latter text, written obviously by another author, assumes the task of providing a sort of make-shift compensation for the uncanny ending of the *Nibelungenlied*. It narrates the reconstruction of the Burgundian realm by the hands of Gunther's and Kriemhild's son. The primary motive for rejecting the *Klage* in modern times was the abyss in terms of literary quality, which separates it from the *Nibelungenlied*. But at the same time, this shift in the reception history may be caused by modernity's propensity, beginning in the age of romanticism, to appreciate the uncanny. The paradoxical background of this appreciation is, according to me, the increased repression that goes along with modernity's particularly high level of civilization. Because modern people firmly believe (or have to believe) in the power of progress, they are irresistibly attracted by the uncanny, but with one qualification: that it be confined to the realm of fiction.

CHAPTER SIX

The Possibility of Historical
Time in the Crónica Sarracina

MARINA BROWNLEE

In a recent essay, Caroline Bynum notes that lately, historical studies have involved "a retreat from the textual: the renewed interest in material culture and physical objects . . . and by a renewed recourse to . . . cognitive explanations for human behavior."[1] I would like to consider a fifteenth-century text by not retreating from the textual, by focusing on one material object in particular, and on cognitive explanations—showing that the interaction of all three features is essential to textual interpretation.

If the past is separated from the dialectic of future, past, and present, it remains an abstraction, as Heidegger reminds us.[2] Or, as Ricoeur explains, "the gap between *the time of the world* and *lived time* [emphasis added] is bridged only by constructing some specific connectors that serve to make historical time conceivable and manipulable."[3] There are three essential connectors that he identifies as conditions of possibility for the articulation of historical time (for linking the subjective time of our experience and the universal time of the world). The first is the calendar, which is likened to a sundial or clock because it emphasizes the fusion of its individual reader's response with astronomical and institutional, political, and social identities. The second is the charting of generations, since it is simultaneously a biological and intellectual expression, "a biological datum and a prosthesis for recollection in the Husserlian sense" (183). The third link is the preservation and analysis of archives and the documents they contain. Only once we have used all three criteria to reconstruct the "world surrounding the relic that today is missing" (184) can we understand its significance.

For Spain, the year 711 provides spectacular material for testing these three "conditions of possibility" of historical time outlined by Ricoeur. That year marks the beginning of a confrontation of Christianity and Islam that lasted nearly eight hundred years, constituting Spain's unique foundational subject matter—on par with the legends Troy or King Arthur. Like them, the retelling of 711 is about the constructing of historical time—forging mythic connections in order to legitimize empire in a temporally remote time frame. Written in the early 1430s, Pedro del Corral's monumental *Crónica sarracina,* whose full title reads *La Crónica del Rey don Rodrigo con la destrucción de España* (The Chronicle of King Rodrigo with the Destruction of Spain) exploits the calendrical, genealogical, and archival mechanisms outlined by Ricoeur to extraordinary advantage.

Attention given to the *Crónica* tends to dwell more on the text's perceived accuracy (or distortion) of the events surrounding the invasion, rather than wondering about its fifteenth-century context of production. Fascinating from many points of view, the *Crónica* has been construed primarily as a masterful conflation of the deeds of Rodrigo—the last Visigothic king prior to the conquest of 711—and of Pelayo, initiator of the reconquest circa 722. The author of this text displays a deep familiarity with the key Christian chronicles—even a prominent Arabic one—and is lauded by such fifteenth-century Spanish intellectual luminaries as Enrique de Villena, who appreciates the text's construction as a sophisticated historiographic *summa*.[4] At the same time, however, it has been immortally vilified by the equally illustrious fifteenth-century Fernán Pérez de Guzmán, in his notorious characterization of the text as a "lie," or *trufa o mentira paladina*.[5] His blatant disapproval of Corral's work is clearly influenced by political events and alliances.

This chapter seeks to explore the elaborate discursive universe Corral constructs using Ricoeur's three criteria for the representation of historical time. The *Crónica* seriously calls into question both historiography and romance composition as viable forms of articulation, as relevant philosophical models in a "fallen" world. During the fifteenth century, each of these forms in Spain had largely played out the transparent ideological possibilities it had served in earlier periods. History and romance are chosen advisedly in the *Crónica* because of their ironically problematic, timely nature. The time in which this text was produced was a time of notably stalled reconquest efforts in the eight-hundred-year enterprise, a time when ceremonial jousting had replaced true chivalric combat.

To a considerable degree, it seems, the *Crónica* has been the victim of periodization. Since neither historical discourse nor that of romance functions in a normative way here, critics of the *Crónica* do not know what to make of it. As Foucault would have it, the Middle Ages represent *similitude*—a resemblance between the sign and what it stands for, an epistemological fullness that, in his view, is not cast into doubt until the seventeenth century, a period that initiated "the age of the deceiving senses." Yet the Middle Ages, which for Foucault belong to a world of transparency, are clearly not so transparent.

The *Crónica* offers us a striking case in point—a text whose conflicting discourses lead to what amount to "contagious" articulations—contradictory representations, versions of iconic figures that call into question the very notion of representation. In addition, these carefully constructed portrayals reflect the most timely political and spiritual abuses of its infamous time of production. Epic history, by definition concerned with nation building, and romance, the utopian vehicle for aristocratic, personal self-aggrandizement, will expose the graft and corruption of Juan II's Spain (1405–54), simultaneously offering a model for justifying the Trastámara usurpation of the throne.

One of the most striking features of this text—relevant both to history and romance composition, as well as to paradigms of authority and authorship—is its alleged compilation. No author is named—not even Pedro del Corral is credited in any of the 217 folios of the many surviving fifteenth-century manuscripts with the authorship of this ambitious work. Instead, two eyewitnesses (obvious inventions of Corral) are posited as the collective authors of the *Crónica* along with a character who discovers the two manuscripts and stitches them together. Meanwhile, in a rather Borgesian manner, Corral presents himself as the editor instead. This is a significant form of identity switching indeed, given that it reveals his devious authority, which makes us wonder seriously about the ultimate veracity of his historiography. Part and parcel of his metaliterariness is his evocation of the miraculously rediscovered lost-book *topos*—stemming from the need to transform himself into an objective third-person authority through the all-important mediation of the editor.

This distancing of Corral from his material, his self-presentation not as the author but rather as editor, is striking. It extends even further, however, pointing to a broader sort of discursive distance regarding the subject addressed by the *Crónica*, one that conforms closely to the features of the pseudo-historiographer's text. Basing himself on a tripartite procedure, Genette identifies three elements that are essential in the production of such narratives: first, "un compte rendu général des faits importants, c'est typiquement le récit sommaire." Second, there is projected a distinct impression of "une réalité plus complexe que celle que l'on expose au lecteur." Such writing "doit laisser (à) deviner au lecteur [cette complexité] sans l'exposer lui-même" (a summary of the important facts; there follows an impression of reality that is more complex than that which the author explicitly offers the reader. Finally, such writing should let the reader decipher this complexity without the author's help).[6]

In accord with the features outlined by Genette, we find a long account of the events surrounding the fall of Spain to the Moors, but also a distinct impression that matters are far more complicated than the expository prose indicates. To offer one example of many contradictory appraisals, Rodrigo is both condemned as the direct cause of Spain's defeat due to pridefulness and greed, but also referred to as an *ombre de gran seso*.[7] Finally, it is the readers' task to wade through the complexities with which they are confronted, given that the contradictions are not addressed directly by the author.

That Corral is constructing an anomalous chronicle that challenges the reader becomes clear from his treatment of narrative authority and its chronological referencing—especially its notable paucity. The authority of the eyewitness narrator is strained at several points. To give one example, of the chronicler Eleastras's obviously devious nature, he claims first that he will scrupulously report everything that transpired, omitting no detail, yet he both does and does not do so in the following entry:

> que lo hazían por se mostrar de buen talante contra los estrangeros . . . E dize Eleastras, a quien el Rey don Rodrigo mandó poner por escripto todas las cosas como pasavan, que más de veinte donzellas de grandes linajes, que aquí no faze mención dellas por quanto no eran de linaje de los godos, dieron este dia muchas joyas a sus caballeros. (1.261)

> Eleastras—who Rodrigo instructed to write down everything that happened, did not mention twenty hig-born maidens who gave their knights many jewels because they were not of Gothic lineage.

Further contradiction is noted when we learn details of episodes where no historian was present, as in the exchange of Luz and Favila. Corral calls the reader's attention to this authorial departure explicitly, indicating that "no avía ombre ni muger sino ellos ambos, e así eran bien seguros que sus poridades no las entendiese alguno" (2.123). Who is in charge of this account if no one is present? Clearly, we are not relying on eyewitness authority here, but on authorial invention. As Ricoeur observes, the historian must play the role of mind reader: "The reader is prepared to accord the historian the exorbitant right to know others minds" (186).

 Even more disturbing in the evocation of historical time is its disregard for the calendar, calendrical referencing, that Ricoeur underscores as being of primordial importance to historical time—here we encounter a programmatic lack of historical specificity to precise years in which momentous events occur. In this long narrative of 518 chapters, however, few such references are made. Occasionally, the day of the month or of the week on which something important happens will be included: May 10 is given as the day when the Duquesa e Loreyna arrives in Toledo to make her request for assistance at Rodrigo's court, but no reference to the year in question is included (1.37), while the wedding for the foreign nobles is arranged for *un lunes,* "a Monday" (1.61).

By contrast, careful attention to the number of days (and even hours of the day) is given in the details of the many jousting tournaments Rodrigo orders.[8] Even here, however, no year is given. Because of these chronological omissions, the excessive time referencing (1.ccliv) with regard to Julián's call to battle seems especially strange: "Esto fue domingo cinco días de abril, que es el mes de la luna, que era el año de los alarabes a Mahomad de su nacencia a noventa e quarto. E a la hera de César setecientos e cinquenta e dos. E a la Encarnación de setecientos e quatorze" (This was on Sunday, April 5th, which is the month of the Moon in the 94th year after Muhammad's birth. It was 752 in the year of Caesar, and 714 in the year of the Incarnation; 1.620). Clearly, this is a case of information overload. The last of the references given (to 714) suffices. The excessiveness of this referencing serves to contrast for the reader the general lack of chronological information in the *Crónica* as a whole. And such profusion of detail in one brief passage in a text where historical dates are notably absent can only be calculated to provoke and even amuse the reader.

What adds to readerly skepticism regarding the authority of this text is the astounding discovery of the manuscript—in the hands of a merchant (1.258). Rather than being miraculously recovered from the ruins of an illustrious library or monastery, it belongs to an anonymous contemporary figure identified with an urban context and personal cash flow—prosaic elements that defy both the epic mentality and the chivalric world of knights and ladies. This is an obvious red flag signaling Corral's new enterprise, his daring recasting of historical time and of romance material and constructs for a vastly altered readership.

By his unorthodox treatment of narrative authority, Corral signals his metaliterary project—playing off the categories Vattimo describes as "archaism" that seeks to return to "origins and mythical knowledge without asking about the 'intermediary' period" and "cultural relativism" evoking "separate and autonomous cultural universes" (here the eighth and fifteenth centuries in Spain), without clearly delineating between them.[9] Corral does this to foreground his awareness of the powerfully deceptive potential embodied by cultural icons (especially

Rodrigo, La Cava, and Julián) and their use. For, paradoxically, as Baudrillard notes, iconolators/iconodules are in fact *"more modern and adventurous"*—more powerful vehicles of skepticism and cultural relativism—than iconoclasts:

> It can be seen that iconoclasts, who are often accused of despising and denying images, were in fact the ones who accorded them their actual worth, unlike the iconolators, who saw in them only reflections and were content to venerate God at one remove . . . The iconolators possessed the most modern and adventurous minds, since, underneath the idea of the apparition of God in the mirror of images, they already enacted his death and his disappearance in the epiphany of his representations (which they perhaps knew no longer represented anything, and that they were purely a game, but that this was precisely the greatest game— knowing also that it is dangerous to unmask images since they dissimulate the fact that there is nothing behind them).[10]

Because of their capacity to represent much more than their initial identities, the foundational genealogy (Ricoeur's second essential form of connection), these icons of Spain's historical identity represented by Rodrigo, his alleged rape victim, La Cava, and her vengeful father, Count Julian, are well-suited as high-profile messengers for Corral's politically charged allegory of Spain's fifteenth-century crisis.

The text is full of dramatic, unanticipated, and contradictory events and assertions that make us rethink the iconic value of the principle characters. One of the most fundamental treatments offered by the text (a crucial one for an epic composition as much as it is for romance), is the issue of free will. Rodrigo, La Cava, and her father the Conde don Julián are the most relevant characters in this context, and they point to some of the challenges posed by Corral's text.

From the start, Rodrigo is a problematic figure, to say the least, even in his earliest historical representations (which began ca. 754). In general, it is challenging indeed to assign much specificity to Rodrigo or to the empirical truth surrounding the events of 711. As Joseph O'Callaghan remarks, "the circumstances that led to the Muslim invasion of the peninsula . . . are involved in extraordinary confusion."[11]

What is known about him is that during a period of seemingly perennial civil war, he was elected to the throne at the royal city of Toledo in 710, in keeping with the Visigothic model for determining kingship—unlike the Hispano-Roman model, which saw the crown as a hereditary office. His nemesis (Akhila, who was his predecessor's son), refusing to accept Rodrigo as legitimate commander, provoked by this perceived usurpation, is said to have sent emissaries to Africa to seek Muslim military reinforcements, thus enabling the Iberian conquest. While Corral describes at length the positive responses of Rodrigo's supporters in this power play, he is more graphic in articulating its long-term tragic consequences as he battles his disapproving compatriots. The narrator's lament is poignant and graphic in detailing the human devastation throughout the text.[12]

From the opening pages to the final words of the text we are repeatedly reminded of the high human cost of this "primera destruición de España de los buenos cavalleros en el tiempo de don Rodrigo" (1.153). Moreover, the pessimism regarding this eighth-century "first destruction" serves as an echo of his own strife-torn situation amid fifteenth-century Spain's protracted civil wars. The dysfunctional nature of the monarchy; dangers posed by the ruling class for the country; stalled reconquest; graft, greed, and corruption on the part of both church and state; as well as a relentless anti-Semitism plagued both periods in Spain's history.

Though his genealogical identity is clear, Rodrigo is full of contradictions. He is described as being brave in war—"andava por la batalla más bravo que nunca fue cavallero" (148)—yet he fled from the battlefield in his final encounter. In the final pages, Corral affirms that "el Rey era muy sabio, asi en Guerra como en otras cosas que rey deve aver" (1.626). Yet in the next breath (in the same sentence), he contradicts this judgment, saying "aunque en algunas cosas no lo fue" (though in some things he wasn't so wise; 1.626).

A stunning lack of *sabiduría* on the part of Rodrigo is given by some as the cause of Spain's fall—namely, his arrogant violation of the Palace of Hercules (1.30). According to legend (both Christian and Islamic) in ancient times, the first king of Spain built a palace, depositing a secret inside it. He sealed the palace with a padlock and instructed each of his successors to add an extra lock so as to ensure the preservation of the secret. After twenty-six kings had followed his instructions, rather than adding his own lock, he violated the order, breaking into the palace—much against the passionate protestations of his councilors. Motivated by a kind of Adamic curiosity and also greed, he broke the locks, entering the forbidden room where he saw a chamber on whose walls were painted Arab warriors brandishing swords and scimitars. A parchment warned that once the violation had been effected, Spain would fall to the enemies. This is what Alfonso X's *Estoria de España* (chapter 553) and other respected sources report. But given this prophesy, the inevitability of Rodrigo's violation seems to suggest predestination at work. The narrative states that the violation was "lo que avia de ser." If such is the case, then, we may ask: To what degree can Rodrigo be blamed personally for the fall of Spain as a consequence of his entry into the palace?

In any event, this legend not only provides a dramatic narrative of magic, exoticism, and prophesy of the kind that appears in romances, offering its readers not only a wonderfully imaginative evocation, but also proof of the author's artistry. From an ideological perspective, it also offers the conquered Christians a scapegoat: they were destined to lose once Rodrigo defied his royal obligation that was preordained. At the same time, his action and the consequent fall of Spain can still be construed by the Christians as the result of the collective *pecado* of the land's inhabitants. This narrative was important to the conquerors, as well—spurred on by the knowledge that their invasion constituted a prophetic fulfillment.

In a striking move, Corral complicates historical time—and space—by reflecting both the empire's enduring Herculean Greek origins and the seven-hundred-year derailing of empire caused by Rodrigo's Gothic hubris. In the violated palace he and his men encounter a bed containing an imposing armed statue with an arm outstretched and holding a parchment. It identifies its bearer as Hercules, explaining that, just as in his tenth labor he slew the reckless warrior Geryon in a three-day battle (thereafter conquering all of Spain), the intruder, namely Rodrigo, would have the opposite effect, causing the destruction of Spain. Though he feigns composure, Rodrigo and his men are mortified.

Nonetheless, they proceed to a second palace of unimaginable beauty and architectural uniqueness, seamless construction, a structure that is also more translucent than crystal. On a pillar (the only content of the room) they find an inscription in Greek indicating that Hercules constructed the palace in the year of Adam, 3006 BCE. Next, he opens the small door on the pillar, finding words this time in Hebrew attesting to the structure's construction by Hercules. Thereafter they discover a jewel-encrusted gold coffer with Greek letters indicating that whoever opens it will—by order of Hercules, the ruler of Greece and Spain—see the future. Breaking the pearl lock on the box, Rodrigo encounters a cloth decorated with Muslim warriors and also the following words: "When this cloth is spread and the warriors made visible, Spain will be conquered by them" (1.180). From this message Rodrigo derives a certain measure of solace, reasoning that he was predestined to undertake this adventure given that: "There is nothing that happens without God's consent" (see fig. 7).[13]

No sooner have they exited this structure than an eagle descends with a flaming sword that utterly destroys it, turning even the building's stones to ash. Next, black birds descend, stirring up the ash to such a degree that it spreads throughout

Figure 7. Rodrigo as depicted in the *editio princeps*, the 1499 edition of Corral's *Crónica*. Courtesy of the Hispanic Society of America, New York.

all of Spain, landing on its inhabitants, which marked them "as if they had been anointed by blood." These multitudes died in battles in which Spain was "conquered and lost—and this was the first sign of the destruction of Spain" (1.181).

Several interesting observations can be made regarding Corral's depiction. First, he distinguishes between the Tower of Babel and the Tower of Hercules (adopted as the coat of arms of the city of La Coruña), where it has been standing since its construction in the second century. Unlike the paradigmatic Tower of Babel, and not in La Coruña but Toledo, Corral is explicit in evoking a tower/ palace with not only countless riches, but also inscriptions in Hebrew and Greek.

This is the structure that burns to ash. It is *not* a figure of Babel where the languages are incomprehensible. It is a prophetic space adorned by clear messages in the most illustrious ancient languages—Greek and Hebrew—whose inclusion serves to remind readers that the *translatio* was not from Greece to Rome to the medieval empires of France, Italy, or Spain, but from Greece directly to Spain. (And, of course, the long-standing Christological association of Hercules is as compelling in eighth-century Spain as it is in the fifteenth century.)

By having two buildings rather than just the Tower of Hercules as it was in Alfonso X's chronicle account, Corral can preserve the enduring presence of the

Hercules/Geryon tower while simultaneously juxtaposing it with the tempo-rary, ultimately destroyed building that heralds Rodrigo's and Spain's demise in 711. Corral is careful to add, however, that eleven years later (in 722) Pelayo will initiate the reconquest from the miraculous Cave of Covadonga, a Hispanicized version of Cueva Dominica/Cave of the Lady/the Virgin. Yet after Pelayo effects his victory, Corral will move his text chronologically backward (unlike chronicle procedure)—ending his work with Rodrigo's death eleven years earlier. Here, too, we see Corral's daring manipulations of Ricoeur's three "conditions of pos-sibility": genealogy, time, and archive.

Rodrigo defied the repeated warnings of his men, entering the palace to plunder it for his battle-related expenses and his extravagant international jousting tournaments. We see here the anachronism at issue regarding the chivalric lifestyle of fifteenth-century Spain, and its outmoded expectations of noble behavior. Knightly combat was vestigial in Corral's time, unlike the eighth century inhabited by Rodrigo. And in the fifteenth century, the much-commented social and moral crisis of the country revolved precisely around the tenuous position of noble pedigree in a bourgeois society, and the equation of money with honor. The climate of civil war and the usurpation of funds for personal pleasure and power exhibited by Rodrigo mirror the waste and moral impoverishment of fifteenth-century Spain. At the same time, however, he is explicitly identified, upon his death, with life everlasting: the church bells begin tolling by themselves—in spite of the symbolically significant devouring of his heart and genitals by a snake.

The figure of La Cava is presented in an equally challenging (and even more contradictory) manner in this labyrinthine political allegory.[14] She is presented as both victim and villain. The historian Sánchez Albornoz believes that the legend of this raped woman originated as an invention of the Goths as a way of masking the Vitizanos collusion with the infidel raiders, while others claim that the legend is Muslim in origin. What is known for certain is that she was not the daughter of the historical Conde don Julián.

Drawing on the tenth-century *Crónica del moro Rasis*, Corral initially intro-duces La Cava as a tool of the Devil, the Evil One who wrought the destruction of Spain that was foretold when Rodrigo defiled the Palace of Hercules: "como ya era dada la sentencia contra el Rey que en su vida fuese destruida España, el diavlo ovo de buscar comienço para que oviese lugar la destruición" (since it had been determined that Spain would be destroyed during Rodrigo's lifetime, the Devil had to find a beginning for the destruction; 1.448), he realizes that La Cava can be the agent of the destruction. She is first presented as an honorable

maiden who finds Rodrigo's amorous advances to be repulsive. She feigns igno-
rance at first, pretending not to understand his immodest proposal, which is
anything but the discourse of a *rey sabio*. His remark regarding his queen and
also God's will is nothing short of grotesque: "si en este tiempo la Reina muere
que yo no avré ninguna otra por muger sino a ti; para ojo bien que Dios te faze
en yo me enamorar de tu fermosura" (if the Queen were to die now, I would not
have any other woman but you; notice that God made you so that I would fall in
love with your beauty; 1.452). In spite of her claims that such an act would constitute treason (1.453) as well as a violation of her will, he rapes her with the aid
of one of his vassals, while she refrains from screaming so that the queen will
not become aware of her defilement and their mutual dishonor (1.455). After her
violation we are told that La Cava loses her beauty, too.

Her single-minded resistance reveals that she is by no means the wicked
woman who seduced an unwilling king, thereby precipitating the demise of the
peninsula when her father colludes with the infidel so as to avenge the dishonor
done to his daughter and their family by Rodrigo. Corral presents her as victim
in his account, and her ghastly death crystallizes the painful conclusion to her
unfortunate life, as she succumbs to an infection brought about by a fishbone
that becomes lodged between her nail and finger. She dies from the infection
after consuming her own flesh in a vain attempt to diminish her suffering. This
is clearly not the death of a romance heroine.

It is, I maintain, a grotesque and anomalous invention created by Corral
himself in order to signal the complexity and originality of his presentation by
comparison with her representation in previous sources. He seeks to demythol-
ogize her as the wicked woman who caused Spain's fall to the infidel, just as he
is not content to present Rodrigo as the clearly victimized monarch. The inclusion of Rodrigo's soliloquies when he confesses, repents, and does penance for
his destructive pride and greed complicates the King's presentation immeasur-
ably, and this is why Corral invents them. In the same way, La Cava's anguished
remarks to her mother regarding her fault in revealing the rape to her father,
that had she maintained silence about this violation Spain would have not been
destroyed, are poignant.

A different reason for the conquest of Iberia is offered by an enigmatic figure
referred to as Count Julian. He is implicated in the Muslim conquest by all the
Arabic chronicles, yet not by the early Christian ones. He is identified variously
either as a Byzantine exarch who ruled Ceuta on the northern coast of Africa, as
a Christian Berber who fought against the Muslims to defend Tangier, or as a
Goth who ruled Algeciras and Cádiz. According to Arabic accounts, he aided in

the Muslim conquest in order to avenge his daughter, whom Rodrigo had raped. Some say Julian betrayed Spain and his lord (Rodrigo) by aiding the Muslim invasion. Yet once Witiza had died and Julian was no longer receiving aid from Rodrigo, he became the vassal of another. So, politically, he was not a traitor in the eyes of some. At the same time, numerous sources indicate that the Muslims had every intention of invading Iberia—irrespective of Julian's wishes. Here, too, Corral is interested in generating doubt, calling into question Julian's culpability. As with Rodrigo and La Cava, in the case of Don Julián the question of agency, especially responsibility for the guilt leading to the destruction of Spain, is problematized. His iconic status, like that of the other two protagonists of the *Crónica*, is obscured and called into question.

Pelayo is the last of the protagonists, and he provides a fascinating portrait in terms of iconicity, free will, and generic affiliation. He serves at the corrective rewriting of kingship, and of Spain's future. While Rodrigo oversaw the country's destruction, Pelayo initiated its reconstruction. Corral, in accord with chronicles that predate his work, presents him as the emblem of Christian resistance. Historically, he—like La Cava, Don Julián, and Rodrigo himself—differed substantially from his depiction both in literature as well as putatively accurate chronicles. Though he is presented as king, he never held that office. He was the son of Duke Favila, he married, and had a son to whom he gave the name Favila as well as daughters, and his son succeeded him. He has been identified alternately as a *gallego, asturiano, cantábrico,* or *cordobés.* It is true that Witiza conspired to assassinate Pelayo's father, and that he journeyed as a pilgrim to Jerusalem, staying there until Witiza died. At that point, Pelayo returned to Spain, serving Rodrigo at the Battle of Guadalete in 711. In 722, Pelayo defeated the Moors at the Battle of Covadonga. His son succeeded him in 737 as governor of Cangas de Onís in Gijón, and when Favila died, Pelayo's sister married Alfonso I of Cantabria, who ruled from 739 to 757.

In Corral's text, Pelayo, whose epithet is *caballero de Dios,* is an otherworldly, messianic figure, replete with mysterious origins. As the child of a clandestine marriage between Luz and Favila, Pelayo is placed into an ark (2.99) that is put into the river so that he may escape King Abarca's wrath. He proves to be an exemplary warrior and defender of those in need (2.xcviii) by saving a merchant, his wife, and daughter from evil *malfechores* with a display of great bravery, thereafter delivering them from a ferocious bear (2.ci). As a result of his extraordinary prowess, the thankful merchant remarks to his wife, "por cierto este infante no es deste mundo, ca sus fechos celestials son" (Clearly, the young knight is not of this world, his deeds are celestial; 2.183). And indeed this is the case. Pelayo's mission is to save his country militarily and spiritually. Part of this otherworldliness involves an impeccable courtliness, but also a total indifference to the amorous longings that humans tend to have: "sin dubda si el Infante requeriera [a] la donzella hija del mercad[o]r de amores no le dixera de 'no,' más a él nunca le vino a la voluntad tan solamente para lo pensar" (Doubtless, if he asked the merchant's daughter for her favors, she would not deny them, but he never even thought of such things; 2.180). As a result of his genteel behavior, Pelayo accepts a ring that the merchant's daughter gives him. While she intends it as a love offering that will be reciprocated, he accepts it not out of *amor encendido* "burning love" but instead "por que las gentes no lo toviesen a mal e a villanía en lo no tomar" (so that people would not think ill of him for refusing it; 2.186–87).

Pelayo never sees the girl again, but she remains steadfast in her love only for him, dying a virgin. Before expiring, however, she writes a book entitled *Contemplamiento de amor* that included meditations "de amores, e de armas, e de las temptaciones de la vida deste mundo, e una parte de las cosas celestiales" (on love and arms and the temptations of this world and a part of heavenly things; 2.187). Here, too, we see a character who defies generic norms: an enamored girl who dies a love martyr, but only after writing a philosophical-theological treatise.

For his part, Pelayo is difficult to categorize, since he does not conform to norms of human behavior. He is in a class by himself in terms of human and divine relationships. He is an impeccable warrior, revealing himself to be also a concerned brother once he learns that his sister Lucencia has married Mimaça, the King of Gijón, who had secretly converted to Islam, convinced that he would pressure her into converting, as well. Lucencia refuses to convert and leaves Mimaça. His shield spells out "Jesús" in Chaldean letters, and his special status is dramatized at the confrontation with Alcamar and Oropas when he is trapped in the Cueva Donga, known more commonly as Covadonga. When it appears that Pelayo cannot possibly survive this attack, God performs a miracle, causing the arrows that the Moors and renegade Christians discharged against him to turn around and kill them. Thereafter, the mountain crashes into the sea, killing those who remained (2.345).

That Corral is interested in generic complexity is evident if we consider the patters of epic, hagiography, and romance. Pelayo is not an epic character because of his superhuman status. He is a paradigm of spiritual devotion but, unlike the lives of saints, he is never tempted by the types of flaws that often beset them, such as hubris, greed, or carnal temptation. Because he is in a class by himself, he is not beset by the self-doubts, setbacks, or inherent flaws of epic heroes.

And his status as perpetual virgin never tempted by carnal desire clearly eliminates him from the realm of romance. He is a total anomaly, an unearthly being. The *Crónica* is invested in dramatizing human complexity not only in historical time as Ricoeur conceives it—through the calendar, genealogy, and archive—but Corral also thereby casts doubt on the viability of generic categories, which tend to oversimplify the representation of history and the implementation of ideology. On the topic of free will, for example, we are told that it is free "sometimes": "Nuestro Señor lo dexa a las vegadas en el alvedrío de las gentes e en su libre poderío que usen del bien e del mal" (1.189). To show some of the complexities inherent in human experience, for example, Corral has captive Christians stone to death Frandina, La Cava's mother. They are reluctant to do so, in spite of the suffering she has caused them. Yet when they are told by King Alahor that they themselves will be stoned to death if they do not comply with his order, they kill her on the spot (2.369).

This narrative gestures toward a demythologizing or destabilizing of epic certainties and of romance values, as well. In the last analysis, we see from Corral's skeptical enterprise that romance proves to be an essential ideological tool that powerfully elucidates the contingencies of history and historical time.

NOTES

1. Caroline Bynum, "Perspectives, Connections and Objects: What's Happening in History Now?," *Daedalus* 138, no. 1 (2009): 77.

2. Martin Heidegger, *The Basic Problems of Phenomenology*, trans. Albert Hofstadter (Bloomington: Indiana University Press, 1982).

3. Paul Ricoeur, *Time and Narrative*, trans. Kathleen Blamey and David Pellauer (Chicago: University of Chicago Press, 1988), 3:182.

4. No Arabic manuscript of the *Crónica del moro Rasis* has survived, nor has the original Portuguese translation. Interestingly, in the three surviving manuscripts used by Diego Catalán in his Castilian reconstruction of the *Crónica del moro Rasis*, the conquest of Spain by the Muslims and the account of the emirate of al-Andalus contained in al-Razi's original are replaced by Corral's account of Rodrigo's reign along with material based on the Portuguese translation of Gil Pérez. See Pedro del Corral, *Crónica del Rey don Rodrigo [Crónica sarracina]*, ed. James D. Fogelquist (Madrid: Castalia, 2001), 1:12–13. Villena takes the *Crónica* seriously as a text worthy of great respect, including it in his "Epístola a Suero de Quiñones" as a reliable meteorological source along with Virgil's *Aeneid* and Guido della Colonna's *Estoria troyana*. See Enrique de Villena, *Obras completas* (Madrid: Turner, 1994), 1:347–48.

5. Fernán Pérez de Guzmán, *Generaciones y semblanzas*, ed. R. B. Tate (London: Tamesis, 1965), 1. Pérez de Guzmán's blatant disapproval of Corral's work was clearly influenced by political events and alliances. When Corral allied himself with Alvaro de Luna soon after pledging his allegiance to the King of Aragon, he incurred the hatred of Pérez de Guzmán, who was imprisoned as a result of his Aragonese affiliations.

6. Gérard Genette, *Palimpsestes*, trans. Channa Neuman and Claude Doubinsky (Lincoln: University of Nebraska Press, 1977), 253.

7. Michael Agnew, "Crafting the Past and Present: The Figure of the Historian in Fifteenth-Century Castile" (PhD thesis, University of Pennsylvania, 2000), 233, observes that: "in more than 200 double-column folios, Corral mentions only 3 precise dates, one of them glaringly incorrect."

8. See, for example, 1.189.

9. Gianni Vattimo, *The Transparent Society* (Baltimore: Johns Hopkins University Press, 1992), 39.

10. Jean Baudrillard, *Selected Writings*, ed. and trans. Mark Poster (Stanford: Stanford University Press, 1988), 169.

11. Joseph O'Callaghan, *A History of Medieval Spain* (Ithaca, NY: Cornell University Press, 1975), 50.

12. In 1.17, for example, he writes: "¡O España triste, cómo hoy este dia eres puesta en condicion de ser destruida para siempre jamás! En fuerte punto nasció tanto orgullo en el noble linaje de los godos que unos a otros así se han de matar y así se viene llegando la gran destruición de toda España, que los sabios antiguos dixeron . . . que en España sería fecho fin de sangre, así como por el mundo fue ya fin de aguas del diluvio" (1.139).

13. Some viewed Rodrigo in such positive terms that, for example, the Catholic Kings, Ferdinand and Isabella, identified with him strongly. In figure 7, taken from the *editio princeps*, Rodrigo is seated on the throne with the windows behind him on the left depicting the mountains that crashed into the sea, crushing the enemy Moors and renegade Christians, while those on the right reveal some politically significant shrubbery in the curiously tall "pineapple trees" that remind the reader of the monarchs' New World conquest. Meanwhile, the border that frames the entire scene showcases the pomegranate (*la granada*; the fruit as well as the Kingdom of Granada) and hence the symbol of their reconquest.

14. For two recent and valuable studies, see James D. Fogelquist, "Pedro de Corral's Reconfiguration of La Cava in the *Crónica del Rey don Rodrigo*," *eHumanista: Monographs in Humanities* 3 (2007): 1–76, and Patricia E. Grieve, *The Eve of Spain: Myths of Origin in the History of Christian, Muslim, and Jewish Conflict* (Baltimore: Johns Hopkins University Press, 2009).

CHAPTER SEVEN

Good Friday Magic

Petrarch's *Canzoniere* and the Transformation
of Medieval Vernacular Poetry

ANDREAS KABLITZ

The reception of Petrarch's work, and especially the reception of his *Canzoniere*, has been, in modern times, largely determined by two tendencies, the temporal coordinates of which have been antithetic, if not, at least at first glance, contradictory. On the one hand, his poetic work is considered to be an important step in the history of emancipation of the subject; it is even presumed to constitute the birth of modern subjectivity—one of its numerous origins that the historians of literature could not help accumulating. It was Jacob Burckhardt who, in the middle of the nineteenth century, in *The Civilization of the Renaissance in Italy*, had called Petrarch the first really modern man. On the other hand, Petrarch's *Canzoniere* has the reputation of being a typical work of Renaissance literature, for it undoubtedly represents, in a paradigmatic way, the phenomenon that has provided its denomination to this period; that is to say, the rediscovery of antiquity. Of course, the presence of the traces of Latin poetry is undeniable in this text, and nobody before Petrarch had introduced the entire world of Greek and Roman mythology into a work of vernacular poetry.[1] Nonetheless, it is more than doubtful that the recourse to these elements of the cultural heritage of a pagan antiquity is identical to their simple semantic rebirth, as if the ideological premises of a Christian world had not at all changed the conditions of meaning of these relics of a polytheistic culture.

At the same time, it could hardly be put into doubt that Petrarch's *Canzoniere* offers the first example of a poetic cycle, containing more than 360 poems, which is centered on the figure of the author. It seems therefore obvious to conclude that in this text emerges the emancipation of subjectivity, a subjectivity that will determine the very constitution of reality in modern times. Yet, as evident as this might appear, the self-representation of the subject of this discourse differs considerably from the epistemological conditions of modern subjectivity, and it looks as if the central position of the author in this poetic work is much more due to the specific conditions of poetry in the Italian trecento, and especially to the work of Dante Alighieri.

The words "Infima inter omnes doctrinas" characterize the *poetica doctrina* for Thomas Aquinas in his *Summa theologiae*.[2] Indeed, the rationalization of discourse by scholastic philosophy had necessarily some decisive consequences for poetic discourse. Its prestige, unavoidably, had to diminish when logic became the essential, if not exclusive, criterion of truth. Nobody reacted to this theoretical provocation with greater radicalness than Dante, who transformed poetry into the very medium of truth. Particularly in his *Commedia*, he claims for his own poem an immediate access to a transcendent truth that will be closed even to philosophy and theology—an access to truth that is accorded only to an exceptional individual, elected by God himself. If competition, the aspiration for artistic excellence, is inherent to the vernacular poetic tradition, this claim for superiority is now transferred to truth. The author, none other than Dante himself, the wanderer across the other world, is granted the privilege of exclusive access to a truth which mankind had lost. This literally incredible revaluation of the role of the author does not aim at an emancipation of subjectivity but is ascribed to divine election, to an exceptional vocation. It is this eccentric position of the "poetic I," claiming a privileged insight, that we will rediscover in Petrarch's *Canzoniere* from the very beginning. On the contrary, the concept of truth represented in this lyrical cycle has considerably changed in comparison with Dante's *Commedia*. Petrarch's truth, the paradoxical and obscure truth of a world ransomed by the Redeemer, whose salvation is nonetheless not yet completed, remains totally inaccessible, and no wanderer across the other world will be able to make it evident. Therefore, in the *Canzoniere*, it will be its author's task to explore the enigmatic character of this truth through an existential erotic passion.

> Voi ch'ascoltate in rime sparse il suono
> di quei sospiri ond'io nudriva 'l core
> in sul mio primo giovenile errore,
> quand'era in parte altr'uom da quel ch' i' sono.[3]

This sonnet starts Petrarch's *Canzoniere*. It is a strange beginning, and hence the irritating singularities of this poem have always aroused the attention of its readers. In particular, the syntactic structure of the first two stanzas has provoked many interpretations. The central philological problem that they pose is the syntactic function of the pronoun *voi*. What is the relation between this address to the poem's readers and the rest of this sentence? It is not at all easy to give an answer to this question, for this address seems to be somewhat separated from the syntactic order of the phrase. Consequently, it has even been argued that the first quatrain of this sonnet constitutes an anacoluthon. Yet, as I will try to demonstrate, it is exactly this initial uncertainty about the syntactic function of the poem's first word that will allow for the deciphering of the meaning of the rhetorical procedures of this sonnet.

The extent of the readers' address, put at the beginning of the poem, is remarkable, for it contains the whole first stanza. But what is its content? Trying to give an answer to this question, one observes another singularity of this sonnet, because three of the four lines that constitute the readers' address in the first quatrain do not mention the addressees of the poem but its poetic I, the author Francesco Petrarca.

The relative clause following the personal pronoun *voi* in "Voi ch'ascoltate in rime sparse" characterizes the addressees as people listening to the poem's sounds; it characterizes them by designating the linguistic object of their attention. Instead, the continuation of the first sonnet aims to identify the content of this *suono*, introduced by the definite article *il*, the referent of which is not easy to determine. For, to define its identity, Petrarch talks exclusively about himself, without revealing the exact nature of this *suono*. It seems as if it is possible to characterize the semantic structure of this quatrain as a continuous *différance*, as the permanent delay of the identification of the referent of *il suono*.[4]

The sonnet starts by an evocation of the addresses whose more detailed characteristics lead to the verses to which they are listening: *in rime sparse*. Yet, precisely speaking, the verses as such are not introduced by these words. Rather, they are presented as the medium that allows for listening to them (*in rime sparse*). On the contrary, the mentioning of the sound leads immediately to their content; that is to say, to the sighs expressed by these verses. But the grammatical form of the sighs, *quei sospiri*, refers to something else, to a relative clause the exact sense of which remains again uncertain: "ond'io nudriva 'l core." This is a metaphor, but a quite enigmatic metaphor that transforms the sound of the verses into a figurative aliment. That, obviously, demands an explanation. This explanation does not take a long time to materialize, and yet neglects to offer the clarification one could have expected: "in sul mio primo giovenil errore." This is no longer a metaphor, but a circumlocution, the meaning of which remains also rather vague. Because what exactly is the error to which it refers? For the very reason that this expression remains vague, it is accompanied by another expression that, again, does not contribute much to the clarification of the meaning of these verses because it contains nothing more than a tautology: "quand'era in parte altr'uom da quel ch'io sono." This subordinate clause is not really informative because it hides rather than reveals what exactly makes the difference between the current and the former state of the poetic I. We would need this information to determine more precisely the nature of the sighs, the origin of which remains enigmatic. Instead of providing expected information, the first quatrain deprives the reader of information by accumulating a series of rhetorical procedures that constantly seem to promise a clarification that, on the contrary, is continuously withheld—a series that finally leads to a tautology. To summarize, the first stanza of Petrarch's first sonnet not only poses the syntactic problem of its relation to the continuation of the sentence it opens, it is also characterized by an irritating semantic structure, by a continuous *différance* of meaning. Is there any connection between both phenomena? We have to wait for the next stanza of this poem in order to answer this question.

If the first quatrain of this sonnet is dedicated to the content of the poems of the *Canzoniere*, the second quatrain talks about the function that the author attributes to his poetry. And if, in the first quatrain, the circumstances that constitute the content of the *Canzoniere* remain rather obscure, every enigma disappears more or less incidentally in the second quatrain:

> del vario stile in ch'io piango et ragiono,
> fra le vane speranze e 'l van dolore,
> ove sia chi per prova intenda amore,
> spero trovar pietà, nonché perdono.[5]

But what is the precise function of this poetry, according to its author? Line 8 seems to give a clear answer: "spero trovar pietà non che perdono." The second stanza also designates clearly all the readers in whom the author hopes to provoke such an effect: "ove sia chi per prova intenda amore." At first, it should be noticed that the persons to whom the poetic I addressed directly in the first quatrain are now designated by a periphrasis. For, undeniably, those who should testify their pity or pardon to him are the addressees of the text. The reason why they are now expressed by a circumlocution becomes clear if we take into consideration in more detail the content of this rhetorical figure.

The word *amore* bluntly calls a spade a spade, whereas the first quatrain long-windedly had circumscribed what now is designated directly. Thus a chiastic structure is to be found in this sonnet. Whereas the first quatrain—which, from its first word, presents itself as a characterization of the poems' addressees—only by periphrasis refers to the content of the *rime*, the second stanza refers to the readers who are addressed directly in the first quatrain by a circumlocution; but, at the same time, this circumlocution uses the proper expression to designate what in the first stanza had been long-windedly circumscribed: *amore*. By this rhetorical strategy, Petrarch implicitly reveals two properties of his readers. On the one hand, he distinguishes between different categories of readers, and on the other hand this distinction is made in a double way. Because, as verse 8 makes clear, those to whom the first quatrain is addressed are not identical to the addressees of line 8 (as the tercets will prove). The first line of this poem is addressed to any reader of Petrarch's rime; line 8, on the contrary, talks about those readers who are able to understand them. And, as far as these readers are concerned, this verse also evokes the conditions of a correct understanding of his poetry, and these conditions depend on the opposition between *ascoltate* . . . *il suono* and *intenda amore*: they depend on the contrast between those who pay attention only to an acoustic phenomenon and those who are competent to understand the poems' meaning. Hence the knowledge of Amor is identical to the competence of comprehension of the language of this poetry.

In this regard, it is significant that, in line 8, the readers wanted by the author are referred to by a circumlocution that on the contrary, as we have seen, directly designates what is at stake in this line; that is to say, *Amor*. In contrast, the first quatrain had referred by a proper expression—the personal pronoun *voi*—to the addressees of the text, concealing at the same time the sense of Petrarch's *rime* in a series of rhetorical devices that, instead of clarifying this sense—*amore*—rather tends to obscure it.

The famous anacoluthon of Petrarch's first sonnet, therefore, begins to make sense. It presents itself as a portrait of the not-so-judicious readers of his poems, who, without understanding their meaning, gloat over their sound. This is why, in the first quatrain, the content of the *rime* is indicated only by enigmatic expressions the resolution of which is constantly postponed. The syntactical form of an anacoluthon and its semantic structure are nothing other than two aspects of the same thing. They both contribute to a characterization of the undesirable readers, for the semantic structure of a continuous *différance* demonstrates the readers' incapacity, and the form of the anacoluthon indicates their eccentricity in relation to Petrarch's poetry, to which they do not really gain access. In a significant way, the proper expression of the *Canzoniere*'s central subject, love, appears for the first time only when Petrarch refers to his desirable readers, who are concealed in a circumlocution. Hence the understanding of these verses presupposes that these readers are able to recognize themselves; it presupposes their rhetorical competence. Already here, a parallel is established between the nature of Amor and the structure of poetic language. Thus the semantic chiasmus, which, as we have described, exists between the first and second quatrain of Petrarch's sonnet, opposes two types of readers: one desirable and combining their knowledge of Amore with their rhetorical competence, and the other undesirable, limiting their attention to phonetic pleasure.[6] By the way, the similarities between the complex structures of poetic discourse and the enigmatic nature of Amor will become evident in the second sonnet of the *Canzoniere*.

Thus in the second quatrain of the first sonnet the enigma that the first quatrain had produced is resolved. But is it actually resolved? Or, to be more precise, is it totally resolved? For, until now, we have not taken into consideration the exact formulation that designates the author's juvenile error: "in sul mio primo errore." This error is characterized by two temporal adjectives: *primo* and *giovenile*. The juxtaposition of these two words presupposes the existence of at least two errors, although it is not clear if the second error is also a juvenile one. But what does this second error consist of? One has to wait until the first tercet to find an answer to this question:

> Ma ben veggio or sì come al popol tutto
> favola fui gran tempo, onde sovente
> di me medesmo meco mi vergogno.[7]

Ma ben veggio or: "Now, but only now, I recognize the error to which I had succumbed." If Petrarch had committed a second error, this error refers to his expectation toward his readers. Instead of having gained their pity, not to mention their pardon, he has rather provoked their mockery. And we should not forget that Petrarch talks explicitly about the *popul tutto*. *Everybody* is laughing about him. Nothing indicates that he has found at least one reader who is able to understand his poetry. On the contrary, it seems to be the case that every reader pays attention only to the sound of his poems. The first error, constituted by the author's passion for Laura, is accompanied by a second one, which consists of the publication of his poetry.[8] It is of particular importance for the whole semantic structure of the first sonnet that the second quatrain combines the two errors committed by the poet:

> et del mio vaneggiar vergogna è 'l frutto,
> e 'l pentérsi, e 'l conoscer chiaramente
> che quanto piace al mondo è breve sogno.[9]

The combination of both errors, which I mentioned, is based on the fact that it becomes impossible to distinguish between them. The first verse, "e del mio vaneggiar vergogna è 'l frutto," seems, at first glance, without any doubt to refer to the preceding tercet, because the substantive *vergogna*, obviously, seems to quote the verb *vergogno*, which concludes the first tercet. But things are not as easy as they seem. The error to which line 12 refers is designated by the verb *vaneggiar*, and this verb refers to line 6, where a more or less identical adjective is to be found twice: "fra le vane speranze e 'l van dolore." And it is undeniable that this verse is referring to the pain caused by Laura's continuous refusal to fulfill his desires. Consequently, at the end of the sonnet it becomes impossible to decide whether the verb *vaneggiar* refers to the errors of love or to the poet's illusion, to which he had fallen victim by publishing his poems.

The same uncertainty applies to the last verse of this sonnet: "che quanto piace al mondo è breve sogno." Is it the recognition of the ephemeral nature of beauty that is expressed in these words—a recognition constituting a metaphysical verdict on Laura's beauty that, for so long time, had captivated the lover? Or is the briefness of pleasure caused by beauty evoked here to point to the only short estimation that the poet enjoyed amongst his readers? (By the way, we should not forget, in this context, the phonetic similarity between the two rhymes in the first and last verse of this sonnet: *suono* and *sogno*.) It is impossible to decide this alternative. Thus the last line of the poem is not limited to a simple reproach of the poet against himself. It is, of course, undeniable that this verse contains a condemnation of the sinful erotic desire that had captured the author during, after all, more than thirty years. Yet, at the same time, this verse contains, implicitly, a reproach addressed to the readers of his poem who relish the beauty of the sound in Petrarch's poetry, although they are mistaken about its meaning.

It is by the words "Vegnendo in terra a 'lluminar le carte ch'avean molt'anni già celato il vero" that Petrarch evokes, in the fourth sonnet of the *Canzoniere*, the salutary effects of Christ's incarnation for an appropriate understanding of the Bible.[10] On the contrary, the decipherment of his poetry is still expected. Obviously, nobody has been able, until now, to seize the sense of his poems, and this lack of understanding proves, at the same time, a sign of the author's singularity or, rather, of his intellectual superiority to all others. As Dante, Petrarch claims exceptional intellectual excellence.

Twice in the first sonnet of the *Canzoniere*, Petrarch uses a metaphor of food: in the second verse, where he talks about the sighs with which "he had nourished his heart," and in verse 12, where his shame is characterized as the fruit of his errors. Probably, these sighs are a hardly nutritious food, for they only prolong an all-consuming passion. By the way, we should not forget that these sighs constitute, together, the poet's rime, for they are expressed only by his poems. However, as soon as these poems fall into the hands of readers, they cast opprobrium on their author.

In his *Convivio*, Dante had mentioned only two conditions that can allow for talking about oneself: the necessity to defend oneself against disgrace or risk and the opportunity to teach other people: "L'una è quando sanza ragionare di sé grande infamia o pericolo non si può cessare . . . L'altra è quando, per ragionare di sé, grandissima utilitade ne segue altrui per via di dottrina."[11] It looks as if Petrarch's first sonnet refers to the second of Dante's conditions for legitimately talking about oneself: self-defense. However, the publication of Petrarch's poems provokes the contrary of its expected effect. Instead of preserving from opprobrium, they earn him dishonor. Yet this effect is not only due to his own mistakes, it is also explained by the incapacity of the readers who do not understand his poems where they could learn something about Amor's nature. If Petrarch, in the first sonnet, uses a metaphor of nutrition conceived as word, he recurs to a biblical expression, according to which man shall not live from bread alone and which Dante had used in his *Convivio* to justify his commentary to his own poetry. On the contrary, Petrarch uses the same metaphor to describe a poetics of love that casts him opprobrium instead of earning him prestige, for readers able to conceive the sense of his *rime* have not (yet) shown up. It is not the insights of philosophy and theology into love's character that the *Canzoniere* will repeat. Its discourse will explore the unfathomable depth of his nature that cannot be reduced to an already well-established knowledge. That is why Petrarch cannot do more than continuously hope to find a reader who, finally, will understand him. Social segregation serves as proof of a superior intellect, but exclusiveness makes loneliness.

At first glance it would appear that the first quatrain of the second sonnet of the *Canzoniere* begins with remarkable rational clarity.

> Per fare una leggiadra sua vendetta,
> et punire in un dì ben mille offese,
> celatamente Amor l'arco riprese,
> come huom ch'a nocer luogo et tempo aspetta.[12]

The event being recounted, namely the *innamoramento*, has a prehistory that allows for the understanding of the motivation for the behavior of the revenge-seeking

Amor. He wishes to put an end to the shame of countless defeats and at last realize a long-hoped-for victory. Amor secretly draws his bow once again and, with
this game of hide-and-seek, clearly accepts that he will thereby be contravening
a sacred principle of knightly combat. Yet the brilliant victory, which will this
time be granted to him, indeed ought to justify his actions. In this respect it would
seem that everything in the first quatrain of Petrarch's second sonnet is of unques-
tionable conclusiveness—that is, if it were not for the presence of something in
the first line that decidedly upsets this logical transparency. It is, namely, the epithet that more closely defines Amor's revenge: *leggiadra*.

How can it be appropriate for his planned act of punishment that his victim
regards it positively as a *leggiadra sua vendetta*? While in the context of Petrarch's
Canzoniere paying so much attention to an oxymoron might seem an exaggera-
tion, phenomena such as *dolci sdegni* "sweet scorn" (204.13) or a *dolce affano*
"sweet breathlessness" (61.5) are among the most common and well-known features of his cycle. Here a deep ambivalence of the experience of love moving between joy and pain, between bliss and despair is expressed, with which Petrarch
himself was able to become acquainted through Latin poetry. Nevertheless, this
reference to the frequency of this rhetorical device in the *Canzoniere* does not tell
us about its function in the section that we are examining. It will, however, become clear that the oxymoron of the *leggiadra vendetta* forms the starting point
for the fundamental problematization of the causalities of the action in both sonnets 1 and 3, which characterizes these poems to a great extent. Above all, the use
of pronouns both personal and reflexive will play a significant role.

However, what is meant exactly by Amor's *leggiadra sua vendetta*? Indeed, we
must concede that it is not possible to ascertain its meaning definitively, and
this presumably somewhat intentional circumstance with regard to this metonymy, of course, opens up at least two different links in the context of both
innammoramento sonnets. What is uncertain is whether the qualification of
Amor's revenge as *leggiadra* relates to the cause or the effect. After all, already in
the fourth sonnet, Laura's eyes are described in line 4 as beautiful, and it is her
eyes that the lover regards as responsible for giving rise to his unbridled love:
"i be' vostr'occhi, donna, mi legaro" (3.4); moreover, the eyes described here as
be' . . . occhi are referred to elsewhere as "occhi leggiadri, dove Amor fa nido."[13]
Amor's revenge may well be a *leggiadra vendetta* in that with love it will produce
an effect that is at least also regarded as agreeable.

In fact, at the end of the third sonnet there is a wholly unexpected if secret
consent on the part of he who has been struck by love, to his love. (It is unexpected because it clearly contradicts the other lamentations in the second as

well as the third sonnet.) In his final address to the lady, it is namely with reference to the god of love:

> però al mio parer non li fu honore
> ferir me de saetta in quello stato,
> a voi armata non mostrar pur l'arco.[14]

This new complaint, however, only makes sense if we assume that because he has in the meantime fallen in love, this new situation does not seem so wrong. Only then can it be understood why he accuses love of not having also brought the lady under his power, since this would have decidedly increased his chances of being able to satisfy his desires. That is to say, love for Laura also gives rise to mainly *pensier' leggiadri*, as it is elsewhere referred to, for instance, in sonnet 148.13. *Leggiadro* qualifies the cause as well as the effect of love.

However, for the final complaint against Amor there is a further explanation: because of his attacks, at this point the god of love is denied honor by the lover. Thus the code of honor is invoked—the code that regulates knightly Agon, and that already plays a role at the beginning of the second sonnet: *celatamente Amor l'arco riprese*. The reference to the secretive nature of Amor's attack indicates the contravention of the knightly code. Thus the accusation of a lack of honor would seem to be completely justified. However, the reproaches that the lover makes to Amor at the end of sonnet 3 do not relate to this aspect of Amor's behavior, but rather to the fact that Amor has only cast him, and not the lady, under his spell. It is not Eros itself that appears reprehensible, but rather the unfulfilled and unattainable desire that is to be avoided. If both sonnets had seemed to suggest a moral reproach against Amor, it now turns out that the defense against love is not morally justified, but rather it arises much more from the fear of the almost endless misery of an unfulfilled longing. Thus it is not due to ethical reservations, as the text initially seems to suggest, but fear of physical harm that in the end appears to determine the assessment of Eros.

Yet, with the assertion that Amor's behavior is a *leggiadra vendetta*, the antagonism—which had at first seemed so unambiguous—between the poet and the god of love, between a helpless victim and a devious perpetrator, disappears. Thus the initial impression that there is a simple logic behind the events has to be qualified. And, as we shall see and have already begun to see, it is precisely this deception of previous assumptions produced by the text itself that constitutes one of its predominant semantic structures. This insight, however, leads to further observations that, in contrast to the original assumptions, increasingly point to the subtle complexity of the text.

As we have seen, the reference to the secrecy of Amor's reaching for his bow alludes to the rules for knightly combat which demand that one acts openly— rules that here have clearly been contravened. However, such combat assumes the fundamental equal status of those who will oppose each other. Yet how can this assumption, which is in itself undeniable, be consistent with the reason for Amor's behavior given in this sonnet: "e punire in un dì ben mille offese"? This position corresponds much more to the behavior of one who is hierarchically superior, to the image of a god who punishes all resistance against his will, with which Amor brings honor to his reputation as the god of love.

However, in vernacular lyrics the pagan god has long since become a rhetorical method, and in the context of the Italian lyric of this epoch, one was decidedly conscious of this method. It was none other than Dante, who in chapter 25 of his *Vita nova* explicitly commented on the status of the figure of Amor, and who explicitly denied the quality of an autonomous *sostanzia* to this ubiquitous figure in his *rime*: "Potrebbe qui dubitare persona degna da dichiararle onne dubitazione, e dubitare potrebbe di ciò, che io dico d'Amore come se fosse una cosa per sé, e non solamente sustanzia intelligente, ma sì come fosse sustanzia corporale: la quale cosa, secondo la veritate, è falsa; ché Amore non è per sé sì come sustanzia, ma è uno accidente in sustanzia."[15] Against the background of this clarification it is especially striking that, by contrast, in this sonnet Petrarch increasingly provides Amor with attributes that stand in the way of his allegorical translation into a psychological trait, and lend him the features of an autonomous person. Nowhere is this more clearly seen than in the fourth line of the first stanza of sonnet 2, where Amor is attributed an action which is morally extremely dubious: "come huom ch'a nocer luogo et tempo aspetta." It hardly seems possible for this characteristic of highly morally questionable behavior to be translated into the characteristic of desire, the allegorical representation of which is indicated by the personification of the god of love. The qualities of the allegorical figure gain more of the upper hand here against the demands of figurative language, and the god of love develops more and more into an autonomous personal authority.

With regard to the specifics of time and place, for which Amor is waiting in order to for his somewhat unphilanthropic intention to achieve success, the speaker at first remains silent. This does not change in the second quatrain, in which we learn of some details regarding the reaction to Amor's *colpo mortal*.

Era la mia virtute al cor ristretta
per far ivi et negli occhi sue difese,

quando 'l colpo mortal là giù discese
ove solea spuntarsi ogni saetta.[16]

As has been mentioned, it is at this point that the pronouns gain particular importance, albeit the game that begins with them here will only become clear from the perspective of the tercets. "The power in my heart was constricted, for me to defend it there and in my eyes" could be a possible translation for lines 5 and 6 of this sonnet. Of course, we have here unambiguously interpreted *vertute* as "power" and not virtue, but this will be reexamined later. Nevertheless, at first it does seem that this is in fact what is indicated, and that this word does relate to the lack of strength that the poet has to defend himself against Amor. Moreover, there is also no reason to doubt that it is the poet's task to defend his heart: "I do not have the power to defend my heart" appears to be the obvious meaning of these two lines. In the possessive pronoun of the grammatical subject, *mia vertute*, lies the logical subject; at least this is how it would seem.

However, in this second quatrain it is already striking how consistently the metonymic representation of the events transforms the causality of the actions. Let's have a look, for instance, at line 7: "Quando 'l colpo mortal là giù discese." But it is not the deadly blow that pierces the heart, but rather Amor's perpetrated *colpo* is the instigator for the movement of the arrow, which then enters the heart. The next line also has this arrow as its theme: "ove solea spuntarsi ogni saetta." Yet, linguistically, the infinitive *spuntarsi* attributes an activity to the *saetta* that does not belong to it. For it is not the arrow that breaks its own point; rather, the point is smashed by the hard-heartedness of the poet. Thus the passive portrays itself as if it were active. In this second quatrain the roles of the actors are almost systematically reassigned. In the following stanza it is shown of what the signal character of these linguistic operations consists.

While in the second quatrain we may still assume that no one except the poet is concerned with defending himself against Amor's attack, in the first tercet the situation looks different indeed.

Però, turbata nel primiero assalto,
  non ebbe tanto né vigor né spazio
che potesse al bisogno prender l'arme.[17]

This sentence has no grammatical subject of its own. Therefore we must assume that the subject is contained in the predicate (*ebbe*) and as such is identical to that in the preceding sentence: *mia vertute*. This assumption is confirmed by the participle *turbata* and its feminine form. What is clearly different from the second quatrain, however, is the circumstance that this grammatical subject now also appears as the logical subject. For *vertute* itself is now the protagonist, who ought to have reached for a weapon, and yet was not in any position to do so. Thus *vertute* appears as the opponent of Amor, albeit as the unsuccessful opponent, whose task it would have been to stand in his way. Yet in the light of this mutation from grammatical to logical subject, the question is raised as to whether the neutral term "power" is still appropriate to the understanding of *vertute*. As the autonomous acting opponent of Amor, it is in fact *virtue* that here so pathetically fails against its adversary. The text itself underlines this conclusion when in line 10 power is given its own name, and is referred to as *vigor*.

The third stanza also brings clarity in another respect. In the preceding stanza the temporal relationship between lines 5 and 6 is not clear, and with this temporal relationship once again the logical relationship is brought into question. Does the named weakness of virtue in line 5 describe the state before Amor's attack, or is it a consequence of a successful attack? In the first case, could it be that the weakness of *vertute* is at the same time an explanation for Amor's swift and brilliant victory? The second quatrain does not enable us to decide between the two possibilities—it is only in the first tercet that clarity is given with the information that virtue was *turbata nel primiero assalto*. If it is the case that the first wave of the attack already results in such confusion that power fails virtue, then it is surely the case that her strength was not well formed to begin with. Thus virtue's weakness is not only a consequence of Amor's attack, but also relates to its prior state.

This is shown not least by the mood: the use of *potesse* indicates the possibility or rather the impossibility of an appropriate counterreaction. Also, the adverbial phrase *al bisogno* has the same effective function. For what is indicated is that *vertute* "in case of need" is simply not capable of defense. Why then is *vertute* now so weak when in the past it was so successful at defending itself? At first it would seem that this question has no answer. However, we can see that the effect of Amor on weak *vertute* is indicated by the term *turbata*. This is not an expression that relates to physical inferiority, but rather is concerned with cognitive failings. Thus virtue is confused. We will return later to this characteristic of inadequacy.

While the first tercet instigated the emancipation of *vertute* from the subject of the poet, the second tercet radicalizes this process:

overo al poggio faticoso et alto
ritrarmi accortamente da lo strazio
del quale oggi vorrebbe, et non pò, aitarme.[18]

All of this is still syntactically dependent on the grammatical subject *mia ver-tute*, and thus there remains no other possibility than to declare the speaker, the poet, as the object of this weak *vertute*. She is not able to free the poet from his *strazio* and she is not in a position to help him, although it is clear that this is her task. And we are even told further that *vertute* did not want to free the poet from all affray, because only now, *oggi*, she would like to do that, yet she is inca-pable of doing so. "Il poggio faticoso et alto," the "high and weary hill" seems to represent allegorically Reason. Thus virtue is unable to defend the poet against Amor's attack, and she is unable to demonstrate to him, in a stoic manner, the substantial irrelevance of Love's pains.

Whereas the poem initially seems to represent an antagonism between Amor and the poet, more and more its verses undermine this assumption, for the poet finally appears to be totally powerless, living at the mercy of the superi-ority of Amor and the weakness of his virtue and being nothing else than the object of their unequal struggle. But why is the text constructed as its continu-ous self-denial? And why, furthermore, is *vertute* so weak? The second sonnet does not give any answer to this question raised by itself, so we must have a look to the third sonnet.

The juxtaposition of the two sonnets, narrating the same event, the *innamo-ramento*, seems to be constituted und contemporarily explained by a theoretical opposition. Sonnet 2 rather refers to the inner motivations of actions, whereas sonnet 3 refers to their determination by outer circumstances. Amor, as we were told in line 4 of the second sonnet, was waiting for the "time and place to harm"; indeed, we find references to both in sonnet 3.

> Era il giorno ch'al sol si scoloraro
> per la pietà del suo Factore i rai,
> quand'io fui preso, et non me ne guardai,
> ché i be' vostr'occhi, donna, mi legaro.
>
> Tempo non mi parea da far riparo
> contra' colpi d'Amor: però m'andai
> secur, senza sospetto; onde i miei guai
> nel commune dolor s'incominciaro.[19]

As far as time is concerned, the opening lines of sonnet 3 make clear that the *innamoramento* takes place on Good Friday: "Era il giorno ch'al sol si scoloraro per la pieta del suo factore i rai." And, as Saint Matthew as well as Luke and

Marc report: "From the sixth hour darkness came over all the land unto the ninth hour." Regarding the place of the *innamoramento*, we have to look at lines 6 and 7 of sonnet 3, where there is an implicit allusion to the local circumstances of Petrarch's falling in love: "onde i miei guai nel commune dolor s'incominciaro." Common sorrow on Good Friday can be mostly found in church, and probably even during the service. Thus we learn why the poet's feeble *vertute* was unable to resist Amor's seduction. The perversion of Petrach's *innamoramento* lies in the fact that just the religious and maybe liturgical grief for the death of Christ, an expression of devoutness, proves to be the cause of his fault. An emotion, although full of piety, the mourning over the murder of God, as an emotion is inevitably a lack of rational control, and therefore becomes the gateway to sin. This is why the *vertute* was called *turbata*, "confused."

The more pressing question of who is Amor requires an answer. Who is this seducer who proceeds with remarkable foresight? As sonnet 2 had revealed, it seems no longer possible to reduce his figure to an allegorical representation of desire; Amor makes an appearance of a personal subject, of a *sustanzia*, to put it in Dante's terms. But it no longer seems reasonable or even possible to identify him with the ancient pagan god. So what is his identity? Isn't it plausible to consider him to be the so-called classical Christian seducer, a figure of the devil? That might be evident, if there were not in the *Canzoniere* some indications pointing in a quite different direction.

As an example, I choose sonnet 62, one of the rare texts of the *Canzoniere* where the poet himself recognizes the fault of his sinful love to Laura:

Padre del ciel, dopo i perduti giorni,
dopo le notti vaneggiando spese,
con quel fero desio ch'al cor s'accese,
mirando gli atti per mio mal sì adorni,

piacciati omai col Tuo lume ch'io torni
ad altra vita et a più belle imprese,
sì ch'avendo le reti indarno tese,
il mio duro adversario se ne scorni.[20]

Let us have a look, especially, at the first two lines of the second quatrain, where really every word looms large: "piacciati omai col Tuo lume ch'io torni ad altra vita et a più belle imprese." The sense of these two lines depends largely on the word that seems to be the most unimportant of all but that on the contrary proves the key to their profound meaning—the temporal adverb *omai*. If Petrarch implores God, from now on, to bring him back to the right way, was it not the same God who had formerly been pleased to expose the poet to Amor's temptations? Referring to a temporal continuity, the adverb *omai*, implicitly makes clear that God's power is omnipresent and that, consequently, nobody other than the omnipotent God hides out behind Amor, who is acting according to his orders. If Amor in the *Canzoniere*, unlike in Dante's *De vulgari eloquentia*, cannot be reduced to a rhetorical device, if he gets a personal autonomy that excludes an interpretation of this figure as an allegorical representation, he, at the same time, appears to be an agent of God. Amor here resembles a little bit the figure of Fortune as designed by Dante in his *Inferno*.

Of course, the Christian God *is* the God of Love. But therefore we might assume that he will not seduce to sin. Yet we should not forget the most troublesome line of the Lord's Prayer: "et ne nos inducas in tentationem" (And lead us not into temptation).

Let us come back to the first sonnets of the *Canzoniere*. We have identified "poggio faticoso et alto" in the second tercet of sonnet 2 as an allegorical representation of human reason, and probably, following a well-established symbolical tradition, we were right to do so; therefore this mountain is called also *faticoso*, arduous—it is difficult to reach its top. But in the context of a Good Friday setting, an arduous mountain probably has a further connotation—it appeals as well to the Calvary. The incapacity of the poet's mind, the sacrifice of his mind, the moral death that is sin, is allegorically represented by a figure of the death of Christ. This symbolic parallel is the deeper sense of the poet's mental powerlessness.

Twenty years ago, when I was working for the first time on the third sonnet of Petrarch's *Canzoniere*,[21] I discovered (but was not sure if I was right to) a parallel between the moment of Petrarch's *innamoramento* and the capture of Christ in the garden of Gethsemane. Today, and maybe not because of greater wisdom but because of greater courage or daredevilry, I will pretend that there is indeed a connection between the words used in Saint John's Gospel to describe the capture of Christ, "comprehenderunt *Jesum*, et ligaverunt eum," and the terms used by Petrarch to describe his falling in love: "e non me ne guardai ché i be' vostr'occhi, Donna, mi legaro." Yes, Petrarch is a *figura Christi*, and the unlimited pains caused by his love to Laura are an imitation of Christ's Passion.

In the last text of the *Canzoniere*, in the *Canzone* 366, Petrarch invokes the mercy of Mary:

Vergine, que' belli occhi
che vider tristi la spietata stampa
ne' dolci membri del tuo caro figlio,
volgi al mio dubio stato,
che sconsigliato a te vèn per consiglio.[22]

How could Petrarch, in his prayer for mercy, remind the Mother of God of her look to the martyred son if he did not presuppose any connection between his own suffering and the Passion of Christ? And if he believes to have acquired the right that grace should be conceded to him, it is the extremity of his pains which seems to justify his claim:

Vergine, s'a mercede
miseria extrema de l'humane cose
già mai ti volse, al mio prego t'inchina.[23]

This extraordinary character of his suffering makes it comparable to the pains of the Son of God.

In a last gradation of the tradition of *fin'amors*, Dante's vernacular lyric poetry presents love, the love to a Beatrice, as the royal road to heaven because the perfect beauty of the earthly (or even no longer earthly) woman represents transcendent perfection and therefore leads to salvation. In the *Canzoniere*, Petrarch continues to praise Laura's unearthly excellence, but this is no longer serious speculation about her actual ontological status. These delusions belong to the *phantasmata* of a lover whose desire transforms the beloved woman into a transcendent person. Every Neoplatonic idea of an earthly representation of transcendent perfection by the lover's object of desire is abandoned; the very concept of *fin'amors* seems to be rejected in Petrarch's lyric poetry. Yet, if the lover in the *Canzoniere* continues to hope to win salvation by his nevertheless sinful desire, it is the immense suffering caused by his love that seems to encourage him in his hope. To put it in theological terms, *luxuria* is a *vitium poenale*, a vice that has its punishment in itself because it produces nothing but pains. And these pains lead to a participation in the pains of suffering Christ, to an *imitatio passionis*. If love continues to be a royal road to heaven, this concept nonetheless constitutes a complete reversal of the traditional *fin'amors*, a reversal that conserves the final destination of love.

It is by this logic that the ambiguous role of Good Friday as the day of the *innamoramento* may be explained. Already in the history of salvation itself, Good Friday is a deeply ambivalent day. It is the day of extreme crime and sin, the murder of God's Son; and yet, precisely because of this incredible event, Good Friday, too, is the beginning of man's redemption. It is this twofold role of the day that is experienced in extremis in Petrarch's encounter with Laura, who will cause unconceivable pains and yet will justify his hope for salvation by these very pains. If God himself might make an appearance as seducer, he is, at the same time, the one who opens the way to redemption by extreme suffering in imitation of his own beneficial pains.

But Petrarch's lyric poetry not only constitutes a reversal of Dante's lyrics, it also refers to his *Commedia*. In his *Divine Comedy*, Dante, the poet, presents himself as the elected man who will bring back to the earth, fallen anew into the moral depravation of a *selva oscura*, the message of its chance to be redeemed once more. This is, of course, a radical answer to the scholastic doubts about the value of poetry that Thomas Aquinas declared to be *infima forma doctrinae*, the lowest form of all knowledge. But by the poet's journey to the other world, poetry in the *Commedia* becomes the highest form of science that allows access to a knowledge refused to any other *doctrina*. The *Divine Comedy* is something like a third testament, and thus the poet himself, bringing back to earth the lost knowledge of its redemption, becomes the figure of a redeemer, a *figura Christi*. As we saw, Petrarch continues to claim a similar role although nothing seems to predestine him to a savior. He remains a poet of the *selva oscura*, and nothing allows for its transgression, for any perspective to overcome its miserable status. A chance of redemption is offered only by the misery of the world itself because the death of Christ has transformed its guilt into the possibility of salvation. Thus, by means of passion, by the participation in Jesus's sufferings, access to heaven might become possible. Petrarch's self-ascertained claim for the role of a *figura Christi* is based on the pretention of the exclusiveness of his pains. This again is a kind of election, but with one remarkable difference. Dante's journey to the other world allowed his readers to benefit from his experience. Petrarch's election to extreme pains may require admiration, but it lost every effect of *doctrina* or *exemplum*. Should this distinction by an exclusiveness of pain be an origin of modern subjectivity?

In the fourth sonnet of the *Canzoniere*, more precisely in its second stanza, after having introduced God as the Creator, Petrarch, as I mentioned already, characterizes the incarnation of Christ: "vegnendo in terra a 'lluminar le carte ch'avean molt'anni già celato il vero, tolse Giovanni da la rete et Piero, et nel regno del ciel fece lor parte." At first glance, rather marginal effects and events of Jesus's incarnation seem to be mentioned here as an illustration of Christ's incarnation. Of course, only by his work of salvation the deeper sense of the Bible, namely its allegorical meaning, became accessible to man, and it is likewise undeniable that

Jesus transformed the former fishermen into his apostles. But why does Petrarch mention precisely these elements of Christ's life and task in the context of this sonnet, where nothing else seems to motivate the selection of just this information about his coming to earth? An answer might become possible, if we apply the hermeneutic principle that Petrarch evokes in this second stanza of sonnet 4— that is, the allegorical structure of the text of the Bible—in his own text.

If Jesus took Saint John and Saint Peter from the nets, on the contrary, Petrarch himself is captured by the net of Amor. In *Canzoniere* 181 we read: "Amor fra l'erbe una leggiadra rete d'oro et di perle tese sott'un ramo." The net is a frequent metaphor of love in the *Canzoniere*, and already in sonnet 3, by an allusion to the capture of Christ, we were told that the lover was bound and taken by Laura's eyes. Whereas Christ's disciples are freed from the net, Petrarch becomes the prisoner of Amor. The story that Petrarch's *Canzoniere* tells us is a reversal of the history of salvation, it is a story taken from the *conditio humana* in the *selva oscura*. If nonetheless the horizon of redemption is not abandoned, this is because Christ's death has transformed the miserable existence of a sinful mankind into a chance of salvation, transforming extreme suffering into the very source of hope for salvation.

In his *Convivio*, Dante had transferred the allegorical structure of the language of the Bible to vernacular poetry; the same allegorical mood is still practiced in Petrarch's lyric. But, whereas the allegories of the Bible lead from the historical sense of the events narrated in the Holy Scripture to the anagogical sphere of heaven, the allegories of the *Canzoniere* lead to the enigma of a world that still might be a redeemed world but whose salvation is hidden in its innumerable paradoxes. Thus a text as the sonnet 2 of the *Canzoniere*, which we have read with particular attention, is characterized by a permanent deception of assumptions the text itself produces. The semantic structure of Petrarch's poems becomes itself a mirror of the enigmatic nature of this world. Unlike the *Commedia*, in the *Canzoniere* poetry is no longer a revelation of transcendent truth, but by its permanent variations of the very same subject it offers continuously new insights into the substantially paradoxical character of the perhaps redeemed but, precisely because of this hope, deeply unfathomable world.

NOTES

1. See for instance Hugo Friedrich, *Epochen der italienischen Lyrik* (Frankfurt: Klostermann, 1964).

2. Thomas Aquinas, *Summa theologiae* 1.1.9, arg. 1: "Illud enim quod est proprium infimae doctrinae, non videtur competere huic scientiae, quae inter alias tenet locum supremum, ut iam dictum est. Procedere autem per similitudines varias et repraesentationes, est proprium poeticae, quae est infima inter omnes doctrinas. Ergo huiusmodi similitudinibus uti, non est conveniens huic scientiae." S. Thomae Aquinatis *Opera omnia*, hg. v. Leonina-Kommission, Rom 1882ff., Bd. 4: *Summa theologiae. Prima pars (Quaestiones I–XLIX)*, Rom 1888, 23.

3. Petrarch, *Canzoniere*, ed. Marco Santagata (Milan: Mondadori, 1996), 5. *Canzoniere* 1.1–4.

4. To avoid any misunderstanding: The term *différance* is used here to illustrate a specific semantic procedure of this quatrain, and not as a general characteristic of linguistic semantics as defined by Jacques Derrida.

5. *Canzoniere* 1.5–8.

6. This distinction, as may be said in passing, seems to refer to the *congedo* of a *canzone* of Dante, "Voi, che 'ntendendo, il terzo Ciel movete," the wording of which is as follows: "Canzone, io credo che saranno radi / color che tua ragione intendan bene, / tanto la parli faticosa e forte. / Onde, se per ventura egli addivene / che tu dinanzi da persone vadi / che non ti paian d'essa bene accorte, / allor ti priego che ti riconforte/dicendo lor, diletta mia novella: / 'Ponete mente almen com'io son bella!' " Dante Alighieri, *Edizione Nazionale*, vol. 3, *Rime* (Florence: Le Lettere, 2002), 3:46. On the contrary, in the case of Petrarch's sonnet, the enjoyment of acoustic pleasure not only constitutes a minor form of reception of his poetry but, as the tercets will clearly declare, leads to a false reaction that proves harmful for their author.

7. *Canzoniere* 1.9–11.

8. This publication seems, therefore, to refer to a circulation of his poems among his readers before the publication of the entire *Canzoniere*. Hence the expression *rime sparse* could have a somewhat different meaning in relation to the one that the commentaries of the *Canzoniere* ascribe to it. This formulation seems to quote a technical term of the troubadour poetry, the *coblas esparsas*, a term that was used to denominate the separate stanzas composed by the troubadours mostly for their *tensos*. Therefore the *rime sparse* of the *Canzoniere* seems to indicate the metrical form of this poetic book, which is made out of 366 poems and does not constitute a continuous poem, as in the case of epic poetry. In this sense, the expression *rime sparse* would present itself as a modesty topos. On the contrary, if we take into consideration the circulation of Petrarch's poetry before the publication of the *Canzoniere*, *rime sparse* means also the poems spread among their readers. Hence the expression *rime sparse*, too, seems to have a double sense.

9. *Canzoniere* 1.12–14.

10. For, by the following words, Petrarch tells the whole history of incarnation in this stanza: "vegnendo in terra a 'lluminar le carte / ch'avean molt'anni già celato il vero, / tolse Giovanni da la rete et Piero, / et nel regno del ciel fece lor parte" (*Canzoniere* 4.5–8).

11. Dante, *Edizione Nazionale*, vol. 2, *Convivio* (Florence: Le Lettere, 1995), 11. Dante, *Convivio* 1.2.13.

12. *Canzoniere* 2.1–4.

13. *Canzoniere* 71.6.

14. *Canzoniere* 3.12–14.

15. Dante, *Le opere di Dante*, ed. Michele Barbi et al. (Florence: Società Dantesca Italiana, 1960), 32. Dante, *Vita nova* 25.1.

16. *Canzoniere* 2.5–8.

17. *Canzoniere* 2.9–11.

18. *Canzoniere* 2.12–14.

19. *Canzoniere* 3.1–8.

20. *Canzoniere* 62.1–8.

21. "*Era il giorno ch'al sol si scoloraro per la pietà del suo factore i rai*: Zum Verhältnis von Sinnstruktur und poetischem Verfahren in Petrarcas *Canzoniere*," *Romanistisches Jahrbuch* 39 (1988): 45–72.

22. *Canzoniere* 366.22–26.

23. *Canzoniere* 366.9–11.

CHAPTER EIGHT

The Identity of a Text

JAN-DIRK MÜLLER

Philologists have to be devoted to detail. As one German author has written, philology is *Andacht zum Kleinen*. New Philology, whatever the enemies say, means dealing with minor details, too, as did Old Philology before. So, in a conference in honor of one of the leading new philologists—or, as he prefers—material philologists, I take the liberty of discussing what is—on its face—a minor problem. My topic is only one stanza, anonymously transmitted in an anthology, and my question is: Under which conditions may we consider these lines a version of one stanza in a famous song by Walther von der Vogelweide? For we have to consider that it is set in a different context and some important details are different.[1] For old philologists the answer was clear: as the majority of words corresponds with those in the stanza transmitted under Walther's name, the text has to be Walther's; only the dialect is different and some lines are corrupted and distorted. Hence its variants have to appear in a critical edition of Walther's songs, even if they do not contribute any detail to the reconstruction of the text the editor believes nearest to Walther's original.[2]

For a new or material philologist the question is open. He or she will print all transmitted stanzas following the different manuscripts without claiming to reconstruct Walther's "original" text by combining different variants from them. But will they take the single stanza as a text of Walther? After all, it is anonymous. Adding Walther's name to it is one of the conjectural procedures new philologists are rejecting. And claiming that Walther composed it means to insist on the principle authorship that New Philology criticized as a projection of modern literature into the Middle Ages. Even to ask the question seems wrong. Therefore New or Material Philology was not very interested to ascribe a text to a certain author. But its theoretical assumptions have consequences for this problem, too.

New Medievalism (or better: the medievalism of the past twenty years) emphasizes the materiality of the manuscript, the mise-en-page, the visual shape and material context of the written text. The program was first developed in the 1990 issue of *Speculum*; an issue that was perhaps the most important event in the history of recent medievalism.[3] Too obvious was the challenge to some of the crucial convictions of traditional medievalists. At stake were concepts like work, authorship, original, traditional hermeneutics. Still to insist on the materiality of manuscript culture and its consequences for literary communication allowed us to comprehend some observations philologists had been making for a long time. In Germany—after a certain lag—the reactions were heavy, but in some regards medievalists felt confirmed in a well-established editorial practice that from the beginning of the twentieth century had turned away from the so-called Lachmann philology. The theses of Bernard Cerquiglini,[4] one of the authorities of New Medievalism (or, at least, this is how his thesis was received) seemed only too radical: the thesis that in medieval literature the concept of a fixed and closed text did not exist at all, that the Middle Ages altogether did not know the idea of authorship, that each manuscript has to be taken as an original and that it should not be interpreted in its dependence on older manuscripts, that no variant is better or worse than another—famous Cerquiglini's apothegm "la littérature médiévale n'a pas de variantes, elle est variance."

But if the radicalism of Cerquiglini's theses was contested, many medievalists agreed with some of their tendencies: that medieval texts are more open to alterations, additions, and abbreviations than modern ones, that the original text is out of reach and an editorial practice combining the variants of different manuscripts creates a hybrid never existing in the Middle Ages, that textual difference does not necessarily mean corruption, and that the medieval author was unable to control his text. Those assumptions were discussed since the beginning of the twentieth century. They entailed editions of medieval texts following the *Leithandschriftprinzip*; that is, editing a text as it is written in a certain manuscript (even though—to the disapproval of Cerquiglini—they added corrections, and even if this manuscript had to be compared in advance with other manuscripts of the same text to find out which one was "better" than the other). The series *Deutsche Texte des Mittelalters* follows this principle in actually more than one hundred volumes. Since the 1970s, the Würzburg School of Kurt Ruh discussed the theoretical frame and underlying editorial assumptions of those editions. It was therefore the members of this very school who argued against the pretense of New Philology being "new" in any way.

Meanwhile the discussion led to some kind of armistice between traditionalists and neologists: Cerquiglini's objections against traditional philology were accepted, while what were called his "exaggerations" were rejected; the

Lachmannian leftovers of the *Leithandschriftprinzip* were gradually abandoned, but critical scrutiny of conceptual flaws and grammatical mistakes in the variants of a text were still required. Nearly all new editions of medieval texts no longer claimed to reconstruct the one hypothetical "archetype" that is thought nearest to the author's "original," but, if possible and necessary, arrange parallel corrected versions of different manuscripts. Prepared by a longer tradition in Germany, New Philology seems accepted.

Yet even the recent editorial praxis is still influenced by assumptions of the Gutenberg Galaxis, especially its concept of "text" and of "authorship," and the linkage between these concepts. I think that some necessary consequences of Material Philology are still unexplored, especially in late medieval tradition, which revises and decomposes older texts and transposes them in different genres or discourses. My example is as mentioned before a famous stanza of Walther von der Vogelweide.

This stanza is comparing meaning and value of the words *wîp* and *frouwe*, "woman" and "lady." I give you the text in the Cormeau edition (after Ms. *A*).

Wîp muoz iemer sîn der wîbe hôhste name,
und tiuret baz denne vrowe, als ich ez erkenne.
Swâ nû deheiniu sî, diu sich ir wîpheit schame,
diu merke disen sanc und kiese denne.
Under frowen sint unwîp,
under wîben sint si tiure.
Wîbes name und wîbes lîp,
die sint beide viel gehiure.
Swiez umbe alle frowen var,
wîp sint alle frowen gar.
Zwivellop, daz hœnet
Alse under wîlen frowe:
Wîp dest ein lop, daz si alle kroenet.

For ever the word *woman* has to be the worthiest name for women; it gives more honor than the word *lady*, as I see it. If any woman is feeling shame because of her womanhood, she should listen to this song and then make her choice. There are nonwomen among ladies, but never among women [I try to imitate the pun]. Both, the name *woman* as the woman herself are delightful. No matter how it may be about all ladies: Women are all ladies, indeed. An ambiguous praise is scorn [disdain], as sometimes the word *lady*. *Woman* is a name which honors [literally crowns] them all.

Difficult are lines 10 and 11, especially the form of the verb *sint*. Old Philology proposed a conjecture, the form *sîn* instead of *sint*: "wîp *sîn* alle frowen gar" (all ladies should be women; i.e., should behave womanlike [emphasis added]), but the three complete manuscripts transmitting the song (*ACe*) let no choice; they write *sint*. Therefore we have to accept "wîp *sint* alle frowen gar" (emphasis added). I try to reword the possible meaning: Normally *lady* is a species of *woman*; the concept *woman* is more comprehensive than the concept *lady*. Here the relation is inverted. The concept *woman* does not include all ladies, for there may be ladies who are not womanlike. But because the name *woman* is ennobling, and the woman herself noble (my understanding of *gehiure*), all women are and therefore have to be called (can demand to be treated as) ladies. The conclusion would be that *lady*—in a moral, not in a social, sense—is the more comprehensive concept. All women are ladies, but not all ladies are women in a more demanding sense. The speaker revalorizes gender at the expense of class.

This basic argument is more pointed here than in other singers, but it is not so unique as some scholars fascinated by Walther's originality make us believe.[5] A comparison between social rank and ethics is a main issue in courtly lyrics, and the praise of the term *woman* at the expense of the term *lady*, which is associated with haughtiness and repudiation, is found in the songs of other singers, too, for instance in those of Heinrich von Morungen or Reinmar; it becomes a commonplace in later lyrics.

The stanza is part of one of Walther's most famous songs, L 48,12.[6] In this song Walther is contesting some ideals and norms of the *grand chant courtois*; he rejects the arrogance of the courtly lady and is pleading for another kind of love. The song is transmitted in three of the great Chansonniers (*ACe*). To give the context, here is the whole text of Walther's song as edited by Christoph Cormeau:

I. Hie vor, dô man sô rehte minneclîchen warp,
dô wâren mîne sprüche fröiden rîche:
sît daz diu minneclîche minne alsô verdarp,
sît sanc och ich ein teil unminneclîche.
Iemer als ez danne stât,
alsô sol man danne singen.
swenne unvuoge nû zergât,
sô sing aber von höfschen dingen.
noch kumt fröide und sanges tac:

wol ime, ders erbeiten mac!

derz gelouben wolte,

sô erkande ich wol die vuoge,

wenn unde wie man singen solte.

II. Ich sanc hie vor den frowen umbe ir blôzen gruoz.

den nam ich wider mîme lobe ze lône.

swâ ich des geltes nû vergebene warten muoz,

dâ lobe ein ander, den si grüezen schône.

Swâ ich niht erwerben kan

einen gruoz mit mîme sange,

dar wend ich vil hêrscher man

mînen nac oder ein mîn wange.

daz kît: mir ist umbe dich

rehte als dir ist umbe mich.

ich wil mîn lop kêren

an wîp die danken kunnen:

waz hân ich von den überhêren?

III. Ich sage iu waz uns den gemeinen schaden tuot:

diu wîp gelîchent uns ein teil ze sêre.

daz wir in alsô liep sîn übel alse guot.

seht, daz gelîchen nimet uns vröide und êre.

schieden uns diu wîp als ê,

daz och si sich liezen scheiden,

daz gefrumt uns iemer mê,

mannen unde wîben beiden.

waz stêt übel, waz stêt wol,

ob man uns niht scheiden sol?

edeliu wîp gedenket

daz och die man waz kunnen:

gelîchens iuch, ir sît gekrenket.

IV. [The quoted stanza]

V. Zwô fuoge hân ich doch, swie ungefüege ich sî,

der hân ich mich von kinde her vereinet.

ich bin den frôn bescheidenlîcher fröide bî,

und lache ungerne, swâ man bî mir weinet.

Durch die liute bin ich frô,

durch die liute wil ich sorgen.

ist mir anders danne alsô,

waz dar umbe? ich wil doch borgen.

swie si sint, sô wil ich sîn,

daz si niht verdrieze mîn.

manigem ist unmære,

swaz einem andern werre:

der sî ouch bî den liuten swære.

Stanza I: The singer recalls better times, when courtly song and courtly order corresponded to each other; only when these times return will he sing as before and his songs will mirror courtly joy. Stanza II: Before, the singer was content if the lady showed him her appreciation (this is the meaning of *gruoz*), but now he demands more and warns her: he will turn away from her because she is too haughty; love has to be mutual. Stanza III: The defect of courtly society consists in the fact that women do not distinguish the different qualities of different men in the same way as men distinguish good and bad women. Stanza IV is the stanza in question, commented above. Stanza V: the singer argues that his angry words only seem to be an attack against courtly values, but in fact he fulfills courtly norms better than everybody else; seeming *ungevüege* (rude), in fact, he has *vuoge*. In each manuscript the sequence of the stanzas differs; for instance stanza II—with its aggressive mode—is the last stanza in *Ce*, and only these two manuscripts have stanza V (*Zwô fuoge*). Thus the line of reasoning is different each time as are its results.[7] But, in any case, the reflection upon *wîp* and *frouwe* is part of a larger discussion about courtly love.

Now we come to our problem. One manuscript (*n*) transmits only the stanza quoted first, or better: a text seeming akin to it, but not under Walther's name:[8]

Wif was ie der hoiste name.

inn prisit bas dan vrauwe. als ich it erkenne.

welich wif sich ir wifheit szame.

die hore minen sanc. in mirke denne.

vndr vrauwen sint unwijf

vndr uuiuen sint si dûre.

wiues name vnd wiues lijf.

dat is vil gehûre.

wie it vmbe allen vare.

wip nimt des hoesten louis ware

vrauwen lof dat honit.

wif is eyn name dat si alle cronit.

The word *woman* always was the worthiest name and gives more praise than the word *lady*, as I see it. A woman feeling shame of her womanhood shall listen to my song and pay attention to it. There are non-women among ladies, but never among women. The name *woman* and the woman herself are delightful. No matter how all that may be, *woman* gets the highest praise. The praise of *lady* [or: of ladies] is scorn [disdain?]; *woman* is a name which honors them all.

The anthology comes from the northern Rhine.[9] Therefore a part is called *Niederrheinische Liederhandschrift*. The whole manuscript contains in a first section (I, *Chronikalischer Teil*) chronicle-like texts and in a second (II, *Poetischer Teil*) different texts: in the first grouping a series of anonymous stanzas from love songs (*Minnesang*) and sayings (*Sangspruch*) and, in addition, in a second grouping—as says the description in the Cormeau edition—"other texts" (*andere Texte*), among them excerpts from the *Virginal*, a heroic epic about Dietrich von Bern and the queen of dwarfs. The label *Niederrheinische Liederhandschrift* sometimes is given to the whole section, sometimes—more adequately—only to its first grouping (folio 91–96).[10] This first grouping is written by one scribe, while the "other texts" are written separately by different hands. So, the first grouping seems to be planned as a unit. In its first part we have twenty-five stanzas about *minne* and appropriate behavior of men and women, then after a vacant line, folio 93rb–94ra, a didactic, yet strophical poem in eighteen stanzas, an atypical Minnerede about nine knights and nine ladies praising each other as model lovers (*Neun Männer, neun Frauen*),[11] then again after a vacant line[12] thirty-one stanzas about different subjects: *minne*, virtues, everyday life, and so on. The Walther stanza is on folio 95vb in the second series. By its contents it would perhaps fit better in the first,[13] but as a whole the subject matter of both series is quite similar: noble and virtuous life including courtly love.

There is no space between the different pieces, no title, and naturally no name of an author. Each single stanza is marked by an indention and begins with a greater initial, alternately a red and a blue one. This is the usual manner to write lyric poetry in the Chansonniers, each stanza separated from the other, but no space between the songs. We find this order for instance in the *Manessische Liederhandschrift*. The Minnerede *Neun Männer, neun Frauen* is presented as a unit, also with indentions between the single stanzas. The excerpted stanzas appear as elements of one greater text, too, even if they are not linked by form or genre.

The verses on folios 91–96 are written continuously. At first glance, there are points to separate the verses (*Reimpunkte*), but we also find points at the end of a syntactic unit, or in order to separate a word from the following one. That means that the metrical order is less important than the syntactic; the texts may be read as prose. This is suggested also by the weak interest in poetic form. Often, the segmentation of the verses is difficult; the texts have many bad rhymes, often the rhythm is corrupt, sometimes a measure of a verse is lacking. In our stanza for instance the order of the rhymes is conform to Walther's song, but the meter seems different. The distribution of accented and unaccented syllables is quite irregular. Walther's first verse has five stresses in MS *ACe*. MS *n* has four. Corresponding verses may be built differently (in our stanza verses 1, 3, 6, and 8). The verse next to the last is missing altogether (or if we take the two verses as one long verse: the last verse is shorter). That means that the text could be sung no more on Walther's melody. In all: even if the rhymes are correct, the stanza is not presented as an artistic specimen of courtly lyric poetry.

Obviously, the manuscript combines different genres. It presents a series of stanzas with a wide range of subjects. The stanzas are different in extent, different in structure, and different in poetical form; some texts tell a story, some give moral instructions, some reflect on social values, some give advice in everyday life. They all seem to be strophic, but very often the strophic order is destroyed; some seem to be complete texts, some fragments of a greater unit. In most cases we do not know the origin of the text, and apparently should not know it. Obviously the patron (or the writer himself) was interested in the subject matter.

I shall sketch the contents, to give an idea of the diversity of subjects and types. It would be necessary to analyze folios 91–96 completely, but I have to confine myself to some pages surrounding the stanza in question. I begin with folio 95r. The first text deals with a kind of pleasure that destroys all which is noble. In the second, the personifications of Faithfulness and Perfidy meet, and Faithfulness complains of the prepotency of Perfidy. Next, it is told how Lady Honor laments (*si klait . . . si klait*) because she is insulted everywhere. Then an anonymous voice is arguing by rhetorical questions of the kind "Waz sal eyn keiser ane recht?" that all classes and professions, beginning with the emperor, neglect to fulfill their duties. Then we have a strophic narrative, a kind of *bîspel* (example), divided in two parts; the first tells a story about an owl and a noble falcon, the second gives its interpretation: the *bîspel* demonstrates how the young nobleman (falcon) is exposed to bad influences (owl). Then again a strophic *bîspel* of a falcon, now a falcon and a jackdaw (folio 95v). The jackdaw knows better to chat (*claffen*), and therefore is fed better; the falcon remains hungry. Here the falcon represents the wise man being less successful than the babbler. Next is a stanza about the ideal lady and the hierarchy of purity and beauty. Then a catalogue of virtues, then verses about the relation of Love (*minne*) and Honor (*êre*), then verses about the inconstancy of many women (*Somelicher wiue unstede*). Next is Walther's stanza, then a piece of advice to good ladies, a complaint about the decay of the world, and so forth and so on: an anthology of good advice and critical remarks about life nowadays, about the duties of a noble man and a noble lady, about the challenges and risks of nobility in a changing world, about the hierarchy of virtues and similar subjects.

Most texts teach directly, but there are some little narratives, too; some texts are allegorical—we have plain statements, a sequence of questions, advice, reflections. Sometimes the single texts seem to be linked by motives (for instance two texts about falcons and their failure in a vile world) or subjects (like the duties of ladies). And in the midst of it all, the sententious stanza about *wîp* and *vrouwe* fits well in this context.

Is Cormeau right to stress the principle of authorship and count the stanza within the tradition of Walther's works? Is it really part of Walther's oeuvre or rather part of a discourse establishing rules for the life of a Christian nobleman? Is it really the same text, only in slightly altered shape? Is its meaning affected by the new frame in the manuscript as described before?

When we regard the main issue, the distinction between woman and lady, there seems to be no difference with Walther's stanza, and likewise when we regard the main arguments. So, in the edition of Walther's songs, the stanza in *n* figures as one of the sources of the edited song, even if only as an additional, not very reliable one. Its variants are listed in the apparatus—as variants of a text of Walther.[14] But this is exactly the point. Modern scholarship assumes beforehand that the principle of authorship is the organizing principle of the textual tradition. In modern times this may be appropriate: Nobody would doubt that some verses by Goethe—for instance, "Wer immer strebend sich bemüht"—published anywhere in a calendar are Goethe's verses, even if they are quoted anonymously and isolated from their context (in this case, the last scene of Goethe's drama *Faust II*), and even if they differ in some details from the text of the critical edition. A text has an author and is his property even after the copyright expires. But these are conditions not existing in the Middle Ages. Are we really right to consider the stanza as a text of Walther?

The smallest problem is its isolation from the remaining stanzas of the song. The relevant unit in the tradition of medieval lyric poetry is the stanza and not the whole song. In many cases the manuscripts confine themselves to only one stanza, and we find isolated stanzas in the oeuvres of many courtly poets. The sententious character[15] of our stanza may have stimulated its separation from the rest of the song and its insertion in a series of didactic texts. This is a common practice if we recall passages from Arthurian romance or heroic epics in a historiographical context.

Those insertions in other texts as a rule are anonymous, as they are here. In addition, medieval lyric poetry often is transmitted anonymously. The songs are sung not only by their authors, but also by other singers; the name can get lost, especially because first the songs seem to have been written without the name of the author. Therefore, even in the great early collections of *Minnesang*, some songs are attributed to different poets or even to persons who probably were only performers. In later anthologies often the name of the author is missing.[16] All the more, anonymity is typical for the kind of didactic manuscript *n* represents. In *n*, all stanzas are anonymous. However, our stanza is well attested as a work of Walther by two of the three great Chansonniers;[17] the third ascribes it to another poet, Reinmar.

Anyway, a material philologist examining the mise-en-page would have to doubt, for he sees a series of short texts all presented in the same manner, without any distinctions. And indeed his doubts can be supported by some other observations. Material Philology is a guide to hermeneutic questions. Those questions are: Are the positions of speaker and recipient identical in both texts? Are the "variants" noted in Cormeau's apparatus really variants of an original text? And is the meaning the same when, on the surface, many words and thoughts seem to be similar?

I begin with the role of the speaker and the meaning of the pronoun *I*. In Walther's song a self-confident *ich* opposes himself to the current norms of courtly love; he claims to give new rules for the relationship between the lady and the courting singer and threatens to leave her. In each stanza the pronoun *ich* and its derivations are prominent. In the beginning, Walther opposes it to the others (*ir, man, si*, etc.), but then he shifts to an integration of the opposite positions: Stanza I stresses *mîne, ich, sing [ich], ich*, even more obviously stanza II: *Ich, ich, ich, ich, mîme, ich mîn, mir, mich, min ich*. But in stanza III *ich* is included in *wir/uns: ich, uns, wir, uns, uns, uns*. In stanza IV (the stanza in question) *ich* is the undisputed authority revaluating the meaning of *wîp* and *frouwe*, suppressing any doubt (*muoz sîn*). It is the authority of the courtly singer giving rules to a courtly society. This is continued in stanza V: the previously rebellious *ich* represents the true values for everybody in the court, here called *fuoge*: "Zwô fuoge hâ ich doch, swie ungefüege ich sî." Walther begins performing the role of the courting knight who protests against the exactions of *minne*, but then he claims that doing so he fulfills better than any other the demands of courtliness. A man who has *fuoge*, who is *gefüege*, is in accord with every situation in every society.

The song is a reflection upon the relationship between the individual and the court, represented in the lady. And in this context Walther compares the concepts *wîp* and *frouwe* and rejects the latter because it implies all those pretensions of rank and all that arrogance against the courting singer, which is criticized in the rest of the song. Without admitting any doubt (*muoz*), Walther plays off gender against class, *als ichz erkenne*, "as I understand." The stanza configures the typical role of Walther, which distinguishes him from all other *Minnesänger*: the rebel against false courtliness and against the decay of courtly values.

In *n* this context is lacking—the discussion of courtly love—but, what is more important, the role of the speaker, what German scholars have called *die Walther-Rolle*,[18] is canceled. Is it possible to identify a text as Walther's, if the voice of Walther's fictional *ich* is speaking no more? When the singer said *als ichz erkenne*, "as I understand it," he claimed the authority of the expert in courtly love. The speaker in manuscript *n* affirms, too, *als ich it erkenne*, but it is not the same voice. It is the anonymous, neutral, only vaguely defined voice of a teacher, an adviser, as it is present all over the manuscript, an authority in all questions of noble life, not the single singer opposing himself to false norms of *minne*. In the following, also anonymous stanza the same neutral voice will continue: "Ich geuen vch vrauwen eynen rait," and in similar way its authority is recalled from time to time in other stanzas.

It is not the only difference to Walther's stanza. Already the first verse is different: "Wif was ie der hoiste name. inn priset bas dan vrauwe." "Walther" demanded what should be (*muoz*), but actually is not the case; in contrast to this the speaker in *n* informs us what has been at all times, that at all times *wîp* has been the highest (i.e., worthiest) name, *der hoiste name*, and not only the highest name for women, but the highest name in general. According to the logic of the scholastic realism the highest name means the most precious substance. This is no more a discussion about courtly love. Discussion is replaced by an authoritative statement.

Then the speaker seems to quote the original text: *die hore minen sanc* (she should listen to my song), but which song, when the metrical-musical structure is destroyed and when the context of courtly interaction is missing? Walther's song required that the lady made her choice between the two titles, "woman" or "lady." In *n*, the addressed women do not have to make a choice between the two names (*kiese denne*), but have to pay attention to the words of the speaker (*in mirke denne*) in order to follow them: The excellence of the woman is beyond dispute.

Walther sung "swiez umb alle frowen var, wîp sint alle frowen gar" (no matter how it may be about ladies, women are all ladies, indeed). Surely, the lines are difficult to understand; this could be the reason that our copyist wrote "wie it vmbe allen vare. wip nimpt des hoesten louis ware" (No matter how all that may be, "woman" gets the highest praise). Again, the speaker cancels the comparison of names or concepts and of class and gender: no comparison at all: *wîp* was, is, and will be always praised (and, one may add, worthy of praise).

Walther called the ambiguous praise of ladies *zwîvellop*. *Zwîvel* (doubt, ambiguity) derives from alternatives. In *n* there are no alternatives; therefore the first element in *zwîvellop* has to be replaced, and so it happens: *vrauwen lof dat honit* (the praise of a lady [of ladies] is scorn). This is a curious statement, far beyond *Minnesang*, which is doing nothing else than praising the (socially or morally superior) woman, the *vrouwe*.

The manuscript does not present a corrupted stanza of Walther, but a didactic text adapting some motives and even some formulations from Walther, directing them to another purpose. The issue is not the distinction between class and gender, not Walther's distinction between the proud courtly lady and the loving woman, not the demand for a better courtly society, but a rather conventional statement about the place of women in aristocratic society.

It happens often in medieval copying that the name of the author is missing, that the poetic structure of the stanza (metrical order, rhyme) is damaged, and that the connection with the other stanzas is cut. Yet, all this taken together with the materiality of the manuscript, here a new text is emerging. There is a change from orality to literacy: the text is no more the statement of a present (identifiable) person (hence his name vanishes); the text is not to be sung but to be read (hence its metrical structures and its rhymes are less important); the stanza is cut from its context (hence it becomes an element in the storehouse of written wisdom where things can be arranged and rearranged corresponding to changing necessities). In this storehouse, differences of genre don't matter (hence nearly all specific features of a courtly song are effaced, and the remaining stanzas are excerpts from different genres). In the *grand chant courtois* it is an individual *ich* who is concerned by courtly ideals, who complains about his fatal service, the pitiless lady and the frustration of love. Even when saying *I*, he claims to speak for courting knights in general, displaying general values. In a didactic discourse the role of the speaker does not matter either (hence this role has to be canceled, too; the *ich* of courtly love is replaced by the anonymous *ich* of an adviser for a good and reasonable life of an upper class man).

The analysis of the manuscript leads to a more proper estimate of medieval textuality. Walther's stanza has become one only element in a series of brief texts in verses, in a unit of a didactic discourse whose elements are linked together by the general subject. Regarding the manuscript, it is no more granted that we read a text by Walther. In its new context the origo of the text is not a certain poet nor a knight courting a lady but the generalized *I* of courtly wisdom. More, I would contest the labeling of this part of the manuscript as *Niederdeutsche Liederhandschrift*, even if some stanzas seem to stem from a courtly song. It contains a selection of sententious stanzas from different genres.

The emerging genres of courtly lyric and courtly romance emphasize authorship, in difference to more archaic genres as heroic epics, sayings, proverbs, and so on. The interest in authorship is mirrored in the great manuscripts. But in the twelfth and thirteenth centuries the principle of authorship still is a weak one and it is weakened again and again by the conditions of literary communication. In the transition from orality to literacy the name of the author has to replace the present singer, but connecting a name and a text for a long time is by no means compulsory. The absent singer can be replaced by another singer, too, who may add something of his own. Writing can support his memory and at the same time vary the text again. Oral repetition and written copy produce variants over variants, and no author can control the shape of his texts once they are distributed. When initially he inscribed himself in a collective (courtly) discourse, his words are swallowed up by this discourse once they are no more sung by himself.

This can concern the identity of a text. As long as literary tradition is oriented to single poets, it may be suggestive to collect all traces of their work. But if one agrees that in the middle ages a text is not necessarily linked to its origins and that everybody can make use of it borrowing a phrase here and a thought there without offending against one's copyright then a stanza like "wif was ie der hoiste name" is at best an example for the reception of Walther's songs, but has to be canceled in the apparatus of the edition. Consequences for the other texts in manuscript *n* vaguely ascribed to other authors remain to be scrutinized.

NOTES

1. This chapter is a complement of a more exhaustive study about the late medieval tradition of courtly lyrics. See Jan-Dirk Müller, "Einzelstrophen–Florilegien–Autorprinzip:

Zur Überlieferung einiger Strophen Walthers von der Vogelweide im Lichte von Überlegungen der New Philology," in *Neuere Aspekte germanistischer Spätmittelalterforschung*, ed. Freimut Löser et al. (Wiesbaden: Reichert Verlag, 2012), 49–62.

2. See Walther von der Vogelweide, *Leich, Lieder, Sangsprüche*, 14th ed., völlig neu bearbeitete Auflage der Ausgabe Karl Lachmann, ed. Christoph Cormeau, Thomas Bein, and Horst Brunner (Berlin: Walter de Gruyter, 1996), 101; *Die Gedichte Walthers von der Vogelweide. Herausgegeben von Karl Lachmann. Dreizehnte, aufgrund der zehnten von Carl von Kraus bearbeiteten Ausgabe neu herausgegeben von Hugo Kuhn*, 13th ed. (Berlin: Walter de Gruyter, 1965), 68.

3. I still remember Eugene Vance's comment "It will happen never more."

4. Bernard Cerquiglini, *Éloge de la variante: Histoire critique de la philologie* (Paris: Seuils, 1989).

5. See Silvia Ranawake, "Der manne muot—der wîbe site: Zur Minnedidaxe Walthers von der Vogelweide und Ulrichs von Liechtenstein," in *Walther von der Vogelweide*, Hamburger Kolloquium zum 65. Geburtstag von Karl Heinz Borck, ed. Jan-Dirk Müller and Franz Josef Worstbrock (Stuttgart: Hirzel, 1989), 177–96.

6. In older editions (cf. von Kraus and Kuhn, *Die Gedichte Walthers von der Vogelweide*, 66–69), this song begins with "Zwô fuoge hân ich doch, swie ungefüege ich sî" (L 47,36) against all manuscripts. Hence the song is normally quoted under this title. Cormeau et al., *Leich, Lieder, Sangsprüche*, reestablish the order of the manuscripts beginning with "Hie vor, dô man sô rehte minneclîchen warp" (L 48,12). The sequence of the remaining stanzas differs in the manuscripts. Cormeau et al., *Leich, Lieder, Sangsprüche*, follow A and add stanza V, which is missing there after C. Admittedly, separate editions of the several versions would be better, but this would make no difference for my argument.

7. See Jan-Dirk Müller, "Die *frouwe* und die andern: Beobachtungen zur Überlieferung einiger Lieder Walthers," in Müller and Worstbrock, *Walther von der Vogelweide*, 127–46.

8. Transcription after Günther Schmeisky, *Die Lyrik-Handschriften m* (Berlin, MS germ. qu. 795) and *n* (Leipzig, Rep. II fol. 70a). Zur mittel- und niederdeutschen Sangvers-Überlieferung. Abbildung, Transkription, Beschreibung, GAG 243 (Göppingen: Kümmerle, 1978), fol. 95vb.

9. About the manuscript, see Schmeisky, *Die Lyrik-Handschriften m*; Cormeau et al., *Leich, Lieder, Sangsprüche*; Gisela Kornrumpf, s.v. "Niederrheinische Liederhandschrift," in *Die deutsche Literatur des Mittelalters: Verfasserlexikon*, 2nd ed., vol. 6, ed. Kurt Ruh (Berlin: Walter de Gruyter, 1987), cols. 995–.

10. The Marburger Repertorium convincingly restricts the name "Niederrheinische Liederhandschrift" on folio 91–96. Franz Josef Pensel, however, calls it "Niederrheinische Liederhandschrift, Sammlung mhd. Dichtung, bestehend aus Sangverslyrik, Minnerede- und Heldenepik-Teilen." Franz Josef Pensel, *Verzeichnis der deutschen mittelalterlichen Handschriften in der Universitätsbibliothek Leipzig* (Berlin: Akademie Verlag, 1998), 91ra–102vb, 337.

11. About this *Minnerede*, see Melitta Rheinheimer, s.v. "Neun Männer, neun Frauen," in *Die deutsche Literatur des Mittelalters* 6, cols. 922–23.

12. Kornrumpf's "Niederrheinische Liederhandschrift," col. 997, has a description of the manuscript that says the *Minnerede* is "framed" by stanzas from songs and sayings with different subjects.

13. Kornrumpf's "Niederrheinische Liederhandschrift," col. 997, describes the content of the second group: "In n III liegt der Akzent mehr auf höfischer Tugendlehre und - mahnung, der Bedeutung der *êre*, allgemeiner Zeitkritik; auch an *gotes hulde* und den Tod wird erinnert."

14. Cormeau et al., *Leich, Lieder, Sangsprüche*, 101.

15. Müller and Worstbrock, *Walther von der Vogelweide*, 129.

16. Kornrumpf, "Niederrheinische Liederhandschrift," col. 997.

17. Cormeau et al., *Leich, Lieder, Sangsprüche*, XXXVI.

18. See Gerhard Hahn, *Walther von der Vogelweide: Eine Einführung*, Artemis Einführungen 22. (Munich: Artemis Verlag, 1986), 86; Christa Ortmann, "Der Spruchdichter am Hof. Zur Funktion der Walther-Rolle in Sangsprüchen mit *milte*-Thematik," in Müller and Worstbrock, *Walther von der Vogelweide*, 17–35, esp. 18–19.

CHAPTER NINE

Conceiving the Text in the Middle Ages

JACQUELINE CERQUIGLINI-TOULET

As though presiding over a new *Marriage of Mercury and Philology*, Stephen Nichols has always succeeded in uniting Mercury—or interdisciplinary dialogue—and Philology, who is, as Martianus Cappella tells us, the daughter of Phronesis, or wisdom. The January 1990 issue of *Speculum* that he edited under the provocative title *The New Philology* had a profound impact on medieval studies. If they had a past, Steve Nichols was instrumental in ensuring their future. The studies he assembled and presented, highlighting the discipline's new interest in manuscript culture, were not, strictly speaking, a manifesto calling for a new school of thought. However, as if bewitched by the word "new," fierce polemics erupted, demonstrating that the volume was in fact read as a manifesto in a restaged quarrel of the ancients and the moderns. That it was published in *Speculum*, the official journal of the Medieval Academy of America, was not insignificant, either for its achievement or for the resentment some felt at losing one of their bastions.

Scienza nuova, as Giambattista Vico called his "new science," philology, in 1725, was for him an all-encompassing discipline thanks to its privileged relation to philosophy. Howard Bloch analyzes the import of that designation in his article "New Philology and Old French" in the *Speculum* issue, and Steve Nichols nods to Vico in his preface. The current New Philology emerged, then, from reflections on the history of the discipline subsequently echoed by the volume *Medievalism and the Modernist Temper* coedited by Howard Bloch and Stephen Nichols.[1]

The new reflections of 1990 reminded philologists not to forget that their work implies a theory of the text, much as they might wish it otherwise. In fact, the practice of critical text editing had attempted to play down, if not deny altogether, the role of the editor as agent. Lachmannians, for example, neutralized agency by subordinating editorial judgment to a mechanical, rule-governed process. At the other end of the spectrum, zealous disciples of Bédier pretended to efface themselves through the lazy expedient of reproducing a single, "best" manuscript. In so doing, both groups severed the link between practice and theory, textual criticism and literary criticism. But what, exactly, is "a text" in the Middle Ages, and how do we locate it in a manuscript culture where each codex is unique? The text is never closed, whether we are editing, where one must address the question of variants, or seeking to decipher and understand the threads of its composition *in praesentia*, where there is direct quotation, or *in absentia*, where we are confronted with the play of echoes and intertextuality. More radically still, we might legitimately ask just where we're supposed to find the text in the manuscript. How does it come to instantiate itself materially as object? And how is its literary identity realized?

For a number of reasons, the question is more complex than it appears. Where are the boundaries? The *incipit* and *explicit* rubrics may be lacking, and we know that we must depend, internally, on a whole strategy of literary markers (which I analyzed in my contribution to *La littérature française: Dynamique et histoire*)[2] to identify the borders of a text. Textual criticism and literary analysis are inseparable. But it has become clear, especially through the work of Steve Nichols, that there is an aesthetics proper to manuscripts: an aesthetics of authors in some cases, or of scribes, or the direct or indirect will of a patron. The return to the manuscript tends to make the text or texts disappear in favor of a global examination of the codex; that is, of an extant material whole: *The Whole Book* according to the title of a volume coedited by Steve Nichols and Siegfried Wenzel.[3] It's the old issue of the miscellany, a genre many of us have addressed theoretically, historically, or critically. I am thinking in particular of the issue of the journal *Littérales*[4] that published the papers of a colloquium at Nanterre in December 1985; or more recently, *Mouvance et Jointures: Du manuscrit au texte médiéval*, which presented results from the Limoges conference (November 2002);[5] or again, issue 16 (2007) of the journal *Babel*, "La mise en recueil des textes médiévaux"; not to mention the two conferences in 2007 at Louvain-la-Neuve and Geneva.[6] How do all these scholars define texts? Or, alternatively, how do texts figure in their analyses? Let me cite some particularly thought-provoking cases.

Christine de Pizan's *Le Livre du Duc des vrais amans* ends with two *explicits*.[7] The first follows line 3556, "Et ycy mon dit deffine," where we read "Explicit le livre appellé le duc des vrais amants" (Here ends the book called the Duke of True Lovers). But the manuscript continues with a commentary by the poet on the versification in this work: "A tous ditteurs, qui savoir / Ont en eulx, celle savoir / Fait qui ce dittié ditta" (To all poets who possess knowledge, she who composed this poem makes known; 3557–59). Following these remarks are nine ballads *de pluseurs façons*, three *virelais*, four *rondeaux* and a *complainte*, and finally the note "Explicit le Duc des vrais amans." Is Christine de Pizan (or her scribes) stuttering? In fact, it is as if, for Christine, there were two ways of thinking about her text: as a story, or *dit*, and as a coffer that contains both the story and examples of versification: in other words, narrative and treatise. In this case, the intention is didactic and authorizes the poet to maintain a certain distance from the love story.

Such cases are not particularly rare and sometimes elicit strange reactions from editors. Let's take another example. In Guillaume de Machaut's *Confort d'ami*, the *explicit* does not signal the end of the work.[8] It simply marks the end of the poet's words of consolation; but then the prince continues with a twenty-six-line response that begins "Explicit le Confort d'amy / Qui esveilla le cuer de my / Es tenebres ou il dormi" (Here ends the Friend's Comfort, which awakened my heart from the darkness in which it slept; 3979–81). These verses unfold on a single note, the rhyming –*mi*, which invokes musical terminology. I agree with the editor, Ernest Hoepffner, that "Mon b mol de be fa be mi / Mis en b dur" (3993–94), constitutes a kind of signature for the poet-musician. As Hoepffner notes in his introduction, "Cette tirade se trouve dans tous les manuscrits à l'exception du manuscrit 994 de la Bibliothèque nationale" (xvii). However, the manuscript that lacks it only includes excerpts from the text anyway. The *explicit* must have reassured the scribe on his choice of excerpts. More perplexing is the hasty affirmation of a modern critic like William Calin, who denies Guillaume de Machaut's paternity of these verses without further explanation.[9] Similarly confounding is the commentary of the text's most recent editor, R. Barton Palmer, who writes, "Unlike the other *explicits* in the composite MSS, this one is followed by more text which belongs neither to *Comfort* nor the next work" (xxxi).[10] In fact these verses do not exist in some kind of *hors-texte*, and the editor later corrects his statement but still reverts, after all, to the idea that Machaut might not have been their author, but only their editor. Does R. Barton Palmer think that the prince wrote them and the poet only collected them? That gives a lot of credit to a fictional character. A systematic examination of the phenomenon of double *explicits* and *explicits* followed by a rhetorical signature— phenomena more common than some critics seem to think—would avoid postulating false premises. By thinking about the text—where it is, and how we conceive it—we can view the manuscript holistically; that is to say, from a viewpoint at once philological, literary, and philosophical.[11]

MS BnF fr. 24301 offers, among other writings, almost the complete works of Robert de Blois. Yet it is presented in a unique way. Robert's didactic and religious works are inserted into the chivalric romance *Beaudous* as the words of the hero's mother. She gives advice to her son, following the model of Perceval's mother, but the advice comes from other works by Robert de Blois: *Les enseignements des princes, Floris et Lyriopé, Les chastoiements des dames,* among others. We know *Beaudous* only from this one manuscript. Apparently, Robert conceived this text as a setting for his entire oeuvre. He didn't think in terms of genres in the manner of modern editors who publish these different texts separately or paste together two parts of a romance that has been chopped up, while purging the other bits, in order to publish it as a chivalric romance.[12]

In many cases, editors do not recognize the text and, as in Pierre Bourdieu's beautiful analysis of the expression, *ne s'y retrouvent pas* (do not find themselves there).[13] *S'y retrouver* is at once to "go back over one's accounts," "recuperate one's stakes," and to "recognize oneself." This comfort of recognition cancels out any attempt to admit that one does not yet understand.

But let's look at the problem the other way around: not according to the modern critic's judgment as to what constitutes a text, but from what the language of medieval works designates as text. The primary meaning of the word is religious. The text is the text of the Gospel in its material form as "the book." We see this in two examples in Chrétien de Troyes.[14] At the coronation of Erec and Enide, there is a procession with "Croiz et textes et encensier" (cross, evangelaries, censers; 6894), and at the funerary procession of Laudine's husband in "Le Chevalier au Lion: Et li texte et li enchensiers" (evangelaries and censers; 1169). We find the term in its modern sense in Jean de Meun.[15] Reason responds to the lover, who is astonished that she should have pronounced a crude word: "n'encor ne faz je pas pechié / se je nome les nobles choses / par plein texte sanz metre gloses" (still, I do not sin if I name noble things in plain text without adding glosses; 1.6926–28). God, she says, has made these things *de ses propres mains* (with his own hands; 6930); she can name them properly *par plein texte.*

Yet how did the Middle Ages recognize a text? A text is that which allows for commentary; text implies gloss. It is perceived as an authority. Its layout on the manuscript page says so. Several case studies have been done. What is designated as text occupies the center of the page, or the double page, and the commentary surrounds it in the margins. The hierarchical relationship is thus clearly established. The phenomenon has been well studied by Laura Kendrick in an article titled "The Monument and the Margin" in a special issue of *The South Atlantic Quarterly* coordinated by Lee Patterson and Stephen Nichols, "Commentary as Cultural Artifact."[16]

I will add a particularly telling example to be found in Christine de Pizan's *L'Epistre Othea.* She consecrates herself as "author" by writing a hundred texts in French, each one followed by a gloss and an allegory and preceded by an image. Some manuscripts have followed this process of self-canonization by introducing a page layout like that of a Latin glossed manuscript: the text is in the center, surrounded by the gloss on the left and the allegory on the right. That's the case for manuscripts Paris BnF fr. 848, Beauvais, Bibliothèque municipale 9, and Cambridge, Newnham College, 070 6. Other manuscripts make a different choice, preferring instead to distinguish among different types of audiences.

One case that is treated differently is that of the French translations of the great Latin authors in the fourteenth century. Translating from Latin into French confers the same monumental status on the translation as the original. The text might have occupied the center of the page, based on the model of juridical texts and their commentaries. This is not what happened. The page layout that is adopted is generally the following: text and gloss, designated by name, alternate in segments. Confronted with this problem, Simon de Hesdin, translator of Valerius Maximus, conceived the following solution:

> Item il est assavoir que partout ou il y a grosse lectre ce sont les paroles de Valerius en propres mos ou en sentence et ou il y a menue lectre, soit en narracion ou exposition ou declaracion, ce sont mes propres paroles ou les paroles de aucun autre, lequel je aleguerai par nom, soit philosophe, poete ou historiographe ou autre de quelconque estat.[17]

> That is, namely, that everywhere where there are large letters, these are the words of Valerius in his own words or sentences and where there are small letters, whether as narration, exposition or declaration, these are my own words or the words of another whom I will cite by name, be it a philosopher, poet or historiographer or another of whatever status.

Perhaps because the problem of how to rule the page for so complex a layout proved insurmountable, scribes did not follow Simon de Hesdin's lead. They simply alternate passages from Valerius introduced by the words *auteur/acteur* or *texte/tiexte*—the equivalence is significant—and the commentary introduced by the term *translateur* or *glose*. I will give an example. It is a passage in Book II dedicated to artistic endeavors:

> *Tiexte* Jusques à ce temps le peuple de Rome estoit content du jeu que on faisoit ou scirque, *Glose* c'est-à-dire une reonde place commune en laquele le peuple se aloit esbatre; et estoit celi jeu.

Text Until that time, the people of Rome were content with the games played at the circus, *Gloss* that is, a communal round plaza where people went to fight, and this was the game in question.

The alternation can be rapid or the gloss can develop at length, but always keeping the same type of alternation. Other scholars showed themselves to be sensitive to the layout of their translations, distinguishing text from gloss. Nicole Oresme's personal manuscript of his translation of Aristotle's *Politics* regularly opposes the text written in *littera formata* to the gloss written in *bâtarde* script. It's an example of the importance of vision and visual layout to which Steve Nichols has given a lot of thought. The manuscript page reads like a musical score.

With this play of text and gloss, thinking about the text turns into thinking about reading. There is in fact a reconstitution of the text through reading, an interaction between the reading *I* and what is being read. The reading *I* brings the text to life, and this begins even with the edition, just as the text brings about a certain type of consciousness within the reading *I*. We might think of Marcel Proust's reflection in *A la recherche du temps perdu*:

> En réalité, chaque lecteur est, quand il lit, le propre lecteur de soi-même. L'ouvrage de l'écrivain n'est qu'une espèce d'instrument optique qu'il offre au lecteur afin de lui permettre de discerner ce que, sans ce livre, il n'eût peut-être pas vu en soi-même.[18]

> In fact, when he reads, each reader is a reader of himself. The writer's work is only a kind of optical instrument that he proffers to the reader to allow him to perceive that which, without the book, he might never have seen in himself.

Here we find the question of interpretation. The reader plays the text, interprets it like a pianist interprets a piece of music, and in return, the text plays the reader, awakening him to himself, and perhaps plays around with him. It is the reader's self-awakening that Paul Ricoeur in his essay "Qu'est-ce qu'un texte?" in *Mélanges Gadamer* calls appropriation:[19]

> Par appropriation, j'entends ceci, que l'interprétation d'un texte s'achève dans l'interprétation de soi d'un sujet qui désormais se comprend mieux, se comprend autrement, ou même commence à se comprendre.

> By appropriation, I mean that the interpretation of a text ends with the self-interpretation of a subject who will henceforth understand himself better, understand himself differently, or even begin to understand himself.

Which definition of a text do we end up with? The text is that which resists immediate comprehension, and that communication cannot dissipate. The text is a monument. The case of the *Roman de la Rose* is exemplary. Copied more than three hundred times, it quickly becomes authoritative. As early as 1290, Gui de Mori, through his reworking of it, raises it to the status of text.[20] He essentially gives a kind of critical edition of it, noting the suppressions, additions, and modifications he makes by way of a system of diacritical signs that he invents: twigs and roses.

Here we run into notions like "original" and "authentic" that need to be defined. The notion of authenticity stems from the concept of truth. As its etymology suggests, *authentic* denotes the authority, worth, and credibility of a text regardless of its origin.[21] The *original* designates the source for the copyist, translator, or secondary writer. Thus we read in the *Grandes Chroniques de France*, "Si sera ceste hystoire descrite selon la lettre et l'ordenance des croniques de l'abaïe de Saint Denis en France . . . car la doit on prendre et puisier l'origenal de l'estoire" (And this history will be described according to the letter and the order of the chronicles of the abbey of Saint-Denis in France . . . for one must take and draw from the original version of the story).[22] The author of the *Tombel de Chartrose* opens his tale with "De la deshonnesté que l'en fist au pappe Formose" (On the dishonoring thing done to Pope Formosus) by saying "Je truis en .I. original / Qu'il ot a Romme un cardinal" (I found in an original that a cardinal had in Rome; 37–38).[23] One of the copyists of the *Roman de la Rose*, Michel Alès, when he was finishing what is now MS Bibliothèque Nationale de France fr. 25525, specifies:[24]

Chi fenist le Romans de la Rose,
Qu'en .V. sepmaines, veritable chose,
Michiel Alès, par hastivesté
Copia, quer la largesce
N'ovoit de tenir l'original.

Here ends the *Romance of the Rose*, which in five weeks, a true fact, Michel Alès,
in his haste, copied, for he did not have the good fortune to keep the original.

This complex set of ideas took shape in French around the *Roman de la Rose*. The romance was analyzed and contested in the event we now call "la querelle du *Roman de la Rose*." This vernacular romance provokes commentary as an integral part of its structure, with its interplay between two authors, text and gloss. These couplings multiply in the fourteenth century. Jean Froissart plays the game in his *Prison amoureuse* with the Prince's dream and its exposition. The verse romance *Les échecs d'Amour* and prose romance *Les Echecs amoureux* by Evrart de Conty operate on the same template. But the original model comes from the relationship that links the Old and New Testaments. Alain Chartier points to this model in his *Livre de l'Espérance*, where he writes, "Le viel Testament propose / Le nouvel preuve et expose / Sur gros texte clere glose" (The Old Testament proposes, the New attests and reveals, a lucid gloss on a great text; PO, 13.38–40).[25] The *Roman de la Rose* finally becomes a medium for commentary when Jean Molinet "moralizes" it; that is, gives an interpretation of it according to the technique of meanings superposed on scripture, "unfolding the text," as it were.

The question of voluntary obscurity is, in part, tied to the notion of the text. One of the reproaches that Martin le Franc, through the words of the Champion of Ladies, addresses to Jean de Meun has to do with the end of the *Roman de la Rose*:[26]

> Je vous respons que tant ouvry
> Le texte qu'il n'y fault ja gloses.
> Ly en la fin: sans que le gloses,
> Te sera proprement advis
> Que devant toy face les choses
> Dont il fait son paillart devis.

> I answer you that the text was opened so far that it will never need glosses. Read to the end: without glossing it, it will be clear to you that these things that he has his tramp talk about are done right in front of you.

Christine de Pizan's reflections on the necessary obscurity of texts is fundamental. She starts with a criticism addressed to her, which she recalls through the mouth of Lady Opinion in *L'advision Christine*: "Les autres dient ton stille estre trop obscur et que on ne l'entent, si n'est si delectable" (Others say that your style is too obscure and that no one understands it, and therefore it is not very pleasing; 2.22). Indeed, the debate extends well beyond Christine. The question of obscurity, and whether it was to be sought after or avoided, animated humanist circles in Avignon that were in contact with the Parisian networks she frequented.[27]

Laurent de Premierfait, for example, favored an obscure style whereas Giovanni Moccia and Jean Muret defended *claritas*. Even for Christine, it was more than a question of using sophisticated figures or Greek words. The obscure style is a gauge of a text's profundity, as well as the beauty and power of polyvalence, which imply a particular kind of reading: subtlety. In fact, any true reading pre-supposes an appropriation, and this appropriation requires effort and decipher-ing. We might entertain the apparent paradox that in her view, a text is only readable if it is obscure; that is, if it encourages interpretation and gloss. Be-tween Christine and her readers who resisted obscurity, two conceptions of the text and of reading collide, two conceptions of pleasure. There must be some-thing in the text that is condensed, as in a dream, so that the reader may play the interpreter and gloss it. It is the thrill of intelligence.

Another paradox stands out in thinking about the text. The text is constituted *qua* text through its commentaries, but may also be destroyed by their excess. A proverb warns of this danger: "On dit voulentiers que la glose d'Orleans si destruit le texte" (It is readily said that the Orleans gloss destroys the text). It alludes to the practices of the schools of Orléans, famous for their commentaries on ancient authors. *Alleguer glose sans texte* (putting forth a gloss without a text) is the re-proach that Lyon Jamet addresses to the *moynes crottez*, or "dung-covered monks" in his *Epistre du Coq à l'Asne*. François Sagon, in his quarrel with Marot, sums up their differences this way: "J'ayme la glose, il hayt tout commentaires" (I like glosses, but he [Clément Marot] detests all commentaries).[28]

Thinking about the text and about texts is rich ground for debate and contro-versy. Perceived as a material object in the earliest instances of the word in French, where it refers to books that contain the Gospels, the text later distin-guishes itself from the book, the volume, the work, and writing. Close to the letter, it brings into play theories of meaning and reading. As a literary object and monument, the text has its own logic, which I have tried to define. For the Middle Ages, the *Roman de la Rose*, in many respects, seems emblematic of it. It's no coincidence that Steve Nichols has devoted himself to this text and its *parerga et paralipomena* with passion. *Rose-enclose*, the rhyme that functions like a refrain for all the texts that invoke the name of the *Roman de la Rose*, identifies the medieval text in its relationship to beauty and the secret:

> Et m'est avis, qui veult drois
> Y visier, qu'on puet entendre
> Qu'a aultre choses veult tendre
> Que le texte ne desclot,
> Car aucune fois on clot
> En parabole couverte
> Matiere a tous non ouverte,

Qui semble estre truffe ou fable,
Ou sentence gist notable.

And it is my opinion that whoever deigns to see it for what it is will understand that other things are intended that the text does not disclose, for sometimes one seals up in cloaked parables material that is not open to all, which seems to be a joke or a fable, but wherein lies notable wisdom.

Thus remarks Christine de Pizan in her *Dit de la Pastoure* (24–32), which, like a good reader of Jean de Meun, she thinks of as a text.[29]

Old and New Philology: the difference lies in their way of thinking about the text, as document or as monument.

NOTES

This chapter translated by Jeanette L. Patterson.

1. R. Howard Bloch and Stephen G. Nichols, *Medievalism and the Modernist Temper* (Baltimore: Johns Hopkins University Press, 1996).

2. Jacqueline Cerquiglini-Toulet et al., *La littérature française: Dynamique et histoire* (Paris: Gallimard, 2007), 1:83–88. See also Jacqueline Cerquiglini-Toulet, *A New History of Medieval French Literature* (Baltimore: Johns Hopkins University Press, 2011).

3. Stephen G. Nichols and Siegfried Wenzel, eds., *The Whole Book: Cultural Perspectives on the Medieval Miscellany* (Ann Arbor: University of Michigan Press, 1996).

4. "La présentation du livre," special issue, *Littérales* 2 (1987).

5. Milena Mikhaïlova, ed., *Mouvances et Jointures: Du manuscrit au texte médiéval* (Orléans: Paradigme, 2005).

6. Tania Van Hemelryck and Claude Thiry, eds., *Le recueil au Moyen Age: La fin du Moyen Age* (Turnhout: Brepols, 2010); and Yasmina Foehr and Olivier Collet, eds., *Le recueil au Moyen Age: Le Moyen Age central* (Turnhout: Brepols, 2010).

7. Christine de Pizan, *Œuvres poétiques*, ed. Maurice Roy (Paris: Firmin Didot, 1896), 3:59–208.

8. Ernest Hoepffner, ed., *Œuvres de Guillaume de Machaut* (Paris: Edouard Champion, 1921), vol. 3.

9. William Calin, *A Poet at the Fountain: Essays on the Narrative Verse of Guillaume de Machaut* (Lexington: University Press of Kentucky, 1974), 130n1, writes, concerning these verses, "a twenty-six-line passage, a reply from *Ami*, which should not be attributed to Machaut."

10. Guillaume de Machaut, *Le Confort d'ami* [Comfort for a Friend], ed. and trans. R. Barton Palmer (New York: Garland, 1992).

11. In discussion, Daniel Heller-Roazen brought my attention to Emmanuel Kant's reflections on this subject.

12. The latest of these editions is dated 2008. Jacques-Charles Lemaire, ed., *Biaudouz de Robert de Blois* (Liège: Editions de l'Université de Liège, 2008). See the felicitous correction offered by Milena Mikhaïlova, *L'école du roman* (Paris: Champion, 2010).

13. Pierre Bourdieu, *Les règles de l'art: Genèse et structure du champ littéraire* (Paris: Seuil, 1992), 439–40.

14. Chrétien de Troyes, *Romans*, ed. Michel Zink (Paris: Librairie générale française, 1994).

15. Guillaume de Lorris and Jean de Meun, *Le Roman de la Rose*, ed. Félix Lecoy, 3 vols. (Paris: Champion, 1965, 1966, and 1970).

16. Lee Patterson and Stephen Nichols, eds., "Commentary as Cultural Artifact," special issue, *South Atlantic Quarterly* 91, no. 4 (Fall 1992): 835–64.

17. MS BnF, fr. 9749, fol. 103vB, cited by Alessandro Vitale Brovarone, "Notes sur la traduction de Valere Maxime par Simon de Hesdin," in *"Pour acquerir honneur et pris": Mélanges de Moyen Français offerts à Giuseppe Di Stefano* (Montréal: CERES, 2004), 183–91, esp. 186.

18. Marcel Proust, *A la recherche du temps perdu*, ed. Jean-Yves Tadié (Paris: Gallimard, 1988), 3:911.

19. Paul Ricoeur, "Qu'est-ce qu'un texte?," in *Hermeneutik und Dialektik: Hans-Georg Gadamer zum 70 Geburtstag*, ed. Rüdiger Bubner et al. (Tübingen: Mohr, 1970,) 2:194–95.

20. Andrea Valentini, *Le remaniement du* Roman de la Rose *par Gui de Mori: Etude et édition des interpolations d'après le manuscrit Tournai, Bibliothèque de la Ville, 101* (Brussels: Académie royale de Belgique, 2007).

21. See Umberto Eco's analysis, beginning with Saint Thomas Aquinas, in *The Limits of Interpretation* (Bloomington: Indiana University Press, 1994), 196.

22. J. Viard, ed., *Grandes Chroniques de France* (Paris: Société de l'Histoire de France, 1920), 1:2.

23. Ewald Kooiman, ed., *Dix-huit contes français tirés du recueil intitulé Le Tombel de Chartrose* (Amsterdam: Academische Pers, 1975), 27:251.

24. See Ernest Langlois, *Les manuscrits du Roman de la Rose: Description et classement* (Lille: Travaux et mémoires de l'Université de Lille, 1910), 64–71.

25. Alain Chartier, *Le Livre de l'Espérance*, ed. François Rouy (Paris: Champion, 1989).

26. Martin Le Franc, *Le Champion des Dames*, ed. Robert Deschaux (Paris: Champion, 1999), 3.12427–32.

27. See, for example, Carla Bozzolo, *Manuscrits des traductions françaises d'œuvres de Boccace, XVe siècle* (Padua: Editrice Antenore, 1973), 6.

28. "Rondeau par contrarietez de l'aucteur a Marot," in *Querelle de Marot et Sagon*, ed. Emile Picot (Rouen: Société rouennaise de bibliophiles, 1920; reprint, Geneva: Slatkine, 1969).

29. Christine de Pizan, *Œuvres poétiques*, ed. Maurice Roy (Paris: Firmin Didot, 1891). The *dit* is on pages 223–94. See verses 24–32.

CHAPTER TEN

Dante's Transfigured Ovidian Models

Icarus and Daedalus in the *Commedia*

KEVIN BROWNLEE

The privileged status of key narratives from Ovid's *Metamorphoses* as model texts for Dante's *Commedia* is well known.[1] In this chapter, I consider a particularly dense double set: Daedalus and Icarus (*Met.* 8.183–235). I argue that the *Commedia* sets up a Daedalus "program" beginning in *Inferno* 17.109–11, where Dante the protagonist, riding on Geryon's back with Virgil, is presented as a corrected Icarus figure, and Virgil, as a corrected Daedalus figure (as artist, as father, as guide). Over the course of the poem as a whole (all the way to *Par.* 33), these two Dantean Christian corrections of Ovidian models are substantially elaborated (even transformed) in terms of the *Commedia*'s ongoing meditation on the problematic status of the mimetic artist and on the potentially salvific activity (for Dante-author) of writing poetry, both within the emerging context of the great poem's Christian cosmos.[2]

My overall interpretive perspective is the vast and heterogeneous nexus of explicit or implicit comparisons of Dante himself to various model characters from the *Metamorphoses*.[3] The master strategy here involves a corrective Christian rewriting of both failed and successful Ovidian heroes in the person of Dante-protagonist, Dante-poet, or both. Within this overall mimetic strategy, the first (and only) explicit mention of Icarus in the *Commedia* occurs, as just noted, in the key central canto of the *Inferno*, as Dante-protagonist is descending from the seventh to the eighth circles on Geryon's back. A double Ovidian metaphor is at issue here, which (among other things) associates from the outset the Dantean Icarus with the Dantean Phaeton.[4] Immediately after an initial comparison of his past fear qua protagonist to that of Phaeton at the fatal moment when he let go of the reins of Apollo's chariot (*Met.* 2.178–200, esp. 2.178–200), Dante-poet evokes that of Icarus (in *Met.* 8.223–30) at the moment he felt his wings melting off:[5]

né quando Icaro misero le reni
sentì spennar per la scaldata cera,
gridando il padre a lui "Mala via tieni!" (*Inf.* 17.109–11)

nor when the wretched Icarus felt his back unfeathered by the melting wax, while his father shouted to him: "You're taking the wrong way!"

In both cases, it is the difference between the pagan Ovidian model and the Christian Dantean protagonist that is stressed: Dante is both a Phaeton made good and an Icarus *in bono*. Unlike them, he has a guide whom he obeys; where they descend to death, he ascends to life. The two Ovidian models are read figurally, but in a contrastive mode: they are correctively inverted, converted in Dante-protagonist's Christian autobiographical narrative; to the degree that they are also exemplary, they are *exempla ex negativo*. At the same time, these infernal references to Phaeton and Icarus initiate programs, for these two Ovidian characters will, on the one hand, function "separately" as models for Dante-protagonist in the other two *cantiche*. In addition, this initial pairing of Phaeton and Icarus will work at later moments in the poem to suggest various associations between these two Ovidian figures.

At the same time, this initial presentation of Icarus stresses the failure of human artifice (figured by Daedalus and his "invention") both with *scaldata cera* in the rhyme position, and by the *hapax* "spennare," "unfeathering," a negative introduction of the "penne motif" which will become crucial as the Icarus program is developed. Finally, the presence (and the perspective) of Daedalus (as failed father, guide, and artificer) is evoked in *Inferno* 17.111 as he cries ineffectively to his falling son, whose "wrong way" (*mala via*) is contrasted to the *diritta via* involved in Dante-protagonist's apparent descent in *Inferno* 17, which turns out to be, paradoxically, a Christian ascent.[6]

Within the basic context of a double contrastive comparison between Dante-protagonist and Icarus on the one hand, and Daedalus and Virgil on the other, numerous details of the Ovidian model text repay further study.

First, the moment of Icarus's fear described by Dante-poet in *Inferno* 17.109–10 constitutes a brilliant epitome of *Metamorphoses* 8.223–30, a passage rich with details relevant to Dante's transformative rewriting. The Ovidian Icarus's fatal solo journey begins with an impulsive, prideful joy which leads him: (1) to treat the flight as an end in itself, rather than as a means to a "higher" goal, namely (in the Ovidian text) escape from his Cretan captivity, described as an "exile" in

Metamorphoses 8.184; and (2) to abandon his guide (presented as *dux*, leader) who is also his father:

puer audaci coepit gaudere volatu
deseruitque *ducem* caelique *cupidine* tractus
altius egit iter.[7]

the boy began to rejoice in his bold flight and, deserting his *leader*, drawn by *desire* for the sky, directed his course higher.

The result of Icarus's unthinking impulse (and filial disobedience) is swift and absolute:

rapidi vicinia solis
mollit odoratas, *pennarum* vincula, ceras;
tabuerant cerae: nudos quatit ille lacertos,
*remigio*que *carens* non ullas percipit auras,
oraque caerulea patrium clamantia nomen
excipiuntur aqua, quae nomen traxit ab illo.[8]

The scorching rays of the nearer sun softened the fragrant wax which held his *wings* [feathers]. The wax melted; his arms were bare as he beat them up and down, but *lacking wings* [oars], they took no hold on the air. His lips, calling to the last upon his father's name, were drowned in the dark blue sea, which took its name from him.

It is important to note that in this Ovidian passage, three and a half lines (8.255–58) are used to describe in detailed sequential narrative the process of "defeathering" that lies behind the single Dantean verbal phrase "spennar per la scaldata cera" (17.110). In the model Ovidian text that lies behind the Dantean phrase, "wings" are indicated both metonymically (*pennae*, wings are composed of feathers) and metaphorically (*remigium*, wings are like oars).

Daedalus is named for the only time in the *Commedia* in *Inferno* 29, in the Bolgia of the Falsatori by the alchemist Griffolino, who explains that he met his death when Alberto da Siena had him condemned to the flames because he failed to make good on his boast that he knew how to fly. Griffolino uses Daedalus's name as a metaphor to signify this boast:

Vero è ch'i' dissi lui, parlando a gioco:
   "I' mi saprei levar per l'aere a volo";
   e quei, ch'avea vaghezza e senno poco,

volle ch'i' li mostrassi l'arte; e solo
perch'io nol feci Dedalo, mi fece
adere a tal che l'avea per figliuolo. (*Inf.* 29.112–18)

It is true that I told him, joking: "I could raise myself through the air in flight";
and he, who had eagerness but little sense wanted me to show him the art; and
only because I did not make him Daedalus, he had me burned by one who loved
him as a son.

In the Bolgia of the Falsifiers, therefore, we have a failed, fraudulent human
artificer who falsely presents himself as a new Daedalus—and fails completely
to imitate his model. We are as far removed as possible from the self-presentation
of Dante in the *Commedia*.[9]

To summarize, in *Inferno* 17, Icarus is named for the only time in the *Commedia* in an explicit comparison with Dante-protagonist. In *Inferno* 29, Daedalus is
named for the only time in the *Commedia* in an implicit comparison with Dante-
poet. This powerful double comparison will be extended and elaborated all the
way to the end of the great poem's final canto—where it culminates in a brilliant,
polysemous fusion. In the balance of the present essay, I will be focusing on three
key elements of this Ovidian program of transformative rewriting in terms of the
new vernacular, transcendent, Christian poetics of the *Commedia*.

First, the "guide motif," carefully structured over the course of the poem as a
whole. The Ovidian model of Icarus/Daedalus is carefully deployed—in a pro-
gressive development—in connection with each of the three Dantean guides
in sequence, in each of the different realms in which they function. First, of
course, with Virgil as Dante-protagonist's guide in *Inferno* (1–34), followed by
the quite different Virgil as guide up the Purgatorial mountain (1–27). Once
Beatrice replaces Virgil in the Earthly Paradise as Dante's new guide in *Purgatorio* 30–33, evocations of the Icarus/Daedalus model text function in a different
(and more complex) way. The qualitative shifts in mimesis and poetics that
characterize *Paradiso* inform the status and the role of the Ovidian model text
in connection with Beatrice as Dante's guide through the Heavenly Spheres to
the Empyrean (*Par.* 1–31). Finally, the semantically enriched Ovidian model text
remains relevant, continues to produce and enhance meaning during the continuing upward trajectory of Dante-protagonist under the guidance of St. Bernard (*Par.*
32–33), from the Celestial Rose, to the Blessed Virgin, to union with God.

The second key motif I will be following is that of "human artifice" in the
Dantean Icarus/Daedalus program, beginning with the programmatic use of

the Daedalan wings to figure mimetic art. In this connection, it is important first of all to note Ovid's initial introduction of the character in *Metamorphoses* 8.159—as inventor and builder of the Labyrinth: "Daedalus ingenio fabrae celeberrimus artis / ponit opus" (Daedalus, most highly renowned for his ingenuity/ skill [*ingenio*; cf. *Inf.* 2.7] in the art of construction / erected the work). Further on, the narrative sequence in which Daedalus fabricates his new invention to escape from Crete is introduced as follows: "dixit et ignotas animum dimittit in artes / naturamque novat" (So saying, he sets his mind at work upon unknown arts, and changes the laws of nature; *Met.* 8.188–89). Next, the Ovidian *opifex* (*Met.* 8.201) proceeds to create, to craft the artificial wings (an imitation of "natural" wings) in order to escape from his Cretan "exile" (explicitly noted as such in *Met.* 8.184, a detail not irrelevant to Dante-poet). The artifact succeeds for Daedalus, in earthly terms, flying horizontally; but fails for Icarus, who attempts vertical (i.e., heavenward) flight. Directly linked to this is the double meaning of the Italian word *penne* (that is, "wings" and "pens"), which is key in this Dantean context, as is the related topos of "writing a poem [pens] is like taking a voyage by ship [oars/sails]."[10] The semantic and figurative links between "wings" and "oars" (and by metonymy "sails") is reinforced by the Latin etymon *remigium*, which is used to signify all three in both Ovid's and Virgil's treatments of Icarus and Daedalus, as we shall see.

My third focus involves the *Commedia*'s use of the deeply suggestive contrast/opposition between the rhetorical and the figural with regard to *penne* and to its near synonym *ali*: literal versus metaphoric wings on the one hand, and material versus spiritual wings, on the other.

Let me now return to the text of the *Inferno* by noting two key passages that semantically "thicken" our program in the first *cantica*, and which both occur between the naming of Icarus in canto 17 and that of Daedalus in canto 29.

In the conclusion of the poem's treatment of the seventh bolgia—that of the thieves—occurs the *Commedia*'s first use of the noun *penna* (*Inf.* 25.144) to signify the pen in the hand of Dante-poet, writing the poem in the present of the time of composition. *Inferno* 25, as we know, is extravagantly and spectacularly self-conscious with regard to its writerly virtuosity, and to the radical newness of its Christian subject matter,[11] with regard to which Dante-poet feels obliged to intervene dramatically in the narrative in order to "excuse" himself:

> e qui mi scusi
> la novità se fior la penna abborra. (*Inf.* 25.143–44)

and here [i.e., at this point in the ongoing composition/transcription of the poem as true verbal artifact] let the novelty [of the subject matter] be my excuse, if my pen goes astray.

This first representation of Dante-poet with pen in hand also initiates a set of three such passages strategically distributed at structurally similar points in each of the three *cantiche*: *Inferno* 25, *Purgatorio* 24, *Paradiso* 24. These function together to add a special emphasis to the sense of *penna/e* = "pen/s" as the instrument used by the poet to produce the extraordinary verbal artifact that is the *Commedia*. I will consider each in sequence focusing on their function of stressing this semantic component in tandem with that of *"penna*/feather," which constitutes the material used by the Ovidian Daedalus to construct the artificial wings that epitomize his identity as *opifex*, as master human artificer.

The second key infernal passage which functions to thicken and to deepen the Icarus/Daedalus program that is my present concern is the justly famous moment in Ulysses's speech that functions (among other things) to recall the flight of Icarus:

> E volta nostra poppa nel mattino,
> *de' remi facemmo ali al folle volo*
> sempre acquistando dal lato mancino.[12]

And having turned our stern to the morning, *we made of our oars wings for the mad flight*, always gaining on the left.

As John Freccero observed in a seminal article, the Dantean phrase *de' remi facemmo ali* echoes the Virgilian *remigium alarum* (the oarage of his wings) used by Virgil to describe the newly abandoned wings that Daedalus dedicates to Apollo in gratitude for his safe landing in Cumae (*Aen.* 6.17), in a temple to Apollo that the master artificer has just constructed.[13] They function thus as the antitype of the "oars made wings" of Ulysses's fatal voyage, as do the "super-Daedalan" spiritual wings of Dante-protagonist.[14]

In the *Purgatorio*, two evocations of the Icarus program frame Dante-protagonist's ascent of the Mountain. The first occurs near the beginning of canto 4, as Dante and Virgil approach the steep, narrow pathway (*calla*, 4.22) through the rock face, which ascends from the first to the second subdivision of the Ante-Purgatory. The difficult climb begins with Dante-protagonist following after his guide (*duca*, 4.23). The voice of Dante-poet then intervenes to contrast the literal climbing of steep mountains on earth, which can be effected by foot alone, with the Purgatorial ascent, presenting the latter, metaphorically and spiritually, as requiring *flight*:

> ma qui convien *ch'om voli;*
> dico *con l'ale* snelle e *con le piume*
>   *del gran disio, di retro a quel condotto*
>   che speranza mi dava e facea lume.[15]

> but here *a man must fly,* I mean with swift *wings* and the *plumes of great desire, behind that leader,* who gave me hope and was a light to me.

Particularly important in this context is the explicit emphasis on the necessity of following the guide (*condotto,* 4.29) as the only possible way of flying up, as opposed to Icarus whose unsuccessful upward flight involved deserting his guide (*Met.* 8.223–24). In addition, this Dantean flight of successful ascent involves intense desire (*gran disio,* 4.29) moving his "wings" upward following Virgil, in contradistinction to Icarus who, through his *cupidne* (*Met.* 8.423), abandons Daedalus's lead in order to fly up alone. Finally, the failure of Daedalus as guide with his son is implicitly contrasted with Virgil's success with his, imparting to him the Christian theological virtue of hope (*speranza*) by showing him the light (*lume,* 4.30), thus emphasizing the Latin *poeta*'s validity as Christian guide, showing his charge the way up to Beatrice and to God.

Near the end of Dante-protagonist's successful ascent of the Purgatorial mountain comes the second evocation of the Ovidian Icarus, which may be seen, I suggest, as forming a frame with the passage just considered. As Dante-protagonist awakens from the third and final Purgatorial dream, Virgil motivates him with the promise that the dawning new day will lead him to the goal of his journey. Dante's reaction is such that his final Purgatorial climb, from the seventh terrace to the threshold of the Earthly Paradise, metaphorically conflates his literal steps with the wings of Icarus. In significant contrast to the Ovidian Icarus, however, Dante-protagonist's "wings" are simultaneously metaphoric and spiritual, rhetorical and figural, looking both diegetically backward to his ascent (under Virgil's leadership) of the Purgatorial mountain, and forward to his ascent in the *Paradiso* (under the guidance of Beatrice):

> Tanto *voler sopra voler* mi venne
>   *de l'esser sù,* ch'ad ogne passo poi
>   *al volo* mi sentia crescer *le penne.*[16]

So much did *desire upon desire* grow in me *to be above*, that at every step I felt my *wings* [feathers] growing *for the flight*.

Again, we see the Dantean emphasis on a suddenly increased (and now—as Dante-protagonist leaves the seventh terrace—corrected) desire/will (*voler . . . voler*, 27.121) to fly up after his guide displacing *in bono* the Ovidian Icarus's cupidinous desire to "abandon" his guide by flying up. At the same time, the success of Virgil as a guide is triumphantly demonstrated at the moment when he will be passing this status to his higher, better, and necessary replacement, Beatrice. The contrast with Daedalus is striking: the master human artificer successfully completed his own flight (in human terms; that is, he liberated his corporeal self from literal exile and imprisonment) in contrast to the reversal of Icarus's transgressive ascent into a fatal descent. Thus, in contradistinction to Virgil, the flying Daedalus was a failure as guide (and as father) for his son, while successful only for himself (at the literal, human level; i.e., with no spiritual dimension). The "ascending" Virgil, by contrast, is fully successful as guide and father figure in fully spiritual terms, for Dante-protagonist (and, indeed, for Dante-poet), while unable to save himself in the literal and figural universe of the *Commedia*.

Between these two passages, which frame the ascent of the Purgatorial terraces with suggestive presentations of Dante-protagonist's upward journey in terms recalling Icarus's flight, there occurs the second *cantica*'s single use of *penne* (here in the emphatic rhyme position) to identify the writing implement of Dante the poet. On the sixth terrace, during his key encounter with Bonagiunta da Lucca—highly significant for the *Commedia* as a whole with regard to its author's self-presentation as a divinely inspired poet[17]—Dante-protagonist responds to his interlocutor's question concerning his earlier authorship of the canzone "Donne ch'avete intelletto d'amore" by describing his own (unique) poetic practice:

> E io a lui: "I' mi son un che, quando
>   Amor mi spira, noto, e a quel modo
>   ch' e' ditta dentro vo significando." (*Purg.* 24.52–54)

And I to him: "I am one who, when Love inspires me, takes note, and goes setting it forth after the fashion which he dictates within me."

Bonagiunta responds by exclaiming that he now understands (as he could not during his life on earth) what distinguishes Dante's *dolce stil novo* (a phrase

used for the fist time in Italian literature here, by Dante) from the work of earlier Italian poets (including himself):

> Io veggio ben come *le vostre penne*
>   *di retro al dittator* sen vanno strette,
>   che de le nostre certo non avenne.[18]

Clearly I see how *your pens* follow close *after him who dictates*, which certainly did
not happen with ours.

There has long been scholarly debate on the precise meaning of the phrase *le
vostre penne* (24.58): whether it should be understood either as an honorific singular or as a plural, and if as a plural, with what referents.[19] I remain open to the
possibility that the expression involves the honorific singular, employed by the
character Bonagiunta (in contradistinction to his earlier use of *tu* for Dante-
protagonist) to emphasize the fact that he has only just learned the full significance of Dante's unique poetic identity.[20] It is relevant in this context to keep in
mind Dante-protagonist's use of the honorific *voi* with both of his two key Italian vernacular model authors: for narrative, Brunetto in *Inferno* 15.30 and, for
lyric, Guido Guinezzelli in *Purgatorio* 26.112. In this case, the plural sense of
penne in *Purgatorio* 24.58 could perhaps be seen as indicating Dante's specific
individual poems, both *Donne ch'avete* and the *Commedia*. In any case, my suggestion is simply that Bonagiunta's expression foregrounds the *penne* (pens/
feathers) in the hand of Dante-protagonist (and, indeed, of Dante-poet) as signifying the act of writing as the result of "divine" inspiration[21] in a way that functions in tandem with *Inferno* 25.143–44 and *Paradiso* 24.25 to create a *Commedia*-
wide "Dante's pen/s" program.

The final moment in the second *cantica*'s development of the Icarus/Daeda-
lus program is in fact a moment of transition. It occurs in the Earthly Paradise
as Dante-protagonist, no longer under the guidance of the now inadequate Virgil, undergoes the painful initiation necessary for him to continue his journey
(his flight) under his new guide, Beatrice.

After the difficult confession of his sins that she has obliged him to undergo
despite his own preconversionary desires (his will), Beatrice reproaches Dante
for his not having recognized the true lesson of the death of her superlatively
beautiful mortal body, after which he erred gravely by letting himself be attracted by a necessarily less beautiful mortal object (*cosa mortale,* 31.53). She
compares Dante's error to the behavior of an inexperienced bird, in contradistinction to that of the mature bird that Dante should have resembled:

Ben ti dovevi, per lo primo strale
de le cose fallaci, *levar suso*
di retro a me, che non era più tale.
Non ti dovea gravar *le penne* in giuso,
ad aspettar più colpo, o pargoletta
o altra novità con sì breve uso.
Novo augelletto due o tre aspetta,
ma dinanzi da li occhi *d'i pennuti*
rete si spiega indarno o si saetta.[22]

After the first arrow from deceptive things, you should have *risen up after me*, for I was no longer such. *Your wings* should not been weighted down, to await more blows, by either a young girl or some other new thing of such short duration. A young bird waits for two or three, but before the eyes of the *fully feathered* (i.e., fully matured bird) nets are spread and arrows shot in vain.

It seems to me that (among many other things in this rich—and much commented—passage) Dante-protagonist is presented as being (in the past) an ineffective, a nonfunctioning Icarus figure, with Beatrice functioning as a Daedalus figure who is not followed, but should have been. In this sense, she was then (in the *Vita Nova*) what she is now revealed to be in the *Commedia*, but was not then listened to on her own terms (verses 56–57 are particularly important in this context). On the one hand, this anticipates directly Dante's (corrected) ascent through *Paradiso*, where he functions as a (corrected) Icarus to Beatrice's (corrected) Daedalus. On the other hand, the past Dante is here being reproached as a protagonist for having had his "wings" weighted down (i.e., not following Beatrice up), and the past Dante-poet, for not writing poetry (correctly) about her with his "pens," depicted in the same way. The lowered *penne* (verse 58) would thus signify simultaneously "wings" and "pens." Finally, the avian imagery of the passage as a whole presents (in contradistinction to the young bird that will not fly up) the "mature bird" that can and does fly up as *i pennuti* (62; "fully feathered"): an implicit recall of Icarus in *Inferno* 17.110. Dante *should* (in the past) have been a corrected Icarus figure.

The enduring validity (and power) of Ovidian poetic discourse for Dante to articulate figurally Christian truth is most elaborately demonstrated in the *Paradiso*. For this *cantica* is characterized by the visible presence of the greatest number of Ovidian models which function to represent the salvific trajectory both of Dante-poet and of Dante-protagonist.[23] Furthermore, the *Metamorphoses* as textual model is particularly relevant to the poetics of Paradise as a whole, which involve transformation and transfiguration in fundamental ways, with regard both to the protagonist's experience and to the poet's language. A fundamental problem is at issue here that is unique to the *Paradiso*, where, by definition as it were, both the human mind of the protagonist and the human language of the poet are profoundly and inescapably inadequate. In both of these contexts, the Ovidian narratives of metamorphosis operate as essential, yet necessarily insufficient and incomplete, figures for Christian transfiguration.[24] The Icarus/ Daedalus program is particularly striking in this context.

The first explicit reference to Daedalus in the *Paradiso*—simultaneously the second and last in the *Commedia* as a whole—is again directly linked with Icarus. In the Heaven of Venus (*Par.* 8.125–26) Charles Martel (eldest son of Charles II of Naples), in his exposition to Dante of the unpredictable diversity of an individual human being's nature, cites four examples of exceptional (and quite different) talents and achievements: Solon, Xerxes, Melchizedek, and, finally, Daedalus by means of the following periphrasis

> quello
> che, volando per l'aere, il figlio perse. (*Par.* 8.125–26)

> he who, by flying through the air, lost his son.

Here again, as in *Inferno* 17, it is the fatal fall of Icarus that is identified, and explicitly associated with his artificer/father's perception of his own failure. The success of Daedalus as artificer for himself alone is contrasted with his failure for his son.

The next key locus of the *Paradiso* in which the Dantean Icarus/Daedalus program functions is toward the beginning of the sustained encounter between Dante-protagonist and Cacciaguida in the Heaven of Mars. Here, again, the transformative Ovidian evocation is implicit, and takes place in the opening speech in Italian by Dante's great-great-grandfather. Cacciaguida describes Dante's heavenly ascent thanks to Beatrice who "a l'alto volo ti vestì le piume" (for the lofty flight dressed you in feathers; *Par.* 15.54),[25] terms that evoke contrastively the fatal flight of Icarus (*Met.* 8.187–216). This implicit presentation of Dante-protagonist as a corrected Icarus both recalls the initiation of the Icarus program in *Inferno* 17.109–11, and continues that program on the qualitatively different mimetic, rhetorical, and spiritual terms of the third *cantica*, with Beatrice substituted both for Virgil as the Daedalus figure at the level of the sustained Ovidian metaphor and, I would suggest, for the literal infernal figure of Geryon, at the level of the *Commedia*'s plot line. Dante's literal ascent in the *Paradiso* is effected by Beatrice.

In this context, Beatrice would be a better (Christian) combination of Donna and Mother than Daedalus was as an (pagan) artificer Father. The complex inadequacy of Virgilio as Father is also at issue here. And all of this takes place, of course, in the central encounter of *Paradiso* in which Dante-son meets Cacciaguida: his redeemed and salvific father figure, both crusader and martyr on the one hand, and authorizer of Dante's exile as a martyrdom underpinning the truth of the writing and the imperative for the public dissemination of the *Commedia* as a whole on the other.[26] The full revelation of Dante's exile in the central canto of the *Paradiso* (17) is, of course, explicitly informed by a key pair of Ovidian models: Phaeton and Hippolytus, who function to "thicken" the increased associative semantic richness provided by the hermeneutic configuration of the Ovidian Icarus-Phaeton- (and now, also) Hyppolytus[27] transformatively rewritten by Dante, and structurally resituated in the *Commedia* versus the *Metamorphoses* so as to function as reciprocal, mutual commentaries on each other within Dante's Christian poetics.

The third and final component of the program of "Dante's pen/s" occurs in *Paradiso* 24.25. Just before examining Dante on Faith, the Apostle St. Peter circles three times around Beatrice, singing "un canto tanto divo / che la mia fantasia nol mi ridice" (a song so divine that my phantasy does not repeat it to me; *Par.* 24.23–24). Because Dante's image-making facility cannot understand this song, his pen does not write it down: "Però salta *la penna* e non lo scrivo" (Therefore *my pen* leaps and I do not write it down).[28] There is thus a restatement here of Dante-protagonist's stance as an eyewitness whose poem is a record of what he has seen, with a particularly strong emphasis on the writing of the material document through the explicit mention of his pen (*penna*). At the same time, this use of *penna* meaning pen involves a clear recall of *Inferno* 25.143–44, which simultaneously sums up the mimetic difference between the two realms: in Hell, Dante-poet records what he has seen, which is true even if it seems to be fantastic; in Heaven, by contrast, what is stressed is Dante's human incapacity to grasp the full experience of what is presented to him, and thus the incapacity of human language to record this experience in the poem.

An additional allusion to the *Commedia*'s central character as a corrected version of Icarus occurs during his interrogation on theology in the eighth heaven. Here Dante-protagonist is about to respond to his second examiner

(St. James, on Hope) when he is interrupted by Beatrice in a way that presents him as a successful version of Icarus and her as a successful version of Daedalus (recalling at the same time the similar presentation by Cacciaguida in *Par.* 15.54, exactly ten cantos earlier). The voice of Dante-poet here refers to Beatrice as "quella pïa che *guidò le penne / de la mie ali a così alto volto*" (that compassionate one, who had *guided the feathers of my wings to such lofty flight; Par.* 25.49–51).[29] It is important to note that this passage (unlike *Par.* 15.23) emphasizes the key role of Beatrice as the effective guide of the upward flight of Dante, as opposed to Icarus, who abandoned his guide by flying upward in *Metamorphoses* 8.223–25.

In *Paradiso* 32.145–46, St. Bernard announces to Dante that it is time for them to turn their eyes to the Primal Love, so that, gazing toward Him, Dante may penetrate, as far as can be, into His effulgence:

> Veramente, *ne forse tu t'arretri*
> *movendo l'ali tue, credendo oltrarti.*
> orando grazia conven che s'impetri
> grazia da quella che puote aiutarti.[30]

> But *lest you now fall back* when, *even as you move your wings, you think that you advance,* imploring grace, through prayer you must beseech grace from that one who has the power to help you.

That is to say, within the semantically expanding context of the Icarus program, that without Christian grace from the Virgin Mary, Dante would risk becoming an Icarus who falls while flapping his wings, thinking that he is flying higher, advancing to new heights (*credendo oltrarti*).

In terms of my present reading, the culmination of the *Commedia*'s Icarus program occurs in *Paradiso* 33. First, near the beginning of the *ultimo canto*,[31] St. Bernard, in his intercessionary prayer to the Virgin, declares (speaking in general terms):

> Donna, se' tanto grande tanto vali,
> che qual vuol grazia e a te non ricorre,
> *sua disïanza vuol volar sanz'ali.*[32]

> You, Lady, are so great and so prevailing that whosoever would have grace and does not turn to you, *his desire would be to fly without wings.*

The final phrase of this citation, *vuol volar sanz'ali* (wants to fly without wings), constitutes a potent and contrastive evocation of Icarus's downward fall. For flying without wings is precisely what the Ovidian protagonist is obliged to attempt as the result of having abandoned his guide. The moment after Icarus's wings have been melted off his body by the heat of the sun, he vainly flaps his unfeathered arms:

> nudos quatit ille lacertos,
> *remigioque carens* non ullas percipit auras.[33]

> his arms were bare as he beat them up and down, *but lacking wings*, they took no
> hold on the air.

St. Bernard's words work dramatically to contrast the very moment that Icarus's fatal fall begins with that at which the final stage of Dante-protagonist's final upward flight is about to begin, an ascent that will succeed in the highest, most absolute terms: union with God.

St. Bernard then turns (rhetorically) to the particular case of Dante, whose cause he pleads to the Virgin on Dante's behalf, begging Her to grant

> per grazia, di virtute
> tanto, che possa con li occhi levarsi
> più alto verso l'ultima salute. (*Par.* 33.25–27)

> by your grace such power that with his eyes he may rise still higher towards the
> last salvation.

The final (and successful) flight (*levarsi*) of Dante-protagonist will take place by means of visual perception and intellection infused with grace (*grazia*), and finally to the union with (Divine) Love, which constitutes true salvation.

At the very end of the trajectory both of Dante-protagonist and Dante-poet, the *Divine Commedia's* final—climactic—polysemous development of its Icarus program represents that program's own inadequacy—and its necessary *dépassement*, its own transcendence. In *Paradiso* 33.139, Dante-protagonist, after looking into the third circle (which figures the Mystery of the Incarnation), wishes to understand that mystery:

> ma non eran da ciò *le proprie penne*:
> se non che la mia mente fu *percossa*
> da un *fulgore* in che sua voglia venne.[34]

> but *my own wings* were not sufficient for that, had my mind not been *smitten* by a
> *flash* wherein came its wish.

I suggest that the word *fulgore* recalls also the Ovidian Phaeton, at the moment of the tragic end of his transgressive flight, without a guide.[35] Jupiter (*pater omnipotens*, *Met.* 2.304), in the "highest vault of heaven" (*summam . . . arcem*, 2.306) from where he habitually "throws his lightning bolts" (*fulmina iactat*, 2.308), now unleashes a mighty one at Phaeton: "intonat et dextra libratum fulmen ab aure / misit in aurigam pariterque animaque rotisque / expulit et saevis conpescuit ignibus ignes" (He thundered, and balancing in his right hand a lightening bolt, flung it from beside the ear at the charioteer and hurled him from the car and from life as well, and thus quenched fire with blasting fire; 2.311–13). The death at the culmination of Phaeton's flight thus contrastively underlies the enhanced and eternal life at the culmination of Dante's flight—in which he is unified with the ultimate guide and the ultimate object of desire: God. This final evocation of the *Commedia*'s Phaeton program thus functions in tandem with its final evocation of the Icarus program: a sublime recasting of the first (and strikingly explicit) pairing of these two guideless, failed fliers in *Inferno* 17.

In this polysemous final evocation of the Icarus program that is the object of the present study, I suggest that a powerful, climactic double mimesis is at issue: Icarus for Dante-protagonist, and Daedalus for Dante-poet. The literal wings (*penne*) of even the corrected Ovidian Icarus are inadequate for Dante-protagonist. And the (metaphorically [and figurally] successful) wings of the corrected Ovidian Daedalus, the master—but *mortale*—artificer, are insufficient for the "full" success of Dante-poet in the figurative mimesis (accommodative metaphor, etc.) of *Paradiso* as a whole, and of the Empyrean in particular. And most explicitly, for the full union with Divine Love, which by definition cannot adequately be articulated in human language—not even in the new grammaticalized Italian illustrious vernacular, infused with Christian Grace, that Dante-poet has invented to figure the journey to *Paradiso* 33. In this sense, it is the writing, the successful construction of the unique verbal artifact, the book, the *volume* of the *Commedia* itself that has reached its own absolute limits, by means of the articulation of which it makes its final move toward closure.

In this sense it is the written composition, the pens (*penne*) of Dante-poet, that surpass, transcend with Christian inspiration, the tools and the ingenuity of Daedalus as *opifex*, as figure for the human artificer. But these Dantean pens/wings can most fully succeed only by finally articulating their own limitations, as is the case with Dante's use of his Ovidian (and, indeed, Virgilian) textual models.

NOTES

1. The bibliography on Dante and Ovid is substantial, and I wish here simply to indicate several key studies that have been useful to me: Ettore Paratore, "Ovidio e Dante," in *Nuovi saggi danteschi* (Rome: Angelo Signorelli, 1973), 45–100 (also published as "Ovidio," in *Enciclopedia dantesca* (Rome: Istuto della Enciclopedia dantesca, 1976), 4:225–36; Rachel Jacoff and Jeffrey T. Schnapp, eds., *The Poetry of Allusion: Virgil and Ovid in Dante's "Commedia"* (Stanford, CA: Stanford University Press, 1991); Madison U. Sowell, ed., *Dante and Ovid: Essays in Intertextuality* (Binghamton, NY: Center for Medieval and Early Renaissance Studies, 1991); Warren Ginsberg, "Dante, Ovid, and the Transformation of Metamorphosis," *Traditio* 46 (1991): 205–33; Michelangelo Picone, "L'Ovidio di Dante," 107–44, and Steno Vazzana, "*Ovidio è il terzo* (Indice dei luoghi ovidiani della *Commedia*)," 123–51, in *Dante e la "bella scola" della poesia: Autorità e sfida poetica*, ed. Amilcare A. Iannucci (Ravenna: Longo, 1993); Pier Paolo Fornaro, "Seconda morte (Dante metamorfico)," in *Metamorfosi con Ovidio: Il classico da riscrivere sempre* (Florence: Olschki, 1994), 145–72; Giorgio Brugnoli, "Forme ovidiane in Dante," in *Aetates Ovidianae: Lettore di Ovidio dall'Antichità al Rinascimento*, ed. Italo Gallo et al. (Naples: Edizioni Scientifiche Italiane, 1995), 239–56; Diskin Clay, "The *Metamorphosis* of Ovid in Dante's *Commedia*," in *Dante: Mito e poesia*, ed. Michelangelo Picone and Tatiana Crivelli (Florence: Cesati, 1999), 239–56; Peter S. Hawkins, *Dante's Testaments: Essay in Scriptural Imagination* (Stanford, CA: Stanford University Press, 1999); Michelangelo Picone, "Dante Alighieri: La riscrittura di Ovidio nella *Commedia*," *Il mito nella letteratura italiana* 1 (2006): 125–75; Giuseppe Ledda, "Semele e Narciso: Miti ovidiani della vision nella *Commedia* di Dante" in *Le Metamorfosi d'Ovidio nella letteratura tra Medioevo e Rinascimento*, ed. Gian Mario Anslemi (Modena: Gedit, 2006), 17–40; Winthrop Wetherbee, "Ovid and Vergil in Purgatory," in *The Ancient Flame: Dante and the Poets* (Notre Dame, IN: University of Notre Dame Press, 2008), 117–57.

2. All citations of the *Commedia* are from the text of Giorgio Petrocchi as found in Charles S. Singleton, *The Divine Comedy*, 6 vols. (Princeton, NJ: Princeton University Press, 1970–75). Translations are from Singleton with selective emendations. Citations from Ovid and Virgil are from Frank Justus Miller, *Metamorphoses*, 2 vols. (Cambridge, MA: Harvard University Press, 1976–77); J. H. Mozley, "*Ars amatoria*," in *The Art of Love and Other Poems* (Cambridge, MA: Harvard University Press, 1969), 12–175; H. Rushton Fairclough, *Aeneid*, 2 vols. (Cambridge, MA: Harvard University Press, 1969–74).

3. See Kevin Brownlee, "The Special Case of Ovid and His *Metamorphoses*," 152–60, in Brownlee, "Dante and the Classical Poets," in *Cambridge Companion to Dante*, 2nd ed., ed. Rachel Jacoff (Cambridge: Cambridge University Press, 2007), 141–60.

4. For the Phaeton program, see Kevin Brownlee, "Phaeton's Fall and Dante's Ascent," *Dante Studies* 102 (1984): 135–44, and Teodolinda Barolini's important and innovative book *The Undivine "Comedy": Detheologizing Dante* (Princeton, NJ: Princeton University Press, 1992), 57, 64, 67.

5. It is the full version of the story in *Met.* 8.183–235 that functions as Dante's primary model text in the *Commedia*'s Icarus/Daedalus program. Also relevant is the other Ovidian version of the story in *Ars amatoria* 2.21–98, as well as the Virgilian version of

Daedalus in *Aen.* 6.13–33, with its brief but important treatment of Icarus in *Aen.* 6.31–33.

6. See John Freccero, "Pilgrim in a Gyre," in *Dante: The Poetics of Conversion*, ed. Rachel Jacoff (Cambridge, MA: Harvard University Press, 1988), 70–92.

7. *Met.* 8.223–25; emphasis mine.

8. *Met.* 8.225–30; emphasis mine.

9. For Daedalus in this context, see Barolini, *Undivine "Comedy,"* 90–91.

10. See Ernst-Robert Curtius, *European Literature and the Latin Middle Ages*, trans. Willard R. Trask (Princeton, NJ: Princeton University Press, 1953), 128–30, on "Nautical Metaphors," where the comparison of "the composition of a work to a nautical voyage" (128) is considered from Virgil, Horace, and Statius through the "poetic and rhetorical tradition of the Latin Middle Ages" (130) to Dante.

11. See Peter S. Hawkins, "Virtuosity and Virtue: Poetic Self-Reflection in the *Commedia*," *Dante Studies* 98 (1980): 1–18. See also Caron Ann Cioffi, "The Anxieties of Ovidian Influence: Theft in *Inferno* 24 and 25," *Dante Studies* 113 (1994): 77–100.

12. *Inf.* 26.124–26; emphasis mine.

13. See John Freccero, "Dante's Firm Foot and the Journey without a Guide," *Harvard Theological Review* 52, no. 3 (1959): 245–81. I here refer to the first part of this groundbreaking piece as reprinted in the first chapter, "The Prologue Scene," in *Dante: The Poetics of Conversion*, ed. Rachel Jacoff (Cambridge MA: Harvard University Press, 1986), 1–28. The second and final part of the initial article appears as chapter 2 in the book (29–54). The passage that concerns my argument at this point carries the subtitle "The Wings of Ulysses (*Inf.* 26.125)," Freccero, *Dante*, 15–24. R. G. Austin, *P. Vergili Maronis: Aeneidos Liber Sextus* (Oxford: Clarendon, 1977), in the commentary to his edition of *Aen.* 6, translates *remigium alarum* (*Aen.* 6.10) as "the oarage of his wings," citing the same phrase used for Mercury's flight in *Aen.* 1.300–301: "volat ille per aëra magnum / remigio alarum." Austin views these two Virgilian uses of the phrase as looking back to Lucretius's "remigi oblitae pennarum vela remittent" (of birds) in *De rerum naturae* 6.743. He further states that "Daedalus' dedication of his wings to Apollo marks his gratitude for a safe [successful] landing and also his retirement from air-travel [and thus from his successful, unique, voyage by air], in the manner of many Greek dedicatory epigrams," including one (*AP* 6.90) "where a retired fisherman dedicates his anchor, oars, and other gear to Poseidon." The primary sense of the Virgilian Daedalus's dedication in *Aen.* 6.10 (the celebration of a successful [horizontal] earthly flight, which Icarus failed at; and in contradistinction to the successful [vertical] flight of Mercury from pagan heaven to earth) may thus be seen to contrast dramatically with the Dantean Ulysses's oars/wings comparison in *Inf.* 26.125 (in connection with an earthly [or watery] attempted voyage from one point to the globe to another), which is a failure.

14. For Dante's Ulysses, see Barolini, *Undivine "Comedy,"* 48–58. Especially significant for my argument is Barolini's powerful presentation of Ulysses as the key figure for transgressive desire in the *Commedia*, and as a privileged figure for Dante-poet in the process of writing the poem: "the poet who has embarked on a voyage whose Ulyssean component he recognizes, fears, and never fully overcomes" (52). For the relation between Ulysses and Icarus in this context, Barolini is particularly insightful on pages 48–51. In

my present reading, I view the Dantean Icarus as a rich *complement* to Ulysses in terms of the poet's presentation of transgression, especially with regard to the "guided vs. unguided journey" motif and the "human artifice" motif, both linked to Daedalus. Dante's Phaeton is also at issue here, as well, ultimately, as Dante's Ovid.

15. *Purg.* 4.27–30; emphasis mine.

16. *Purg.* 27.121–23; emphasis mine.

17. See especially Barolini, *Undivine "Comedy,"* 52–53. See also Robert Hollander, "Dante's 'dolce stil novo' and the *Comedy,*" in *Dante: Mito e poesia,* ed. Michelangelo Picone and Tatiana Crivelli (Florence: Cesati, 1999), 143–51.

18. *Purg.* 24.58–60; emphasis mine.

19. For a good treatment of the debate in terms of Dante's representation of his predecessors, see Hollander, commentary on *Purg.* 24.55–63, a well as *Purg.* 26.112. It is worth noting that several of the early commentators seem to understand the Dantean *voi* as an (honorific) singular in *Purg.* 24.

20. In the present context, it is only the meaning of this phrase that concerns me. For the contrary interpretation, cf. Chiavacci Leonardi's commentary on *Purg.* 24.58 and 26.112, where she argues that Dante-protagonist uses the plural rather than the honorific singular *voi* in referring to Guinizzelli's *li dolci detti vostri,* in what she sees as a meaningful parallel with the plural sense of Bonagiunta's *le vostre penne.* In this context, I (on the other hand) find useful Mark Musa's interesting reading of the implicit *voi* in *Purg.* 24.58 as the honorific singular, with the plural *penne* in *Purg.* 24.58 signifying "wings." See Mark Musa, "The 'Sweet New Style' That I Hear," in *Advent at the Gates: Dante's "Comedy"* (Bloomington: Indiana University Press, 1974), chap. 6, 111–28, esp. 122–24. While it has encountered some critical opposition, Musa's reading is suggestive for my current endeavor in that it is aware of what I view as the key double meaning of *penna/e*—"pen/s" and/or "wings"—and its function in the poetics of the *Commedia.* See also Lino Pertile responding to and expanding Musa in the context of falconry, "Il nodo di Bonagiunta, le penne di Dante e il Dolce Stil Novo," *Lettere Italiane* 41 (1994): 44–75. For a contrasting view, see Luciano Rossi, "*Purgatorio* XXIV" in *Lectura Dantis Turcensis* (Florence: Cesti, 2001), 377–87, and especially Michelangelo Picone, "Il 'Dolce Stil Novo' di Dante: Una lettura di *Purgatorio* XXIV," *L'Alighieri* 23 (2004): 75–95, esp. 93–94.

21. I understand this divine inspiration to mean, following Hollander, "Dante's 'dolce stil novo' and the *Comedy,*" that of both *Amore* (Cupid) and of *Caritas* (The Holy Spirit), as well as the one leading to the other (i.e., the erotic leading to the spiritual, as part of the Dantean poetics of the Incarnation), which is the defining characteristic of Dante's love of Beatrice.

22. *Purg.* 31.55–63; emphasis mine.

23. See Brownlee, "The Special Case of Ovid and His *Metamorphoses,*" and Michelangelo Picone, "Dante argonautica: La recezione dei miti ovidiani nella *Commedia,*" in *Ovidus redivivus: Von Ovid zu Dante,* ed. M. Picone and B. Zimmermann (Stuttgart: M & P, Verlag für Wiss. und Forschung, 1994), 173–202.

24. See Brownlee, "Pauline Vision and Ovidian Speech in *Paradiso* I," in *The Poetry of Allusion: Virgil and Ovid in Dante's "Comedy,"* ed. Rachel Jacoff and Jeffrey Schnapp (Stanford, CA: Stanford University Press, 1991), 202–13, 286–89.

25. See Hollander's commentary to *Par.* 15.54, as well as to *Par.* 15.72 and 15.81 (416–17), which he considers to constitute what he refers to as a "Daedalus program" in this part of *Paradiso*, viewed by him as "bordering on the obsessive." See also his *Il Virgilio dantesco: tragedia nella "Commedia"* (Florence: Olschki, 1983), 135–36.

26. See Jeffrey T. Schnapp's notion of Dante's "poetics of martyrdom" in the *Paradiso* (especially in the Cacciaguida episode) as set forth in chapter 5: *The Transfiguration of History at the Center of Dante's "Paradise"* (Princeton, NJ: Princeton University Press, 1986), 170–238, esp. 215–38.

27. See Margaret Mills Chiaranza, "Time and Eternity in the Myths of *Paradiso* XVII," in *Dante, Petrarch, Boccaccio*, ed. Aldo S. Bernardo and Anthony L. Pellegrini (Binghamton, NY: CEMERS, 1983), 133–50. See also Brownlee, "Phaeton's Fall and Dante's Ascent," 137–39, and Giuseppe Ledda's insightful "Autobiografismo profetico e costruzione dell' identità: Una lectura di *Paradiso* XVII," *L'Alighieri* 36 (2010): 87–113.

28. *Par.* 24.25; emphasis mine.

29. Emphasis mine. See Hollander, commentary to *Par.* 25.49–51 (694), where Beatrice is presented as a new Daedalus, and pens and wings are viewed as coterminus. See also Ledda, "Autobiografismo profetico e costruzione dell' identità," 91n10, for the key link between *Par.* 15.54 and 25.50, provided by the repetition of the *Commedia's* only two uses of the phrase *alto volo*. Ledda sees this (quite rightly) as a correction in Dante's heavenly ascent of the *folle volo* of the negative models provided by Ulysses and by Phaeton.

30. *Par.* 32.145–48; emphasis mine. Hollander (commentary to *Par.* 32.145.48) points out that Dante-protagonist here functions as a corrected Icarus and St. Bernard as a successful Daedalus.

31. For the opening of the final canto, see Ledda, "*Vergine madre figlia del tuo figlio*: *Paradiso* XXXIII 1–57," in *Lectura Dantis Scaligera* 2005–2007, ed. Ennio Sandal (Rome: Antenore, 2008), 97–135.

32. *Par.* 33.13–15; emphasis mine.

33. *Met.* 8.226–27; emphasis mine.

34. Emphasis mine. Cf. *Inf.* 17.108, *possa*.

35. I am here considering the Ovidian term for "lightning" based on the Latin etymon *fulgor*, *-oris* together with that based on *fulmen*, *-inis*. The latter is used repeatedly in Ovid's Phaeton story; the former occurs once in Ovid's Semele story (*Met.* 3.300), followed in quick succession by the latter (*Met.* 3.301, 3.305).

CHAPTER ELEVEN

Ekphrasis in the Knight's Tale

ANDREW JAMES JOHNSTON

Chaucer's *Knight's Tale* is one of the poet's most insistent engagements with classical antiquity. Emulating and sometimes even surpassing his direct source, Boccaccio's *Teseida*, Chaucer highlights and simultaneously problematizes not only his deep immersion in the classical but also the extent to which that immersion is already predicated on representational strategies and devices themselves part of the ancient tradition. For a writer like Chaucer, familiar both with the tradition of the *roman d'antiquité* and with the budding early humanist discourse on classical culture, to deal with antiquity meant also to deal with classical notions of representation and with the way these had been adapted by his medieval predecessors. Few subjects offer a richer site for such an engagement as does ekphrasis. After all, not only is ekphrasis a typically epic topos, one that, seen from a late medieval perspective, potentially invokes a Virgilian tradition of political narrative and narrative politics (and equally potential Ovidian responses), but it also constitutes a topos ideally placed to probe into issues of representation themselves—and, from the earliest times (i.e., from the *Iliad* onward), ekphrasis has been used to that particular purpose. This then is the issue I wish to discuss in this article: the question of how the *Knight's Tale* makes use of ekphrasis in the service of a specific narrative politics of representation, a politics in which the visual and the verbal on the one hand, and the classical and the medieval on the other, are locked in ineluctable conflict.

But before I proceed, a few brief words on ekphrasis seem appropriate, since this phenomenon has many different facets, and hence critics tend to view it from a plethora of divergent perspectives. The type of ekphrasis I wish to focus on here is the one James Heffernan defines as "visual representation of verbal representation."[1] This is a concept that goes back to Homer, if not in terms of an explicit definition of the phenomenon then certainly as regards the way it is conceptualized performatively in the epic's narrative. And, within the last half century or so of literary studies, this is what ekphrasis has consistently been narrowed down to by major critics. By contrast, in classical antiquity and in the Middle Ages the use and the theoretical discussion of the term "ekphrasis" focused on the problem of the lifelikeness of detailed descriptions in general. In other words, the literary tradition of ekphrasis as evidenced in a vast number of premodern literary texts was not, for a long time, theorized as ekphrasis at all.[2]

Moreover, the particular variety of ekphrasis which matters in the context of this article is that which John Hollander has called "notional ekphrasis"; that is, the verbal depiction of fictional images rather than of real ones.[3] The distinction is important for my analysis, since it helps us to see ekphrasis not simply as an engagement between verbal and visual art—as in "poems for paintings" for instance[4]—but rather as an engagement that is always already fictional itself and does not, therefore, have to refer to anything real outside the text.[5] Consequently, it aspires to a highly developed degree of poetic self-reflexivity, a self-reflexivity that, as Margaret Bridges has shown, by no means depends on the lifelikeness or pictorial quality of the ekphrasis in question. Indeed, an instance of ekphrasis in the sense used here might actually be presented in considerably less a pictorial and image-like fashion than an example of what one might call an "ordinary" description.[6]

It is the specifically self-reflexive quality of ekphrasis that has tempted one critic to state that it "has a strong claim to consideration as the most narcissistic mode of literary discourse," since it becomes "a mode in and by which literary language gazes at the visual as a lens upon the beauty of its own performance."[7] True as this indictment of ekphrastic narcissism may, to a certain extent, be, it should not, however, lead us to the conclusion that ekphrasis of this particular self-reflexive kind constitutes, by definition, a depoliticized style of representation. On the contrary, even as poetry thus performatively meditates on its power to purvey aesthetic pleasure and hence may lay itself open to charges of narcissism, it nevertheless fully retains, I would suggest, its capacity for critiquing the purposes to which this aesthetic pleasure is put and, more importantly, its capacity for problematizing the means by which this aesthetic pleasure is achieved. The issue is of considerable relevance amongst other things because of a recent debate on the specifically *literary* importance of Lollard writing, a debate in which ekphrasis has loomed large. Defending the aesthetic complexity of Lollard texts against James Simpson's banishing them from the realm of the literary in his volume of the *Oxford History of English Literature*,[8] Bruce Holsinger has pointed out the extent to which Lollard texts—for all their claims to aesthetic simplicity and iconoclasm—skillfully employ the rhetorical techniques of ekphrasis to play out their theological and ethical iconophobia in the service of attacking the official Church's tendency toward ever-increasing forms of lavish aesthetic display. Holsinger is undoubtedly right in drawing attention to the fact that Lollard writing, too, possesses sophisticated rhetorical and poetic qualities and thus not merely merits but actually demands being treated as "literature" and not simply as a body of propaganda material or as a corpus of theoretical tracts systematizing a given set of ideological tenets. Yet it is important to note that the instances of ekphrasis Holsinger discusses in this context are ekphrastic merely in the sense that they concern the lifelikeness of the verbal representation, rather than being ekphrastic in the more specific sense of a verbal representation of visual representation. Thus the Lollard ekphrases Holsinger marshals in support of his critique do not participate in the literary conversation on fictionality and literariness that is so typical of medieval ekphrasis. Whereas James Simpson takes Lollard anti-aesthetic claims at face value and, consequently, Lollard iconophobia, and underestimates the poetic dimension of Lollard writings, Holsinger's defense of Lollard rhetoric unnecessarily reduces the self-reflexive to the narcissistic—and, by implication, denies it political relevance. If, as Bruce Holsinger has shown, it is at our peril that we take Lollard iconophobia literally, then, at the same time, we would err no less if we took for granted the aestheticist pose so glaringly prominent in much ekphrastic self-reflexivity. This point, I feel, is one Chaucer is at pains to make, commenting thereby not only on a chivalric politics of violence, on the relationship between the classical and the medieval, and on that between the visual and the verbal, but also, albeit very obliquely, gesturing toward the question of Lollard iconophobia.

Chaucer's most prominent example of ekphrasis is to be found, of course, in the descriptions of the temples in the *Knight's Tale*. At the very end of these descriptive passages, he makes what one might call a typically ekphrastic joke. This concerns the final detail of the images in the Temple of Diana, which is a woman giving birth to a child:

> A womman travaillynge was hire biforn;
> But for hir child so longe was unborn,
> Ful pitously Lucyna gan she calle
> And seyde, "Help, for thou mayst best of alle!"
> Wel koude he peynten lifly that it wroghte;
> With many a floryn he the hewes boghte,[9]

The irony of this scene has many layers. Even as Emilye, the romance's principal female character, is on the brink of imploring the goddess to help her maintain her chastity, the deity is visually associated with the pains and labors of motherhood. Moreover, the narrator describes the silent image as crying out and thus makes a conventional ekphrastic move proclaiming the lifelikeness of an image supposedly being depicted verbally. This move consists in making the image do something that, as an artifact of visual representation in extratextual reality, it would never be capable of doing.

In her recent book on the visual object of desire in late medieval England, Sarah Stanbury has commented on this final ekphrastic scene:

> The image is so lifelike it appears to speak. Or is it that the image is so lifelike it *does* speak? The image might be said to illustrate the drama of life-likeness, but also—in the picture of the woman trapped in childbirth—a terrible stasis, the place of the undead, the inability to bring to life. This final ekphrasis bespeaks a number of very different responses, highly ambivalent, toward images as it resolves on an image, lodged between life and death, of death-dealing nascent life.[10]

Stanbury's perceptive reading teases out the complex ambiguities and ambivalences inherent in this narrative representation of a fictional image. By referring to the question of "life-likeness," she addresses the issue much along the lines ancient and medieval rhetoricians would have used, focusing on the way poetic language can vividly bring to life an object existing only in the imagination. Thus ekphrasis is discussed within the context in which the term itself originates, that of detailed description, a notion of ekphrasis that is not necessarily linked to the description of visual art in verbal art, let alone to that of purely fictional works of art in narrative poetry. Stanbury's reading proves less interested, then, in the particular conventions of ekphrasis as are to be witnessed in the epic tradition handed down from Homer. Thus, even as she acquaints us with the subtleties of the verbal picture, her interpretation emulates the vagueness and ambiguity we encounter in the image itself. After all, what do we actually see? Do we see the "picture of a woman trapped in childbirth," as Stanbury suggests, or do we see a woman trapped in an *image* of childbirth? This, it would seem, is what Stanbury's use of the term "stasis" implies. In that case, the entrapment we are confronted with would not so much be a question of the liminal state of childbirth being prolonged beyond what is bearable— "But for hir child so longe was unborn"—but rather a fundamental problem of visual representation itself. The trap that the woman has been caught in is the *supposed* inability of the image to truly capture the temporal. What we see is the stasis of an image *trying to tell a story*, yet being incapable of transcending the confines of the picture. In order to represent action—movement in time—a painting must seek to show the "pregnant moment" in a sequence of events, a moment that makes it possible for the viewer to imagine all that went before and, more importantly, all that is still to come: "the concentration of action in a single moment of energy."[11] And what moment could, literally, be more "pregnant" than that of a woman giving birth?[12] Because an image—be it a sculpture or a painting—appears to be literally encapsulating what it seeks to represent, ostensibly freezing what it attempts to bring to life, this pregnancy will be drawn out indefinitely and thus illustrate what Bruce Holsinger has called the "frozen cruelty in ekphrastic writing, a refusal of empathy that sustains the poetics and prosaics of ekphrasis as both genre and mode."[13] And, indeed, one cannot help feeling that Chaucer is seeking to give expression to and comment on that "frozen cruelty," first by permitting his narrator to stress the pathos of the situation—"Ful pitously Lucyna gan she calle"—and second by subsequently letting him switch his focus to the purely aesthetic issue of lifelikeness before, third, making him speculate callously on the question of how much money the painting may have cost. Not only does the narrator remind his readers that it is, after all, only a picture they see, but he simultaneously forestalls too intensive an engagement as he withdraws from the artifact emotionally by highlighting not only its materiality but also its ultimate origin in processes of economic exchange.[14]

But of course, this reading is based on an analysis of visual representation's exigencies that is both culturally specific and ideologically charged. It looks as though the Knight—and it is the Knight as narrator that seems to be highlighted here—were anticipating Gotthold Ephraim Lessing's famous distinction between literature as an essentially temporal form of representation—*Zeitkunst*—and visual art as a fundamentally spatial one—*Raumkunst*. Moreover, the Knight seems to share the value judgments traditionally attached to these concepts. According to the eighteenth-century German dramatist and literary theorist, verbal representation was superior to visual representation because the former was capable of unfolding in time and thereby of representing action in narrative, whereas visual art did not possess the potential for sequentiality required for storytelling: "It remains true that succession of time is the province of the poet just as space is that of the painter."[15]

Lessing's distinction remained highly influential right down to the late twentieth century, when it came under attack by W. J. T. Mitchell, who argues that it is impossible to distinguish between verbal and visual representation on the basis of space and time. According to Mitchell, both forms of representation are mixed forms in which the temporal and the spatial merge inextricably, as do the verbal and the visual: "all media are mixed media, and all representations are heterogeneous; there are no 'purely' visual or verbal arts, though the impulse to purify media is one of the central utopian gestures of modernity."[16]

In a recent discussion of Lessing, Italian archaeologist and historian of classical art Luca Giuliani has argued that what distinguishes verbal from visual representation is not so much that one unfolds in time and the other in space, but rather that verbal representation has a stronger tendency to guide the audience's reception in time: "The crucial difference between a text and an image does not consist in the text's being read in a successive mode while the image is observed in an act of simultaneous reception, but rather in the text's reception taking place as a process in time that is subject to a form of guidance [*Steuerung*] dependent on the structures of its medium—something that is not the case with images."[17] Lessing's general concepts did not originate with him. His distinctions are inherent in the tradition of the *paragone* itself, in this case: in the competition between the verbal and the visual arts. Poets would invariably claim to be winning that contest whenever they turned their pens to ekphrasis. This is a fundamental feature of the epic tradition of ekphrasis; it starts with Homer's shield of Achilles and continues all through literary history. By making pictures move, sing, or speak or by depicting things that could not possibly be represented within a single image, poets since Homer, especially epic poets, have implicitly been making Lessing's point. Ostensibly, this is a game that the Knight, too, is playing by introducing elements into the descriptions of his images, which would never have been visible on an ordinary panel, mural, relief, or statue.

One of the *Knight's Tale*'s most significant examples of ekphrasis—apart from the one just quoted—is to be found in the descriptions of the images in the Temple of Mars. Here we see a mural depicting a second temple of Mars from the outside that contains frescoes which are described in detail, even though these paintings must to all intents and purposes be invisible to the viewer's eye—simply because it is impossible for the viewer to see things inside a building supposedly represented from the outside only. Similarly, in the *House of Fame*, Chaucer gradually turns into a visual experience the text of the *Aeneid* inscribed on tablets of brass adorning the walls of the temple of Venus.[18] In as much as the Knight, too, employs these typically ekphrastic devices with considerable skill, he demonstrates that he is following the epic tradition of letting the verbal triumph over the visual. He, too, has grasped the basic competitive thrust of ekphrasis and is enjoying the opportunity to stage his own "narcissistic exhibition of writerly prowess."[19] And we could simply leave it at that. But within the narrative economy of *Knight's Tale*, I suggest, ekphrasis has significance greater than being a mere exercise in literary tradition.

We begin to realize this when we encounter the ekphrastic mode of telling even in cases that do not constitute verbal representations of visual art at all, because, for all intents and purposes, within the narrative's fiction, the objects being referred to are supposed to be real. Hence, in the detailed descriptions of the kings Lygurgus and Emetrius, we hear the Knight say "There maistow seen,"[20] as though he were taking us through a gallery of paintings or a hall of frescoes.

This fits a pattern. After all, in the *Knight's Tale*, the relationship between vision and narrative is charged with political meaning. As Susan Crane has shown, Theseus's theater betrays all the visual potential of Jeremy Bentham's *Panopticon* as seen through the eyes of Michel Foucault.[21] And then there is the Knight's gleeful highlighting both of his own voyeurism and of the reader's voyeurism in the scene of Emilye's ritual ablutions. Through its celebration of narratorial power both vis-à-vis the characters of the story and—just as impressive—vis-à-vis the readers who are unwittingly turned into the narratorial voyeur's accomplices, this scene bespeaks a cynicism that renders suspect what has often been interpreted as the supposed innocence of the Knight's narratorial ineptitude.[22] Hence the Knight's voyeurism calls into question the thoughtlessness of his compliance with the denial of subjectivity inherent in chivalric ideology, a denial which plays the central role in Lee Patterson's reading of the tale.[23] Far from being a straightforward example of chivalric society's inability or unwillingness to address the issue of subjectivity, the Knight actually provides a commentary on that problem, albeit an oblique one that is implicit in his cunning narratorial stratagems, stratagems amongst which ekphrasis features prominently.

Especially in the *Knight's Tale*, then, Chaucer seems to be doing more to ekphrasis than merely playing by its narrative and poetic rules as inherited from the epic tradition, starting with Homer, whom he did not read, through Virgil and Boccaccio, with interesting detours through Ovid and the *Roman de la Rose*, all of whom he did read. Chaucer, I argue, is drawing attention to the very temptations of the *paragone* and to the easy victories it always seems to promise to the *poeta doctus* who has ekphrastic tradition at his fingertips and knows how to deal out the cards in a game always already stacked in his favor. That is, a poet who has grasped the ultimately facile technique of including in the verbal depiction of a visual work of art things that could not possibly be there. A typical instance is Homer's description of the shield of Achilles in the eighteenth book of the *Iliad*, where there are far too many of these things to fit into the space they have been put in and where these things or beings start moving or singing or engaging in sequential action. An equally famous instance consists in Virgil's shield of Aeneas, which depicts events destined to happen in a glorious future, thereby self-consciously breaking the frame of the narrative action.

Another brief look at the first book of the *House of Fame* confirms both Chaucer's mastery of the art of *paragone* and his tendency not simply to imitate the tradition but rather to conceptualize the *paragone* itself as a space of artistic rivalry. Starting off with a translation of the *Aeneid* inscribed in brass tablets, Chaucer addresses three different zones of aesthetic conflict at the same time. Moving from the verbal to the visual, he stages an ekphrastic *paragone*, while switching from the script on the tablets to the narrator's words, he alludes to the tensions between writing and the oral. Finally, seemingly abandoning Virgil for Ovid, he turns to the competitive politics and the political competitiveness of the classical tradition itself. Ekphrasis here is but one of many competitive structures whose threads become so tangled that it is impossible to unravel them. Juxtaposing and merging these traditional sites of artistic rivalry, Chaucer problematizes the issue of aesthetic competition as such.

This seems to be also his concern in the politics of ekphrasis we encounter in the *Knight's Tale*. Here, Chaucer makes his narrator exaggerate those competitive principles that determine the game, and exaggerate them, moreover, in a conspicuously gratuitous fashion. Hence the Knight's description of the statue of Venus gives us a figure "fletynge in the large see."[24] Thus the statue turns into something more composite than a mere statue since it is depicted with a background as though it were a relief or a painting. And, as I have already mentioned, the Temple of Mars represents a visual impossibility: depicting, as it does, images *in the interior* of a building that is visible *merely from the outside*; that is, "an ekphrasis within an ekphrasis."[25] Readers are here plunged into a kind of ekphrastic hall of mirrors or, rather, into a set of ekphrastic Chinese boxes in which one ekphrasis contains the next until readers become confused about which level of ekphrasis they actually find themselves on. What the ekphrasis within the ekphrasis draws attention to is the ultimately mechanical nature of ekphrastic *impossibilia*, is the fact that one ekphrasis could, in theory, be layered onto the next ad infinitum because, at the end of the day, each ekphrasis is capable of framing a second one and so forth. If anything, then, the effect is to highlight self-reflexive narrative excess, self-consciously putting on display the very narcissism so unattractive to some modern critics. This narrative excess fits well with some of the *Knight's Tale*'s more prominent aesthetic characteristics. Here, as in so many other of the tale's features, the epic pathos of the *Knight's Tale* seems to be segueing into something close to operatic ridiculousness.[26]

Yet, especially when it comes to the Temple of Mars, that operatic excess gives vent to something more powerful than mere poetic narcissism, since what ekphrasis as an aesthetic mode derives from is a culture depicted as grounding its basic values in rivalry and competition. The tale's narrative, we must remember, centers on the way Palamon's and Arcite's self-destructive male rivalry seeps over into a quarrel between the gods, and ends up by becoming an extension of the antagonistic policies that led to Theseus's imperialistic subjugation of the reign of Femenye in the first place. If, in the *Knight's Tale*, rivalry and aggression are the fundamental principles of chivalric politics and (anti-) subjectivity, they also become the basic principles of chivalric narrative as exemplified by the *Knight's Tale*'s telling. And this is particularly true of the relation in epic between the verbal and the visual. The manner in which the story is told establishes epic poetry as being locked in an interminably violent conflict against the visual even as it seeks to emulate the visual—or perhaps precisely because of its attempts at emulating the visual. Since ekphrasis as a narrative and rhetorical ploy encapsulates, at the very least, a double rivalry, that between visual and verbal representation and that between a poet and the literary tradition that precedes him, it provided the ideal mode for narrating an epic-cum-romance that derives its principal thrust from chivalric competitiveness, be it erotic or political or both. And so it is no coincidence that the most glaring example of ekphrasis should be found in the description of the Temple of Mars, dedicated to the god who like no other embodies that epic rivalry the *Knight's Tale* proves incapable of containing. In the ekphrastic absurdities of the Temple of Mars, with its potentially endless series of verbal representations of visual representations, or in the pregnant woman's piercing and potentially never-ending cry, Chaucer literally envisions a narratorial approach indicative of a cultural impulse that seeks to suppress all forms of dialogue and conceptualizes cultural exchange as an infinite chain of one-upmanship. It is a cultural stance capable of imagining its poetic and narrative engagements with the past only within an endlessly repeated binary of victory and defeat, of triumph and surrender, just as Theseus first subdues the Reign of Femenye, then conquers and destroys Thebes, and can think of no other solution to the problem of Palamon and Arcite than a carefully staged mass combat.

But even this is not quite all. As we have seen, the ekphrases proper of the temples are contrasted with scenes that are ekphrastic in tone and style without, however, being verbal representations of visual representation. Instead, they are verbal representations of imaginary visual scenes that emulate the actual ekphrases and sometimes outstrip them in terms of pictorial quality. One of the best examples of this characteristic is the description of Lygurgus and Emetrius, the two exotic kings in their outlandish garb who have come to participate in the tournament, one fighting for Palamon, the other for Arcite. The first to be depicted is Lygurgus.

> Ther maistow seen, comynge with Palamoun,
> Lygurge hymself, the grete kyng of Trace . . .
> Ful hye upon a chaar of gold stood he,
> With four white boles in the trays.
> In-stede of cote-armure over his harnays,
> With nayles yelewe and brighte as any gold,
> He hadde a beres skyn, col-blak for old.
> His longe heer was kembd bihynde his bak;
> As any ravenes fethere it shoon for blak;
> A wrethe of gold, arm-greet, of huge wighte,
> Upon his hed, set ful of stones brighte,
> Of fyne rubyes and of dyamauntz.[27]

The second king to be portrayed is Emetrius, the ruler of India.

> With Arcita, in stories as men fynde,
> The grete Emetreus, the kyng of Inde,
> Upon a steede bay trapped in steel,
> Covered in clooth of gold, dyapred weel,
> Cam ridynge lyk the god of armes, Mars.
> His cote-armure was clooth of Tars
> Couched with perles white and rounde and grete;
> His sadel was of brent gold newe ybete;
> A mantelet upon his shulder hangynge,
> Bret-ful of rubyes rede as fyr sparklynge;
> His crispe heer lyk rynges was yronne.[28]

As mentioned above, the narrator begins his description by addressing the reader with the phrase "Ther maistow seen," as though he were speaking not to a distant reader encountering a textual representation but rather as if he were turning to his audience as one fellow witness to another sitting on the theater's curving benches and cheering the brilliant spectacle unfolding before their eyes.

But what is perhaps most fascinating about the two kings' description is that their outer aspect forms a marked contrast to the diligently expounded principles according to which Theseus's theater is constructed. With its evenly rising rows of seats arranged in perfectly concentric circles the building's very structure claims the ability to exert rational control over the visual.

> That swich a noble theatre as it was
> I dar wel seyen in the world there nas.
> The circuit a myle was aboute,
> Walled of stoon, and dyched al withoute.
> Round was the shap, in manere of compas,
> Ful of degrees, the heighte of sixty pas,
> That whan a man was set on o degree,
> He letted not his felawe for to see.[29]

Walled with stone and "dyched al without"—rather like a castle surrounded by a moat—the building succeeds in being two things at the same time: first, a typically medieval defensive structure protected by a wall and a ditch and adorned not only with three chapels but also with a tower containing the third of the chapels, that of Diana. Second, the narrator's words evoke an equally typical ancient building glorying in its geometrically reinforced circularity— "in manere of compas"—a circularity that would have been largely unknown to the medieval architectural imagination, except, that is, in the form of archaeological relics from classical antiquity.[30] The building's very architectural nature thus seems to be embodying conflicting aesthetic and historical principles, juxtaposing mutually exclusive cultural traditions and thus perfectly encapsulating the dilemma of classical narrative as told by a medieval crusader.

It is into this perfectly geometrical, yet also oddly medieval, edifice that the two oriental kings ride, there to do battle according to the violent imperatives of chivalric culture. Hence, as an architectural attempt to police and regulate visual experience, the theater pits the rational against the sensual in the experience of vision. Like the building's contradictory architectural aesthetics just discussed, this is a binary opposition literally built into Theseus's theater.[31] In the theater, the strictly geometrical framing of the visual can be read as a self-consciously rational response to the potentially unruly corporeality of the visual, a corporeality represented by the two exotic kings in their fantastic oriental physicality. This sensuous physicality is rendered especially conspicuous by the narrator's insistence on the expensive materials and colors as well as by his fascination with the animals accompanying the kings and by his generous use of animal imagery in his description.

The Theater is thus styled as a building that regulates the visual geometrically, which subjects the sensual and animal side of vision to the mathematical reason of optics. But since we are not, after all, dealing with a real theater, but merely with one that comes into being through architectural ekphrasis, at the narratorial level this policy translates into a clear directive: the visual must be subjected to the verbal. The Knight thus styles himself as a Virgilian narrator whose aim it is, in the words of Stephen G. Nichols, "to subordinate sensate image to rational idea."[32]

So, what we face is a twofold situation: on the one hand, there are the temples with their strictly circumscribed, though exaggerated, ekphrases in the conventional epic sense, and on the other there is the fact that the visual and the pictorial seem to be very much a feature of the tale as a whole, but a feature that can assume a decidedly troubling quality requiring strategies of containment and control, as is the case with the two foreign kings. If, then, in the ekphrastic set pieces of the temples, we are presented with something like a semblance of verbal representation's victory over visual representation repeating itself over and over again in a succession of extreme examples of the *paragone*, it is as though the text were inserting these instances of clear-cut and pitched ekphrastic battles into a general environment where the pure distinctions between the verbal and the visual are constantly threatened. The temples thus serve as miniature framing devices within the larger narrative. And within these self-contained framing devices in the narrative, the verbal is granted a reassuring power over the visual that has long been called into question in the story as a whole. The temples and their excessive ekphrases thus seem to offer the false promise that the borders between the verbal and the visual can still be effectively policed and that an undisputed victory can still be awarded to the verbal—a verbal closely identified with the rational as opposed to the sensual, which is implicitly linked to the visual. Hence the theater expresses that "impulse to purify media," which W. J. T. Mitchell has identified as one "of the central utopian gestures of modernity."[33] Yet at the same time as the circular edifice embodies that impulse it also shows this impulse already doomed to failure, a failure that becomes particularly evident in the narrator's enraptured response to the grand entrance of Lygurgus and Emetrius: "There maistow seen."

My use here of military metaphors such as "pitched ekphrastic battles" is deliberate. We must not forget that it is a late fourteenth-century English knight who is supposedly telling the story. The English during the Hundred Years War appeared to be invincible as long as they were in a position to choose their own battlegrounds and confront the enemy in regular engagements; that is, in pitched battles. They failed, however, when it came to developing an adequate response to Bertrand du Guesclin's guerrilla tactics.[34] In a similar way, the Knight as narrator is at his most triumphant when he is capable of occupying a position that makes it possible for him to subject visual representation to his verbal superiority in conditions carefully designed for that specific purpose. The temples with their ekphrases thus assume the character of a tournament-style battleground on which the *paragone* can be staged in a manner most favorable to setting off the superiority of verbal representation. No wonder then that these temples are themselves set into the walls of Theseus's theater, that vast and all-encompassing tournament site or battle ground. After all, this is a feature where Chaucer consciously departs from his source, Boccaccio's *Teseida*, which does not link the temples to the theater at all. Just as Duke Theseus seeks to contain and even harness chivalric violence by attempting to channel it into the theater's civilizing frame, the Knight as narrator tries to verbally fix the visual in the frame provided by the temples and their murals. Hence "Chaucer's translation of the temples to Athens itself" does not mean that the poet is shifting "the significance of the ekphrasis from the semiotic to the political,"[35] but rather that the text is at pains to highlight the extent to which the semiotic itself is always already political.

But as we know, Theseus's civilizing mission fails. The Gods themselves intervene and cynically reverse the decision of the tournament battle. And of course, at the visual level, Emetrius and Lygurgus in their exotic attire suggest that the theater's architectural rationality is ultimately incapable of containing the power of the image. Arcite, the rightful victor, must die and it is Palamon who gets Emilye in the end. Just as, in the final analysis, chivalric violence proves unmanageable in the *Knight's Tale* as a whole, at the narratorial level the visual always threatens to overcome the verbal. Self-consciously staging his close-to-absurd ekphrases, the Knight as narrator attempts at best to win a few paragonal battles while he is losing the representational war. When, as Lygurgus and Emetrius enter the scene, the Knight utters his spellbound "There maistow seen," the carefully circumscribed sphere of verbal dominance over visual representation is broken apart, and Theseus's theater reveals the Gothic and castle-like aesthetic hiding behind the ostensible classicism of its geometrical regularity.

The verbal, Chaucer seems to be implying, always already contains the visual, just as the medieval will always betray its presence in a classical tale told by a chivalric narrator. Like W. J. T. Mitchell, Chaucer is fully aware of the way the verbal forms a constant presence in the visual and vice versa, and he employs this awareness in order to critique chivalric ideology's claim to be capable of making use of violence and yet keeping it under control. If we were to see this as an oblique comment on Lollard iconophobia, then it would amount to a shrewd analysis rather than a simple critique of that iconophobia, an analysis bent not on a defense of images, but rather one pointing out the futility of seeking to banish or even merely to contain the visual.

NOTES

1. Heffernan, *Museum of Words*, 3.

2. Wandhoff, *Kunstbeschreibungen und virtuelle Räume*, 15; Klarer, *Ekphrasis*, 4–7.

3. Hollander, *Gazer's Spirit*, 4–9.

4. Surprisingly, despite the long-standing debate on ekphrasis, some critics still see ekphrasis primarily in terms of "poems for paintings," thus largely cutting themselves off from the ancient tradition and its specific potential for a critique both of the politics of narrative and that of representation. For a recent approach to ekphrasis in these rather limited terms, see Cheeke, *Writing for Art*, 3.

5. There are, however, limits to the usefulness of the concept of "notional ekphrasis," as Gabriele Rippl, *Beschreibungskunst*, 64n20, points out, since even the description of actually existing works of art can always represent only the describer's mental picture of a given work of art and not the work of art itself. The reason why the term nevertheless retains a considerable analytical potential in our context is because notional ekphrases possess a tendency to flaunt their fictionality, and hence the fictionality of the texts they occur in, and this cannot be said of ekphrases of real—that is, actually existing—works of art.

6. Bridges, "The Picture in the Text," 152.

7. Holsinger, "Lollard Ekphrasis," 67–89, esp. 75.

8. Simpson, *Reform and Cultural*, 371, declares: "A literary history is clearly not the place for any extended account of this movement [i.e., Lollardy], whose writings almost without exception set out to be discursively stable, unimaginative, and instrumental."

9. *Canterbury Tales*, fragment 1, lines 2083–88. All quotations from Chaucer's works are taken from Benson, *Riverside Chaucer*.

10. Stanbury, *Visual Object of Desire in Late Medieval England*, 105.

11. Steiner, *Colours of Rhetoric*, 41.

12. As Heffernan, *Museum of Words*, 5n12, points out, the term "pregnant moment" derives from Lessing, "who asserts that painting can represent only a single moment of action." Both Murray Krieger and Wendy Steiner adopted this idea for a characterization of ekphrasis itself. Heffernan, *Museum of Words*, 5, is critical of this projection of picto-

rial stasis onto a mode of verbal representation and insists on "language by its very nature" releasing and stimulating a "story-telling impulse." He does not, however, object too much to the basic idea of visual representation being hampered by stasis.

13. Holsinger, "Lollard Ekphrasis," 75.

14. For an in-depth discussion of how this ekphrasis in bound up in an acute Chaucerian analysis of the social and political functions of art, see Epstein, "'With many a florin he the hewes boghte,'" 49–68, esp. 61–62.

15. Lessing, *Laocoön*, 91.

16. Mitchell, *Picture Theory*, 5.

17. Giuliani, "Laokoon in der Höhle des Polyphem," 20: "Der entscheidende Unterschied zwischen einem Text und einem Bild liegt also nicht darin, dass der Text sukzessiv, das Bild simultan wahrgenommen würde, sondern vielmehr darin, dass die Wahrnehmung des Textes als Vorgang in der Zeit einer medienimmanenten Steuerung unterliegt, die des Bildes hingegen nicht" (my translation).

18. *House of Fame*, book 1, 119–467.

19. Holsinger, "Lollard Ekphrasis," 76.

20. *Canterbury Tales*, fragment 1, line 2128.

21. Crane, *Gender and Romance in Chaucer's* Canterbury Tales, 34.

22. Johnston, *Performing the Middle Ages*, 107–16.

23. Patterson, *Chaucer and the Subject of History*, 169–230.

24. *Canterbury Tales*, fragment 1, line 1956.

25. Epstein, "'With many a floryn he the hewes boghte,'" 52.

26. Another typical example is the funny description of the sylvan gods' panic as they are deprived of their natural habitat when the trees are cut down to provide fuel for Arcite's funeral pyre (*Canterbury Tales*, fragment 1, lines 2925–30).

27. *Canterbury Tales*, fragment 1, lines 2128–29, 2138–44.

28. *Canterbury Tales*, fragment 1, lines 2155–65.

29. *Canterbury Tales*, fragment 1, lines 1885–92.

30. This is not entirely true, since there are medieval buildings that suggest an attempt to achieve the geometrical perfection of the circle. But precisely because these buildings are so uncommon in the Middle Ages have later scholars sought to explain them away in terms of precursors of the Renaissance—such as Frederick II's octagonal Castel del Monte in southern Italy. But as David Abulafia has pointed out, there need not necessarily be anything classical about an octagonal structure in the thirteenth century. In the case of the Castel del Monte, the geometrical structure resembles not so much that of a classical amphitheater or even of the Roman Pantheon but the typical column as is to be found in any Gothic cathedral that deserves its name (Abulafia, *Frederick II*, 280–89).

31. As Kolve, *Chaucer and the Imagery of Narrative*, 122, observes, the conflict between the geometrical order on the one hand, and the unruliness of the visual on the other is played out also on the level of the narrator's description of the images in the temples, which are "experienced as modally indeterminate, spatially unfixed, and devoid of any clear internal structure."

32. Nichols, "Ekphrasis, Iconoclasm, and Desire," 147.

33. Mitchell, *Picture Theory*, 5.
34. Allmand, *Hundred Years War*, 20–24.
35. Epstein, "'With many a floryn he the hewes boghte,'" 55.

BIBLIOGRAPHY

Abulafia, David. *Frederick II: A Medieval Emperor.* Oxford: Oxford University Press, 1988.
Allmand, Christopher. *The Hundred Years War: England and France at War c. 1350–c. 1450,* 20–24. Cambridge: Cambridge University Press, 1988.
Benson, Larry D., ed. *The Riverside Chaucer.* Reissued with a new foreword by Christopher Cannon. Oxford: Oxford University Press, 2008.
Bridges, Margaret. "The Picture in the Text: Ecphrasis as Self-Reflexivity in Chaucer's Parliament of Fowles, Book of the Duchess and House of Fame." *Word and Image* 5 (1989): 151–58.
Cheeke, Stephen. *Writing for Art: The Aesthetics of Ekphrasis.* Manchester: Manchester University Press, 2008.
Crane, Susan. *Gender and Romance in Chaucer's* Canterbury Tales. Princeton, NJ: Princeton University Press, 1994.
Epstein, Robert. "'With many a florin he the hewes boghte'": Ekphrasis and Symbolic Violence in the *Knight's Tale.*" *Philological Quarterly* 85 (2006): 49–68.
Giuliani, Luca. "Laokoon in der Höhle des Polyphem: Zur einfachen Form des Erzählens in Bild und Text." *Poetica* 28 (1996): 1–47.
Heffernan, James. *Museum of Words: The Poetics of Ekphrasis from Homer to Ashbery.* Chicago: University of Chicago Press, 1993.
Hollander, John. *The Gazer's Spirit: Poems Speaking to Silent Works of Art.* Chicago: University of Chicago Press, 1995.
Holsinger, Bruce. "Lollard Ekphrasis: Situated Aesthetics and Literary History." *Journal of Medieval and Early Modern Studies* 35 (2005): 67–89.
Johnston, Andrew James. *Performing the Middle Ages from* Beowulf *to* Othello. Turnhout: Brepols, 2008.
Klarer, Mario. *Ekphrasis: Bildbeschreibungen als Repräsentationstheorie bei Spenser, Sidney, Lyly und Shakespeare.* Tübingen: Niemeyer, 2001.
Kolve, V. A. *Chaucer and the Imagery of Narrative: The First Five Canterbury Tales.* Stanford, CA: Stanford University Press, 1984.
Lessing, Gotthold Ephraim. *Laocoön: An Essay on the Limits of Painting and Poetry.* Translated with an introduction and notes by Edward Allen McCormick. Baltimore: Johns Hopkins University Press, 1962.
Mitchell, W. J. T. *Picture Theory: Essays on Verbal and Visual Representation.* Chicago: University of Chicago Press, 1994.
Nichols, Stephen G. "Ekphrasis, Iconoclasm, and Desire." In *Rethinking the Romance of the Rose: Text, Image, Reception.* Edited by Kevin Brownlee and Sylvia Huot, 133–66. Philadelphia: University of Pennsylvania Press, 1992.

Patterson, Lee. *Chaucer and the Subject of History*. Madison: University of Wisconsin Press, 1991.

Rippl, Gabriele. *Beschreibungskunst: Zur intermedialen Poetik angloamerikanischer Ikontexte (1880–2000)*. Munich: Wilhelm Fink Verlag, 2005.

Simpson, James. *Reform and Cultural Revolution: The Oxford English Literary History*. Vol. 2, *1350–1547*. Oxford: Oxford University Press, 2002.

Stanbury, Sarah. *The Visual Object of Desire in Late Medieval England*. Philadelphia: University of Pennsylvania Press, 2008.

Steiner, Wendy. *The Colours of Rhetoric: Problems in the Relations between Modern Literature and Painting*. Chicago: University of Chicago Press, 1982.

Wandhoff, Haiko. *Kunstbeschreibungen und virtuelle Räume in der Literatur des Mittelalters*. Berlin: Walter de Gruyter, 2003.

CHAPTER TWELVE

Montaigne's Medieval Nominalism and Meschonnic's Ethics of the Subject

JACK ABECASSIS

In the words of Henri Meschonnic, "Nominalism is the only [theory of language] that permits an ethics of subjects, thus a politics of subjects. It was already in the sentence of Montaigne: 'Each man carries the entire form, of the human condition.'"[1] My concern in this chapter is to link Montaigne's formal arguments concerning the name and the sign to practical questions concerning ethics and politics, or more precisely, to the modalities of engagement in politics for a nominalist-skeptical thinker in the world as it is—"vivre du monde, et s'en prevaloir, tel qu'on le trouve" (to live in the world, and to take advantage of it, just as one finds it; III.10.1057).[2] The primary thesis of this chapter is that nominalism allows for Montaigne's skeptical yet active and constructive engagement with political realities, even those of cruel religious civil wars that were raging in France during the period of the writing of the Essais, 1562–98. These political realities cannot be underestimated as the palpable impetus behind the Essais' break with previous discourses about the self in the world. Moreover, Montaigne's alignment of language theory, ethics, and politics anticipates Henri Meschonnic's central thesis that language theory necessarily possesses historical and ethical dimensions; thus the title of his last book, Langage, histoire, une même théorie.[3]

Throughout Montaigne's Essais there lies a single and urgent series of questions: How does a critical thinker, who is also a self-styled aesthete, conduct his life amidst the folly of the world, amidst what he aptly designates as this universal shipwreck, cet universel naufrage? What forms and what range of self-stylization are available to a critical and aesthetic agent who must live out his life in a determined social and historical context? What exactly would philosophically warrant such a dissonant existence? Could linguistic nominalism, namely the idea that ahistorical "universals" are empty concepts devoid of any reality, except for wishful thought, become the theoretical foundation for a critical ethics of the subject (instead of an ethics of essentialized abstractions, collectivities) in the midst of vicious civil wars of religion?

In the *Essais* we encounter a series of answers to this tragic question; discourses written in the form of the "essayistic," rather clear answers to these questions. Yet these answers are occluded perhaps by a certain surface profusion of diverse opinions, myriad quotations, anecdotes seemingly unrelated, jokes, and laughter already anticipating the baroque self-conscious narratives of Lawrence Sterne, Montaigne's closest "fictional" analog.[4] The essayistic is a new discourse, a new poetic manner of posing and partially answering the most fundamental of philosophical questions concerning the contingency of becoming in real historical time, the plurality of sound opinions, the susceptibility of opinions and beliefs—the tension, in sum, between a critical *logos* and a custom-based *praxis* and the multiple expressions one Michel de Montaigne could give these perennial yet urgent questions.[5]

Nominalism, in particular in its medieval resonances better known as the *Quarrel of Universals*, plays a major role in Montaigne's conceptualization of the dissonances between thought and action, between the possibility of many realities and the crushing weight of a given reality not of one's choosing, a reality that we always misperceive, a reality that is always arbitrary and misnamed in some absolute sense—if indeed such reality existed and were available to us.

The apparent absence of the Middle Ages from Montaigne's *Essais* has often been noted. Montaigne was, for the most part, the product of his Hellenistic and Roman readings, a product of the moral imagination of Plutarch and Seneca, among others. And in good Renaissance fashion Montaigne pretended to skip over the medieval period, as if it did not exist. Yet at least three times in the *Essais* Montaigne explicitly engages nominalism, a theory of language, or rather I would contend, a mode of thought, an ethics and a politics, clearly derived in his case from multiple medieval sources, though Occam's conceptual semantics seem to dominate Montaigne's discussions of nominalism. The first instance is the essay "Des Noms," which starts with the pithy sentence "Quelque diversité d'herbes qu'il y ait, tout s'enveloppe sous le nom de salade" (No matter the diversity of herbs, everything envelops itself under the name of a salad; I.46.296) to which we will frequently make reference, with further elaborations in "De la gloire" (II.16), in which Montaigne decouples the notion of glory from the romance of the name. And then there is of course the centerpiece of the *Essais*, "L'Apologie de Raimond Sebond" (II.12), itself being of medieval vintage on two counts: first, its explicit engagement with late medieval natural theology and second, its ubiquitous engagement with nominalism. Antoine Compagnon sums up the "Apologie" with his characteristic precision in asserting that:

> the "Apologie" contradicts both Saint Thomas and the rational theology of Ray-
> mond Sebond and Natural theology, by deploying arguments similar to those of
> nominalism and following the same postulate of the separation of God from cre-
> ation, of the *potentia absoluta* from the *potential ordinate*. The primacy of evidence
> or of the sensible intuition end up being identical to fideism, as an ultimate re-
> course of man before God's *potentia absoluta*. And when Montaigne pronounces
> the irrevocable divorce of reason and faith, he is assuredly closer to Occam and the
> French nominalists, Nicholas, D'Autrecourt, Jean de Mirecourt ou Jean Gerson,
> than to Skeptics or Pyrrhonians.[6]

This medieval nominalism is foundational to Montaigne's enterprise of cre-ating a new mode of writing, the essay, a mode of writing that uses language that by its nature is "une masse d'argent vif" (a mass of mercury; III.13.1113), and whose subject is the capturing of this *branloire perenne*, the disorienting sto-chastic movement of a flowing Heraclitian world devoid of Platonic metaphysi-cal essences, and especially devoid of Hegelian historical totalizations of any kind. The essayistic "meaning" is in its flowing "form," expressed by a language whose own historicity is all too painfully evident to Montaigne, impervious to all clarity just as mercury is impervious to all pressure to conform. As per Henri Meschonnic's definition of poetry, the essay is precisely "a form of life trans-formed by a form of language and a form of language transformed by a form of life."[7] Few instances in world literature could offer a more vivid illustration of this definition of a poem writ large than Montaigne's *Essais*.

This radically and dynamic historicity of the sign is what some call today the "arbitrariness" of the sign. And the essayistic is the poetic form of discourse that is all too aware of this historicity/arbitrariness, a poetic discourse capable of expressing the swerve of having to act in a world dominated by fast-changing uncertainty.

Nominalism is known for its formal linguistic and logical dimensions. There are good reasons for this quarantining of nominalism to logical formalism, for, initially, the difference between realists and nominalists was born from the epistemological problem of the relation of thought to reality, the relationship of language to reality. The symbolic and pragmatic stakes here are enormous. To briefly sum up the realist/nominalist difference: realists believe that universals (especially, abstract ideas, general concepts that invite capital letters like God, Man, Humanity, the People, the Good, or even the Triangle) possess a reality before the thing and within the thing—*ante re* and *in re*. And, even more importantly, realism considers the existence of these essential realities that are independent of naming, independent of the material and concrete sign, as ontologically superior. The sensible name, whatever its quality, is always ontologically inferior to the intelligible essence. Many attributes (words, signs) may refer to one reality, whence the possibility of synonymy.[8] Thus *many* names, *many* sounds, *many* signs for *one* truth. The most felicitous destiny for an attribute is to cohere as closely as possible its contingent behavior with the essence of which it is but a secondary attribute; that is, to remain consistent and self-aware of its meaning, referent—its unchanging essence. When we say "Socrates was a Man" and then "Aristotle was a Man," the concept of Man is a universal of which Socrates and Aristotle are derived secondary instances or attributes—two individuations of that real singular, universal, and essential substance to which refers the name "Man."

You will have noticed in the logical realist position that universals exist independent of language. Language in fact constitutes a linguistic doubling of the Platonic ontology, where the questions inherent in the plurality and contingency of the sensible (e.g., multiple and imprecise languages) are resolved in the ontology of the "real" real, the forms, the essences.

The nominalists, on the other hand, refuse any realism of the essences, any attribution of reality to the essence. Nominalists claim that real existences can only be attributed to individuals, to particulars. What we naively assume to be an essence on the existential level is but a naive effect of language, a sort of infantile wish-fulfillment fantasy, and possesses an existence only *in voce*. Nominalism may be defined by two trenchant axioms: "Universals are words; only individuals exist."[9] Socrates and Aristotle were singular individuals who shared some attributes, attributes that by semantic analogies we call Man, which chain of analogies is really nothing but the hypnotic and narcissistic and megalomaniac effects of language. As the nominalists claimed, essences are just *flautus vocis*, literally breath of the sound, and thus a mere word, without a corresponding objective reality. Logical realists claim that we often mistake the particular for the general; nominalists claim that we often mistake the general for the particular. For the nominalists we are often victims of the fantasy of invisible universals, which somehow paradoxically we can name. The universals are nothing but the product of our desire for certainty and stability. Plato versus Heraclitus, in sum. Nominalists view Platonic ontology as a more sophisticated version of the primitive magical circle. It answers all questions as it provides a coherent narrative where, in reality, only stochastic randomness exists. Logical realism quiets the mind, bewildered as the mind is by the questions that arise from the randomness of real experience in the sensible, contingent world.

Nominalists were not far from the truth regarding the primacy of the particular over the universal, of movement over stasis. Only things are even more complicated.

For there is after all something logically and existentially necessary about assuming essences, attributing to essences an "as if" status, even if it is just by means semantic analogies (more about that below). We must allow, or rather pretend, that essences exist, all while being critically aware that they are just *flautus vocis*, that the logical realist dreams of drowning language's historical origins, its anthropological and historical specificities, in all manner of truth eternal, endowed languages with an amazing imperial reach. This is Montaigne's chief complaint against metaphysical thought throughout the *Essais*. In "Des Boyteux" he describes yet again our endless capacity for *flautus vocis*:

> Nostre discourse est capable d'estoffer cent autres mondes, et d'en trouver les principes et la contexture. Il ne luy faut ny matiere ny baze. Laissez le courre : il bastit aussi bien sur le vuide que sur le plain, et d'inanité que de matiere, *dare pondus idonea fumo* [*susceptible de donner poids à la fumé*]. (III.11.1072)

> Our discourse has capacity enough to provide the stuff for a hundred other worlds, and then to discover their principles and construction! It needs neither matter nor foundation; let it run free: it builds as well upon the void as upon the plenum, upon space as upon matter: *dare pondes idonea fumo* [likely to give heaviness even to smoke]. (Screech, 1161, modified)

Like Occam, Montaigne's arguments come down to this one: "the very notion of a singular entity present in a multiplicity of particulars is a contradiction in terms."[10] Again, this logical contradiction cannot really be existentially overcome, as it is impossible for us to think of particulars outside of a certain ontological realism, just as it is impossible to think of essential and totalized concepts outside of particulars, whence the eternal problem of God. When you or I think of concepts such as Good and Evil, Justice—or even a person—though we may pretend to think of them in their possible plurality and arbitrariness, their historical differences, in truth, both you and I have recourse to notions that we cannot but assume to be universal. (But we may assume these universalities in different ways, as we shall see below.) Logical realism must exist as a foil to any nominalism; or, alternatively, the two theories of language and meaning have a parasitical dependency on each other since Plato and Aristotle. They are alternative perspectives on languages, but alternatives that imply radically opposed systems of ethics.

Indeed, much of our current political debates and cultural posturing boils down to this inherent tension, often dissonant, between our desire for individualized and localized difference (cultural nominalism) and our de facto universalist judgments (logical realism). Think of the debate about female circumcision as a jarring starting point of playing this out in your mind. Montaigne's last sentence in "Des canibales": "tout cela ne va pas trop mal: mais quoy? ils ne portent point de haut de chausses" (All this is not too bad: but what? they do not wear breaches; I.30.221) always served in my mind as an important corrective to the apparent relativist thrust of the bulk of the essay. Is it a funny throwaway line? Montaigne's equivocal last line signifies what could be paraphrased as follows: "this radically other culture is all very interesting and entertaining. But the cannibals are so historically different than us that their worldview, and thus their conduct could in no account be considered normative with regard to our mores, as absurd and cruel as our mores may indeed be."[11] And, in a sense this same "yes, but" logic is the essence of what Antoine Compagnon shows in such fine detail in his book about Montaigne's nominalism. Montaigne, for example, intellectually understands the arbitrariness of proper names, his theoretical anti-romance of proper names. But when it comes to his own proper name and the relationship of his name to his father's name (Michel de Montaigne to Pierre Eyquem), nominalism takes a back seat to his vanity, his desire for difference and distinction, the poetic difference and distinction of the noble son against the prosaic merchant father, no matter how intrinsically inane and futile he ultimately knows these differences, these signifiers, to be. Or, seen differently, and perhaps more interestingly, being a good nominalist, Montaigne believes in the materiality of the sign, that the "meaning" of the sign resides in its signifier, and therefore there is indeed a world of social and historical difference between a Pierre Eyquem and a Michel de Montaigne. At least there and then in 1562 Gascony, the name is the thing—and probably today, too.

This necessity to think in terms not exclusively individual and the necessity to have recourse to universalist concepts, even if these universalist concepts are in the final analysis just wind, just (useful) words, is why nominalism does not reject in practice abstract entities such as Man in favor of purely concrete, singular and discrete entities, which would be sheer nonsense. It is one thing to say with Montaigne that *"Distinguo*, est le plus universel membre de ma Logique" (*Distinguo* is the most universal member of my Logic; II.1.355) and quite another to lead a life on the razor edge of pure Heraclitian continual movement and difference. Montaigne's sincere wish for dynamic and individuated distinction, the real time savoring of all the individual herbs instead of the collective salad, is a charming and utopian antidote to our natural narcissistic tendency to essentialize and totalize and collectivize our beliefs and desires—the ideological "salad" so typical of our daily lives, our common discourses—and no more so in times of vicious religious civil wars.

At any rate, nominalism understands more general concepts, let us call them "nominalist generalities," as instances of implied comparisons, with their potential for classifications by analogies, and so on. "Occam substitutes for universal the resemblances among individuals: the universal is nothing but that which can be predicated from a class of individuals by way of their resemblance, a mode of classification that stems from the mind [esprit], warranted by their resemblances, *actus intellegendi* or *intentio animae.*"[12] Of course, the logical impasse in nominalist thinking comes down to explaining away in nominalist terms the synthetic nature of comparative terms. For how can synthetic comparisons function outside of general ideas, upper- or lowercase universals? The predicates of a resemblance are not after all independent of other preexisting ideas, even more general. Upon close inspection most comparisons, most predicative analogies fall short, just as Montaigne emphatically insists that "La resemblance ne faict pas tant un comme la difference faict autre" (Likeness does not make things "one" as much as unlikeness makes them "other"; III.13.1111; Screech, 1208, modified). He then undercuts the notion of generalities as species existing on the basis of implied analogies, since he vehemently insists in his most lucid moments that "Toutes choses se tiennent par quelque similitude: Tout exemple cloche. Et la relation qui se tire de l'experience, est tousjours defaillante et imparficte: on joinct toutefois les comparaisons par quelque bout" (All things are connected by some similarity; yet every example limps and any correspondence which we draw from experience is always feeble and imperfect, we can nevertheless find some corner or other by which to link our comparisons; III.13.1116; Screech, 1213, modified). So the whole notion of a predicative analogy, a comparison of A and B that is capable of being projected and generalized to other terms, indeed the basis of so much of our practical daily thought, is undermined in Montaigne, even if he himself cannot escape using them. Nominalist semantics are superior to the logical realist position, notwithstanding the impossibility of purely thinking in terms of particulars; nominalist semantics are the best we can do with this imperfect tool of language, provided that we always remain skeptical or even ironic vis-à-vis its deployment, as Montaigne does throughout the *Essais*, which explains, at least in part, the comical dimension of the *Essais*.

You will have noticed by now that linguistic arguments about the nature of language are formal and logical in nature and have been almost always framed that way, both in sophisticated discussions of analytical philosophy as well as in continental histories of philosophy.[13] But already in the late Middle Ages the debate between logical realism and nominalism (or the "quarrel of universals") was pregnant with the potential for theological and eventually social heresy. Take for example the pivotal doctrine of original sin. How can one in fact account for original sin unless one asserts the ultralogical realist position that Man, Adam, is the substantial unity of many individuals: "Homo est multorum hominum substantialis unitas"?

The crucial difference here is that for logical realists the essential and totalized real is primary and language is its secondary attribute, akin to the Platonic difference between reality and appearance, where—and this is crucial—appearance nevertheless refers to a real essence, albeit obliquely or incompletely. Semantic nominalists, however, decouple language from any necessary correspondence to the nonlinguistic real; they attribute to language an autonomy vis-à-vis the real. In Occam's conceptual nominalism, nothing is a universal except by its signification to human speakers; in other words, through a historical process. Words become "universals" by the semantic process of attribution of similarities among disparate things. Culture is language indeed. The question for Occam is not as it was for Socrates, "What is X," say what is "virtue" *in re* and *ante re*, but rather what is the signification of the arbitrary word "virtue" in a given historical context as it is actually used by real speakers in specific discourses? What is the "universality" of an entity "X" as it can be inferred by analysis of comparisons and analogies and predicated from such an analysis in a given time and place? So, was Adam's sin universal in all senses of the word? Are we all just fragments of the (broken) unity that Adam possessed as an essentialized totality? Hardly . . . for that would be incompatible with even a "weak" nominalism where word or concept is transposed from the ontological to the historical presence of a situated human speaking, where "Vérité au deça des Pyrénées, erreur au delà" (Truth on this side of the Pyrenees, error on the other side)[14] primes over eternal truths and unities. In other words, there is in nominalism a serious decoupling between words and their seemingly logical realist meaning, even simply when they are uttered on "just" the opposite sides of the Pyrenees, let alone before and after Adam's sin. This is why nominalism always risks heresy, be it religious or political.

Nominalism posits that words and their meaning in the world of things are disunited in a radical fashion, regardless of our everlasting desire to reunite them: "Il y a le nom et la chose: le nom, c'est une voix qui remarque et signifie la chose; le nom, ce n'est pas une partie de la chose, ny de la substance: c'est une piece estragnere joincte à la chose" (There is the name and the thing: the name, [it] is a voice that remarks and signifies the thing; the name, [it] is not a part of the thing, nor of the substance: it is a foreign piece joined to the thing; II.16.655). There are two ways of understanding this statement. First, the arbitrariness of signifiers is a perennial formal aspect of language, absolutely and perennial discontinuous aspect of the sign, as structuralist semiology would have it. Second, and to my mind a more interesting understanding, the arbitrariness in signifiers is a byproduct of dynamic historical processes, vigorous evolutions by fits of discontinuation and accelerations, which renders the relationship of signifiers to meaning in an absolute sense unstable, seemingly arbitrary at the level of synchronicity, as Meschonnic would have it in his historical understanding of the arbitrariness of the sign.[15] This lexical tension within language can only be circumvented by the invention of a new form of discourse, the essay, where signifiers are set to a specific movement, a stylized swerve, within writing which endows the whole with specific, intelligible, and historical meaning. Part of this discourse, nevertheless, is its self-awareness of the problematic nature of its lexical and referential dimensions, its self-awareness of its mercurial contingency, self-awareness of its radical historicity.

Montaigne's nominalism and relativism are thus alloyed. And so is his desire, need, perhaps even his self-serving duty to act decisively in a sociohistorical world where almost all social and political actors act as if their language cohered with universal and essential truth not of their (historical) making. This is why Montaigne cannot but repeatedly decry the hollowness of official, ideological languages, their potential for pure gibberish if we cling to the logical realist position:

Nostre contestation est verbale. Je demande que c'est que nature, volupté, cercle, et substitution. La question est de parolles, et se paye de mesme. Une pierre c'est un corps: mais presseroit, Et corps qu'est-ce? Substance; et substance quoy? ainsi de suitte: acculeroit en fin le respondant au bout de son Calepin. On eschange un mot pour un autre mot, et souvent plus incongneu. (III.13.1116)

Our controversies are verbal. I ask what is nature, pleasure, circle or substitution. The question is about words: it is paid in the same coin. "A stone is a body." But if you argue more closely: "And what is a body?" "substance." "And what is substance?" and so on, you will eventually corner your opponent to the last page of his lexicon. We change one word for another, often for one less known. (Screech, 1213, modified)

In other words, the question to which Montaigne returns over and over again can be summed up as follows: if the logical realist conception of language is correct, why, when pressed for precise definitions in discussions of formal, logical philosophy, do we just exchange words for words? We define one universal for another; for example, *virtue* is doing the *good*, and the good is what is *right*, and so on. The identity of a "universal" is always established by displacements, similarities, analogies—all imperfect, all blunt tools, all circular at the end of the day. "On eschange un mot pour un autre mot, et souvent plus incongneu." (We exchange one word for another, and often more unrecognizable.) Each thoughtful reader of dictionaries knows that the only precise information in a dictionary entry concerns the etymological and historical discussions of the usage of a given word. If languages in the most abstract sense (*Langue*) were transparent and referred to universal concepts then their meaning with respect to nonlinguistic reality, which is always historical and contingent, would have been more easily available. Philosophical ontology would have reigned supreme over historical philology and poetic discourses. But the opposite is true, even among contemporaries belonging to the same culture, living in the same place: "Jamais deux hommes ne jugerent pareillement de mesme chose. Et est impossible de voir deux opinions semblables exactement: non seulement en divers hommes, mais en mesme homme, à diverses heures" (Never did two men ever judge identically about anything and it is impossible to find two opinions which are exactly alike, not only in different men but in the same man at different times; III.13.1114; Screech, 1210, modified). Most discussions among us concern what we (really) meant when we said something. Even at the most intimate and mundane level, the meaning of words, gestures, tone, body language just vacillate, their meaning constantly negotiated, like a mass of mercury trying to be squeezed by two speakers.

But if words, as Montaigne believed, were at once material and contingent, referring only to individuals and/or partially true analogies, even when in the guise of general ideas, if one presupposed the *in*existence of essences and of their totalizations in language and acts, then the ethical and political implications would be of major import. There would be the possibility of a nominalist ethos, which is precisely one of the most strident leitmotifs of Montaigne's third book of the *Essais* where, within essayistic discourse, skeptical modalities and linguistic nominalism are explicitly translated to the realm of social practice.

Let me first paint the difference of nominalism and realism with respect to individuals and humanity in stark terms: I am quoting here a passage from Henri Meschonnic's book *Heidegger ou le national essentialisme*:

From the realist point of view, humanity exists, and men are fragments of humanity. From the nominalist point of view, individuals exist, and humanity is the
ensemble of individuals. The example confirms that concerning language, as
Saussure says . . . there are but points of view. Here, the two points of view . . . are
true. But the logical, ethical and political consequences are not at all the same.
Realism, about humanity, presupposes a generalized essentialization, as a precon-
dition. The individual is melted into this mass, indistinctly . . . There are cultures
where the notion of an individual does not exist, he is but an element of the group.
As in the *oumma*, in the religious fusional sense in Islam.[16]

At heart, says Meschonnic, and he is absolutely right, give me your theory of
language and I'll surmise your ethics and your theory of history. The self in
nominalist thought can never accomplish itself in the becoming of the community, be it Rousseauist or Islamist, can never fuse itself in the totalized identity
of the community, race, country to the detriment of all else.

Meschonnic again:

The logical realism of Heidegger is the linking of a chain of essentializations. There
is the essentialization of the infinitive *to be* and of the German people. And the *self*
only accomplishes itself in the "becoming of the community, of the people—*das
Geschehen der Gemeinschaft, des Volkes*" [Being and Time, §72], as a community of
destiny, *Schicksal*. The essentialization of the language. German.

And Meschonnic continues:

We should recall the example of the medieval discussions about *humanity*. The
cult of real essences. The essentialization of the group, it is the group first, the
individual is just a fragment of it. Logical consequence: ethics is obsolete [*cadu-
que*] as a thought and as a stake [*enjeu*] of subjects. The group is synthesized in the
"thought of the race," *Rassegedanke*, underlining *Gedanke*, thought.[17]

For the realist, this chain of essentializations culminates in the complete
dehumanization of the enemy per se, and all the devastating consequences
therein—the Saint-Barthélemy massacre, for example, where individuals, fragments of a false humanity (that is, no longer subjects of any kind) were liqui-
dated one by one, fragments of an essentialized falsehood. But in contradistinction, to the extent possible, the nominalist remembers that essence is just an
effect of language, a historically constructed and highly mutable *flautus vocis*,
the illusion that the metaphorical and classificatory capacity of language confers upon speakers who project their wishes upon a fantastic, transcendental

realm. In nominalism, language is a contingent factor and real individuals, Pierre and Jacques, exist apart from the essentializations attributed to them by language, namely Catholicism, Protestantism. This is true even in extreme circumstances such as religious civil wars where for historical or pragmatic reasons, essences are pragmatically assumed on a certain rhetorical level, where it becomes most efficient or expedient to essentialize contingent differences.

It is in this fragmented, Heraclitian light that the very equivocal sentence "Chaque homme porte la forme entière, de l'humaine condition" (Every man carries the entire form, of the human condition; III.2.845) makes nominalist sense within the internal logic of Montaigne's *Essais*, as opposed to the sentence's possible logical realist sense. In the logical realist reading this sentence signifies that each individual carries within himself an irreducible essence that corresponds to human essence writ large independent of concrete human existence, *ante re* and *in re*. This sounds good in a decontextualized vacuum. What happens, however, when two subsets of "humanity which is one" are set on annihilating each other precisely because the other subset is presumably no longer a part of the real covenant of humanity, the spirit of the time, the officially sanctioned *geist* of the moment, the "right" direction of History. Nominalism is interested precisely in this kind of a messy situation, and its reading of "Chaque homme porte la forme entière, de l'humaine condition" would then signify the following: Each person possesses the potential for a bewildering range of emotion, judgment and action, thus for change, for difference within that which is human. Our individuating potential to adapt tactics, to construct strategies to confront what is presented to us as the real is paradoxically our truest and most authentic "universal." "The universal," says Meschonnic, "is the infinite diversity of specificity, to be realized each time for itself, by itself, to be recognized as such by all other specificities."[18] The "universal" is a dynamic and historical capacity for action, thought, and passion. The universal is not a preexisting essence containing a set of positive propositions that dictates our lives as if from the outside. It cannot be subsumed by the collective, as if it were an ontological genetic code invisibly dictating its essence onto our seemingly contingent actions. The essence is not something out there to which we must correspond, call it God or Being or Spirit—or the true essence of the French or especially German *Langues*. The enemy in front of me, though at times I must fight him for real and legitimate reasons (think of the United States circa 1860), is an individual, just as human as I am who in the flux of historical time, by accident or by choice, has adopted tactics and strategies that set him on a collision course with me. For Montaigne, such "enemies" may have been members of his own family who sided with the Protestant camp. And therefore on the most practical level—a fight there might be, but there can be no undue cruelty, no vicious violence, no torture, no slow burning of the live person at the stake, no gratuitous subsuming of the particular into the whole.

Again, each of the two interpretations of "la forme entière, de l'humaine condition" makes sense in its own right. Each, understood in an extreme manner—that is, that meaning exists only in the universal or that only individuals exist—is ultimately a utopian position, for individuation can only exist as a foil of an assumed universality and, conversely, assumed universality can only be experienced in terms of individuations directly or by elaborate analogies, be it God or the Platonic Forms of the Pure Language of the Race, as per Heidegger. We are, I would say, almost biologically hardwired to think in terms of the logical realist "universality" and therefore hardwired to resist nominalism. It takes much more energy and discernment to think and act along nominalist norms of perception, judgment, and action. The universals, and the thought that we might correspond to and defend their essence in our historical lives, constitute a set of propositions just too congenial with our penchants toward lazy thinking, narcissism, and aggression, penchants toward being blind as to why we do what we do. Universality of meaning is assumed, one way or the other. The only truly critical question, therefore, pertains to whether this "universality" (generalized analogy) is of our human and historical making (nominalism) or whether it has an independent existence outside of the human mind (logical realism).

For Montaigne, it seems to me, the human condition for an active agent, endowed with a critical mind and with a sharp sense of an aesthetic self-fashioning, is that of ironic self-consciousness clothed in the mantle of duty and honor. "J'ay peu me mesler des charges publiques, sans despartir de moy, de la largeur d'une ongle, et me donner à autruy sans m'oster à moy" (I have been able to engage in public duties without going even a nail's breath from myself, and to give myself to others without taking myself away from me; III.10.1053; Screech, 1139). This is baroque irony, not romantic irony. This is the constructive irony of an active agent, a courtier of sorts, engaged at times with the center of power, not the petulant irony of resentment of someone living at the margins of civil society. This irony runs more along the lines of Gracian than Rousseau.

Now, let us transpose this reading of the *l'humaine condition* to the level of politics and war. The group demands, as prerequisite to (violent) action, a belief in essences. The group may also demand, and for legitimate reasons at times, to wage war against another group. I am thinking here especially about civil and religious wars where there most often is shared belief on both sides that the enemy is no longer a part of humanity, that the enemy by its beliefs and actions, is essentially no longer human, a fallen humanity made up of fragments, each of which—that is, each individual within the enemy group—representing a full totalization of the fallen nature of the group and therefore condemned a priori as an individual, no longer endowed with any subjectivity, and thus not a sub-ject of ethics. But, what we call today "identity" is always at variance with the critical individual's awareness of the nonsense of the social world, its contin-gency, its arbitrariness, his or her awareness that what is *Vérité en-deçà* is also *erreur au-delà*. This is exactly the point in Montaigne where nominalism, skepti-cism, and relativism conflate and create the possibility of an ethics, an effective ethics of the subject, ethics for individuals, as opposed to an ethics for groups (if an "ethics of the group" is not oxymoronic to begin with).

It follows then that action within the nominalist perspective, even in the most necessarily violent of circumstances, must be subjected to ethics of the subject whenever possible. It also follows that outside of individuals living and acting in real time and place, no theory of ethics makes sense. This is what Meschonnic means by the ethics of subjects as opposed to the ethics of essences. For there is no ethics of *Being*. It is a symptom of a totalitarian mirage. Heidegger, Nazism, being its epigones.

So only if we understand humanity as an ensemble of individuals can "Chaque homme porte la forme entière de l'humanité"—in any meaningful sense. Otherwise, this is just another hollow platitude, soon forgotten in the heat of the struggle for power. This is the nominalist understanding of this crucial sentence in Montaigne. This is also why Montaigne, as we shall now see, chose the Theban general and statesman, Epaminondas, subject of one of the *Lives* of Plutarch, as his exemplum for moral compass, as the ultimate example to broker the continual negotiations we must always undertake between means and ends, between *l'utile* et *l'honnête* in this universal shipwreck, *cet naufrage universel*.

In the first essay of book III of the *Essais*, entitled "De l'utile et de l'honeste" (On the Useful and the Honest), Montaigne poses the same urgent question present through all the *Essais* concerning the possibility of humane, reasonable and practical conduct in a violently insane world. In fact the first essay of book III mirrors the same concerns of the very first essay of book I "Par divers moy-ens on arrive à pareille fin" (By diverse means we reach the same end); namely, what could be the practical criteria for conduct, we would call now "decision making" under extreme duress and uncertainty. In "De l'utile et de l'honeste," Montaigne starts with a classical Ciceronian topos, the opposition between utility and honesty. The question addressed here regards the optimal relationship between *means* and *ends* in the context of necessary action in a world that cannot be radically reengineered to cohere with a single idea of the Good. *Utility* will be akin to unconstrained instrumental thinking; *honesty* (decency, honor, uprightness) will be akin to adherence to a strict code of historical morality, of ethics, of class ethos whenever possible. Under normal circumstances our actions are an admixture of both. But in civil religious wars, a limit case of ethics, *l'utile*, the useful, the expedient, the purely instrumental is all too often exercised with malice precisely because each and every individual member of the classification designated as the enemy is a fragment of an essentialized totality that must be destroyed. The heretic. The infidel. The traitor. Brothers, after all, are the most vicious of enemies. In war, the *distinguo* just disappears, sometimes overnight, as we saw in so many recent cases from the Balkans to Rwanda to Iraq and Syria, and others. To repeat Meschonnic yet again: on the level of practical ethics, logical realism presupposes a generalized essentialization, and thus the individual is melted in this mass of what some may fantasize as being the historical *geist*, indistinctly—and ethics, understood as ethics of the subject, ethics with regard to real, distinct individuals just disappears, becomes a nonquestion. This is precisely what Montaigne resists. And this explains why Montaigne starts this essay on ethics with the seemingly too general, equivocal sentence "Personne n'est exempt de dire des fadaises: le malheur est, de les dire curieusement" (No one is free from uttering stupidities: the harm lies in doing it curiously; III.1.829, Screech, 891), which I take to mean in this context: We must live in this world as it is, none is exempt from the unpleasant idiocy of acting, taking positions, eventually making mistakes in "cet universel naufrage"; but that does not mean that we must act *curieusement*, that we act viciously, that we fall pray to the narcissistic delusions of essentialized tribalism, fanaticism of every hue. To avoid acting *curieusement* we must avoid attributing to particular herbs the status of a totalized and essentialized salad, which confusion leads to the commission of indiscriminate violence such as the massacre of the Saint-Barthélemy and countless other acts of gratuitous violence carried out during Montaigne's life.

Given our fallen nature, and given the right set of circumstances, there indeed is nothing more natural for human beings than to act violently, Montaigne concedes—he is a close reader of Augustine. Our narcissistic and aggressive penchant in such circumstances is to essentialize differences and to totalize particulars so that we may legitimize our sadism—and no cruelty can match the one occasioned by religious, sectarian civil wars. The narcissism of little differences precipitates grand cruelty. "Ils nomment zele, leur propension vers la malig-nité, et violence" (They name zeal, their propension toward malice, and violence; III.1.833). Montaigne is lucid and sanguine in his philosophical anthropology:

> Nostre estre est simenté de qualité maladives: l'ambition, la jalousie, l'envie, la vengeance, la superstituion, le desespoir, logent en nous, d'une si naturelle pos-session, que l'image s'en recognoist aussi aux bestes: voire et la cruauté, vice si desnaturé: car au milieu de la compassion, nous sentons au-dedans, je ne sais quelle aigre-douce poincte de volupté maligne, voir souffrir autruy: et les enfans la sentent. (III.1.830)

> Our being is cemented together by qualities which are diseased. Ambition, jeal-ousy, envy, vengeance, superstition and despair lodge in us with such a natural right of possession that we recognize the likeness of them even in animals too— not excluding so unnatural a vice as cruelty; for in the midst of compassion we feel deep down some bitter-sweet pricking of malicious pleasure at seeing others suffer. Even children feel it. (Screech, 892)

Violence thus is *not* an error in judgment, as we naively think all too often today. It is actually what comes most naturally to us, just as Saint Augustine explained in the *Confessions*—and children are not exempt, nor is Montaigne him-self who includes himself in the *nous* that experiences the "aigre-douce poicte de volupté maligne [de] voir souffrir autruy."[19]

So the struggle for Montaigne is really triple. First, we must accept that the tautological real is what it is and that no angelic positions or posturing is possi-ble. Second, we must theoretically resist the essentialization of each and every particular, thus the nominalist and skeptical formal arguments as the theo-retical bedrock for a nominalist ethics. Third, we should strive to overcome our innate violent penchants, for which, incidentally, there is no better alibi than identity or racial essentialization and totalization. The combination of the tautological cruelty of the real, the desire to essentialize and the pleasure taken in inflicting pain make it all but impossible to escape the "machine" of total vio-lence, the lot of every war, but especially of civil wars and revolutions. And this is why the main ethical point in "De l'utile et de l'honeste" concerns the active management of "cet universel naufrage." And this also is why the historical ex-ample of Epaminondas, subject of one of Plutarch's *Lives*, is the "pivot point" of this essay on ethics. Montaigne deploys Epaminondas in order to become ex-plicit in his rejection of any ethics that is not an ethics of the subject, an ethics of *distinguo. La raison d'état*, in all its variants, what Montaigne calls *l'interest commun*, should never subordinate our capacity to discern particulars, individuals, subjects. This pivotal passage is worthy of full quotation:

> Ne craignons point après un si grand precepteur [Epaminondas], d'estimer qu'il y a quelque chose illicite contre les ennemys mesmes: que l'interest commun ne doibt pas tout requerir de tous, contre l'interest privé: *manente memoria etiam in dissidio publicorum foederum privati iuris [le souvenir du droit privé survivant même en pleine dissolution des traités entre Etats]*
>
> > *et nulla potentia vires*
> > *Praestandi, ne quid peccet amicus, habet:*
> > [*et aucun puissance n'a la force de contraindre un ami à mal agir*]
>
> Et que toutes choses ne sont pas loisibles à un a homme de bien, pour le service de son Roy, ny de la cause generale et des lois *Non enim patria praestat omnibus officiis, et ipsi conducit pios habere ciues in parentes. [En effet la patrie ne prévaut pas sur tous les devoirs et il lui importe de compter des citoyens respectueux envers leurs parents.*] C'est une instruction propre au temps: Nous n'avons que faire de durcir nos courages par ces lames de fer, c'est assez que nos epaules le soyent: c'est assez de tramper nos plumes en ancre, sans les tramper en sang. (III.1.843)

> After so great a preceptor [Epaminondas] let us not fear to think that some things are unlawful even when done to enemies or that common interest cannot require all men to sacrifice all private interest always: *manente memoria etiam in dissidio publicorum foederum privati juri* [the memory of individual rights subsisting even in the strife of public abominations] *et nulla potentia vires*
>
> > *praestandi, ne quid peccet amicus, habet*
>
> [no might has the power to authorize a friend to act wickedly] and that not all things are legitimate to a man of honor at the service of his king for the cause and commonwealth and its laws. *Non enim etiam patria praestat omnibus officiis, et ipsi conducit pios habere cives in parentes* [The claims of our country are not paramount over all other duties: it is to have citizens who are dutiful to their kindred]. There you have a lesson proper for our own times. It is enough that the ironplate of our armor should give us calloused shoulders, there is no need to make our minds callous as well; it is enough to plunge our pens in ink without plunging them in blood. (Screech, 905)

What is the function of Epaminondas in Montaigne's argument? He exemplifies nominalist ethics of the subject carried out in the flux of time, particularly of violent times. The following propositions are easily deduced from Montaigne's deployment of the exemplum of Epaminondas:

1. That some vicious actions are even illicit against legitimate enemies. Moral and ethical rules do not bind us only with respect to allies—friendship, for example, primes over politics, wherever and whenever possible.

2. That there is permanent and inherent tension between public interest and private interest; no Heideggerian fusion of the self into the "Becoming of the community" is ever possible—nor imaginable nor even desirable.

3. That a free man (*un homme loisible*) must not blindly obey the wishes of his prince, nor even the implied actions seemingly required by the formal application of impersonal law.

4. That there will always be a gap between our private and public personae; that even when actions are taken we can certainly lend our shoulder to a rightful cause but we do not necessarily need to merrily slaughter (*ces lames de fer*).

In sum, Epaminondas, reputed for his mercy in battle and especially mercy toward his vanquished enemies, shows the concrete functioning of a nominalist ethics; he is the exemplum that warrants an ethics of individual ethical *distinguo*, whenever and wherever possible. Epaminondas is hardly then this relic of times long gone, of a nostalgic yearning for nobility as some critics may see it.[20]

Montaigne identified with Epaminondas because he recognized in the Theban general and statesman a grand exemplum of *distinguo*, a form and a life of measured sanity lived out in the violent flux of history. In the French wars of religion the enemy might have been your brother, your wife's uncle, your next-door neighbor, your colleague and close collaborator. Epaminondas, for Montaigne, is the name for discernment in a world gone mad; a world where naming leads to killing, where naming and labeling are killing.

What kind of ethics can there be for a person who is engaged in politics and at the same time, in his *arrière boutique* as Pascal will call it, resists all essentializations and totalizations, all salads and envelopes? Here is Montaigne's Epaminondas-like response:

> Pour moy, je sçay bien dire: Il fait meschamment cela, et vertueusement cecy. De
> mesmes, aux prognostiques ou evenements sinistres des affaires, ils veulent, que
> chacun en son party soit aveugle ou hebeté: que nostre persuasion et jugement,
> serve non à la verité, mais au project de nostre desir. (III.10.1058–59)

> For my part I can easily say, "He does this wickedly, that virtuously." Similarly,
> when the outlook or the outcome of an event is unfavorable, they want each man

to be blind and insensible toward his own party, and that our judgments and convictions should serve not the truth but to project our desires. (Screech, 1146)

In other words, *distinguo* is the name for an ethics of the particular, of the subject precisely because the subject is the opposite of essentialized totalities that want to subvert all thinking and judgments to the interest of the group. Ethics can only exist where there are individuals, perceived and dealt with as such, with discernment—as subjectively subjects.

This is how a most abstract medieval controversy about the nature of language had such a pivotal impact on Montaigne's poetics, ethics and ethos, just one more example of how certain aspects of the Middle Ages, both religious and secular, far from representing relics surmounted by the Renaissance, Enlightenment, and Modernity, continue to be present in Montaigne and in a powerful contemporary thinker like Henri Meschonnic, pertinent and urgent today, just as it was for Montaigne.

NOTES

1. Henri Meschonnic. *Heidegger ou le national-essentialisme* (Paris: Editions Laurence Taper, 2007), 14. All translations of Compagnon and Meschonnic are mine.

2. All references to Montaigne's *Essais* refer to the new Pléiade edition: Michel de Montaigne, *Les Essais*, ed. Jean Balsamo, Michel Magnien, and Catherine Magnien-Simonin (Paris: Pléiade, 2007). Unless otherwise noted, I used, with occasional modifications, the following translation of Montaigne: Michel de Montaigne, *The Complete Essays*, trans. M. A. Screech (London: Penguin Books, 1991). Where Screech is not referenced, the translation of Montaigne is mine.

3. Henri Meschonnic, *Langage, histoire, une même théorie* (Paris: Verdier, 2012).

4. My readings of Cervantes, Sterne, and Diderot and eventually their relationship to the essayistic models of Montaigne have been much informed by Robert Alter's seminal book on this subject, *Partial Magic: The Novel as a Self-Conscious Genre* (Berkeley: University of California Press, 1979).

5. This formulation of the philosophical moment as well as the question/answer "problematology" implied throughout this essay is inspired by my readings of Michel Meyer, in particular here, *Pour une histoire de l'ontologie* (Paris: Quadrige, 1999). First published 1991 by PUF.

6. Antoine Compagnon, *Nous, Michel de Montaigne* (Paris: Seuil, 1980), 23.

7. Henri Meschonnic, *La rime et la vie* (Paris: Gallimard, 2006), 430.

8. Ferdinand de Saussure, *Ecrits de Linguistique Générale* (Paris: Gallimard, 2002), 74–75.

9. Compagnon, *Nous, Michel de Montaigne*, 25.

10. Ibid.

11. Specifically, I am thinking here about the concluding comments in favor of relative conventionalism made by the speaker designated as "B" in Diderot's *Supplément au voyage de Bougainville*, which undermine the thrust of all the previous seemingly universal arguments.

12. Compagnon, *Nous, Michel de Montaigne*, 27.

13. See for example, Claude Panaccio, *Les mots, les concepts et les choses: La semantique de Guillaume d'Occam et les nominalismes d'aujourd'hui* (Paris: Vrin/Bellarimin, 1992), 19.

14. Blaise Pascal, *Pensées*, ed. Michel Le Guern (Paris: Gallimard, 1977), 72.

15. Meschonnic, *La rime et la vie*, 79.

16. Meschonnic, *Heidegger ou le national-essentialisme*, 12–13.

17. Ibid., 148–49; see in the text of Meschonnic the precise page references to Heidegger.

18. Meschonnic, *Langage, histoire, une même théorie*, 726.

19. Saint Augustin, *Confessions*, book 3.

20. See for example Philippe Desan, *Montaigne, les formes du monde et de l'esprit* (Paris: PUPS, 2008), 164.

CHAPTER THIRTEEN

The Pèlerinage Corpus in the European Middle Ages

Processes of Retextualization Reflected in the Prologues

URSULA PETERS

Present-day medieval literature scholars have come to acknowledge the great extent to which medieval literature is a textual practice of rewriting.[1] This concept exceeds by far what has, until recently, been taken as a feature of medieval literature production, performance, and manuscript tradition, subsumed under the notions of editing, multiple versions, or variance. In fact, it denotes the basic specificity of medieval textuality, which Stephen G. Nichols—as early as the late 1980s—defined as "Material Philology."[2] He illustrated this using example cases of textual productivity constitutive of medieval manuscripts. The implications of this textual concept have since been extensively and controversially debated in terms of the history of manuscript tradition and the theory and practice of text editing; however, not so much in terms of its implications regarding poetics and literary systematics.

This can be clearly seen in the literary-historical treatment of texts, which—like the so-called *Pèlerinage* corpus—trace back to the work of one known author, namely the *Pèlerinage de vie humaine*, written around 1330 by the Cistercian Guillaume de Deguileville,[3] a Cistercian monk of Chaalis. The text was rewritten multiple times throughout the following centuries and unfurls in a variety of textual formations.[4] However, in the world of scholarly research, the text still tends to be referred to under the name of Guillaume de Deguileville, the author of the original text; it is "simply" taken to have undergone an extraordinarily varied spread and development, ultimately triggered by the author himself.

The internal transformation processes have only come into focus in recent years. In her seminal contribution from 2003, Fabienne Pomel[5] illuminated

these processes, examining the prologues and incipits of some of the French
Pèlerinage texts in terms of their poetological and functional historical aim.
However, looking at the *Pèlerinage* corpus in particular, it does not make sense
to limit one's view only to the French section, since *Pèlerinage* texts have been
translated into various other languages and were continually rewritten from the
early fifteenth century onward. These texts must also be regarded as genuine
constituents of the *Pèlerinage* corpus, giving it a decidedly European dimension.[6] In the following, I would like to illustrate ten stages of these retextualization processes.

Stage 1: From its very beginning, the textual history of the *Pèlerinage* corpus
was one of retextualization. It did not undergo a material rewriting of an existing text as such, but was rewritten on a conceptual level of discourse traditions.
The very first *Pèlerinage* text by Guillaume de Deguileville, the *Pèlerinage de vie
humaine* written in 1330/31, is set upon the backdrop of the *Roman de la Rose*
even in the opening verses of the prologue: "En veillant avoit lëu, / Considere et
bien vëu / Le biau roumans de la Rose. / Bien croi que ce fu la chose / Qui plus
m'esmut a ce songier / Qui ci apres vous vueil nuncier" (While I was awake, I
had read, studied, and looked closely at the beautiful Romance of the Rose. I am
sure that this was what moved me most to have the dream I will tell you about
in a moment; 9–14; Clasby, 3). Thus it sets up a particular range of expectations,
in which the following dream allegory positions itself anew.

Simultaneously, there is a definite ideological recoding of the dream report
typical of the genre: The Cistercian's Jerusalem dream leads to an arduous path
of the dreamt first-person *pelerin* persona, pointing to the spiritual perils of
human life from birth to death. In any case, Guillaume de Deguileville systematically overwrites the *Roman de la Rose* adventures of the *amant* persona
in the garden of love with the spiritual counter-concept of the *Pèlerinage de vie
humaine.*[7]

Stage 2: Exactly at this point, the next stage of the rewriting sets in, since
some of the many manuscripts offer a significantly different version, the so-
called second edition. It seems to have undergone quite a pronounced editing
process, even showing content-related changes from the first transcript of the
Pèlerinage dream of 1330: in a new prologue,[8] the persona of the first-person narrator reports to have written down the dream immediately upon awaking, still
somewhat *sommeilleus* (sleepy; 22), in order not to forget it and despite not having fully grasped its meaning. However, before having a chance to *corrigier et
ordener* (amend and adjust; 36) the whole of it, as was his original plan, the text—
tout mon escript (my whole text; 32)—had been taken from him and circulated

without his knowledge and against his will. He explains that only now, after such a long time, despite having forgotten much of the dream, will he attempt a revision (*amendement*; 60) of it.

This *Pèlerinage* dream correction,[9] positioning itself expressly in 1355, has been called the final authorized second *Vie* version. It was in circulation up until the sixteenth century. It did not, though, achieve the same outstanding success as the first version.

Stage 3: This ideological "revision" from 1355 shows a close connection to the two subsequent texts: the *Pèlerinage de l'ame*[10] and the *Pèlerinage de Jhesu Crist*.[11] Intratextual evidence suggests that they also date from the late 50s in the fourteenth century.[12] For this reason, medieval literature scholars assume that the *Pèlerinage* author, Guillaume de Deguileville, went through a second phase of extensive literary activity of rewriting and text continuation; this took place around the years 1355–58, a good twenty-five years after the writing of his first dream allegory, thus leading to the accruement of the *Pèlerinage* corpus. This corpus of texts was subsequently passed on in a variety of manuscript combinations until the beginning of the sixteenth century.[13]

The *Pèlerinage* texts were translated in the first part of the fifteenth century, possibly even at the very beginning of the century. Although the increasing bundling of the three texts during the fifteenth century would lead us to assume that the complete trilogy corpus would have been translated, it was in fact—with the exception of the Latin prose trilogy of the Arsenal Codex 507[14]—only the case with the individual texts: the two versions of the *Vie* texts as well as the *Ame* and *Jhesu Crist* continuations. They were translated into English, German, Dutch, Spanish, and Latin, both in verse and in prose versions.[15]

Stage 4: In France, however, the 1465 prose *Vie* version[16] constituted a definite break. According to its dedication prologue, it originates from an unnamed cleric from Angers, who claims to have been commissioned to write it by his patroness Jeanne de Laval, second wife of René d'Anjou. This prose version, rather than the 1330/31 verse version, ended up determining the print history of the *Pèlerinage de vie humaine*.[17] These print versions very accurately distinguish between the *Prologue du translateur* (prologue of the translator), that is, the dedication prologue of the prose editor of Angers, and the real *prologue* of the prose *Vie* text. The writer behind this is the original author, the author known by the name Guillaume de Deguileville. He is identified as the *acteur*. The speech of this *acteur* then turns into that of the *pelerin* within the embedded narrative of the dream. Toward the end, after the awakening and reflections on the general meaning of this pilgrimage dream, the character of the *acteur* becomes apparent again through the first-person narrator's requests for possible corrections of this dream report.

The prints thus offer a subtle differentiation of the various textual voices of *translateur– acteur–pelerin* through the distinct rubrication of speech.

Stage 5: The prints of the second *Vie* version are a different matter. The Parisian printers/publishers Anthoine Vérard[18] and Berthold Remboldt (in cooperation with Jean Petit)[19] use the second verse edition of the *Pèlerinage de vie humaine* at the beginning of the sixteenth century. It is the first part of a large *Pèlerinage* trilogy, namely a revised version by an unnamed Cistercian from Clairvaux.[20] This Clairvaux editor gets his own strophic *prologue*, in which he explains his textual source, his intentions, and poetic activities. He claims to base this print version on the second *Vie* edition of 1355. He justifies his choice in the editor's prologue, recapitulating the textual history of the *Pèlerinage de vie humaine* as consisting of three steps from the authentic work by one known author, the deterioration, and restoration: He says that the *Pèlerinage* text by Guillaume de Deguileville was originally written in good and nicely set rhymes, that it was subsequently *beaucoup deprauee* (badly damaged; 18), but now "bien reparee a moult grans peines et travaulx" (well repaired through great effort and hard work; 21) by a monk of Clairvaux. He holds the unnamed prose editor (of Angers) responsible for this literary decline. He claims that the prose editor translated the original verse text into prose using his *plaisant stile* (good style; 48), but into a *prose mal ordie* (disorderly prose; 52). Moreover, he reports that this poor prose edition is based on the first *Vie* version, to whose faultiness the author himself testifies in his prologue: "Raison adonc est quon la reiecte / Puis quainsi a verite derogue" (It is therefore reasonable to reject it since in this way it has degraded the truth; 63).

So there are two levels of reasoning: first, a poetological-rhetorical level, emphasizing the antithesis between verses as *bonne rime* (good rhyme; 18), *plaisant stile* (good style; 48), or *compose bien elegamment* (elegantly written; 3) and prose as *langue rural* (country language; 38); second, a thematic-ideological level, taking into account the original author's intent and its authorization of the second edition.

Stage 6: This second *Vie* version from 1355, however, had been translated into English verse[21] in the years 1426–28, even before the successful French prose edition of 1465. The most important points of this translation are found in a *prologue off the translatour* (5), whose author has often, but somewhat rashly,[22] been taken to be John Lydgate: This unnamed translator provides information about the famous source in his address to "ye worldly folk" (1): "the book Pyl-grimage de Movnde," full of moral instruction and virtue, offering profound matter (114–18). He names "my lord / Of Salysbury, the noble manly knyht, / Wych in France, for the kyng ys Ryht, / In the were hath meny day contunye" (122–25) as the patron of the English translation; this is Thomas Montague, 4th Earl of Salisbury and second husband of Alice Chaucer, granddaughter of Geof-frey Chaucer. Apparently, the said Montague regularly sojourned in France in the 1420s as the supreme commander of the armed forces and an ambassador of the Duke of Bedford, the king's brother and at that time the regent of France.[23] He found himself in France in 1426, specifically when he—*beying at Parys* (157)—commissioned the translator to translate the book.

The English verse translation of the preface of the second *Vie* version sets in with the subsequent *prologue of the auctour* (6): the reflections of the author regarding the provisional notes of a dream, written in a groggy state, which have been spread throughout the world against his will. This *auctour*-prologue is followed by the first-person narrative of the Jerusalem dream under the header *Here begynneth the pelgrym* (9). This instance also shows the subtle dif-ferentiation of levels of narration typical of certain parts of the *Pèlerinage* tradition.[24]

Stage 7: It is certainly no coincidence that from the closer social circles of this English verse translation of the second *Vie* edition—that is, the highest nobility of England, Latin, and French prose versions of the second text, the *Pèlerinage de l'ame*—also emerge. For during Duke John of Bedford's time as the regent of France, more precisely between 1422 and 1427, the cleric Jean Galloppes—*dit le Galois* (known as *le galois*)—claims to have been commissioned by this Duke not only to produce a prose version of the French *Pèlerinage de l'ame*,[25] but also a Latin translation.[26] Even the layout of the French version shows an impressively rubricated, tiered beginning of the text. It differentiates between the prose edi-tor, the *composeur en prose*, and the *translateur* (translator). This *translateur*, how-ever, serves as the speaker of the original prologue; that is, he appears in the first person adopting a self-reflective gestus of the dreamer and writer, who, in the *Pèlerinage de l'ame* version, is otherwise called *acteur* (author).

The Latin translation solves this problem of first-person narrator categoriza-tion differently: the translator, Jean Galloppes, figures as *actor*, whereas the first-person narrative by the original author, the highly revered Cistercian prior Guillaume, is not categorized any further. In any case, the *Ame* version diverges significantly from the *Vie* version in terms of its speaker margins.

A recent examination of the Parisian Arsenal Codex 507, an early sixteenth-century collection of three different parts,[27] has given rise to the assumption that Jean Galloppes, who is also known to have translated Ps.-Bonaventura's *Meditationes Vitae Christi*, had possibly even translated the complete *Pèlerinage* corpus into Latin. Up until then, it had often been presumed to contain only a Latin *Ame* version. However, it offers a Latin *Peregrinatio* trilogy (fol. 117r–270v) containing the very dedication prologue of the French and Latin prose versions of the *Pèlerinage de l'ame*.[28]

Stage 8: The *Pilgrimage of the Sowle*, the English prose *Ame* version,[29] stands somewhat apart from these transformations of *Pèlerinage* texts belonging to the second phase of retextualization of 1355–58. In its early manuscripts it has also been passed on under the title of *Grace Dieu* (God's Grace). Its explicit clearly dates this version to 1413; this gives rise to the assumption that it stems from the original *Ame* text of Guillaume de Deguileville, and has thus arisen independently of the French prose version by Jean Galloppes. But it also seems to hold a somewhat exceptional position within the retextualizations of the *Pèlerinage*, which the publisher Rosemarie Potz McGerr has called "Englishing" (xxix–xlv). This version does not give evidence as to any preceding text or author, and dispenses with the usual prologue link to the *Pèlerinage de vie humaine*; however, it starts with an autonomous dream report and subsequently diverges quite significantly from the French source. This detachment of the *Grace Dieu* from the *Pèlerinage* cycle does not seem to have worked well in terms of its reception. In any case, at least one manuscript[30] is preceded by the *Pilgrimage of the Lyfe of the Manhode*, an English prose translation of the *Pèlerinage de vie humaine*,[31] presumably dating back to around 1430.

Stage 9: The *Pèlerinage* corpus has, however, made its way into the German and Dutch linguistic and literary area especially via the initial text.[32] The Rhenish-Franconian and the Cologne area have even produced two versions. The first one, the Cologne *Pilgerfahrt des träumenden Mönchs* (Pilgrimage of the Dreaming Monk),[33] offers a programmatic first-person prologue by the translator, explaining about the author and the high prestige of the French source, who, in the face of his humble abilities, is planning to translate from French into German for *den ungeleerden luden* (for the unlearned; 36) with the help of God's grace. We can quite confidently deduct the identity of the author of this German 1430 verse version through intratextual evidence and an additional rhymed preface concerning the activities of the translator. It is clearly Peter von Merode: He was recorded as being a Cologne priest, a canon to Cologne's

Chapter of St. Severin, secretary to the Counts William I and Reinald IV of Jülich and Geldern and once an interpreter for Duke Louis of Orléans.[34] In a countermove to the translator's originally outlined frame, this textual mediator subsequently proceeds to write himself so strongly into the first-person narrative of the preceding text, that he ends up taking over the level of the dream's experience throughout. He keeps this role right through to the end without falling back into the role of the translator.

However, the second verse version of the Berleburg illuminated codex[35] does not show any evidence as to a separate translator—quite possibly because the initial part of this manuscript is missing. It begins right in the middle of the *Pèlerinage* prologue with his report about the dream of Chaalis Abbey, which the first-person narrator declares to have recently experienced. From there onward, this version also completely foregoes any adaptation of the historical and biographical information regarding the translation's circumstances. This verse version is the basis for two manuscripts from the mid-fifteenth century containing prose versions of the *Pilgerfahrt*.[36] Those two do not seem to contain an autonomous preface by the translator, either—if we follow the complete Darmstadt version.

Stage 10: The Dutch prose versions,[37] however, turn the author's prologue of the *Pèlerinage de vie humaine* into a preface by the translator. He asks St. Mary for strength and meaning in order to be able to translate *dit gloriose werck* (this glorious work; 185.22) titled "De pelgrimagien vander menscheliker creaturen" (The Pilgrimage of the Human Creature; 185.22) from French *in Dietscher talen* (into German; 185.23), which has been written by a holy father, a Chaalis Abbey monk. All other information given by the first-person narrative of the source's prologue is provided in the third person: The translator tells about the *Roman de la Rose*, read by the monk, which—as the monk himself relays in his prologue—seems to have spawned a dream vision, which may be helpful to all. This is followed by a marked cut and the dreamer's embedded first-person narration. Just as in the Cologne verse version, this perspective persists until the end without going back to the translator's initial frame.

The Dutch print versions even do away completely with any frame in the form of a translator's preface. In terms of their design, which serves to establish an order, they also take decidedly different paths from the more or less contemporary French print version. The French version has the distinction of differentiating between the *translateur* (prose editor) and the *acteur* (original author of the *Vie* text) in the layout of the text. Thus it not only elucidates the internal structure of the text, but also the complex textual history of the source. The

Dutch print versions do not contain this technique of creating a textual hierarchy to explicitly outline their structure.

In the print version of Jacob Bellaert (Haarlem, 1486),[38] however, it is the picture cycle that establishes a hierarchy within the text and its narrative levels. The majority of woodcuts consist of two parts: the specific illustration of the text, always including a sleeping figure in the left or right margin of each picture. Throughout the picture cycle, this figure serves as a constant reminder of the framing prologue pointing to the dream to follow; additionally, it provides the text with a continuous commentary. It explicitly refers to the embedded narrative as a report of a dream.

These ten stages provide an overview of the *Pèlerinage* corpus on the European field of retextualization, at least in terms of complete texts. Finally, I would like to bring up some of the points that have arisen during the examination of the materiality of each textual transformation, and look at them in some detail.

Textual productivity through possible combinations: At the beginning, the two verse versions of the *Pèlerinage de vie humaine* tended to be handed down as single texts; however, toward the end of the fourteenth century they were increasingly transmitted in connection with the succeeding texts, as a *Pèlerinage* trilogy, but occasionally also as a combination of the *Vie* and *Ame* texts. The range of combinations of the French prose versions is somewhat narrower: Other than the single dominant tradition of the prose *Pèlerinage de vie humaine* of 1465, there are few manuscripts with the same kind of connection to the prose version of the succeeding text by Jean Galloppes.[39] There also does not seem to be a prose trilogy that contains the *Pèlerinage de Jhesu Crist* in French prose.

The French print edition concentrates even more heavily on the single prose *Vie* text. Only Anthoine Vérard seems to have produced a combination of the *Vie* and *Ame* prose texts in 1499.[40] In the early sixteenth century, the three *Pèlerinage* texts are only printed as a verse trilogy under the title *Roman des trois Pèlerinages* (Romance of the Three Pilgrimages). It contains, in a special form, the second *Vie* edition as the first part, edited by an unnamed Cistercian of Clairvaux.[41]

Since the translations concentrate only with some exceptions on the first version of the *Pèlerinage de vie humaine*, this single text tradition naturally dominates both manuscripts and print versions. Only the English prose *Pilgrimage* tradition shows a connection with the two original *Pèlerinages*; this is similar to that of the French area. Additionally, the Parisian Arsenal Codex 507, even offers a Latin prose trilogy with a prologue by Jean Galloppes, who figures here as the translator of the three *Peregrinationes*.

Technical book design and layout: The manuscripts tend to be magnificently illustrated. Clearly the technical book design and layout plays an exceptionally determinant role with regard to the text. The primary purpose of the design of pictorial decorations, categorization, rubrication, speech structure, and metatextual commentary, is to establish an order. These elements place the respective texts differently. To start, the two versions of the *Pèlerinage de vie humaine* differ strongly already on the material level of the illustration technique. In the case of the first text, a number of manuscripts use a frontispiece and categorized commentary to directly call upon the backdrop of the *Roman de la Rose*. In the second edition, however, the frontispieces mask this literary allusion and tend to make reference to the learned world of spiritual instruction.[42] In another instance, the frame of royal patronage is used: Some of the magnificent manuscripts use their dedication frontispiece to incorporate the prose version of the first text, as well as the French and Latin *Ame* prose texts, into this frame.

The complete print tradition, however, foregoes a pictorial unfolding of this level, despite the fact that these texts also contain a dedication prologue of the prose editors including detailed information regarding their respective patrons. These print versions, on the other hand, have perfected the functional possibilities of the layout technique of establishing a registral structure through headers, book and chapter indices, summaries, rubrication of speech, and captions. Thereby they seem to subject the *Pèlerinage* texts to a veritable scholarly systematization.

The voices of rewriting: The complicated first-person narrative typical of dream allegory texts undergoes a remarkably varied differentiation of textual voices throughout its various stages of rewriting: There is a basic distinction between *acteur/aucteur* and *pelerin* speech through distinct subcategorized graphic markings of speech within the embedded narrative of the dream's story. It also includes the marking of characters by captions and thus lays bare a downright narratological differentiation between the narrative levels of the dream's protagonist and the narrative voice, in the same way as the *Roman de la Rose* tradition.[43] This is not true, however, for the translations. Most of them do not show a pronounced terminological marking of the internal levels of the first-person narrative comparable to the *acteur* marking.

The French tradition of the *Pèlerinage* corpus, however, successively expands on this very technique of textual speech marking. Thus the prose tradition not only distinguishes between the first-person narratives of the *pelerin* and the *acteur*, but also denotes that of the *translateur*, the unnamed prose editor.

The print editions systemize finally these distinctions through a marking of the various narrative levels of the prose *Vie* version: The *pelerin* character figures on the level of the embedded narrative of the dream; the *acteur*, as Guillaume de Deguileville, is located on the level of the discourse frame of the prologue and epilogue; and, finally, the *translateur* is the prose editor—the "I"—of the dedication prologue. The Remboldt and Vérard prints of the second *Vie* version even set in with a programmatic prologue by a *correcteur* (corrector), which is preceded by the *Prologue de lacteur* (author's prologue). But not all editors feature so prominently in the textual authorship; some are just mentioned in the explicit; for example, the 1499 print version of Mathias Husz talks about a *messire Pierre Virgin* (master Pierre Virgin), who is said to have it "diligentement veu et corrige jouxte le stile de celluy qui la tourne de rime en prose" (meticulously revised and amended according to the style of the person who transformed it from rhyme into prose).[44]

In the end, the various translators and (prose) editors of the translations remain mostly anonymous, even if some translator prologues do exist. Only the Latin prose *Ame* version, even the complete Latin *Peregrinato* trilogy of the Arsenal Codex, contains a dedication prologue featuring the very Jean Galloppes who also seems to be responsible for the French prose version of the *Pèlerinage de l'ame*. The Cologne verse translation of the *Vie* text hints at the identity of its author. These hints are easily decoded. Also, the Spanish print of the prose *Vie* text dating back to 1490 mentions the translator explicitly in the colophon as Vincente de Mazuelo.[45]

Verse and prose: The earliest prose versions do not refer to the core text of the corpus, but to its successor, the *Pèlerinage de l'ame*. It was possibly translated into English prose as early as the beginning of the fifteenth century, in the year 1413. The French and Latin prose versions also refer to this general period: the 1420s. This time preference of the prose version becomes even more obvious in the first *Pèlerinage* text. It had been translated into English prose (1430) even before the unnamed cleric of Angers claimed to have begun working on his French prose edition (1465). However, the third *Pèlerinage*, the *Pèlerinage de Jhesu Crist*, which is translated into Dutch verse, does not seem to have been given a prose edition at all, at least not as a separate text.[46]

The German *Pèlerinage* adaptation, however, goes somewhat against the grain of these early prose translations. It does not start with a prose version, but rather with a verse translation (circa 1430). This seems to be followed midcentury by a second independent verse translation, which itself turns into the source for two prose solutions (1470/80), thus showing the beginnings of an independent corpus formation.

Finally, the English verse translation of the second *Vie* edition holds a special position in the *Pèlerinage* corpus formation. It was also written in the 1420s and is based on a version that does not seem to have been translated otherwise.

The future of the reception of the *Pèlerinage de vie humaine* in France belonged to a 1465 prose edition. It seems to have determined the complete print history with only few exceptions. This means that the first *Vie* version is the formative source of its late medieval reception. This is also true for the translations into other languages. They are also based on the first *Vie* version, with the exception of the 1426 English verse translation.

The second version, in contrast, does not seem to have received a prose edition. On the contrary: both early sixteenth-century print versions seem to downright propagate, through their decidedly poetological verse prologue of the unnamed Cistercian editor, a programmatic connection of this *Vie* version to great style, authentic content, and verse. Thus this version not only receives special prestige, but also a marginal position in the late medieval *Pèlerinage* corpus.

From manuscript to print: The process from manuscript form to print editions meant a significant reduction, not only of the textual basis, but also of its possible textual combinations. The printing focuses on separate texts, primarily the *Pèlerinage de vie humaine*: in Romance languages, it is primarily the prose version of 1465. Anthoine Vérard and Berthold Remboldt are the only ones to have printed the (edited) verse version of the second *Vie* edition in the beginning of the sixteenth century. It is, however, only the first part of a *Pèlerinage* trilogy.[47] In the Netherlands, the print versions of the late fifteenth century are based on the prose *Pelgrimagie*, whereas the German *Vie* texts of the *Pilgerfahrt des träumenden Mönchs* (Pilgrimage of the Dreaming Monk), as well as the Latin *Peregrinatio* (Pilgrimage) texts, do not seem to have been printed at all. In England, however, the early 1413 *Ame* translation was printed by William Caxton in 1483.[48] A corpus compilation of several printed *Pèlerinage* texts remains a definite exception for which there is only proof within the French tradition.

Function and literary historical context: From its very beginning, this textual corpus about a dream allegory is, through the functional proposition of all prologues and epilogues, inscribed with highly prestigious spiritual teachings about life and the soul. Even the Cistercian author of the very first text stresses the relevance of his dreams to all mankind, thus writing it down for the good of all. The editors and translators continue this line of reasoning and point to the "dignite de la sapience dessus dicte et le grant prouffit qui puet ensuir de la cognoistre" (dignity of the foresaid wisdom and the great benefit which could be the result of knowing this),[49] the "materys ful profovnde" (profound matter; 11), "so contemplatyff" (which induces contemplation; 119), "notable to be rad and songe" (which brings one to a higher level through reading and singing; 118),[50] which, according to the Cologne translator, "den wech der wairheit leert" (teaches the road to truth; 23) and thus makes a translation worthwhile. In the end, the print versions even put these ambitious functional goals of "bons exemples et salutaire enseignement" (good examples and teachings to reach salvation)[51] of the prose prologue into the titles and headers: "Cy commence le tres prouffitable et vtile liure pour cognoistre soy mesmes" (Here begins the very useful and profitable book which leads to self-knowledge)[52] "si vtilement pour le salut de lame" (so useful for the soul's salvation)[53] or "ful of deuoute maters touchyng the sowle" (filled with devotional material concerning the soul).[54] Through this self-description, the separate textual editions tie into an overall claim of spiritual validity and thus establish a European *Pèlerinage* corpus incorporating all separate texts.

These myriad *Pèlerinage* texts, however, also belong to a variety of very distinct literary historical contexts, from which they derive their specific literary significance. Thus Guillaume de Deguileville's *Pèlerinage* trilogy specifically ties into the fourteenth-century allegorical dream tradition prevalent in France since the success of the *Roman de la Rose*,[55] whereas the English *Pèlerinage* translations originating from royal circles compete with the prestigious texts by Geoffrey Chaucer, Thomas Hoccleve, or John Lydgate.[56] Through its recourse to the French source, the textual corpus of the *Pilgerfahrt des träumenden Mönchs* (Pilgrimage of the Dreaming Monk) takes a special position within the German literary scene of the fifteenth century and seems to owe its existence to local nobility taking an interest in the reception of French literature on the basis of their family relations to French dynasties.[57] This is similar to the case of the *Chanson de geste* adaptations in the circles of Elisabeth of Nassau-Saarbrücken.[58] And the Spanish printed prose version of the *Pèlerinage de vie humaine* (1470) seems to be a part of specific devotional literature in Dominican circles in the late fifteenth century.[59]

Most strikingly noticeable, however, is the lack of any Italian *Pèlerinage* translations. It may be the case that the overwhelming presence of Dante's *poema sacro*, the *Divine Comedy*, is responsible for this lack; it may have fully soaked up any literary imagination of the fifteenth century as conveyed by the *Pèlerinage* dream allegory. But this is a problem of regional literary interests, which have to be examined on a broader level.[60]

NOTES

An enlarged German version of this chapter has been published: Ursula Peters, "Das *Pèlerinage*-Corpus im europäischen Mittelalter: Retextualisierungsprozesse im Spiegel der Prologe," *Zeitschrift für deutsches Altertum und deutsche Literatur* 139 (2010): 160–90.

1. See for instance Douglas Kelly, *The Conspiracy of Allusion: Description, Rewriting and Authorship from Macrobius to Medieval Romances* (Leiden, Köln: Brill, 1999); Franz Josef Worstbrock, "Wiedererzählen und Übersetzen," in *Mittelalter und frühe Neuzeit: Übergänge, Umbrüche und Neuansätze*, ed. Walter Haug (Tübingen: Niemeyer, 1999), 128–42; Britta Bußmann et al., eds., *Übertragungen: Formen und Konzepte von Reproduktion in Mittelalter und Früher Neuzeit* (Berlin: de Gruyter, 2005); Joachim Bumke and Ursula Peters, eds., "Retextualisierung in der mittelalterlichen Literatur," special issue, *Zeitschrift für deutsche Philologie* 124 (2005).

2. See, as a continuation to the discussion of the "New Philology" concept of the issue of *Speculum* (January 1990), Stephen G. Nichols, "Why Material Philology? Some Thoughts," in "Philologie als Textwissenschaft: Alte und neue Horizonte," ed. Helmut Tervooren and Horst Wenzel, special issue, *Zeitschrift für deutsche Philologie* 116 (1997): 10–30.

3. J. J. Stürzinger, ed., *Le Pèlerinage de vie humaine de Guillaume de Deguileville* (London: Nichols and Sons, 1893); Eugene Clasby, trans., *Guillaume de Deguileville: The Pilgrimage of Human Life* [Le Pèlerinage de la vie humaine] (New York: Garland, 1992).

4. See the survey of Edmond Faral, "Guillaume de Digulleville, moine de Chaalis," in *Histoire littéraire de la France*, Tome 39 (Paris: Académie des Inscriptions et Belles-Lettres, 1962), 1–132, and recently the most important anthology, Frédéric Duval and Fabienne Pomel, eds., *Guillaume de Digulleville: Les Pèlerinages allégoriques* (Rennes: Presses universitaires, 2008), and the two (forthcoming) *Pèlerinages* volumes, Marco Nievergelt and Stephanie A. Viereck Gibbs Kamath, eds., *The Pèlerinages Allegories of Guillaume de Deguileville: Authority, Tradition, and Influence* (Woodbridge, 2013); Andreas Kablitz and Ursula Peters,, eds., *Mittelalterliche Textualität als Retextualisierung: Das Pèlerinage-Corpus des Guillaume de Deguileville im europäischen Mittelalter* (Heidelberg: Winter, 2013).

5. Fabienne Pomel, "Enjeux d'un travail de réécriture: Les *incipits* du *Pèlerinage de Vie humaine* de Guillaume de Digulleville et leurs remaniements ultérieurs," *Le Moyen Age* 109 (2003): 457–71; see also Philippe Maupeu, *Pèlerins de Vie humaine: Autobiographie et allégorie narrative, de Guillaume de Deguileville à Octovien de Saint-Gelais* (Paris: Champion, 2009).

6. For the relations of the French, English, and Latin versions, see Richard K. Emmerson, "Translating Images: Images and Poetic Reception in French, English and Latin Versions of Guillaume de Deguileville's Trois Pèlerinages," in *Poetry, Place, and Gender: Studies in Medieval Culture in Honor of Helen Damico*, ed. Catherine E. Karkov (Kalamazoo: Medieval Institute Publications, Western Michigan University, 2009), 275–301.

7. See, for instance, Sylvia Huot, *The Romance of the Rose and Its Medieval Readers: Interpretation, Reception, Manuscript Transmission* (Cambridge: Cambridge University

Press, 1993), 207, and Sarah Kay, *The Place of Thought: The Complexity of One in Late Medieval French Didactic Poetry* (Philadelphia: University of Pennsylvania Press, 2007), 70–94, 198–202.

8. See Philippe Maupeu's transcription of the prologue in the manuscript Paris, BNF, fr. 377, fol. 1r/1v: Duval and Pomel, *Guillaume de Digulleville*, 40, et seq.:. I am grateful to Philippe Maupeu for providing me with his manuscript transcription of the second version of the *Vie* text in advance of the publication he is planning together with Graham Robert Edwards.

9. See above all Huot, *Romance of the Rose*, and Kay, *Place of Thought*.

10. J. J. Stürzinger, ed., *Le Pèlerinage de l'ame* (London: Nichols and Sons, 1895).

11. J. J. Stürzinger, ed., *Le Pèlerinage de Jhesucrist* (London: Nichols and Sons, 1897).

12. The *Pèlerinage de l'ame* between 1355 and 1358; the *Pèlerinage de Jhesu Christ* in 1358.

13. See Géraldine Veysseyre, "Liste des manuscrits des trois 'Pèlerinages' de Guillaume de Digulleville," in Duval and Pomel, *Guillaume de Digulleville*, 425–53.

14. See note 28 below.

15. See the (incomplete and somewhat erroneous) list of manuscripts and prints of the French *Pèlerinage* texts and their translations in Clasby, *Guillaume de Deguileville*, xxxv–xliv, and especially the introductions to Nievergelt and Viereck, *Pèlerinages Allegories of Guillaume de Deguileville*, and Kablitz and Peters, *Mittelalterliche Textualität als Retextualisierung*.

16. It is not yet edited, but there exists a sort of summary on the basis of the picture cycle of one of the manuscripts: Anne-Marie Legaré, *Le Pèlerinage de Vie humaine en prose de la reine Charlotte de Savoie* (Bibermühle, Rotthalmünster: Antiquariat Tenschert, 2004).

17. See Michael Camille, "Reading the Printed Image: Illuminations and Woodcuts of the *Pèlerinage de la vie humaine* in the Fifteenth Century," in *Printing the Written Word: The Social History of Books circa 1450–1520*, ed. Sandra Hindman (Ithaca, NY: Cornell University Press, 1991), 259–91, and Maupeu, *Pèlerins de Vie humaine*, 305–32.

18. Paris, 1511: Paris, BNF, Rés. Ye 24; see http://gallica2.bnf.fr/ark:/12148/bpt6k722 969; my quotations are from Harvard, Houghton Library, FC. G 9455 D. 511v.

19. Paris, 1517: Paris, BNF, Rés. Ye 213; see http://gallica.bnf.fr/ark:/12148/bpt6k714 54p. For the relation to the Vérard print, see Edmond Faral, "Guillaume de Digulleville, Jean Galloppes et Pierre Virgin" in *Études romanes dédiées a Mario Roques par ses amis, collègues et élèves de France* (Paris: Droz, 1946), 89–102, who seems to favor the idea that Remboldt printed his *Pèlerinage* trilogy in about 1500, which means before Vérard (97). But see the arguments for 1517 of Maupeu, *Pèlerins de Vie humaine*, 316n1, which are more convincing.

20. The trilogy print of Remboldt/Petit ends with a reference to Clairvaux: "Cy finist des pelerinaiges / lutile et notable romant / En sentences et en langaiges / Tout gay mygnot et tout plaisant / Et touteffoyz denotement / Traitant tout ce quest necessaire / A chascun por son sauvement/Acquerir et pour a dieu plaire. A dieu graces. Clereualx" (Here ends the useful and valuable Romance of the pilgrimages, which in both its teachings and language is totally agreeable and pleasant and is always precisely dealing with

232 Rethinking the New Medievalism

everything which is necessary to obtain salvation and please God. By the Grace of God. Clairvaux; 433).

21. F. J. Furnivall, ed., *The Pilgrimage of the Life of Man, englisht by John Lydgate, A.D. 1426, from the French of Guillaume de Deguileville, A.D. 1335,* edited from three fifteenth-century manuscripts in the British Museum: Cotton, Vitellius, C XIII (vellum, imperfect); Cotton, Tiberius, A VII (vellum, a fragment); and Stowe 952 (paper, completed by John Stowe about 1600), vol. 1 (London: Kegan Paul, Trench, Trübner, 1899; reprint, Millwood, NY: Kraus, 1978).

22. See Kathryn Walls, "Did Lydgate Translate the 'Pèlerinage de vie humaine'?," *Notes and Queries* March-April (1977): 103–5, but also the reference to Lydgate's translation in a book list from 1466: Carol M. Meale, "Reading Women's Culture in Fifteenth-Century England: The Case of Alice Chaucer," in *Mediaevalitas: Reading the Middle Ages,* ed. Piero Boitani and Anna Torti (Cambridge: D. S. Brewer, 1996) S. 81–101, esp. 86.

23. See Jenny Stratford, *The Bedford Inventories: The Worldly Goods of John, Duke of Bedford, Regent of France (1389–1434)* (London: Research Committee of the Society of Antiquaires of London, 1993), and recently Frédéric Duval, "La mise en prose du *Pèlerinage de l'âme* de Guillaume de Digulleville par Jean Galopes," *Romania* 128 (2010): 394–427, esp. 403–10; 129 (2011): 129–60.

24. For the differentiation of these voices, see Stephanie Anne Viereck Gibbs Kamath, "Periphery and Purpose: The Fifteenth Century Rubrication of the 'Pilgrimage of Human Life,'" *Glossator* 1 (2009): 36–55, esp. 42, etc., and her new book *Authorship and First-Person Allegory in Late Medieval France and England* (Woodbridge: Boydell and Brewer, 2012), 147, etc.

25. See the dedication prologue in Paris, BNF, fr. 602, fol. 1rv; transcription by Duval, "La mise en prose" (2011): 149–52.

26. See the dedication prologue in London, Lambeth Palace Library, F 13, fol. 1r–2r. A Latin version of the *Pèlerinage de l'ame* must have been completed before April 7, 1427, because it is on this day that the Parisian cleric Jean Thomas got twenty-two *livres tournois* (for having copied two books) from the Duke of Bedford. One of these books is a "livre en latin intitule le pelerinage de lame en prose; le quel contient XII cayers de parchemin" (a Latin book titled the pilgrimage of the soul in prose, which has twelve quires in parchment). A certain "J. Galoys" (obviously Jean Galloppes, *dit le Galois*) estimates the cost of these books; see this notice in the Bedford papers, in *Letters and Papers Illustrative of the Wars of the English in France during the Reign of Henry the Sixth, King of England,* ed. Joseph Stevenson (London: Longman et al., 1864), 2:415; or Stratford, *Bedford Inventories,* 12n43.

27. The collection assembles print and manuscript parts: The second part is a manuscript with a Latin *Peregrinatio* trilogy (fols. 117r–270v), which goes back to the fifteenth century. For a detailed examination of the codex, see Frédéric Duval, "Du nouveau sur la tradition latine de Guillaume de Digulleville: Le manuscrit-recueil Paris, Bibl. de l'Arsénal 507", *Scriptorium* 64 (2010): 251–67.

28. In a slightly different form referring to the two other *Pèlerinage* texts of the trilogy: The comment on the "libro peregrinacionis anime" (book of the pilgrimage of the

soul; London, Lambeth Palace, F 13 fol. iv) is expanded in this manuscript to "libro de peregrinatione humana ac secundo volumine intitulato de peregrinatione anime tertio intitulato de peregrinatione Jhesu Cristi" (book of the human pilgrimage and the second volume titled pilgrimage of the soul and the third volume titled pilgrimage of Jesus Christ; Paris, Ars. 507, fol. 117r). For a short discussion of this Latin copy, see Frédéric Duval, "Deux prières latines de Guillaume de Digulleville: Prière à Saint Michel et Prière à l'ange gardien," in Duval and Pomel, *Guillaume de Digulleville*, 185–211, esp. 187; more detail is provided by Duval, "Du nouveau sur la tradition latine," and Sebastian Riedel, "In latinum redegi: Zu den lateinischen Transformationsprozessen der *Pèlerinages* des Guillaume de Deguileville," in Kablitz and Peters, *Mittelalterliche Textualität als Retextualisierung*.

29. Rosemarie Potz McGerr, ed. *The Pilgrimage of the Soul: A Critical Edition of the Middle English Dream Vision*, vol. 1 (New York: Garland, 1990).

30. MS M: Melbourne, State Library of Victoria, ˣ096/G 94.

31. Avril Henry, ed. *The Pilgrimage of the Lyfe of the Manhode*, vol. 1 (Oxford: Oxford University Press, 1985).

32. In the context of *Pèlerinage* translations, it is remarkable that there exists a translation of the *Pèlerinage de Jhesu Crist* of about 1470 in Middle-Netherlandish verse; see MS Bruxelles, Bibliothèque Royale, 15657.

33. Adriaan Meijboom, ed., *Die Pilgerfahrt des träumenden Mönchs: Nach der Kölner Handschrift* (Bonn: Schröder, 1926).

34. On the documentary evidence of this Peter von Merode, see Hans J. Domsta, *Geschichte der Fürsten von Merode im Mittelalter* (Düren: Dürener Geschichtsverein, 1974–81), 1:234, 2:442, 2:455; 2:470; 2:481; 2:499–502.

35. Aloys Bömer, ed., *Die Pilgerfahrt des träumenden Mönchs: Aus der Berleburger Handschrift* (Berlin: Weidmann, 1915).

36. Darmstadt, Hessische Landesbibliothek, 201; Hamburg, Staats- und Universitätsbibliothek, Cod. germ. 18 (not complete); see the microfiche edition of this prose version: Ulrike Bodemann, ed., *Guillaume de Deguileville: Die Pilgerfahrt des träumenden Mönchs: Farbmikrofiche-Edition der Handschrift Hamburg, Staats- und Universitätsbibliothek, Cod. Germ. 18* (Munich: Lengenfelder, 1998).

37. Ingrid Biesheuvel, *Die pelgrimage vander menscheliker creaturen: Een studie naar overlevering en vertaal- en bewerkingstechniek van de Middelnederlandse vertalingen van de Pèlerinage de vie humaine (1330/1331) van Guillaume de Digulleville met een kritische editie van handschrift Utrecht, Museum Catharijneconvent BMH 93* (Hilversum: Verloren, 2005).

38. See Ingrid Biesheuvel, ed., "Het boeck vanden pelgherijm," 2005, http://www .dbnl.org/tekst/_boe007boec01_01/colofon.php.

39. MS S: Soissons, Bibliothèque municipale 208; see Legaré, *Le Pèlerinage de Vie humaine*, 235–37.

40. See Faral, "Guillaume de Digulleville, Jean Galloppes et Pierre Virgin" 95.

41. The Vérard print of 1511 promises with its title "Romant des trois pelerinaiges" (Romance of the Three Pilgrimages) and in the table of content a trilogy, but only the first text is actually printed.

42. See Ursula Peters, *Das Ich im Bild: Die Figur des Autors in volkssprachigen Bilderhandschriften des 13. bis 16. Jahrhunderts* (Köln: Böhlau, 2008), 147.

43. See especially Sylvia Huot, "'Ci parle l'aucteur': The Rubrication of Voice and Authorship in *Roman de la Rose* Manuscripts," *SubStance* 17, no. 2 (1988): 42–48.

44. Paris, BNF, Rés. Ye 26, fol. M 6r; see also Le Noir (Lyon 1506): Paris, Ars., 4° B, 2848, fol. U6r; for the role of this Pierre Virgin, see Maupeu, *Pèlerins de Vie humaine*, 310.

45. Maryjane Dunn-Wood, "*El pelegrinage de la vida humana*: A Study and Edition" (Ph.D., University of Pennsylvania, 1985).

46. An exception seems to be the Latin prose trilogy of Paris, Ars., 507, with a prose version of a *Peregrinatio Jhesu Cristi* (Pilgrimage of Jesus Christ; fol. 229r–270v).

47. In the case of Anthoine Vérard, it is only a plan; see note 41 above.

48. Katherine Isabella Cust, ed., *The Booke of the Pylgremage of the Sowle: Translated from the French of Guillaume de Deguileville, and Printed by William Caxton an. 1438 with Illuminations Taken from the Ms. Copy in the British Museum* (London: Basil Montager Peckering, 1859), xvii; see also the complete digital edition by Fred van Vorsselen, *The Pilgrimage of the Sowle*: http:// pilgrim.grozny.nl.

49. Prose version of the *Pèlerinage de l'ame* by Jean Galloppes; see Duval, *La mise en prose* (2011):150.

50. English version of the second *Vie* edition; see Furnivall, *Pilgrimage of the Life of Man*.

51. Matthias Husz (Lyon, 1485): Paris, Ars. 4° 2847, fol. A4v.

52. Matthias Husz (Lyon, 1499): Paris, BNF, Rés. Ye 26, fol. A1r.

53. Berthold Remboldt/Jean Petit (Paris, 1517): Paris, BNF, Rés Ye 213, unfol.

54. Cust, *Book of the Pylgremage of the Sowle*, xvii.

55. For this literary context, see Fabienne Pomel, *Les voies de l'au-delà et l'essor de l'allégorie au Moyen Age* (Paris: Champion, 2001) and Maupeu, *Pèlerins de Vie humaine*.

56. And we should not forget that all three authors figure as translators of *Pèlerinage* material: Geoffrey Chaucer and Thomas Hoccleve extracted pieces of Marian poetry from the *Pèlerinage* texts and translated them into English (Chaucer's *ABC* and Hoccleve's *Compleynte*). And John Lydgate is thought to be the translator of the second *Vie* version; for the English tradition, see Kamath, *Authorship and First-Person Allegory*.

57. This seems to be the case with the Cologne *Pilgerfahrt* (Pilgrimage), which possibly arose because of Marie d'Harcourt, the wife of Reinald IV, Duke of Jülich-Geldern. She was a member of the Norman Harcourt family, which owned the collegiate chapter La Saussaye, where Jean Galloppes was dean; see Ursula Peters, "Das *Pèlerinage*-Corpus des Guillaume de Deguileville: Eine europäische Textgeschichte des Spätmittelalters," in Kablitz and Peters, *Mittelalterliche Textualität als Retextualisierung*.

58. For this discussion, see Wolfgang Haubrichs and Hans-Walter Herrmann, eds., *Zwischen Deutschland und Frankreich: Elisabeth von Lothringen, Gräfin von Nassau-Saarbrücken* (St. Ingbert: Röhrig, 2002), esp. Wolfgang Haubrichs, "Die 'Pilgerfahrt des träumenden Mönchs': Eine poetische Übersetzung Elisabeths aus dem Französischen?," 533–68.

59. This is the result of the historical-biographical research that Florian Meyer (Cologne) did on the Castilian translator Vincente de Mazuelo; see his paper in Kablitz and Peters, *Mittelalterliche Textualität als Retextualisierung*.

60. In the last years, Andreas Kablitz and Ursula Peters have examined this issue in the context of the research project "Medieval Textuality as Rewriting: The Corpus of the 'Pèlerinage de la vie humaine' in the Context of the European Middle Ages from the 14th to the 16th Century" funded by the German Research Foundation; see their forthcoming paper "The *Pèlerinage* Corpus: A Tradition of Textual Transformation across Western Europe," in Nievergelt and Kamath, Pèlerinages *Allegories of Guillaume de Deguileville*, 25–46.

CHAPTER FOURTEEN

Narrative Frames of Augustinian Thought in the Renaissance

The Case of Rabelais

DEBORAH N. LOSSE

In his contribution to *The New Medievalism*, Giuseppe Mazzotta comments that "Renaissance scholars . . . have long been aware of how blurred the dividing line between 'medieval' and 'Renaissance' culture is."[1] And yet, Rabelais, with references to *le temps . . . tenebreux* (the dark time), the age of the "infélicité et calamité des Gothz" (the infelicity and calamity of the Goths), invites us to partition the old from the new.[2] Contemporary scholars, as distinct from our nineteenth-century counterparts, approach such partitioning mindful of the limitations of categorization (46).

Stephen G. Nichols has contrasted the methodology of the nineteenth-century scholars who established the field of medieval study with contemporary methodology. With the discipline's early focus on philology, literary historians such as Émile Littré focused on *le dit*—the said, the historically determinate "fact and artifact."[3] In the past twenty years, scholars have focused on *le dire*—the speech act in context—with special attention to the relationship between enunciating subject and the audience (31).

Writing as he did at the dawn of what we call the French Renaissance, Rabelais encouraged us to believe that his pedagogical project dismissed the work of scholasticism and the Church fathers, and yet he masked the influence of the Church fathers such as Saint Augustine in his pedagogical and devotional project. To better understand major portions of *Gargantua* and the *Tiers Livre*, we need to return to the works of Saint Augustine, and in particular, to the *Confessions* to see the relationship between the believer and the interlocutor, in this case God.

The emergence of printing and the consequent anxiety between the writing subject and the new and changing audience brought with it a growing consciousness of the speech act as it unfolds within the triple domain of the sender, the receiver, and the context.[4] The nineteenth-century scholars who undertook the study of medieval texts from a philological viewpoint did not have access to the broad theoretical writings on the history of printing that have so informed the work of medieval and early modern scholars of the late twentieth century: the works of Paul Zumthor, Michel Zink, Jacqueline Cerquiglini-Toulet for the Middle Ages and François Rigolot, Terence Cave, and Michel Jeanneret for the Renaissance, among others.

By silencing the name of Saint Augustine in his work and so openly attacking scholastic pedagogy and scholarship, Rabelais conceals a potential key to understanding both essential portions of the sequence on the Abbaye de Thélème and on the plight of Panurge. Taking the text as fact or artifact without exploring intertextual connections with the *Confessions* and other writings by Saint Augustine, literary historians of the late nineteenth and early twentieth century, sniffing Rabelais's proverbial marrow bone, failed to detect the scent of the Church fathers and explored what they judged to be more fruitful tracks: Platonism, disbelief, reform ideology, humanist pedagogy. What R. Howard Bloch has said for the Middle Ages is equally true for reform-minded authors of the early modern period: "if I had to indicate a specific direction in which medieval theory might make the greatest impact not only in the understanding of medieval literature but on modern thought as well, it would be in the return to the master theoreticians of the Middle Ages, the Church fathers, a return which, already underway, signals one of the essential directions of contemporary medieval studies."[5] Paul Oskar Kristeller foreshadowed Bloch's observation about the importance of the Church fathers throughout the Middle Ages and the Renaissance when in 1941 he alerts us to the persistent influence of Saint Augustine from the Middle Ages into the fifteenth and sixteenth centuries: "The Augustinian undercurrent in theology and philosophy continued throughout the fifteenth and sixteenth centuries, and the popular religious literature continued to show Augustine's influence."[6]

Following on Kristeller's thoughts, the present study aims not at establishing a one-to-one correlation between Rabelais's reading and individual works of Saint Augustine but showing how much Augustine's thought had shaped late medieval and early humanist thinking as exemplified in the works of François Rabelais. The evangelical reform of which Rabelais was so much a part is grounded in a skepticism about knowledge and about the complex relationship between science and faith, and finally in a belief in the individual's responsibility to overcome presumption, egocentrism, and overreaching curiosity.

Kristeller shows how two major themes of the early modern era—humanism and Platonism—are founded not on pagan classical origins but on Christian interpretations of the classical and platonic thought as filtered through Augustine (9). He demonstrates how such humanists as Petrarch and Vives take hold of the "personal form of Christian religion" so that the element of self-knowledge informs faith and pursuit of divine truth" (8–9). Augustine used classical learning to defend his views against attacks by other theologians. As humanists such as Vives, Lefèvre d'Etaples, and Erasmus develop a reading program, Augustine is included with other Church fathers alongside the classical authors, whereas the medieval theologians are brushed aside (10).

As for Platonism, according to Kristeller, Ficino reveals that he came to it through Saint Augustine. Ficino states his aim to "produce an image of Plato most similar to the Christian truth" (12). His concept that the intellect is subordinate to the will and to love derives from Augustine's *Confessions*. The intellect is driven by an appetite for the truth and goodness embodied in God and yet not disconnected from self-knowledge (12).

I turn now to Rabelais—whose scorn for medieval scholastic theological methodology knows no bounds. Yet his belief in the centrality of self-knowledge to the quest for faith and *caritas* leads him back to Saint Augustine. To illustrate the complex relationship between knowledge that leads to presumption and faith that ultimately leads to self-knowledge, Rabelais constructs the complex friendship between Pantagruel and Panurge. Kristeller's contention that the humanist fascination with Platonism is filtered through Augustine is evident in the ways in which Rabelais illustrates the conundrum in which Panurge finds himself—eager to get married but fearful of being robbed, beaten, and cuckolded by his future wife.

It should come as no surprise that Rabelais opens his *Tiers Livre* and the subsequent exploration of Panurge's marital situation with the praise of debtors. In the *Confessions*, Augustine describes his mother's fervent prayers that the young Augustine would one day have faith. He depicts the visions and assurances God sent to his mother that he would in fact become a believer and accept God's willingness to become a debtor to those who have faith: "For, since your mercy endures for ever [Ps 117], by your promises you deign to become a debtor to those whom you release from every debt."[7] Although Panurge does not yet have the understanding or self-knowledge to grasp the Christian concept of *caritas*, he nonetheless connects the interreliance of both the microcosm and the macrocosm with lending and borrowing. At the outset of the *Tiers Livre*, Panurge's belief in the value of lending grows out of self-interest: "Doibvez tousjours à quelq'un. Par icelluy sera continuellement Dieu prié vous donner bonne, longue et heureuse vie, craignant sa debte perdre" (Do you always owe something to someone? By him will God be continually implored to give you a good, long, and happy life, fearing to lose his debt; *Le Tiers Livre* 88/267).[8] As long as he owes money, his lenders will pray that he live to repay the debt. Panurge's belief in charity is linked only to the notion of self-preservation and social interdependence. It is not yet tied to divine grace and a belief in the abounding love of God—a love of humankind that does not interfere with free will: "Brief, de cestuy monde seront bannies Foy, Esperance, Charité, car les homes sont nez pour l'ayde et secours des homes. En lieu d'elles succederont Defiance, Mespris, Rancune, avecques la cohorte de tous maulx" (In short, from this world will be banished Faith, Hope, Charity, for men are born to aid and succor men. In place of these will succeed Mistrust, Contempt, Rancor, and the cohort of all evils; *Le Tiers Livre* 96/269–70).

Panurge's pursuit of the marriage question is also motivated by self-interest—the desire to see his lust satisfied, the desire to have his needs attended to, and the desire to see his name perpetuated through children: "'Voire mais,' dist Panurge, 'je n'aurois jamais aultrement filz ne filles legitimes ès quelz j'eusse espoir mon nom et armes perpetuer'" ("All right," said Panurge, "but in no other ways would I ever have legitimate sons and daughters, in whom I would have hope of perpetuating my name and coat of arms"; *Le Tiers Livre* 136/283). Explaining to Pantagruel his strange choice of costume that looks more like a monk's garb than the dashing attire of a suitor, Panurge announces that lust drives his search: "Je ne l'ay prins qu'à ce matin, mais desja j'endesve, je deguene, je gresille d'estre marié et labourer en diable un dessus ma femme, sans craincte des coups de baston" (I put it on only this morning, but already I'm wild, I'm unsheathing. I'm sizzling to be married and to go to work like a brown devil upon my wife, with no fear of sticks or beating; *Le Tiers Livre* 122/278).

As Augustine recounts his own journey to the self-knowledge that leads to love of God, he details the obstacles that kept him from joining his will to God's will. He describes lust in terms of habit—blind servitude. "The enemy held my will in his power and from it he had made a chain and shackled me. For my will was perverse and lust had grown from it, and when I gave in to lust, habit was born" (*Confessions* 8.5.164). Love of God is a free choice, but in Augustine's path to belief, his will was divided between lust and divine love: "So these two wills within me, one old, one new, one the servant of the flesh, the other of the spirit, were in conflict and between them they tore my soul apart" (8.5.164). As long as Panurge remains chained to the habit of lusting, he will be divided between his desire to marry and his fear of cuckolding. When the theologian Hippothadée inquires of his lust:

> —Sentez vous importunement en vostre corps les aiguillons de la chair?"
> —Bien fort (respondit Panurge) ne vous desplaise notre pere.
> —Non faict il (dist Hippothadée), mon amy. Mais, en cestuy estrif, avez-vous de Dieu le don et grâce speciale de continence? (*Le Tiers Livre* 302/348)

> "Do you feel importunately in your body the prickings of the flesh?"
> "Very strongly," replied Panurge, "no offense to you, Father."
> "No offense taken," said Hippothadée, "but in this turmoil in which you find yourself, has God given you the gift and special grace of sexual abstinence?"
> (translation modified)

Let us return to the question of self-awareness and self-knowledge preparing one for the spiritual journey that leads to serving God freely within the context of holy matrimony. Augustine speaks of trying to find truth outside of himself: "Yes I was walking on a treacherous path, in darkness. I was looking for you outside myself and I did not find the God of my own heart. I had reached the depths of the ocean. I had lost all faith and was in despair of finding the truth" (*Confessions* 6.1.111). More than one of Panurge's interlocutors remarks that the answer to Panurge's marriage question lies within himself. It is a question of will. Pantagruel is the first to point out the uncertainty that comes with looking to others for a decision as opposed to self-reflection:

> Aussi (respondit Pantagruel) en vos propositions tant il y a de Si et de Mais, que je j' n'y sçaurois rien fonder ne rien resoudre. N'estez vous asceuré de vostre vouloir? Le poinct principal y gist: tout le reste est fortuit et dependent des fatales dispositions du ciel. (*Le Tiers Livre* 138/284)

> "Accordingly," replied Pantagruel, "in your proposition there are so many if's and but's that I can't possibly base or resolve anything upon them. Aren't you certain of your will? The main point lies there: all the rest is fortuitous and dependent on the fatal dispositions of heaven."

Further on, as Panurge loses his composure after consulting the dying poet Raminagrobis, Epistemon counsels him to take control of himself: "je me esbahys de vous, que ne retournez vous à vous mesmes et que ne revocquez vos sens de ce farouche esguarement en leur tranquillité naturelle" (I'm amazed at you, that you don't come back to yourself and recall your senses from this wild distraction back to their natural tranquility; *Le Tiers Livre* 252/325). The firmest rebuke aimed at Panurge's lack of self-direction comes from Pantagruel as he tries to interpret in clear detail the advice of Raminagrobis:

> Il veult dire sommairement qu'en l'entreprinse de mariage chascun doibt estre arbitre de ses propres pensees et de soy mesmes conseil prendre. Telle a tousjours esté mon opinion et autant vous en diz la premiere foys que m'en parlastez. Mais vous en mocquiez tacitement, il m'en soubvient, et congnois que Philautie et amour de soy vous deçoit. (*Le Tiers Livre* 298/347)

> He means, in sum, that in the undertaking of marriage each man must be the arbiter of his own thoughts and take counsel of himself. Such has always been my opinion, and I told you as much the first time you spoke to me about it. But you were tacitly making fun of this, I remember, and I recognize that *philautie* and self-love is deceiving you.

Panurge has taxed his friend's patience by patently failing to hear—to comprehend—to take for himself his friend's advice. In Augustine's terms, Panurge is unable to understand the nature of free will in Christian terms. It is a question of knowing that we are free, and that one characteristic of free will is for us to choose to commit our will to serving Christ: "But [Augustine states] during all those years, where was my free will? What was the hidden, secret place from which it was summoned in a moment, so that I might bend my neck to your easy yoke and take your light burden on my shoulders, Christ Jesus, my Helper and my Redeemer?" (*Confessions* 9.1.181). As the inhabitants of the Abbaye de Thélème (*Gargantua*, chapter 57) do, we can choose to submit to the common good, to act together in the service of God. Eugène Portalié notes that freedom of choice, even under the influence of efficacious grace, was always safeguarded by Saint Augustine.[9]

Free will within the Augustinian context comes to us through divine grace. Grace is the gift of God to choose freely: "For you do what you will and you grant me, as you always will, the grace to follow you gladly" (*Confessions* 10.35.243). The inhabitants of Thélème in *Gargantua* are motivated by *caritas*, "louable emulation de faire tous ce que à un seul voyoient plaire" (laudable emulation all to do what they say a single one liked), and Rabelais makes it clear that this mutual affection and respect have nothing to do with *vile subjection et contraincte* (vile subjection and constraint).[10] Instead, as Pantagruel makes clear above, *philautia* or self-love blinds Panurge and keeps him from experiencing the freedom to follow God "gladly." Until he frees himself from the chains of self-doubt, he will be stuck in indecision.

And so, when the theologian Hippothadée addresses Panurge, he asks him to look to himself for advice: "Mon amy, vous nous demandez conseil, mais premier fault que vous mesmes vous conseillez" (My friend, you ask advice of us, but first you must advise yourself; *Le Tiers Livre* 302/349). But Panurge is afflicted by conflicting emotions—sexual desire or "les aiguillons de la chair" and his fear that his wife will be unfaithful. His discussion of marriage and child rearing is focused on his own needs and reputation—not on the mutual respect and emulation that makes Christian marriage the reflection of celestial harmony. Hippothadée advises him:

> que jamais vostre femme ne sera ribaulde, si la prenez issue de gens de bien, instruicte en vertus et honnesteté, non ayant hanté ne frequenté compaignie que de bonnes meurs, aymant et craignant Dieu, ayant complaire à Dieu par foy et observation de ses sainctz commandemens. (*Le Tiers Livre* 306/ 350)

> that your wife will never be a wanton, if you take her descended from good people, brought up in virtues and decency, having associated with and frequented only company of good moral conduct, loving and fearing God, loving to please God by faith and observation of His holy commandments.

For marriage to be free of deception, the couple's love is central to their relationship but comes secondary to their love of God. The woman obeys her husband "le cherir, le servir, totalement l'aymer *après Dieu*" (cherish[es] him, serve[s] him, love[s] him totally *after God* [emphasis added]; *Le Tiers Livre* 306/350). Two things make him unready for marriage: his slavery to lust and his inability to abandon self-love (*philautia*) for Christian charity (*caritas*). Marriage based on *caritas* allows one to give up love of self for conjugal harmony—always centered on the love of God and the observation of his commandments: "aymant complaire à Dieu par foy et observation de ses sainctz commandemens" (*Le Tiers Livre* 306). Hippothadée returns to the notion of subordinating one's conjugal love to love of God: "Le sainct Envoyé (dist Hippothadée) me semble l'avoir plus apertment declairé quand il dict 'Ceulx qui sont mariez soient comme non mariez; ceulx qui ont femme soient comme non ayans femme'" (The Holy Apostle, said Hippothadée, seems to me to have stated it more clearly when he said, "Let those who are married be as if unmarried, let those who have a wife be as if they had no wife"; *Le Tiers Livre* 342/364). In the notes to the edition of *Le Tiers*

Livre, Guy Demerson remarks that this passage from St. Paul, I Corinthians 7:29, was often cited in Erasmian circles as an appeal for the Christian's freedom in regard to attachment to earthly goods (342n11). Marriage, as Augustine shows in reference to his mother's marriage, need not deter the Christian from bringing his or her faith in harmony with God's will.

Panurge's desire to protect his own reputation in love and marriage blinds him to the possibility that virtuous women exist. Augustine leaves us the example of his mother—who modeled her behavior to bring her husband to virtuous action and to the love of God. Augustine describes his father as unfaithful to his mother: "He was unfaithful to her, but her patience was so great that his infidelity never became a cause of quarrelling between them. For she looked to you (God) to show him mercy, hoping that chastity would come with faith" (*Confessions* 9.8.194). Augustine interprets her willingness to ignore her own disappointment and feelings in favor of conjugal harmony and the wellbeing of the family as an act of faith and Christian love—set in opposition to self-love or *philautia*.

Panurge fully admits that he is incapable of sacrificing his own reputation for the uncertainty that accompanies the joys of marriage. In speaking with the philosopher Trouillogan, he asks, "Mais qui me fera coqu?" (But who will make me cuckold?). Trouillogan responds, "Quelqu'un" (Someone). Panurge responds in anger, "Par le ventre beuf de boys, je vous froteray bien, monsieur le quelqu'un" (By the ox-belly of wood, I'll give you a good drubbing, Mister Someone; *Le Tiers Livre* 348/366). He would not be able to forgive his wife's infidelity in the manner of Saint Augustine's mother, who hoped that her faith in God and her good example would transform her husband's behavior.

Without illumination that comes from within, Panurge can have neither the self-mastery to set the example for his wife, as Hippothadée explains is essential to a harmonious marriage, "Ainsi, serez vous à vostre femme en patron et exemplaire de vertus et honesteté" (Thus shall you be to your wife as a model and exemplar of virtues and decency; *Le Tiers Livre* 308/351), nor the faith and trust in God to know that his wife will be faithful "Et continuement implorerez la grace de Dieu à vostre protection" (And you shall continually implore God's grace for your protection).

Panurge is on a quest to foresee the future. Yet man is incapable of seeing what does not exist. As Augustine states, "So when we speak of foreseeing the future, we do not see things which are not yet in being, that is, things which are future, but it may be that *we see their causes or signs, which are already in being*" (*Confessions* 11.18.268, emphasis added). Augustine asks, "But how do you reveal the future to us when, for us, the future does no exist?" (Is it that you only reveal present signs of things that are to come?; *Confessions* 11.19.268). The signs that Panurge will be beaten, robbed, and cuckolded by his wife are all present—and readily apparent to all but Panurge. He does not yet have the faith to receive God's grace to see the truth—a strength and a gift that can not come from himself, but only from God. As Augustine explains his own revelation, "I have not the strength to comprehend this mystery and by my own power I never shall. But in your strength I shall understand it, when you grant me the grace to see, sweet Light of the eyes of my soul" (*Confessions* 11.19.268).

Interpreting the future, interpreting revealed language even in the case of Moses, is foolish. Augustine explains: "And I realize that when a message is delivered to us in words, truthful though the messenger may be, two sorts of disagreement may arise. We may disagree either as to the truth of the message itself or as to the messenger's meaning" (*Confessions* 12.23.300). It is folly for the individual to try to interpret the words, "When so many meanings, all of them acceptable as true can be extracted from the words that Moses wrote, do you not see how foolish it is to make a bold assertion that one in particular is the one he had in mind?" (*Confessions* 12.25.303). Augustine invites us to consider all possibilities—to keep our minds open rather than closed: "For this reason, although I hear people say, 'Moses meant this' or 'Moses meant that,' I think it more religious to say 'why should he not have had both meanings in mind, if both are true?'" (*Confessions* 12.31.308). The Bishop of Hippo understands the dialogic nature of Moses's writing.

Within the Augustinian context, suddenly Trouillogan's "Ne l'un ne l'aultre et tous les deux ensemble" makes sense (*Le Tiers Livre* 348). Until Panurge puts his faith in God's strength, he will misinterpret the revealed signs and continue the foolish path of trying to interpret revealed truth in a monologic fashion. What Augustine calls "mischievous arguments" (*Confessions* 12.25.303) work against Christian love: "Do you not see how foolish it is to enter into mischievous arguments which are an offence against that very charity for the sake of which he [Moses] wrote every one of the words that we are trying to explain" (*Confessions* 12.25.302).

It is most often assumed that Gargantua, after hearing the obscure dialogue between Trouillogan and Panurge, is criticizing the philosopher Trouillogan:

A ces motz Gargantua se leva, et dist: Loué soit le bon Dieu en toutes choses!
A ce que je voy, le monde est devenu beau filz depuys ma congnoissance premiere. En sommes nous là? Doncques sont huy les plus doctes et prudens phi-

losophes entrez on phrontistere et escholle des Pyrrhoniens, Aporrheticques, Scepticques et Ephecticques. Loué soit le bon Dieu. (*Le Tiers Livre* 350/367)

At these words, Gargantua rose and said, "Praise be to the good God in all things. As far as I can see, the world has grown pretty sharp since first I knew it. Is that where we stand? So then today the most learned and prudent philosophers have entered the think-tank and school of the Pyrrhonists, aporrhetics, skeptics, and ephectics. Praise be to the good Lord!"

Panurge is caught up in the foolish and pointless debate and fails to see that God alone can provide guidance. His prince, Pantagruel, evokes the image of the mouse stuck in pitch to describe Panurge's dilemma: "Vous me semblez à une souriz empegée tant plus elle s'efforce soy depestrer de la poix, tant plus elle s'en embrene" (You seem to me like a mouse ensnared in pitch, the more it tries to get free of the pitch, the more it gets stuck; *Le Tiers Livre* 354/369). Held down by earthly concerns—lust, self-love, external reputation, Panurge will never see the "Light that never changes casting its rays over the same eye of my soul, over my mind" (*Confessions* 7.10.146). This is the light that leads to the love of God, to the experience of putting one's free will in harmony with God's will. Augustine describes his release into the place where he chooses Christian *caritas* over the earthly alternatives: "At last my mind was free from the gnawing anxieties of ambition and gain, from wallowing in filth and scratching the itching sore of lust. I began to talk to you freely, O Lord my God, my Light, my Wealth, and my Salvation" (*Confessions* 9.1.181). Panurge is stuck—his pursuit of future knowledge is at the expense of freedom to align his will to the will of God. At the end of the *Tiers Livre*, Panurge sets his sights on the oracle of the *Dive Bouteille*—another external source of revelation. Still trusting in the power of interpretation instead of embracing holistic meaning, he proposes to make a dictionary of *lanternais* for Pantagruel so that he can understand the oracle.

In the end, it is Gargantua who interprets Panurge's problem. In wishing that Pantagruel express the inclination and desire to get married—"Mais je vouldroy que pareillement vous vint en vouloir et desir vous marier"—he notes that Panurge has come to an impasse in forcing the marriage question: "Panurge s'est assez efforcé rompre les difficultez qui luy pouvoient estre en empeschement" (Panurge has striven enough to break down the difficulties that could have been an obstacle to him; *Le Tiers Livre* 426/398). For Pantagruel, the answer is simple, marriage is a decision that is left to the parents: "Tous Legislateurs ont ès enfans ceste liberté tollue, ès parents l'ont reservée" (All lawgivers have withheld this free-dom from children and reserved it for the parents; *Le Tiers Livre* 428/398). Gargan-tua praises God for the good sense of his son and pledges to find him a suitable wife while Panurge and Pantagruel go off in the vain pursuit of the *dive bouteille*.

We recall R. Howard Bloch's call to revisit the Church fathers as we reread texts from the Medieval and early modern period. "Indeed, the writings of the Church fathers, once dismissed under the twin paralogisms of theology and scholasticism, have become increasingly to be seen as essential to our own es-thetic and intellectual senses" (173). In the "new medieval optic," Bloch argues for an anthropological approach to the study of the early Church. He urges us to place the readings of the Church fathers outside of the confines of "narrow in-tellectual history" and to focus on the "anthropology of the formative Christian period" (173).

Rabelais himself creates such an anthropological reading of marriage—by removing it as a purely "religious ideal" (Bloch's term) and "placing [it] within the broader perspective of social, political, legal, and economic institutions" (174). It is here that we might add another influence to the Augustinian reading of Rabelais's *Tiers Livre*. Stephen Nichols juxtaposes Augustine's view of mar-riage, and that of the Latin Fathers, with the Greek perspective on marriage as exemplified in the work of Johannes Scotus Eriugena (ca. 810–77), translator of Christian Platonism in the court of Charles the Bald. "Marriage for Augustine and the Latin Fathers was problematic precisely because, in authorizing sexuality, it seemed to authorize the body as eroticized space, where the sexual act ritually repeated Eve's remaking of Adam in her own image."[11] Rather than creating a binary opposition between mind (male) and body (female), Eriugena espouses the concept taken from Greek Christian Platonism in which mind (*nous*) and sense (*aisthesis*) are contained in every human.[12]

Rabelais, as well as his theologian Hippothadée, have fused the teachings of Augustine with concepts from Greek Christian Platonism to forge the positive image of marriage, which neither diminishes Christian piety nor disregards the woman's constructive role in the marriage pact. Nichols adds, "Further-more, it is the so-called feminine quality of the senses, *aisthesis*, that integrates the outer being to the inner as a kind of messenger of shuttling back and forth between [outer and inner being]."[13] The wife that the theologian Hippothadée recommends to Panurge has in fact the qualities mentioned both by Augustine, in describing his mother in the context of her marriage, and by Eriugena in describing the fusion of the *nous* and the *aisthesis*. She should be virtuous, hon-est, God loving and God fearing, respectful, and observant of his holy laws (*Le*

Tiers Livre 306/350). If the woman reflects the virtue of her husband—"Elle n'en reçoit que du Soleil, son mary, et de luy n'en reçoit poinct plus qu'il luy en done par son infusion et aspectz" (she receives it from the sun, her husband, and receives from him no more than he gives her by his infusion and aspects; *Le Tiers Livre* 308/351)—she is also the one who brings equilibrium to the union. We remember that Augustine's mother was cast in the mold not of the moon but the sun, reflecting virtue and forgiveness to guide her unfaithful husband (*Confessions* 9.8.194). Yet until Panurge, as he chooses a wife, surrenders his will to God and to his sovereign prince, in the absence of a parent, he will remain stuck and immobile—a reluctant observer rather than an active participant in the marriage contract.

In setting the marriage question within its anthropological context, Rabelais has left us a key to understanding the importance of the Church fathers in his work. Marriage is no longer a disembodied religious ideal examined within a narrow intellectual history, but a social institution that functions within the context of a vibrant and changing Christian community. If Rabelais is reluctant to mention Augustine by name, the Bishop of Hippo finds his voice in the companions and consultants of Panurge as well as in the evangelical teachings of the eponymous evangelical theologian, Hippothadée.

NOTES

1. Giuseppe Mazzotta, "Antiquity and the New Arts of Petrarch," in *The New Medievalism*, ed. Marina S. Brownlee, Kevin Brownlee, and Stephen G. Nichols (Baltimore: Johns Hopkins University Press, 1991), 47.

2. François Rabelais, "Points," in *Pantagruel*, ed. Guy Demerson (Paris: Éditions du Seuil, 1995), chap. 8, 118–60. All citations are from the Demerson paperback edition. Translations are from *The Complete Works of François Rabelais*, trans. Donald M. Frame (Berkeley: University of California Press, 1991); my modifications to Frame's translation are noted. The books are referenced by title.

3. Stephen G. Nichols, "Modernism and the Politics of Medieval Studies," in *Medievalism and the Modernist Temper*, ed. R. Howard Bloch and Stephen G. Nichols (Baltimore: Johns Hopkins University Press, 1996), 31.

4. For a broader discussion of the anxiety of the writer who contemplates the as-yet unfamiliar audience, see Deborah Losse, *Sampling the Book: The Prologues of the French Conteurs* (Lewiston: Bucknell University Press, 1994).

5. R. Howard Bloch, "Old French Literature and the New Medievalism," in *The Middle Ages: Medieval Literature in the 1990s*, ed. William Doremus Paden (Gainesville: University of Florida Press, 1994), 173.

6. Paul Oskar Kristeller, "Augustine in the Renaissance," *International Science* 1 (1941): 8.

7. Saint Augustine, *Confessions V, 10* (London: Penguin, 1961), 103.

8. Francois Rabelais, *Le Tiers Livre*, ed. Guy Demerson (Paris: Éditions du Seuil, 1997), 88.

9. Eugène Portalié, *A Guide to the Thought of Saint Augustine*, trans. Ralph J. Bastian (Westport, CT: Greenwood Press, 1975), 197.

10. François Rabelais, *Gargantua*, ed. Guy Demerson (Paris: Éditions du Seuil, 1997), 374–76/126.

11. Stephen G. Nichols, "An Intellectual Anthropology of Marriage in the Middle Ages," in *New Medievalism*, 78–79. Nichols cites Augustine's *The City of God against the Pagans*, Loeb Classical Library 414, trans. Philip Levine (Cambridge, MA: Harvard University Press, 1966), 4:13–21.

12. J. P. Migne, *Patrologiae Cursus Completus*, Series Latina (Paris: J. P. Migne, 1853), 122:54B, cited by Nichols.

13. Nichols, "An Intellectual Anthropology of Marriage in the Middle Ages," 81.

CHAPTER FIFTEEN

From Romanesque Architecture to Romance

R. HOWARD BLOCH

In the year 1143, Abbot Suger, who had been born into a poor family and, through education, rose to become head of Saint-Denis, toward the end of the first phase of a remarkable building project that had begun in 1136, undertook to make a written record of what is recognized to be the construction of the first Gothic cathedral.

> In the twenty-third year of our administration, when we sat on a certain day in the general chapter, conferring with our brethren about matters both common and private, these very beloved brethren and sons began strenuously to beseech me *in charity* that I might not allow the fruits of our so great labors to be passed over in silence; and rather to save for the memory of posterity in pen and ink, those increments which the generous munificence of Almighty God had bestowed upon this church, in the time of our prelacy, in the acquisition of new assets as well as in the recovery of lost ones, in the multiplication of improved possessions, in the construction of buildings, and in the accumulation of gold, silver, most precious gems and very good textiles.[1]

The story of what was done under his administration is remarkable not only as a record of a medieval patron of the arts, but also because it is not a universal history in the mode of early medieval historical writing, a history of world since Creation, but a history of the present. Suger is interested in the everyday and in current events. He is interested not just in what happened but *how* it happened. For Abbot Suger, history is a composition, a construction in which the building blocks of words are analogous to the stones of the cathedral: "We thought fitting to begin, in its proper place, our tale about the construction of the buildings and the increase of the treasures with the body of the church of the most blessed Martyrs Denis, Rusticus, and Eleutherius" (41). And, in a phrase on which one could build both a cathedral and a book, Suger justifies the recording of current events in terms of linking what has happened with what will come to be: "The recollection of the past is the promise of the future" (53).

Much of twelfth-century humanism can be seen to be latent in what is a new order of language and in the relation of words to being. This order involves not only a continuous relation of past, present, and future, but a concept of the relation of the material to the spiritual as a continuum. Suger expresses a desire to behold sacred reality with bodily eyes, with the assumption that it is no longer necessary to turn one's back on the material world, but "to transcend it by absorbing it."[2] Such a view represents a turning away from the Platonic dichotomy between material and spiritual worlds, between things and the Idea or Ideal of things, which will culminate in a naturalism of the High Middle Ages, new interest in science, in how things of this world relate and work, and in nature itself, as seen in the scientific and encyclopedic spirit of the thirteenth century, the *Roman de la Rose*, Saint Francis and the spiritualism of the natural world in which all that is in nature—birds, fire, chickens—is sacred.

In a startling example of medieval materialism, Suger glories in precious objects and materials:

Into this panel, which stands in front of his most sacred body, we have put, according to our estimate, about forty-two marks of gold; [further] a multifarious wealth of precious gems, hyacinths, rubies, sapphires, emeralds and topazes, and also an array of different large pearls—[a wealth] as great as we had never anticipated to find. You could see how kings, princes, and many outstanding men, following our example, took the rings off the fingers of their hands and ordered, out of love for the Holy Martyrs, that the gold, stones, and precious pearls of the rings be put into that panel. (55)

Suger, cataloging the gems of Saint-Denis, sounds like a miser hoarding gold:

when I was in difficulty for want of gems and could not sufficiently provide myself with more (for their scarcity makes them very expensive): then, lo and behold, [monks] from three abbeys of two Orders—that is, from Cîteaux and another abbey of the same Order, and from Fontevrault—entered our little chamber adjacent to the church and offered us for sale an abundance of gems such as we had not seen in ten years, hyacinths, sapphires, rubies, emeralds, topazes . . . freed from the worry of searching for gems, [we] thanked God and gave four hundred pounds for the lot though they were worth much more." (59)

Suger's estimate that he bought gems for four hundred pounds, "though they were worth much more," points in the direction of worth itself as a relative value. And it implies a vision of the self that is double, like the great high wall of the first Gothic cathedral, both outside and inside, open and hidden. He is aware of the true worth of the gems, though he says nothing, and that nothing is invisible to the seller, who may himself have had thoughts that remain unspoken. It has been suggested that the sellers come from one of the austere Cistercian houses, whose head, Saint Bernard, condemns the building of large churches and the display of wealth in no uncertain terms, and even may have had Suger in mind when he speaks of:

> major abuses, so common nowadays as to seem of lesser moment. I pass over the vertiginous height of churches, their extravagant length, their inordinate width and costly finishings . . . As for the elaborate images that catch the eye and check the devotion of those at prayer within . . . But as a monk I ask my fellow monks the question a pagan poet put to pagans: "Tell me, O priests, why is there gold in the holy place? Tell me, O poor men," say I—for it is the meaning, not the measure that concerns me—"tell me, O poor men, if poor you are, what is gold doing in the holy place?"[3]

Bernard is not interested in the measure, but only the meaning, of rich church decorations, which he condemns in absolute, not relative, terms.

The inscription on the door of Saint-Denis testifies to Suger's esthetics of glitter, light, and enlightenment: "Nobile claret opus, sed opus quod nobile claret / Clarificet mentes, ut eant per lumina vera" (Bright is the noble work; but, being nobly bright, the work / Should brighten the minds, so that they may travel, through the true lights; 46) Just as the reliquary adorns the remains of saints, the church adorns the reliquary; together they transport those who behold them closer to God: "For the generosity of so great Fathers, experienced by ourselves and all, demands that we, most miserable men who feel as well as need their tutelage, should deem it worth our effort to cover the most sacred ashes of those whose venerable spirits, radiant as the sun, attend upon Almighty God with the most precious material we possibly can: with refined gold and a profusion of hyacinths, emeralds and other precious stones" (107). In a cultural shift that could not be further from Saint Bernard's emphasis upon the abstemious and the spare, Suger maintains that the best material provides for the best spiritual access: "Whether thou wants it or not, we want it of the best" (107). It's what the saints would have wanted: "so many [gems and pearls] were brought to us for sale from nearly all the parts of the world . . . that we should have been unable to let them go without great shame and offense to the Saints" (107).

Architecturally speaking, Suger had been born into the world of the Romanesque, characterized by massive and massively thick walls that support the weight of vaults and roof; thus the smallness of the windows and openings and the lack of light. Visually speaking, the optic against which Suger defines the architectural modernity of the mid-twelfth century is characterized by a certain two dimensional passive frontality, promoting the illusion of massive, defensive impenetrability, the church as a projection of a castle as in the example of the castle of Loches. Associated with the north, Gothic was, of course, an international style found in England, Italy, Spain, Germany, the Lowlands, even central Europe and Scandinavia, and France; and, in France, primarily in the Parisian basin: to wit, Henri Focillon's dictum that Gothic architecture is the "Romanesque of the Ile de France." And the Gothic project as conceived by Suger is related to monarchic power. Saint-Denis, the place that supposedly housed the *gonfanon de France* mentioned in the *Chanson de Roland* and represented in the stained glass of the choir, Saint-Denis, the burial place of kings, constituted itself as national art. The dedication ceremony, in Suger's account, unites the bishops of France.

> Our Lord King Louis himself and his spouse Queen Eleanor, as well as his mother, and the peers of the realm arrived on the third day. Of the diverse counts and nobles from many regions and dominions, of the ordinary troops of knights and soldiers there is no count. But of the archbishops and bishops who were present the names are placed on record as follows: Samson, Archbishop of Reims; Hughes, Archbishop of Rouen; Guy, Archbishop of Sens; Geoffroy, Archbishop of Bordeaux; Theobald, Archbishop of Canterbury; Geoffroy, Bishop of Chartres; Jocelin, Bishop of Soissons; Simon, Bishop of Noyon; Elias, Bishop of Orléans; Eudes, Bishop of Beauvais; Hughes, Bishop of Auxerre; Alvise, Bishop of Arras; Guy, Bishop of Châlons; Algare, Bishop of Coutances; Rotrou, Bishop of Evreux; Milon, Bishop of Térouanne; Manesseh, Bishop of Meaux; Peter, Bishop of Senlis. (113)

Each of the chapels was consecrated by a dignitary whose participation in the rite of consecration was a performance of religious and national unity, not unlike the epic catalogue in which the syntactic juxtaposition of the names of noble knights, each attached to land, works to fuse territorial unity in the *Chanson de Roland.*

Chief among the characteristics of the new Gothic architecture of the cathedral is the element of light. In the "Celestial Hierarchies" of Denys the Pseudo-

Aeropagite, which is the founding text for Saint-Denis, God is light: the more light one has, the closer one is to God; the less light, the further away; shadows being proof of the mediation of screens. In the *Celestial Hierarchies* of Denys the Aeropagite, we read of the doctrine of light and illumination:

> Calling, then, upon Jesus, the Light of the Father, the Real, the True, "Which lighteth every man that cometh into the world, by Whom we have access to the Father," the Origin of Light, let us raise our thought, according to our power, to the illuminations of the most sacred doctrines handed down by the Fathers, and also, as far as we may, let us contemplate the Hierarchies of the Celestial Intelligences revealed to us by them in symbols for our upliftment: and admitting through the spiritual and unwavering eyes of the mind the original and super-original gift of Light of the Father Who is the Source of Divinity, which shows to us images of the all-blessed Hierarchies of the Angels in figurative symbols, let us through them again strive upwards towards Its Primal Ray.[4]

Suger, speculating on light in architecture, observes that "the whole [church] would sing with the wonderful and uninterrupted light of most luminous windows, pervading the interior beauty" (101).

Gothic architecture is the translation of the doctrine of light into architectural form, and in this relation of structure and appearance, walls are a key. The Romanesque wall is thick and opaque, and covered with painting, as seen in the image of the crypt of the Église Notre-Dame, Etampes. In the Gothic wall, painting is subordinate to architectural skeleton. The Gothic wall is thinner, lighter, porous, transparent, not an impenetrable surface to be painted, but a source of light. The Gothic cathedral is full of windows, stained glass as in the example of the west facade of Chartres Cathedral, as seen both from the inside, and from the outside, where the openness of the window can be seen in the tracery patterns of the royal portal. The rose window of the south facade shows Isaiah, Daniel, Ezekiel, and Jeremiah carrying on their backs the Evangelists Matthew, Mark, John, and Luke, who have come to bear witness to the accomplishment of the Scriptures, not their abolition.

Gothic architecture is busy and active, full of visual and perspectival energy, in contrast to the heavy inertness of Romanesque. Again, the Gothic is a visual rendering of Dionysian philosophy, the translation of the theology of light into style, which will culminate in the mid-thirteenth-century Saint-Chapelle in Paris. The dynamism of Gothic is apparent in its reaching toward light, its verticalism, which reverses laws of gravity. We see such height in examples from the Bourges Cathedral, north side of choir and nave; or, again, looking east, straight down the nave. There is in Gothic architecture a general increase in lateral volume, but also in height to produce in Jean Bony's phrase a "mysticism of soaring lines." Bourges reaches 157 feet, Chartres 130 feet, and Reims 135 feet.

How did they do it? (1) By the reinforcement of piers. (2) By an externalizing of the support for the high wall, part of twelfth-century functionalism in the form of flying buttresses, which unite the inside and outside of the building in an organic whole. The first High Gothic style denies Romanesque frontality. (3) By use of a bay pattern, construction in modules. Gothic building is associated with multiplicity, fragmentation, modular accretion, a grid system, a network, repetitive all-over pattern. The division of the nave into successive identical units, bays with analytic partitioning, results in a modalism of construction. In fact, the quality of regular modules that can be substituted for each other has led to the comparison of Gothic architecture to scholastic philosophy, which seeks to find in logic a language into which ideas can be inserted and substituted for one another. Art historian Gottfried Semper's remark that "Gothic architecture is scholasticism in stone"[5] is most fully elaborated in Erwin Panofsky's *Gothic Architecture and Scholasticism*.[6] The rise of Gothic architecture is linked to the new science and learning of the twelfth and thirteenth centuries, and nowhere more so than in the arrival of Euclid in the West right around the time of the construction of Saint-Denis. Gothic architecture is full of movement, as compared to the static quality of Romanesque, which some have assimilated to the Platonic world of fixed ideas. Optically, Romanesque forms are "frontal," Gothic are "diagonal," involving a multiplicity of points of views. Romanesque establishes boundaries, while Gothic relief abolishes them, embraces the viewer, comes forward from the core of the wall in continuous recession. In some large, crude way, Romanesque reproduces being, while Gothic transmits a sense of becoming. Its forms are organic and incomplete, its double-wall system transmits a sense of depth, a relativism of perspective in keeping with a changing universe of particulars that can be seen as the architectural embodiment of the philosophical nominalism that grew in the shadows of the cathedrals of the Ile-de-France.

As in scholasticism itself, Gothic architecture from the start represents an attempt at harmony, synthesis. In Suger's remarkable phrase, "the admirable power of one unique and supreme reason equalizes by proper composition the disparity between things human and Divine; and what seems mutually to conflict by inferiority of origin and contrariety of nature is conjoined by the single, delightful concordance of one superior, well-tempered harmony" (83).

Not only are past, present, and future a continuum—"The recollection of the past is the promise of the future"—but their contiguity, through the Gothic building, yields a higher synthesis: "In carrying out such plans my first thought was for the concordance and harmony of the ancient and the new work" (91). If what is known for better or worse as the Renaissance of the twelfth century is synonymous with the revival of classical culture beginning around the 1140s, there is no element of that revival more essential than the topos of *translatio studii*, the belief that knowledge, and by implication power, was born in Greece, migrated to Rome, then reached France in its inevitable journey west. Suger participates in such a motif in the rivalry he imagines with Byzantium. He interrogates those who have returned from the East as to "whether the things here could claim some value in comparison with those there" (65). And in the case of an unfavorable comparison, he imagines that among the wary warlike Greeks, "it could happen that treasures which are visible here, deposited in safety, amount to more than those which had been visible there, left [on view] under conditions unsafe on account of disorders" (65). And in his search for suitable columns for the building of Saint-Denis, Suger speculates about how "we might obtain them from Rome (for in Rome we had often seen wonderful ones in the Palace of Diocletian and other Baths) by safe ships through the Mediterranean, thence through the English Sea and the tortuous windings of the River Seine" (91).

By the time the *translatio studii et imperii* was first explicitly articulated in a literary text, Chrétien de Troyes's *Cligès* (mid-1170s), it was already over a decade old. The classical romances of midcentury—the *Roman de Thèbes*, *Roman de Troie*, *Roman d'Alexandre*—not only bore witness to a return to the ancient world, but from the start, implicitly thematize the westward thrust via the retelling of Virgil's *Aeneid* in the *Roman d'Eneas*, written by an anonymous Norman clerk at the court of the Plantagenets around 1160. The *Roman d'Eneas* is a tale of at least three cities: first Carthage and Laurentium, and then—via the lineage of Lavinia and Eneas—of Rome, as if, from the start, romance, which originally marked the difference between works written in the vernacular and Latin, were looking toward Rome.

The *Roman d'Eneas* makes free use—some translation, but for most part adaptation—of the *Aeneid*, which its author follows directly. In this it is the least "unfaithful" of the romances of antiquity. Classical mythology is not suppressed, but subaltern deities such as Eolius, Cupid, Allecto, as well as Olympic councils and natural and social "machinery" (Aeneas's dream, Hector's apparition, the opening of the gates of the temple of Janus, or the funeral games for

Anchises) are eliminated. Virgil's secondary characters are also absent—Laocoön, Palinurus—as is all of Book 3. The *Roman d'Eneas* does open with the Judgment of Paris, and its author dwells at length upon the suffering of Dido (1,600 verses) as well as the internal amorous struggle of Lavinia and of Eneas. Yet, little remains of the *Aeneid*'s national, dynastic, religious even, spirit; little remains of the high lyric tone and style of Virgil, whose founding epic, an epic of foundation, is transformed essentially into the narration of a love story, a courtly romance that is also set in a culture much closer to a twelfth-century aristocratic circle than to that of the classical world.

In terms of the *translatio studii*, the *Roman d'Eneas* contains what seems to me to be a remarkable twist that makes it clear that this is one of those seminal texts that not only affords a glimpse of how literature from its inception should be read, but of how medieval literature both reflects—and, more importantly, enables—wider changes in the way the world is perceived and, therefore, the way not only culture but social institutions are made. Eneas and his men, after seven years of struggle at sea following their escape from Troy in flames, arrive before the walls of Carthage:

> Li mur erent espés et halt,
> qui ne criement negun asalt;
> cinc cenz torz avoit anviron
> estre lo demoine donjon;
> devers la vile erent trifoire
> li mur, a ars et a civoire,
> o granz pierres de marbre toz.[7]

> The walls were thick and high, and feared no assault; not counting the main dungeon there were five hundred towers all around; towards the town the walls were filled with entryways, archways, and vaults of great marble blocks.

Founding literature seems to begin with walls—the walls of Troy in the *Iliad*, the walls of Saragossa in the *Chanson de Roland*—as if the site of an impossible siege signals the failure of the unreflective military response, the projection of violence outside of the community, and marks a turning toward mediated forms of social exchange and the arts. Carthage is no exception. Though its walls *ne criement negun asalt* (fear no assault), they are here presented as more than simply a defensive site, more than the city as walls to protect and keep invaders out, more, in other words, than mere castle. Looking beyond defenses are arcaded walls (*trifoire*) whose arches (*ars*) in the Old French are homophonous with the "arts," as Carthage is seen from the start to contain a certain kind of excess: tacked to the functionality of the castle is something like architecture, design:

> De chieres pieres naturalz
> ot un mui enz el mur asis,
> et set mile esmalz i ot mis
> es pilers, es antailleüres,
> es oiseries, es volsures,
> es columbes, es fenestriz,
> es verrines et es chasiz. (verse 508)

A great quantity of precious stones were set in the wall, and seven thousand enamels were put there, in the pillars, in the window frames, in the aviaries, in the vaults, in the columns, in the windows, in the panes, in the doorframes.

Carthage as surplus contains the essence of esthetic intention and is allied with the nonfunctional, the excessive, superfluous, luxurious, as if its *oiseries* (aviaries) made synonymous, and here the plasticity of Old French justifies it, the raising of birds and "laziness," just as the functional window frames—the *antailleüres*—are also sculptures. Nor, once one admits of such surplus is there any end: to the surplus of architectural design is added that of decoration:

> Li mur sont fait a pastorals,
> a pilerez e a merals,
> a bisches, a oisiaus, a flors;
> o le marbre de cent colors
> sont painturé defors li mur,
> sanz vermeillon et sanz azur. (verse 427)

The walls are made of posts and pillars and compartments, with animals, birds and flowers; the outer walls are painted with marble of a hundred colors without vermillion or azure.

The walls of Carthage are a version of what in Alain de Lille's *Complaint of Nature*, in Chrétien de Troyes's *Erec et Enide*, and in Guillaume de Lorris's portion of the *Roman de la Rose*, is the motif of Nature's robe, a text containing the representation of all that nature contains—part of the encyclopedic spirit of the age.

More importantly, this passage holds a key to our understanding of what it is that Eneas discovers in Carthage; what it is, further, that romance uncovers to its audience; what it lays down as its own new structure, new law, of perceptual relations, indeed of relation itself. Such a demonstration hangs on what seems like a minor philological point, which turns out to be not so minor after all. One could read the last line of the above passage—"sanz vermeillon et sanz azur"—to mean literally that, of the hundred colors of the walls, those of vermilion and azure are not represented, a reading which hardly makes sense. We must, I think, assume that these two colors are included among the myriad of hues. But the real question is that of where these hues, the colors, actually reside—on the surface of the marble or as part of it? The passage might be understood to mean that the "marble is painted on the outside with a hundred colors." But what do we do then with the "sanz vermeillon et sanz azur," which indicates the lack of color added on? This last sentence forces us to read the preceding two lines not as indicating that the "marble is painted with a hundred colors," but literally as, "with marble of a hundred colors the walls are painted on the outside." Such a reading is supported by lines 422–26:

> Li carrel sont de marbre bis,
> de blanc et d'inde et de vermoil;
> par grant anging et par consoil
> i sunt asis tot a compas;
> tuit sont de mabre et d'adamas.

> The stones are of grey, white, blue, and red marble, placed all around with great skill and care; they are all of marble and of diamond.

These lines are significant, for not only do we find ourselves before the phenomenon of architecture and decoration, both excesses upon the functional defensive walls of a castle, but before the possibility of the same material—marble—producing different effects upon the eye. Which is another way of saying that two different qualities—color—inhere in the same substance—marble.

This is a detail, but the proper of romance is a shifting of the relation of details to the whole; and the importance of such a paradigm cannot be underestimated. On the contrary, the law of inherence—from the structure of the walls of Carthage right down to the law of gender difference and to the notion of what the human being can be said to be—is a widely operating principle within the *Eneas*. The epic world is one of moral and historical absolutes, of categorical differences between good and bad and of inescapable historical prescription: "Li crestiens unt dreit, et li paiens unt tort"; "Roland est preux, et Oliviers est sage." There is no middle term, no possible synthesis between opposites. Some have read the *Chanson de Roland* as a parable of failed binarism, of a failure to find a third term, of a lack of synthesis or compromise, except perhaps at the very end with Thierry's suggestion to execute Ganelon and to spare his thirty relatives. Romance, on the other hand, is dialectical; that is to say, structured in many instances around the search for a median term between opposite extremes, Suger's conjoining "by the single, delightful concordance of one superior, well-tempered harmony."

Romance is a syllogistic genre synonymous with the necessity of moderation. Roland, it will be remembered, is a character whose character can best be defined by a lack of measure—*démesure*. The romance character, if one can posit such a type, however, is one whose contrasting elements occupy the same psychic space and are to be modulated. This is to say that within romance we find a completely different notion of what constitutes human character. To the epic allegory of character, where character as allegory has only a single dimension and humans can only act singly, as if they were under some sort of demonic possession, we find in romance a mixing of emotions: good mixed with bad, pain mixed with pleasure. And not only is fortune considered to deposit joy and pain in the same space, but even love is defined in terms of a dialectical, reciprocal, copresent relation of opposites—a *bon mal*. Indeed, Lavinia's mother's description of love is the very opposite of Roland's unassimilable binarism:

> Et ja est ce tot soatume.
> Soëf trait mal qui l'acostume;
> se il i a un pou de mal,
> li biens s'en suist tot par igal.
> Ris et joie vient de plorer,
> grant deport vienent de pasmer,
> baisier vienent de baaillier,
> anbracemenz vient de veillier,
> grant leece vient de sospir,
> fresche color vient de palir.
> El cors s'en suit la granz dolçors
> qui tost seinne les maus d'Amors;
> sanz herbe boivre et sanz racine
> a chascun mal fet sa mecine;
> n'i estuet oignement n'entrait,
> la plaie sane que il fait;

se il te velt un po navrer,

bien te savra anprés saner. (verse 7957)

And soon is it [love] all sweetness. The one who gets used to pain will know pleasure; s/he feels a little hurt, but the pleasure follows suit. Laughter and joy come
from crying, great pleasures from fainting, kisses from yawning, embraces from
waiting, great lightness from sighing, high color from paleness. Great sweetness
returns to the body to cure the pains of Love; without drinking herb or root it
works its cure on every ill; no need for ointment, it cures the wound it makes; if it
wants to wound you a bit, it knows later how to cure.

The emotions become in romance the site of a balance, as moderation constitutes not only a social ideal, but a corporeal ideal, as well. Romance promulgates
a moderated view of the passions as a mixture of right or wrong, strength and
wisdom, good and bad, of pleasure and pain, to be reconciled.

This is another way of saying that romance is the site of psychology, of psychology as depth as opposed to the asymptotic gestural quality of the epic. A
place of optimism to be sure, of an optimism engendered precisely by a commingling of opposites through time in which pain is always sooner or later relieved
by its opposite:

Molt doit l'en bien sofrir d'Amor,

qui navre et sane an un jor . . .

Se tu t'en plainz et tu t'en dials,

totes voies t'anbelira;

si an as mal, bien te plaira. (verse 7998)

One must suffer from Love which wounds and cures in the same day . . . If you
complain and you suffer, he will improve you in any case; if you suffer ills, he will
please you.

If romance is the site of psychology, that psychology itself has a diegetic site
in the direct discourse that comes to characterize romance as opposed to epic.
Indeed, the inner monologue becomes the place where the individual, endowed
with two voices as opposed to the unidimensional emblematic psychology of a
Roland, comes into conflict with him- or herself, a conflict out of which emerges
something resembling an act of will. To the receding spatial planes of Gothic
architecture correspond the self as a receding psychological space. And just as
history in romance is reversible, the individual, too, seems to remain free to

change his or her mind, as indeed is the case when Eneas first vows to kill Turnus, then spares him (verse 9796); and, finally, upon glimpsing Pallas's ring on
his enemy's finger, slays him in the end.

Romance implies, of course, the integration of the feminine within the wholly
masculine world of epic. And this from the beginning. Eneas's arrival in Carthage
contains an unmistakable reference to the epic beginning with a siege (*Iliad*,
Chanson de Roland), as we catch a glimpse of a walled city ruled, and herein lies
a crucial generic difference defined by gender, by a woman:

> Li mesagier ont tant tenu
> lo grant chemin, qui larges fu,
> Cartage virent, la cité,
> dont Dido tint la fermeté.
> Dame Dido tint le païs;
> miaus nel tenist quens ne marchis;
> unc ne fu mais par une feme
> mielz maintenu enor ne regne. (verse 373)

> The messengers so pursued the big highway, which was wide, that they saw the
> city of Carthage of which Dido keeps the keep. Lady Dido holds the country all
> around better than a count or marquis; never was a fief or realm better held by a
> woman.

There are several strong women in the *Roman d'Eneas*: Dido, Camille, Lavinia,
the Queen of Latinum. Yet even the concept of gender defined in this first romance offers another example of what we have begun to see as something on
the order of a dialectical model of the person as not only deep but conflicted, a
sum of opposite tendencies held in tension.

If romance implies depth psychology and, by extension, a certain optimistic efficacy of the will, it is only because there is a curious connection, despite
the present-day resonance of romance with the irrational (evasion, dream),
between the romance genre and logic. Indeed, the commingling of opposites
defines a world in which logic—anticipation, prospective reasoning, hypothesis,
calculation—permit the individual, conceived to possess a depth out of which
the dialectical relation of competing principles produces a correct perception
of the world, to distance him- or herself from it. The queen mother, for example,
in opposing the marriage of Lavinia to Eneas and favoring a union with Turnus,
counsels a dilatory anticipation that is connected to a dialectical concept of the
emotions:

Un po atant,
li termes ert prochenemant
que la bataille an estera,
et se il voint, il te prendra;
donc i vendras bien a tot tens;
sofre un petit, se sera sens;
et se il est morz et veincuz
et Turnus soit a ce venuz
qu'il te doie a feme prendre,
sel pooit savoir ne antendre
que eüsses cestui amé,
toz tens t'avroit mes an vilté. (verse 8731)

Wait a bit, the date fixed for the battle is near, and if he wins, he will take you; you will be with him forever; hold out a bit, it makes sense; and if he dies and is conquered and it happens that Turnus must take you for a wife, and if he learns or hears that you loved the other one, he will hold you in scorn for all time.

In a world that admits chance, romance is calculation, assessment of the other's emotion, as Eneas makes clear by his reaction to the letter shot to him by Lavinia on an arrow:

Et nequeden feme est molt sage
d'enginier mal an son corage;
il puet bien estre que Turnus
a de s'amor ou tant ou plus,
et qu'ele est a seür de lui;
parler püent ansanble andui,
s'amor li a puet c'estre ofert,
si com a moi tot an apert;
une chose nos fait antandre,
li quels que l'aviegne au prendre,
que ele l'ait ainçois amé;
del quel qui l'ait vialt avoir gré;
fame est de molt male voisdie. (verse 8997)

And in any case woman is very clever at imagining hurt in her heart; it could well be that Turnus has more or less enjoyed her love, and that she is sure of him; she has perhaps offered him her love as clearly as to me; she makes us understand the same thing, and the one who gets her, she will have loved first; whichever one gets her she will have recognized; woman possesses a dangerous cleverness.

Romance enables calculation, prospective reasoning, and its vision implies perspective not only depth psychology, but also a world with some early version of depth perception. And a world in which, because some things are in front of others, unlike the *Chanson de Roland,* where there is neither private space nor is anything hidden, some things are not at all times visible; which is another way of saying that things are not always what they seem. As in Suger's negotiation over the price of precious gems, unseen motives, empty spaces, and hidden corners, the spatial version of chance, come to share pride of place with the public spaces of battlefield and court.

Old French romance, often considered to be naïve, is a cradle of skepticism and an early avatar of the scientific spirit, and it is no accident that the walls of Troy depict a world in which the sciences and technology exist alongside of the arts:

Tot anviron ot fet trois rans
de mangnetes par molt grant sens
d'une pierre qui molt est dure;
la mangnete est de tel nature,
ja nus hom armez n'i venist
que la pierre a soi nel traisist:
tant n'an venissent o halbers,
ne fussent sanpre al mur aers. (verse 433)

All around one had placed with great care three rows of magnetic stones, which are very hard; the magnet is of a nature such that never could an armed man come near that it did not draw him to it: those who came in their halberks were immediately attracted to the wall.

Romance implies an interest in the natural world, in the nature of things, a heightened awareness of causality, an offering of explanations right down to a cognizance of the medical realm. Love is pictured in the *Eneas* as elsewhere as an "incision in the body." Indeed, the *brievet* that Lavinia sends to Eneas stresses the fact that writing as an abbreviation, a foreshortening of Being, opens a gap in both the textual and physical corpus. Wrapped around an arrow aimed at her lover, the "brief" becomes a wound in his body:

Non voir, cop ne plaie n'i pert,

mais li brievez qui antor ert

m'a molt navré dedanz le cors. (verse 8971)

It is true that one sees neither blow nor wound, but the billet that was around it
has grievously wounded me in the body.

And a wound that elicits medical attention:

A sa male li mires vait,

prent une boiste, si a trait

del ditan, se l'a destempré,

boivre li fist; quant l'ot passé,

la saiete s'an est volee

et l'espalle sanpres sanee;

aneslopas toz sains refu.

Li ditans est de tel vertu

et li chevros a tel nature,

quant navrez est, tot a droiture

cort al ditan, a sa mecine;

soit de foille, soit de racine,

des qu'il en a lo col passé,

si a son mal tot resané,

et quant li fers li est el cors,

par cel l'an estuet voler fors. (verse 9559)

The doctor goes to his bag, take a box, pulls out dictame [?], mixes it, makes him
drink it; as soon as it passed his throat, the arrow flew out and his shoulder was
cured; he was immediately cured. The dictame has such a force that the roebuck
is of a nature that when it is wounded it runs to dictame as its medicine; as soon
as it has passed its throat, whether the leaf or the root, it is cured of its ill, and
when the metal is in its body it automatically flies out.

This is another of the key passages in the poem. First, because the efficacy
of medicine implies degree, an intermediary stage between life and death,
and such degree implies the reversibility of biography as well as narrative about
it. The epic world, determined by a force outside of the will of characters, in the
case of the *Chanson de Roland* by Christian Providence, is one which moves only
in one direction, or a world in which history can be only repetition, as if it were

inscribed in some temporal notion of *eternitas*, which contrasts mightily with notions of time, much more like the *tempus* of the secular world, within romance. There are no doctors in the *Chanson de Roland*; for just as words, once spoken, lead inevitably to deeds, the body, injured, is as good as dead. Wounds in romance are not only not necessarily fatal, sickness or "lovesickness" as often as not being psychological, but romance works are filled with doctors, not the *vilain mires* of the fabliaux, but genuine miracle workers. This is, of course, a way of saying that romance is optimistic but, more importantly, it offers from the beginning a vision of a life as reversible.

Finally, this is a passage that emphasizes the observation of nature in the behavior of the *chevreuil* along with the transfer of knowledge gained from observation of nature to the human realm in what is another example of romance interpretative, hypothetical, or strategic thinking. The romance world reveals a renewal of interest in the natural sciences as they existed in the classical world (Aristotle, Pliny, Lucretius). Whereas in the *Chanson de Roland* natural phenomenon such as the earthquake and darkening of the sun occur, they are there to be witnessed but not interpreted. Their meaning is given, univocal, unequivocal. The romance eye, on the contrary, is the eye of the observer in a world in which the meaning of signs is no longer evident and interpretation is necessary. The author, not content merely to attest to events, is compelled to look carefully and to analyze.

The romance spirit of observation is nowhere more evident than for Lavinia, who, it is true, first falls in love with Eneas by hearsay; but hearsay is confirmed by a long look, close observation. It makes sense where romance is concerned to speak of a gaze, which is as often as not female, but which is decomposed, presented as occurring in diverse phases of a process of enamoration, just as the symptoms of love will be observed on the body. To Lavinia's question "est donc amors anfermetez?" (verse 7916) the queen mother replies:

Nenil, mais molt petit an falt,
une fievre quartaine valt.
Pire est amors que fievre agüe,
n'est pas retor, que l'an an süe;
d'amor estuet sovant süer
et refroidir, fremir, tranbler
et sospirer et baallier,
et perdre tot boivre et mangier
et degiter et tressaillir,
müer color et espalir,

giendre, plaindre, palir, penser
et sanglotir, veillier, plorer:
ce li estuet fere sovant
qui bien aimme et qui s'en sent. (verse 7917)

No, but not far from it, it's like a quartaine fever. Love is worse than an aigu fever, one gets no relief unless one sweats; with love one must often sweat and cool off, shake, tremble, sigh, yawn, and lose all appetite, and become agitated and shudder, change color and grow pale, groan, complain, blanch, crash, sob, lay awake and cry: s/he who loves well and feels it does all this quite often.

Romance is synonymous with a symptomology of love and a close observation of its effects upon the body, effects to be read as if the body were itself a text. With the spirit of observation and analysis come a range of other arts and techniques spread throughout the *Roman d'Eneas*. Not only architecture, but also certain refinements of architectural technique right down to the question of acoustics in the capitol:

Par merveillos angin fu faiz;
molt fu biaus et larges dedanz,
voltes et ars i ot dous cenz;
ja n'i parlast hom tant an bas,
ne fust oïz eneslopas
par tot lo Capitoille entor. (verse 534)

It was made as a result of technological skill; it was very beautiful and large inside, with two hundred vaults and arcs; no matter how low a man might speak, his voice would be immediately heard throughout the capitol.

Or, to focus upon another example, we find not only an interest in decoration, but in the art of color, more precisely, in dying and the question of the origin of dye and of the digestive habits of crocodiles:

En cele mer joste Cartage,
iluec prent l'an, a cel rivage,
d'une maniere pesonez,
ne gaires granz, mes petitez;
l'en les taille sor les coëtes,
si an chïent roges gotetes;
de ce toint l'an la porpre chiere.

Pou sont peison de lor maniere;
l'an les nome conciliuns.
Del sanc de ces petiz peisons,
dunt iluec avoit a merveille,
de ces ert la porpre vermoille;
le noires refont an Cartage
del sanc d'un grant serpant evage,
que l'en apelle cocadrille,
dunt molt a iluec an une isle;
serpanz sont granz a desmesure
et de molt diverse nature;
quant a sa proie devoree,
donc si s'endort gole baee;
il nen a noiant de boiel;
el cors li antrent li oisel
et pasturent an son dormant
ce que mangié ot de devant;
ne s'espurge pas altrement,
car n'a mie de fondement. (verse 471)

In the sea by Carthage, one catches on the shore a kind of fish, not too big, rather small; one cuts their little tail and out comes red droplets: with this one dyes precious purple cloth. Fish of this kind are rare, one calls them "conchylium." With the blood of these little animals which live there in abundance one gets purple vermillion; they make black [dye] in Carthage from the blood of a great water serpent called a crocodile with which an island is covered. These are enormous reptiles and of a curious nature; when it has devoured its prey, it goes to sleep mouth open; as it has no intestine, birds enter the opening and graze while it is sleeping on what it ate before; it does not eliminate otherwise because it has no bottom.

To say, of course, that romance is one of the places where in the twelfth century one can observe the importance of observation is not to say simply that what we think of as a scientific or empirical spirit came to take its place alongside of the Platonic idealism or "examplarism" (D. E. Luscombe) that characterized the early Middle Ages. What I am suggesting is that in this new relation of the eye to its object we can see the shifting of a way of thinking, a change in mental structure, a reorientation of world view with far-reaching implications. Indeed, we can see a turn in the way the world is conceived, which, importantly in this instance, also involves a reorganization of the internal economy of perception. This new emphasis upon the eye of the observer cannot be detached from an emphasis evident throughout medieval romances upon experience, upon the particular, upon the particularity of every and everyday experience. It implies an emphasis upon perspective, upon the validity and the indeterminacy of different, competing, parallel, perspectives, upon the natural world, and, therefore, what we think of as a certain subjectivity of the novelistic vision (what in most general terms is high medieval modalism)—the assumption that the meaning of things depends less on a given nature of the thing itself than on its context and on the perspective from which it is seen. Indeed, at a certain point there is no distinguishing between the perspective of the observer and the nature of the thing itself.

What I have been describing all along with respect to the *Roman d'Eneas* looks awfully like the beginnings of a return of Aristotelian thought, according to which the individual object contains different and sometimes even opposite qualities. Where psychology is concerned, the romance self is articulated theoretically in Abelard's *Ethics*, where the meaning of any individual deed is perspectivized, that is, is divested of absolute moral significance, and is placed within the context of relativized modes of ethical action. Good and bad inhere in every individual, and are activated within the framework of particular situations. Such a mode of thought can be seen elsewhere in the scholastic categories, in the primacy of logic and dialectics over the other arts of language (grammar, rhetoric), in the rise of fixed poetic forms, and, of course, in the modal grammars of the terminists of the fourteenth century. And, as we have seen, it is part of the depth of field, the dynamic perspectivism, the recessionism of the Gothic cathedral.

Carthage offers a whiff of the Orient, only suggested at the end of the *Chanson of Roland* via the figure of Thierry. For, as robust, all business, intractable, and masculine as Roland was, Thierry, his defender in the trial of Ganelon, cuts a slimmer, darker, more subtle, logical, feminine figure; and he is also more finely dressed, as if the epic hero had already been replaced by that of romance even before the end of the first *chanson de geste*. Continuing in this direction, the *Eneas* is filled with rich, luxury goods like Dido's coat and the worked jewelry upon it:

> Une nosche i ot mervoillose,
> unques ne fu plus preciose,
> et un mantel qui most fu chiers;
> la penne en fu a eschaquiers,
> d'une bisches de cent colors;
> d'autres plus riches et meillors

fu bien orlez li mantiaus toz
devant et a porfil desoz;
most fu chiere la forreüre
et most valut mialz la volsure:
toz fu batuz a or defors;
sol li atache et li mors
et li boton et li tassel
valoient plus que troi chastel. (verse 739)

It had a marvelous brooch, the most valuable that ever there was, and a rich mantel. The fur was checkered, coming from beasts of a hundred colors; with others even richer and better the coat was bordered in front and hemmed at the bottom; the fur of the lining was even more valuable; the whole outside was of beaten gold; the hooks and the buckles and the buttons and the fringes were worth more than three castles.

The walls of Carthage are synonymous with wealth, economic surplus, accumulation, as if the poet were signaling the kind of economic surplus that, beginning in the twelfth century, created cities with their markets, division of labor, and circulation of luxury goods beyond the necessities of subsistence. The city is the site of commerce, markets, and roads:

Li chemins alot par desoz;
grant marchié i avoit toz dis;
la vendoit an lor vair, lo gris,
coltes de paille, covertors,
portpres, pailles, dras de color,
pierres, especes et vaiselle;
marcheandie riche et bele
i pooit l'an toz tenz trover;
ne se poüst hom porpenser
de richece que el mont fust,
dont en cel leu planté n'eüst.
Granz rues ot an la cité
et palés riches a planté,
borjois menanz, sales et tors
et aleors et parleors;
bels menages a grant plenté
ot la dedanz an la cité. (verse 448)

The road passed beneath; there was a great market there every day; there one sold furs, rough cloth [*petit-gris*], mattresses of silk, covers, less rich furs [*porpres*], silk cloth, colored cloth, stones, spices, and dishware; one could find rich and beautiful merchandise there at all times; nor could one imagine richness in the world that was not in this place. The city had great streets and an abundance of rich palaces, bourgeois dwellings, rooms and towers, and galleries and public rooms. In the city there were beautiful structures aplenty.

But the passage that describes Dido's jewelry also suggests something slightly more theoretical—that is, a compression, the compression of labor that is the essence of a money economy—the very principle of equivalence or exchange: the clasp, the buckle, the button, and the tassel alone are worth more than three castles.

One would be hard pressed, I think, to disentangle the kind of exchange implicit to this passage—the equation of clasp, buckle, button, and tassel with three castles—from a more generalized rule of economic exchange according to which one can establish relative values, quantitative equivalence, between objects that are qualitatively different. And one would be hard pressed to disengage it from Suger's insistence, with which we began, both upon the importance of material things, upon their value relative to each other, and upon the very idea of exchange that made Saint-Denis a center of trade beginning with the famous *foire du Lendit* and culminating in the perspectivism of the first Gothic cathedral.

NOTES

1. Abbot Suger, *On the Abbey Church of St.-Denis and Its Art Treasures*, ed. and trans. Erwin Panofsky (Princeton, NJ: Princeton University Press, 1979), 41. All quotations are from this volume.

2. Erwin Panofsky, "Introduction," in *On the Abbey Church of St.-Denis*, 19.

3. Pauline Matarasso, ed. and trans., *The Cistercian World* (London: Penguin, 1993), 56.

4. Dionysius the Areopagite, *The Celestial Hierarchies* (London: Unwin Brothers, 1949), 29.

5. Cited in Paul Frankl, *Gothic Architecture*, rev. Paul Crossley (New Haven, CT: Yale University Press, 2000), 295.

6. Erwin Panofsky, *Gothic Architecture and Scholasticism* (New York: Meridian Books, 1963).

7. J.-J. Salvedra de Grave, ed., *Eneas: Roman de XIIe siècle* (Paris: Champion, 1964), 441. All subsequent references are to this edition.

JACK ABECASSIS, Pomona College

R. HOWARD BLOCH, Yale University

KEVIN BROWNLEE, University of Pennsylvania

MARINA BROWNLEE, Princeton University

ALISON CALHOUN, Indiana University

JACQUELINE CERQUIGLINI-TOULET, Université de Paris-Sorbonne
(Paris IV) and the Institut Universitaire de France

DANIEL HELLER-ROAZEN, Princeton University

ANDREW JAMES JOHNSTON, Freie Universität Berlin

ANDREAS KABLITZ, University of Cologne

JOACHIM KÜPPER, Freie Universität Berlin

DEBORAH N. LOSSE, Arizona State University

JAN-DIRK MÜLLER, Ludwig-Maximilians-Universität München

STEPHEN G. NICHOLS, Johns Hopkins University

JEANETTE PATTERSON, Princeton University

URSULA PETERS, University of Cologne

GERHARD REGN, Ludwig-Maximilians-Universität München

GABRIELLE M. SPIEGEL, Johns Hopkins University

Page numbers in italics refer to figures.